THE
KINGSTON TRIO
ON RECORD

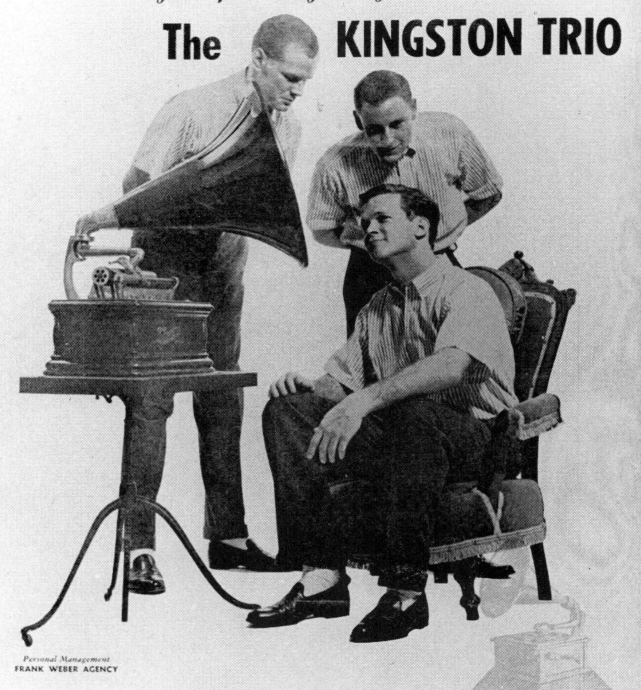

Once again . . .

thanks to everyone for everything . . .

The **KINGSTON TRIO**

Personal Management
FRANK WEBER AGENCY

NATIONAL ACADEMY OF RECORDING ARTS AND SCIENCES
SECOND ANNUAL AWARDS

THE
KINGSTON TRIO
ON RECORD

by
**Benjamin Blake, Jack Rubeck
and Allan Shaw**

With special contributions by:

*William Bush
Floyd Garrett
Paul Surratt
Elizabeth Wilson*

**With a Foreword by Nick Reynolds
and an Epilogue by John Stewart**

Published by

Kingston Korner, Inc.

6 S. 230 Cohasset Rd.
Naperville IL 60540

Library of Congress Catalog Card Number 85-50660

ISBN 0-9614594-0-9

First printing: June, 1986

Printed in the United States of America

Publisher: Kingston Korner, Inc.
            6 South 230 Cohasset Road
            Naperville, IL 60540

   Printer: The Review - Frank H. Gildner Jr.
             Rural Route One, PO Box 77
             Evansville, WI 53536

*This book is dedicated to
the members of The Kingston Trio,
past and present,
as a small thank-you for
the soundtrack they have given
to our lives.*

TABLE OF CONTENTS

Bobby Shane, November 7, 1981. Photo by Jack Rubeck.

FOREWORD:

An Appreciation of Bobby Shane

I have known Bobby Shane for more than thirty years, and I'm *still* as fascinated with the magic of this man as I was the day I first met him back at Menlo Business College. I'll never forget it: walking into my first accounting class and spotting this guy in the back of the room sound asleep, with a book propped up in front of his face so that the professor couldn't see him snoozing. I figured that anybody who had the guts to do that, I *had* to get to know. We have been brothers ever since.

Over the three decades of the Trio, Bobby has been more than simply the "sound" of the group, He has been its *spirit;* that devil-may-care, let's-have-a-good-time and to-hell-with-convention attitude. In retrospect, attitude was so much of what the Trio was all about — a very positive viewpoint of life that translated to the music and ultimately to our fans.

As a musician and an entertainer, Bobby is the best there is. He can create as much excitement "on the natch" as a whole symphony can through years of practice. He's not studied, never practices; it's just *there* — a totally natural talent that does what he does instinctively. Call it magnetism or charisma or whatever, but Bobby's *got it.*

Bobby will be proud of this book, as we all will. It's a document not just of our recordings, but of our lives for so many years. I thank all involved in the project, and just leafing through the pages brings back so many great memories.

I treasure the years we sang and traveled together. I treasure our friendships. I treasure Bobby Shane. Like I said, we're brothers — and we always will be.

NICK REYNOLDS
Port Orford, Oregon
February, 1986

Illustration by Jeff Fessenden.

The Kingston Trio At A Glance:
Organizational Chart 1957 - 1986

(NOTE: From 1969-1976 the group was billed as "The <u>New</u> Kingston Trio")

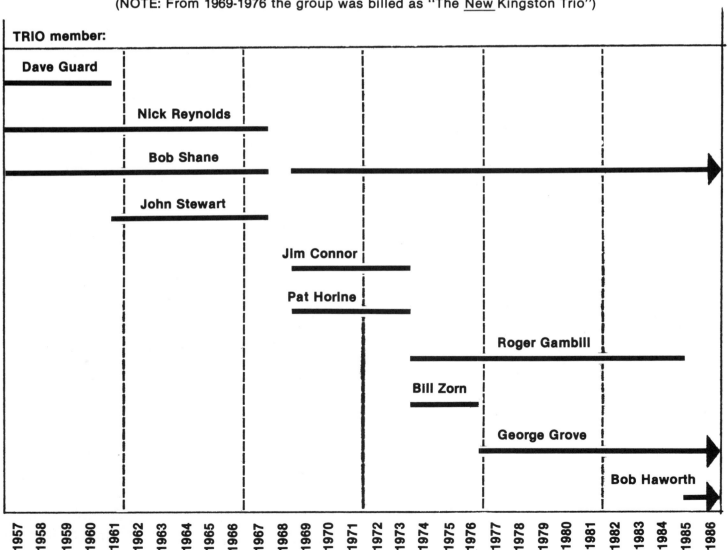

An Introduction to
The Kingston Trio On Record

This brave little volume should not be taken by the reader to be a serious attempt at biography, nor is it a price guide to Kingston Trio collectibles. You will not find their places or dates of birth or favorite colors listed here, anymore than you will discover the going rate for a "mint, still-sealed, stereo copy" of their most elusive LP. Our purpose is to discuss the recordings that form the legacy of one of the greatest musical phenomenon of our age, not that an account of their lives — individually or as a group — would not make for stirring reading. Just such a work was completed a few years back by Richard Johnston, and no doubt it will someday be the basis for the screenplay of a Hollywood megabucks extravaganza. It will be published, according to the author, once the Kingston Trio name has been retired. *The Kingston Trio On Record* is intended to be a companion volume to just such a biography. In the meantime, we highly recommend an excellent in-depth article on the Trio by William Bush (a contributor to this book) that appeared in the June and July, 1984

issues of *Frets, The Magazine Of Acoustic String Instruments,* just one of the many magazines to feature the KT on its cover during the past quarter century.

Yes, there are a thousand stories in the naked Trio, but you will not encounter many of them here. For instance, we will not tell you about the time in Australia that a kangaroo hopped off with the Trio's concert earnings. There will be no discussion of the legend of the alleged pilfering of Tom Dooley's headstone by two Trio members, who shipped it C.O.D. to their startled manager. And we will most definitely not go into detail about the near-crash of the group's plane during a blizzard on an Indiana turkey farm, nor what immortal question a certain Trio member then shouted at the startled farmer!

As fascinating and colorful as such fact-based legends may be, it is the group's music that is our mission, or at least that sizable portion of it that was forever captured in the hearts of a generation,

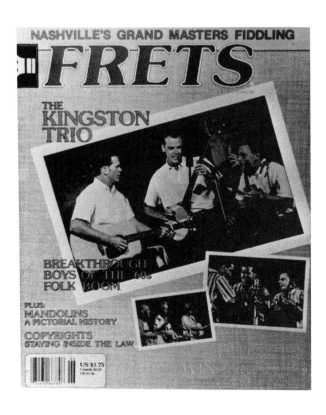

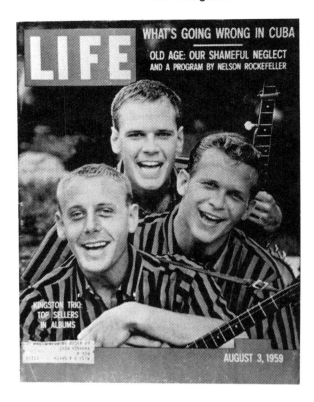

and on recording tape by Voyle Gilmore and a few other talented technicians. *The Kingston Trio On Record* is pretty much a chronological journey through the past quarter century or so with a group of talented individuals who at one time were the most popular performing and recording group in the United States of America.

At this point we will give you *our* definition of The Kingston Trio. It may differ from yours, and we know it differs among the members of the Trio, themselves. For the purposes of this book, "The Kingston Trio" is a group of three individuals (one of whom is Bob Shane) who play guitars and banjos and sing *Tom Dooley* and *M.T.A.* With that given, as we go to press there are ten men (see "Organizational Chart") who are former or current members of the Trio. Eight of them have thus far participated in the group's recordings, and some of those more so than others. We make no judgment on which configuration of the Trio was, or is, "the best".

At least one modern-day journalist has referred to the original Kingston Trio of Dave Guard, Nick Reynolds and Bob Shane as "The Beatles of Folk Music."[1] We agree. There are a great many parallels and common bonds between these two supergroups. Both spawned countless imitations, many of which became successful. The Kingstons influenced an entire generation of young people to start playing guitars, priming them for The Beatles,

who simply encouraged the same bunch (and their younger siblings) to plug their instruments into electrical amplifiers, and grow longer hair. Britain's Beatles ended commercial folk music's domination of the American record business by re-introducing rock and roll to the country of its origin. It is no coincidence that the Trio's record sales dropped dramatically — and permanently — when the British "invasion" of early 1964 began. The Trio induced hundreds of thousands of people to buy long-play record albums and began the swing of the industry away from singles as its staple product, allowing The Beatles a ready-made audience of disc jockeys eager to program entire albums, and young people ready to purchase them.

Certainly The Beatles were bigger than The Kingston Trio. Certainly Elvis Presley was bigger than The Kingston Trio. And we grudgingly acknowledge the fact that Michael Jackson's THRILLER album has outsold all Trio LPs *combined*. Only fools debate the obvious, so how about "Best Folk Group Of All-Time" then? Maybe, but the Trio would tell you *that* honor belongs to The Weavers (Ronnie Gilbert, Lee Hays, Fred Hellerman, Pete Seeger), hands down. And we would not argue with those among you who feel strongly that Peter, Paul & Mary (Peter Yarrow, Noel Paul Stookey, Mary Travers), or The Limeliters (Lou Gottlieb, Alex Hassilev, Glenn Yarbrough), or even the short-lived Journeymen (Scott MacKenzie, John

[1]Eric Zorn, *Chicago Tribune Magazine,* February 21, 1982.

Phillips, Richard Weissman) were just as talented a collection of individuals as the Trio.

Peter, Paul & Mary certainly have as much right to the title of "Best Selling Folk Act" as the Trio does, but it should be taken into account that P, P & M were admittedly molded in the Trio's image, that they inherited an audience of record buyers and college concert goers that the Trio *created,* and that there were more potential customers for albums during P, P & M's peak years (1962-63) than at the height of "Triomania" (1959-60).

For some comparisons between the groups, see our nearby "Battle of the Bands" page. These statistics are paraded forth in an attempt to establish the futility of anybody ever winning this so-called battle that has raged in some commer-

cial folk circles for over two decades. (There were few punches thrown among the principals. Nick Reynolds was one of P, P & M's biggest boosters.) The only thing the charts clearly establish is that Peter, Paul & Mary were both a singles *and* album act, while the Trio's main output was LPs. But even on that concession we should add one final footnote: *Tom Dooley* by itself probably sold more 45s than all of P, P & M's 45s put together. Capitol Records reportedly stopped counting at three million copies, and international sales are thought to have at least doubled that figure. The list of awards for both groups would fill several pages, but the Grammy Awards are of special significance because they tend to reflect the attitude of their recording industry peers. In this

category, P, P & M have a clear edge.

Both groups took it on the chin from the folk "purists" about the "damage" they were doing to the traditional folk process. What the purists could not see was the *positive* side. In a 1962 essay titled "In Defense of Commercial Folksingers", which appeared in the magazine *Sing Out,* Steve Fiott (later the leader of his own folk group, the White Mountain Singers) summed-up the debate this way:

> "Are their versions traditional? Do they follow simple basic chord structures? Are all the lyrics 'folky' enough? The answer to those questions is NO. So what! If they are good enough to use a more complex arrangement and revise lyrics to fit the song, all well and good. Tradition is fine. I myself stick to tradition as much as anyone, but don't condemn the commercial singer for not doing this. Obviously people like the music. They buy it; but more importantly, they sing it. And after all, folk means people. People make traditions — maybe the Trio has started a new tradition."

It should be said of Peter, Paul & Mary that they were able to survive the British invasion that basically did-in the KT. P, P & M had already dethroned the Trio at the top of the folk heap, largely because they took themselves more seriously on stage than the Trio ever had. The happy-go-lucky stage presence of Nick, Bob and (by then) John Stewart, and their largely non-

"Battle Of The Bands"

(Illustration by Rod Harrington)

The Kingston Trio vs. Peter, Paul & Mary

Albums: The Kingston Trio placed fourteen of its LPs in the "Top 10", with five of them reaching #1, and seven remaining a year or more on the charts. Peter, Paul & Mary had five of their albums hit the Top 10, two of them going to the top; six of them stayed charted for more than a year.

Singles: The Trio had ten "Top 40" hits, two of which aspired to the Top 10. P, P & M had twelve Top 40 singles, six of them in the Top 10. Both groups hit #1 only once, the Trio doing it with its first hit record (*Tom Dooley*) and P, P & M with their last (*Leaving On A Jet Plane*).

Gold Records: A dead tie: one million seller for each group (the aforementioned #1s) in the singles category, and seven gold albums each. (Note: these were the days before "platinum" awards were handed out, signifying album sales of over one million units. Best estimates indicate the KT was entitled to two — possibly four — platinum LPs, and P, P & M earned at least five.)

Grammy Awards: The Kingston Trio was nominated for eight Grammys, winning twice. Peter, Paul & Mary were nominated fourteen times, taking home the recording industry's highest award five times.

political, non-controversial song policy actually worked against them during the Civil Rights era (while it had *helped* them in earlier, simpler years), while Peter, Paul & Mary were quick to embrace Bob Dylan's songs and "get involved". By the time the KT finally *did* manifest its conscience after the assassination of President Kennedy (with the album TIME TO THINK), it was too late. When Dylan and The Byrds "invented" folk-rock in 1965, Peter, Paul & Mary rode out the wave that washed away The Kingston Trio.

But this book is not about Peter, Paul & Mary; or The Beatles. Those of you who have read this far are either well-paid reviewers or genuine Kingston Trio fans and knowledge-seekers, and it is for this latter group that we have assembled this book. For those among you who are repulsed by dates and numbers, we ask you to bear with us when they crop-up. Believe it or not, there are many record collectors out there who would toss this tome into the circular file if we left out such information. Breaking up the tedium are revealing interviews with former Trio manager Frank Werber and former group members Dave Guard and Nick Reynolds.

Regretfully, we were unable to ask some timely questions of former Trio producer Voyle Gilmore, who passed away while this book was in the early planning stages. And coming down the home stretch, we were shocked into reflection (and re-write) by the untimely demise of Trio member Roger Gambill, as well as the passing of former KT accompanists David Wheat and Stan Kaess.

Why a book devoted to The Kingston Trio in the first place? After all, this is an act that has not had a charted record since 1969 and has become largely ignored or forgotten by music critics and historians, not to mention most of the thousands of middle-aged middle Americans who once swooned over them in concert and were card-carrying members of "The Kingston Trio Fan Club." First of all, the people involved in the creation of this book have all in some way had their lives changed by the Trio. None were paid for their work, so we can honestly call *The Kingston Trio On Record* a labor of love. Secondly, *someone* had to do it, and quite frankly we were tired of waiting. If there can be fifty books about The Beatles, there certainly should be at least *one* about these guys. (In the interest of historical accuracy we must report that there *was* a book published in 1960 by Random House, titled *The Kingston Trio.* Weighing in at thirty-three pages and sporting the STRING ALONG cover photo, this item was once accurately described by Dave Guard as "a concert program tha got a bit out of hand." Indeed, it was sold almost exclusively at Trio concerts. It, and some of its soft cover descendants are pictured nearby.) And the fact that the group has been mostly forgotten, in itself would be proper justification for such a work. But it goes much deeper.

The Kingston Trio had *class.* The various members of the group were and *are* spirited, gifted performers. At the peak of its power, the group had no peer. About a half-dozen Trio albums deserve to

rank among the very best works of popular music this country's recording industry has ever turned out. (We will leave it to KT fans everywhere to debate *which* half-dozen!) Those works sound as fresh and exciting today as they did twenty years ago. The group has been acknowledged as an influence on the subsequent music of such groups as The Beach Boys, Buffalo Springfield, The Eagles, Abba and Fleetwood Mac.

It is the particular bias of the people who put this book together that the Trio gave this land of ours its greatest living songwriter, John Stewart. (Please, no nasty letters from Irving Berlin lovers!) The KT deserves credit for all of the great songs they introduced — or re-introduced — to radios and concert halls across the country, but perhaps most significantly they should be remembered as the happy catalyst that awakened America at a time of musical boredom, and that actually got thousands of young people involved in *making* music, as well as listening to it.

Perhaps the best news we could bring you is that the kind of movement the Trio started in the late Fifties seems to be surfacing again in the mid-Eighties, and most noticeably in the eastern part of the United States. Radio programs like "Music Americana" in Washington, D.C., with host Dick Cerri, and "American Folk Theatre" in Rochester, New Hampshire (pending syndication on National Public Radio), with host Brownie Macintosh, and a host of others all over the country seem to be stirring not only we nostalgia buffs, but a whole new

generation of eager folk who would rather listen to sound lyrics and clever acoustial artisans instead of the unpleasant fare they have been offered of late. In the print media, *Sing Out* is still going strong, and the previously-mentioned *Frets* always makes for good reading. *Kingston Korner* (more about us later) publishes a newsletter that keeps Trio and John Stewart fans happy. In New York City, something called the *Fast Folk Musical Magazine* (half magazine, half LP) just brims with great new talent in each issue. In Washington, D.C., "The World Folk Music Association" sponsors concerts and publishes a fine newsletter that spotlights both the old (Limeliters, Brothers Four, Tom Paxton, Bob Gibson, Ian Tyson and others are still active, and the WFMA recently reunited the Chad Mitchell Trio for a special performance) and the new (acts like Schooner Fare, Suzanne Vega, Washington Squares, Christine Lavin, White Mountain Singers are starting to make some national noise).

It has been little more than four years since PBS first aired "The Kingston Trio & Friends: Reunion" (March, 1982), and it may well be that it was that television program that revitalized the movement. The moving documentary feature film about the Weavers, "Wasn't That A Time", received rave reviews that same year. Peter, Paul & Mary, reunited, have now celebrated their quarter century mark in the entertainment industry. Folk era artists like Tom Rush, Eric Andersen and John Prine (not to mention John Stewart), have all formed their own labels, much to the delight of their many fans.

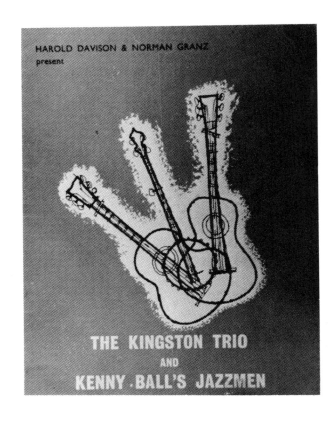

HAROLD DAVISON & NORMAN GRANZ
present

THE KINGSTON TRIO
AND
KENNY BALL'S JAZZMEN

The list of today's pop music stars who got their start in the Sixties folk field includes such names as John Denver, Bob Dylan, Judy Collins, Joan Baez and Kenny Rogers. Pete Seeger is still going strong. In short, we seem to be in the midst of a mini folk boom, and long may it last.

Both Nick Reynolds and John Stewart have utilized the word "attitude" in their respective writings for this book. The attitude of the Trio is perhaps best described as: "We're having a heck of a good time, and we want you to share it with us". It shows in live performances, and it comes through on their records. Bob Shane has said it many times: "We're entertainers".

And of course, The Kingston Trio will continue. Not surprisingly, it is our contention that when the history of American Popular Music is finally written, an entire chapter should be devoted to the legacy of our favorite group — a legacy that will live on as long as Bob Shane can still strum a "C" chord, and hopefully for as long as intelligent beings still listen to intelligent music.

* * * * * * * * *

The Kingston Trio, Dave Guard, Bob Shane, Nick Reynolds, Kingston, Rhode Island, circa 1959.

Frank Werber, the man behind The Kingston Trio. Nick Reynolds in background. Photo courtesy: Archives of Music Preservation.

The Frank Werber Interview

by
Paul Surratt

PS: Without you, we feel there would have been no Kingston Trio. Could you give us a little bit of personal background on how you came to manage the Trio and how you got into that line of work in the first place?

FW: I drifted into San Francisco about 1949, broke on my ass, and scuffled around for many months until I ran into a little club called *the Hungry i*. It had just been bought by Enrico Banducci. It was love at first sight for me, and that's sort of where I got started into the business. Anyway, to make a long story short I came to work for Enrico at *the Hungry i*, and I worked there through the time that we built a new club into which I got involved into putting all the sound and the lights and really getting into the shows. And for a period of six or seven years there I spent every night in the club — minimum of three, sometimes four shows — and I evaluated it to myself or for any of the acts that were interested in what this young punk had to say, and I paid close attention to what the audiences did or didn't like. For background, I would say that was my schooling. I also saw how many of the acts got messed-over by the agencies and management they were signed with . . . Nobody in those days really seemed to get into the act. Everybody was more interested in getting the job signed-up, taking their commission and sending you an opening-day telegram, saying, "We love you, sweetie!"

In 1956, I left *the Hungry i*. I'd left periodically. Enrico and I enjoyed a very close relationship — almost father and son. It was very volatile, and I quite often got fired and I quite often quit, but I always wound up coming back. So 1956 I quit once and decided I didn't want to do that trick anymore. So I got into what was called Public Relations — I became a press agent, and since night life had been my beat, so to speak, I wound up working for

most of the nightclubs in North Beach, which was quite an active cabaret area at that time . . . the night life of San Francisco.

And it was during that time that someone told a friend of mine who worked at the *Purple Onion* (one of my accounts) that a group had auditioned, and that they hadn't gotten a job but that he thought they would be worth looking at. The group was called "Dave Guard and the Calypsonians" — I forget how I was put in touch with them, but anyway I went down to Menlo Park one night to a place called the *Cracked Pot* and met with Dave, Nick . . . about three or four other young dudes, and the *Cracked Pot* was sort of a gathering place where this original group had germinated from. At the time when I met them there really wasn't any strict form to it. They would meet on a certain night, as I remember, and they would sing for beer, and sometimes two would show, sometimes four, sometimes more. Out of that Dave had formed kind of a stricter group, which was Dave, Nick, Barbara Bogue and Joe Gannon, and they got a one-night booking at a place called the *Italian Village* — a club in San Francisco. They invited me to come see them because I had come down to Menlo Park, and I had professed some interest in a sense that I wasn't an agent or a manager, I just had a lot of time on my hands and very little money. Anyway, prior to the performance we had a conversation, and I think I pointed out to them that I could probably help them, and I would like to help them but that four of them would be too tough to get jobs for. Three of them seemed to be all that they needed and that the bass player really wasn't helping them very much — and he wasn't. And they informed me that the girl was an important, integral part of that group, was going to marry the bass player, and if they cut him loose she would leave. And as I recall at that time, we sort of parted company with me saying, "Well, if you ever do that, let me know and we'll see what we can do." I mean it wasn't like I saw the future, and looking back I felt that just scale for three was easier to obtain than scale for four.

So a short while later, Dave and Nick came to see me — I had a little loft office over the *Purple Onion* in this tiny garrett — and they said they had let Joe go and that Barbara had quit, and that a friend of theirs who had been working in Hawaii and had been at Menlo before and had gone back to Hawaii — was working at *Pearl City Tavern* doing Elvis imitations — and was coming back to join them, and that we should all get together. That was Bob Shane. And that's kinda the intro into how all that happened.

PS: *That was around what time?*

FW: This is all happening at the beginning of '57, because from the time of Bobby's arrival and our shaking hands on the agreement — I don't even remember exactly what it was, but the main thing that we ascertained was that they used me as the authority figure. In other words, they *gave* me the authority. They were all pretty much college alcoholics — they were really into drinking beer and smoking. We cracked down on that and some

of the carousing, and they really pulled it together. And I sort of laid it out that I would like to go for it if they really wanted to go for it, and they did. We worked from that winter of '57 through June almost daily on rehearsals and this Wollensac I'd purchased. I sent them to a vocal coach I knew — Judy Davis — and they started that, and we worked every day, rehearsing, taking pictures. The *Purple Onion* — Phyllis Diller bowed out of a date and they needed a fill-in, and we managed to pursuade them to put the group in, and we all went on a major campaign of plastering the Peninsula with paper, letting the college crowd know that one of their kind was going to be at the *Purple Onion*. We did quite well, and as a matter of fact from that break, got a regular job there — under scale, of course. I think they paid us something like $118 for everybody.

PS: *A week?*

FW: A week! And we managed to make it on that. We did seven months there, daily. We would do every job with a clipboard, and I would say I choreographed every song. Every move was planed, every line . . . and the character of the performance was developed in seven months of three and four shows a night, six nights a week, and a

Barbara Bogue, Dave Guard, Joe Gannon, Nick Reynolds. The Kingston Quartet, a.k.a. Dave Guard & The Calypsonians, 1957. Photo courtesy: Guard Collection, Meir Library, University of Wisconsin-Milwaukee.

session after each show — football/basketball team style. They totally dedicated themselves; there was no resistance of any kind . . . the changes . . . the tightening-up . . . My sphere of reference never included records. I was knowledgeable in performance, communication across the stage . . . I never considered that this was to be a "record hit act." I was really focusing on performance and projection and music, of *course*, but *Tom Dooley* . . . I could never say I planned that!

PS: You were looking for a very visual thing, then?

FW: Totally . . . the communication of that act of music, yes. The tunes, yes, in so far as they related to that. To me that was it. You came on; you had so many minutes and you had to get inside those people's heads, leave your mark and get off.

PS: We have heard the Trio's original contract was drawn-up on a paper napkin, or is this just Hollywood nonsense?

FW: Well, as a specific it's nonsense, as a metaphor it isn't. We just kind of made an agreement at first amongst ourselves, and that agreement was later translated into a partnership, so as a metaphor it refers to that.

PS: How much do you think Dave Guard's departure hurt the financial side of the Kingston Trio, and what directions do you think the Trio would have taken if Nick and Bob had gone along with Dave's ideas and he had stayed with the group?

FW: I . . . I don't think that it had any financial effect on the Trio, except for the requirement that it took to bail Dave out, and I don't mean to degrade Dave's contribution or ability by that in any way . . . I want to qualify that: how can I say what would have happened? I don't know . . . of *course* it changed. How would it have gone if it had gone the other way? It was my belief that it could not have gone *too* well, because the other two members were tired of being led and moved to the degree to which they were being moved. I felt their success was in their ability to enjoy themselves perform and project that, and that the combination that had cosmically been joined was capable of doing certain things. Dave wanted to take it into a direction that would satisfy his personal appreciation or would help his pride or whatever, and I don't know that they could have made it . . . I knew that they were uncomfortable at trying too hard. There would have been a great amount of friction, it seems to me, and Dave probably would have wound up getting some people who could execute his wishes — that's what he was really after. But I can't say this was the right move; it would be

presumptuous of me.

But we did all right and economically I think it went very well and it didn't peak there. It didn't peak until afterwards. As a matter of fact, I think it's amazing how well John just dovetailed right into that space. It was as if he'd been understudying Dave anyway.

PS: What part did you play in choosing Dave's replacement?

FW: I chose John. Everybody who stepped forward was seriously considered, but I think John had been warming-up in the wings.

PS: Are you still friends with Dave, Nick, Bob and John?

FW: Well, you'd have to ask *them* that. (laughter) As far as I know I am. There's no animosities between David and I — we've long since been together many times. I never believe anybody's right and the other person's wrong; we've both got some of that. I've tried to help Dave a few times with some of his projects and I see him once in awhile. Nick and I've stayed tight the longest — we're still in the business together, and I see Bobby now and again every time he comes through. John, I probably see the least. In fact the last time I saw John, he was working here at this club, and I said "Hi" and he just giggled, just kept on giggling. Now I don't know if that is good or bad — you'll have to ask him sometime. (laughter)

PS: How did you go about getting the original recording contract with Capitol?

FW: During the long performance at the *Purple Onion* we started getting overtures from people from Los Angeles who would come up to see us. We were approached by Liberty, Vee-Jay or Valiant — something like that — and this gentleman came in and said he could deliver Capitol Records, and the man's name was Jimmy Saphier, a television agent who is now dead. He got us Capitol Records.

We went down and recorded the whole first album. It cost them $980, studio time, tape, everything — that's what the cost was for the album. They didn't know what the hell to do with three guys playing acoustic instruments. They couldn't believe it; they didn't know how to handle it. They didn't know how to record it . . . they just didn't know. They kind of *amused* us. They only printed about a thousand albums . . . they didn't have it when it broke loose. Capitol Records is a (expletive deleted) company. Capitol's got a great history — E.M.I. had to *force* them to release the Beatles . . . that's Capitol Records, folks! That's how Vee-Jay got in there, because Alan Livingston, *genius* of the industy, turned the Beatles down . . . didn't want that stuff on his label, he said. (laughter)

PS: Do you know if they have any unreleased Trio material in the vaults?

FW: I imagine they would have some. Each session had some . . . I don't know. They were so anxious, so many albums — they might have packaged that. There's some stuff in there I doubt they'd have the guts to put out! (laughter)

PS: Was it difficult being both producer and manager to the Trio after they left Capitol?

FW: That's the easiest. I think manager and producer is the same. Once you understand the technical requirements and what's needed, I think — as in many phases of the business — if you're capable, it just requires one title.

PS: How much influence did Voyle Gilmore have on your producing techniques?

FW: He must have had considerable because I sat next to him every time — that's where I started to learn. Nice man, nice gentle soul . . . he did some great Sinatra dates. He was an old line producer: got the songs, did the arrangements, took care of the band, and when the star came in said, "Here's what you're doing" . . . that's what producers were like then.

PS: You also produced You Were On My Mind, a million-seller for the group We Five. Was it greatly different working with them after so many years of the Trio sound?

FW: Not because of the sound, but because of the times and the people. Yes, greatly.

PS: Did you agree with their decision to disband after the second LP?

FW: Oh, I agreed with their decision to disband

prior to the second LP. They couldn't keep it together, and I didn't want to do that again. I didn't want to be Mr. Favor riding herd . . . I'd done enough . . . Bev Bivens, great singer, way before Grace Slick. She'd blow Grace right off the stage — and she just decided not to do that anymore.

PS: Which of the Trio's albums remain your personal favorites from an artistic viewpoint?

FW: It would be hard for me to say. I'd pick it more selectively — bits and pieces of various albums. Really, for an all-in-all picture of the Trio I think the best album is the Sahara-Tahoe concert Tetragrammaton double album I put together — ONCE UPON A TIME. I tried to capture what was their state-of-the-art at that time . . . the personalities and the tunes. It worked real well, and I think that's possibly my favorite because it's the most intricate. It was the most demanding.

PS: There have been about a dozen "greatest hits" packages of Trio material marketed by various record companies. If you could package an LP of your own KT favorites, what would you include?

FW: I'd have to sit down a little bit and look them up . . . I might miss one I really like . . . I mean I know I'd have *Flowers* in there. I know I'd have *Scotch And Soda, Sloop John B. Tom Dooley* was really one of my favorites, melodically. After awhile you get burned out on it, but before it ever happened it was probably my favorite song. *Corey, Corey . . . I'm Going Home* . . . but I can't answer that question properly off the top of my head. I never sat home and played the albums.

PS: Are there any special memories connected with the Trio that you would like to share with the readers of this book?

FW: Well, there was that time in a motel room in Seattle — no, I don't think the readers are ready for that one! (laughter) I've shared a lot with you today that we can't put on this tape, but then again . . . if you want some more you'll have to wait for the release of *my* book, soon to be out, called "Intimate Moments With The Kingston Trio: Backstage And Between The Covers." Every day there were intimate moments, to answer that question. The whole thing was one long intimate moment in an intimate association that went on for a long time. None of it was *cold* . . . As I said, they worked and there wasn't a day they didn't show up, and when somebody violated the work and health rules they drew penalties. Bobby was usually the one that had to be propped up at times, but they just got better and better.

It was like they focused and the moment was right. That's how I believe it happened. It was a moment in time that all these forces came together and none of us dissipated it. We all went for it full on . . . We were working *the Hungry i* for the biggest money we'd ever made — $750 a week — second on the bill to Irwin Corey. Capitol had recorded us and nothing had happened, and I was buying the album from the distributor and selling it at the club, and we were making the mark-up and dividing it between us. That was the only record earnings we had because they didn't do bull — they didn't know what to do with us. Again, Capitol is a parasite, not only with me but with others, unfortunately.

Anyway, some DJ in Salt Lake City played a cut our of the album — they played *Tom Dooley* — and they got a lot of phone action and they did it again, and this guy went home and left it for is friend to play on *his* show, and when he came back that night, it was out of control. He called me at *the Hungry i* from the station and said, "You know something? I think you guys got something going. You better get a hold of Capitol — I can't get nobody." So I got hold of Voyle and, "Yeah-well we'll check it out . . ." And sure enough. And then they found out it was in Salt Lake City! "Yeah-well, don't get excited . . ." That was their attitude. "Sometimes these things happen — we don't want to jump too fast."

And then it started happening in Miami, because this DJ called his friend there, and then — boom! Then one record store in Salt Lake City sold six thousand copies of the album — and Capitol had to press them because they didn't have them — before they ever got a single out. That's how hot it got right off the bat, and after that, it moved out . . . but Capitol had to be snowballed on it before they would move. We were the very first group to reach an audience that bought albums in the quantities that other audiences had only bought singles.

"A," we didn't put out singles, and "B," we didn't have that 45 appeal. We were more a show . . . Capitol *induced* me; it was my stupidity for going along with them. I was a bit naive . . . I've no complaints about what I did. As I said with hindsight: they'd been around a lot longer than I had, and that was no way to do an artist — three or four albums a year!

PS: We understand you converted the Trio's famous Trident Restaurant into a health food restaurant several years ago. Has it been successful?

FW: Extremely. As the Trio did to music, the *Trident* has done to restaurants. It has single-handedly in the last decade changed the restaurant business. I would say there's not too many places in the country I can go today that I don't find some influence: the menu, the decor, the people, the treatment, the approach — it's been very well copied . . . it's an old idea now.

PS: From your point of view as one of the most successful managers in the history of music, who do you feel has been managed most effectively in the music business in the past couple of decades, and who do you feel could have been managed better?

FW: *Many* could be managed better. I would say that I didn't appreciate Epstein's ability totally until he passed away, and I think his genius was revealed by his absence and the consequential change of direction. He kept the thing in balance — not that it went *bad* afterwards, but in retrospect, I really felt his force. Management is a much-encompassing term. In that sense, the Colonel managed Elvis, and I don't think anybody did it better. It's like nobody sells hamburgers better than McDonald's, but I don't want to sell hamburgers, you understand. Say the Colonel as opposed to Epstein: Epstein was naive in the way of the Colonel — development, promotion — but he lent a strong force to this unit that functioned. That to me is what management . . . that's how I related to it, since I wasn't *trained* for it. It was a matter to me of nourishing and sustaining and keeping this thing together and moving forward in a positive direction as best I knew how then. Today I've got to do it better; I've got twenty-five years under my belt.

Now who's managed *well?* (long pause) I'll tell you this: the acts that are successful both in their presentation on and off stage are managed well. Those who can keep their family stuff together and have some privacy and are covered in many ways unbeknownst to us — I'm sure that there's somebody there that's managing them well. That's how it *stays* like that, because it doesn't require

Frank Werber confering with Voyle Gilmore, Nick Reynolds, and Bob Shane (other person unknown) in the Control Room of Capitol Records Studio B. Photo courtesy: Archives of Music Preservation.

that other energy. That's one of the things I worked at pretty hard for the Trio was to keep them sort of separated from a lot of the bull. It was a *pure* presentation, and it was my wish that it *stay* pure, and they *did* stay pure. They were very untamed. They didn't get a chance to get jaded. That's not the direction we took.

PS: What are your current projects and future goals?

FW: I've been involved with Pay TV in the creation and development of new programming. I've been out in the woods for the last several years. I moved out to New Mexico in the wilderness, lived fifty miles from the nearest town and three miles up the river canyon. I've crossed the river eleven times and raised some kids out there and lived self-sufficiently for all that time. My goal would be that my children grow up as healthy, emotionally-balanced beings and somewhat capable in dealing with the world, and perhaps that I have a hand in leaving them a world that I won't be ashamed of. Amen. Alright, chorus, hit it!

PS: In closing, how would you sum-up the Kingston Trio's influence on the popular music of the past twenty years?

FW: As the primary motivating force for all of it. I would say as *they* said: "If it wouldn't have been for the work of the Weavers . . ." Well, if it wouldn't have been for the work of the Kingston Trio . . . I mean they scratched a multitude, a generation. They plowed a field . . . We were the force that took that form of expression and threw it out to as many people as possible, and the feedback was — what happened was the same as what happened in sports since certain sports have become more available to *everybody:* tennis, gymnastics . . . It's become, "Hey, look how many champions are coming out of the woodwork." And that's kind of what the Trio did. They sort of put it out there, and then all the young influenced their siblings and got it on. Hey, no Dylan without the Trio. And it's amazing . . . there's some people out there that readily say, "Yeah, the Trio really turned me on," but I never heard anybody really heavy stop and say, "I bow my head for a minute in thanks to the Lord and the Kingston Trio." (laughter) . . . Hey, Dylan, how about giving thanks to the Trio? And they had a lot to do with Peter, Paul and Mary. As a matter of fact, Nick supported Peter, Paul and Mary very strongly.

PS: Lindsey Buckingham of Fleetwood Mac . . .

FW: That's the only reason John ever got a semi-hit. With that soundtrack, *I* could have had a hit

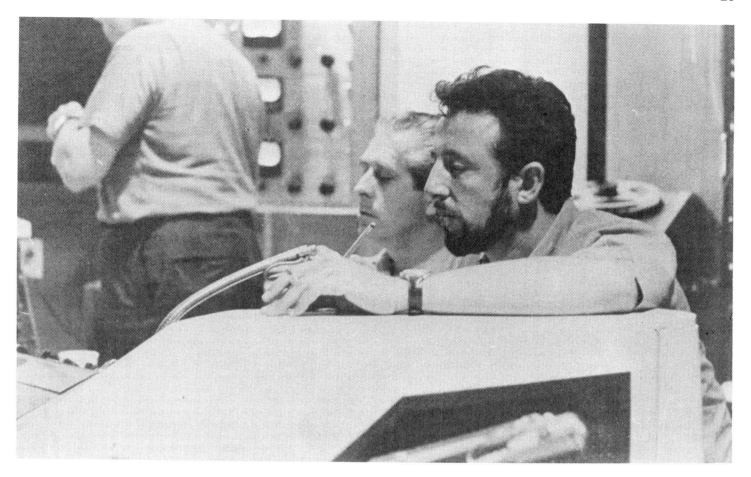

Frank Werber, Producer at work. Photo courtesy: Archives of Music Preservation.

putting my voice in front of that! (laughter) In fact, I think I could have done better! I mean that was Fleetwood Mac on that side and it was discernable.

PS: Lindsey said that he learned by listening to John's licks.

FW: That's what I mean, and the gratitude of that he evidenced, which is really nice and fair and in balance. What I am saying is there are hundreds out there who could do that. It's just that clear a connection.

Dave Guard, Bob Shane and Nick Reynolds, 1958. Early publicity photo. Photo courtesy: Guard Collection, Meir Library, University of Wisconsin-Milwaukee.

The Capitol Years
Part One (1958-1961)
by
Benjamin Blake & Jack Rubeck

Dave Guard, Nick Reynolds and Bob Shane became a recording act for Capitol Records in a roundabout way. Frank Werber has touched on part of the story, but at this point let's put it all into perspective before discussing the group's first Capitol releases.

Dave and Bob grew up in Hawaii and went to high school together, and both attended California colleges. Bob and Nick (a California native) attended the same college, Menlo, while Dave was nearby at Stanford. Late 1956 found Bob back in the Islands playing various clubs as a solo performer. Dave and Nick had formed a group of fluctuating number who at various times labeled themselves Dave Guard & The Calypsonians, The Dave Guard Quartet, The Kingstons and the Kingston Quartet. On February 10, 1957, they officially became a four-member act, consisting of Dave, Nick, Barbara Bogue and Joe Gannon (at one point Nick was briefly replaced by Don MacArthur). Their college friends flocked to such California nightspots as the *Cracked Pot* and *Facks II* to hear them play.

Our sources have ascertained that this group recorded two demonstration discs (of the 10-inch acetate variety) in early 1957. One contained seven songs: *Lolly To Dum, Without My Lover, Fast Freight, Cha Cha Boom, Come Back Lizzy, Jamaica Farewell* and *Kisses Sweeter Than Wine.* The other contained only two songs, *Run Joe* and *Without My Lover.* On the basis of these discs and their live performances as a back-up act at the *Purple Onion* nightclub, James Saphier (who was famous in the entertainment industry for being Bob Hope's agent) signed Werber and the group on April 15, 1957, to let him represent them as a television and record act. Bob Shane finished his club commitments and joined the group on May 1. Then Barbara Bogue and Joe Gannon left (years later, Joe would return as the Trio's road manager, as would Don MacArthur), leaving behind what became known as The Kingston Trio, a name chosen because it sounded both Calypsonian and collegiate.

In July of 1957, the Trio became the headline act at the *Purple Onion* and began taking voice lessons. At Werber's urging, the group recorded a more professional demonstration disc in early September, consisting of ten songs: *Hard, Ain't It Hard; Tom Dooley; Go Where I Send Thee; Coplas; Fast Freight; Sloop John B; Tic, Tic, Tic; South Coast; Tanga Tika/Toerau; Wimoweh.* All of these titles would eventually show up (in more refined performances) on their Capitol LPs. The ten-tune demo made the rounds of the Los Angeles-based record companies, and Dot, Capitol and Liberty all expressed some degree of interest. It is not known what happened to the Liberty proposal, but Dot offered the Trio a "singles deal" (45s as opposed to LPs) which Werber rejected. On September 20th, Capitol producer Voyle Gilmore returned the demo (in person) to the group at the *Purple Onion,* and he was immediately impressed with their "star" quality. On-and-off negotiations between Capitol, Werber and Saphier began.

In the meantime, The Kingston Trio Sound continued to evolve. By year's end, Dave was heavily into banjo lessons, an instrument Bob was already familiar with. Werber booked them into the Holiday Hotel in Reno, Nevada, in early 1958, where they learned to perform winningly before *unfriendly* audiences, singing as many as sixty-five songs per night. It was in Reno that someone suggested they needed a bass player to "fill in the bottom line," and the group hired David Wheat, who came equipped with both a Bachelor Of Science In Music from Columbia University and a $3,000 upright bass.

On February 15, 1958, Saphier and Werber signed a Capitol recording contract for The Kingston Trio, and Voyle Gilmore was assigned to produce their first album.

David "Buck" Wheat, circa 1959. Capitol Records Photos.

It should be noted that David "Buck" Wheat and Voyle Gilmore were probably the two best things that ever happened to the Trio's recording career. Wheat's musical knowledge and taste were productively exploited in the group's arrangements, and his obvious skill with bass and guitar added an extra dimension to the group's sound. Gilmore was the consummate producer, inventor of the recording technique commonly known today as "overdubbing", and who possessed a fine ear for what was simultaneously "good" *and* "commercial". Without the contributions of these two gifted individuals and the whip-cracking Werber, the legacy of The Kingston Trio would no doubt be greatly diminished.

* * * * * * *

The group's first album was recorded in just four days (February 20-23, 1958) in Los Angeles at Capitol's Studio B. The Trio's instrumentation and vocalization would remain basically the same throughout their recording history: all three played guitar, Dave and Bob played banjo, Nick played bongos and conga drums (for a complete analysis of the group's instruments see a later chapter in this book, "The Kingston Trio: Their Instruments"). Vocally, Bob sang most of the leads, Nick provided the high harmony and Dave filled in the low parts.

For reasons unknown, David Wheat was not utilized on this first LP session, and *Purple Onion* bassist Buzz Wheeler was recruited to fill his spot. As Frank Werber has stated, it was an entirely new experience for Capitol Records, since the group brought in its own arrangements, and no elaborate accompaniment was required. Despite the initial confusion, THE KINGSTON TRIO was reportedly Voyle Gilmore's favorite KT LP because of the high level of enthusiasm and excitement the group manifested during the recording of it.

Oddly enough, Capitol held off on releasing the album until June 1. The *first* Capitol release by The Kingston Trio was a 45 — *Scarlet Ribbons,* recorded later in Denver, Colorado, and released on April 14 with a full-page ad in *Billboard* promoting the fact that the group would perform the song on the May 1st edition of CBS TV's *Playhouse 90.* Dave, Nick and Bob portrayed World War II bomber pilots in the teleplay titled "Rumors Of Evening", thus receiving their first national exposure. While the record received airplay in some parts of the country, *Scarlet Ribbons* did not become a hit. The first song actually released from the album was the single's B side, *Three Jolly Coachmen.*

Scotch And Soda, which Bob Shane acknowledges as his favorite Trio song, has an interesting story behind it. This is the only tune on THE KINGSTON TRIO that actually credits Dave Guard as its writer, but it would be more accurate to say that Dave became its *caretaker.* Dave and Bob first learned the song while on a 1953 date in Fresno, California. Dave's date's parents had heard it nineteen years earlier on their honeymoon in Phoenix, Arizona, from an anonymous piano player at their hotel lounge. Since no one knew who wrote it, Dave put his name (after all, it was *his* date!) on what was to become Bob's most famous solo, but all concerned assumed — and genuinely hoped — that the writer would step forward and claim his loot once the song achieved popularity. Over thirty years later, the songwriter's name is still a mystery, and *Scotch And Soda* has been a mainstay of every Trio show since the beginning.

The acts the Trio most admired in the music business are represented in many of the first album's selections: *Fast Freight* (Easy Riders), *Saro Jane* (Gateway Singers), *Sloop John B* (Weavers). Pete Seeger is also reported to have had a hand in Dave's arrangement of *Bay Of Mexico. Hard, Ain't It Hard* was only the first of many Woody Guthrie classics the group would record (and it also had the distinction of being the first track the Trio ever cut for Capitol Records). The tunes on this album eventually found their way into the songbags of countless singers. Years later, an up-tempo version of *Sloop John B* would become a top ten hit for the Beach Boys, who also adopted the Trio's striped shirts.

During the Trio's June 3-30 engagement at San Francisco's *Hungry i* nightclub, Capitol dispatched a crew to record two evenings (four shows) for a future "live" LP. Recording anything outside of the studio was unusual in 1958. It is also significant to note that this recording was done only a few days after the release of the group's first album, an indication that Capitol always intended to give the group more than just a one-shot chance. Throughout the booking at the *Hungry i,* Frank Werber was selling copies of THE KINGSTON TRIO at the door.

Chronologically, the next event in the Kingston's story proved to be the turning point in their careers, changing Guard, Reynolds and Shane from talented performers having a good time and making a living, into wealthy, internationally famous celebrities.

On June 19, 1958, at radio station KLUB in Salt Lake City, Utah, disk jockey Paul Colburn played a cut from the THE KINGSTON TRIO album. He soon received phone requests to play it again — and again. *Tom Dooley* was soon the most requested-song on the station's playlist. A Salt Lake City record store sold thousands of copies of the album because record buyers were unwilling to

wait for the single to be released. Other stations added the album track to their playlists, and Capitol finally released it as a single on August 8. *Tom Dooley* went slowly up the national charts, finally hitting the top just before Christmas, and it was awarded a gold record for over one million copies sold on January 21, 1959. It was the biggest-selling record the group would ever have, as well as the corner stone of their career, and the catalyst for what soon became known as "The Folk Era." *Tom Dooley* forced their LP onto the national album charts in late October of 1958, and it eventually hit the very top. The Trio's first album remained charted for nearly four years, although it held the top spot for just one week.

A gold record for "Tom Dooley". Photo courtesy: Guard Collection, Meir Library, University of Wisconsin-Milwaukee.

Like *Scotch And Soda,* the Trio's aquisition of *Tom Dooley* also has a story behind it. They added it to the repertoire after hearing it from a middle-aged man on August 20, 1957, at an afternoon *Purple Onion* talent audition. He didn't win the audition, no one got his name, and they never saw him again. It became one of seven songs on the LP credited as "Traditional — arranged by Dave Guard". Some arrangements of the song dated back almost one hundred years to the events that legend says inspired it (the hanging of young Civil War veteran Tom Dula, a convicted murderer), so the Trio felt they were safe in copyrighting their own arrangement. Once it became obvious that the record was going to be a monster hit (and that the songwriting and publishing royalties were going to run into the big money), a New York publishing company — claiming prior ownership of a similar arrangement — brought suit against Dave Guard and the Trio's publishing. Four long years later the court found against Dave, and *Tom Dooley* was assigned to the New York publisher, with the ar-

side one:

1   Three Jolly Coachmen
2   Bay of Mexico
3   Banua
4   Tom Dooley
5   Fast Freight
6   Hard, Ain't It Hard

side two:

1   Saro Jane
2   Sloop John B
3   Santy Anno
4   Scotch And Soda
5   Coplas
6   Little Maggie

rangement officially credited to "F. Warner/J. Lomax/A. Lomax".

FROM THE "HUNGRY i", the Trio's second LP, was released in January of 1959, while *Tom Dooley* was still high on the charts. The eleven tracks were culled from the best of the performances that Capitol had recorded the previous June. This album was an immediate best seller, yet it fell just one notch short of the number one spot on the *Billboard* listings. Both FROM THE "HUNGRY i" and THE KINGSTON TRIO eventually sold nearly 800,000 copies each, and achieved gold album status by 1960.

The second album's song line-up continued to reflect the Trio's main musical influences, with Burl Ives' *New York Girls,* and several songs from the Weavers' repertoire: *Wimoweh, Lonesome Traveler* and *When The Saints Go Marching In.* The latter title, which finishes out the album, became the Kingston Trio's traditional concert finale. *Wimoweh* became a smash hit a few years later for the Tokens, as *The Lion Sleeps Tonight.*

This album also made Dave Guard's reputation as an "intellectual" comic, thanks to his often lengthy speeches between tunes. This was actually a device Dave learned from Lou Gottlieb of the Gateway Singers (later of the Limeliters) to keep the audience entertained while the group tuned-up between numbers.

Trio members are credited on this album with only two copyrighted arrangements: *Dorie* and *Gue, Gue.* They originally tried to claim *Shady Grove,* but that adaptation was eventually credited to folk singer Jean Ritchie. *Gue, Gue* is described in the liner notes as "... a French lullaby whose beauty leaves the audience hushed and hanging on every phrase ..." There is good reason why we don't hear the otherwise fairly rowdy crowd on this track: it was recorded in the studio! Apparently the Trio had a rough time getting the proper blend for the tune's accappella intro at any of the shows taped, so they resorted to this minor deceit for the sake of their listeners.

Oddly enough, none of the album's tunes were released as singles. By far the most popular cut with DJs was *The Merry Minuet,* written by Sheldon Harnick, who later became famous for *Fiddler On The Roof* and other Broadway shows. A special 45 of the song was sent to radio stations but was never released to the record-buying public.

With the excitement of *Tom Dooley* blasting out of every jukebox in the land, the group was anxious to get back into the studio and record a follow-up hit single. On January 10, 1959, Capitol released *Raspberries, Strawberries* as the third 45 by The Kingston Trio. The song was written by Will Holt, but collectors will be interested to learn that

the labels on early radio station copies listed Guard, Reynolds and Shane as the writers. Voyle Gilmore once stated that this was his personal favorite of all Trio 45s, and it was a great disappointment to all concerned when it failed to crack the national top forty chart. From our present-day perspective it would appear that Capitol released the record too soon, as *Tom Dooley* was still being heavily programmed in many parts of the country. It would not be inaccurate to say that this little record just got lost in the wake of the monster.

It is likely that the single record version of *Raspberries, Strawberries* was the last Kingston Trio release that was *not* recorded in sterophonic sound. All of the recordings we have thus far discussed were recorded monophonically (hereafter these terms will be identified as "mono" and "stereo"). Besides *Raspberries, Strawberries, Scarlet Ribbons* and the twenty-three tracks that comprise the first two albums, there were a few other mono releases that should be noted at this point. *Ruby Red, Como Se Viene, Se Va* and *Sail Away Ladies* were apparently all recorded at the same studio session that produced *Gue, Gue,* probably sometime in July of 1958. *Ruby Red* was released as the B side of *Tom Dooley. Sail Away Ladies* and *Como Se Viene, Se Va* were finally released in July of 1959 on an extended-play 45

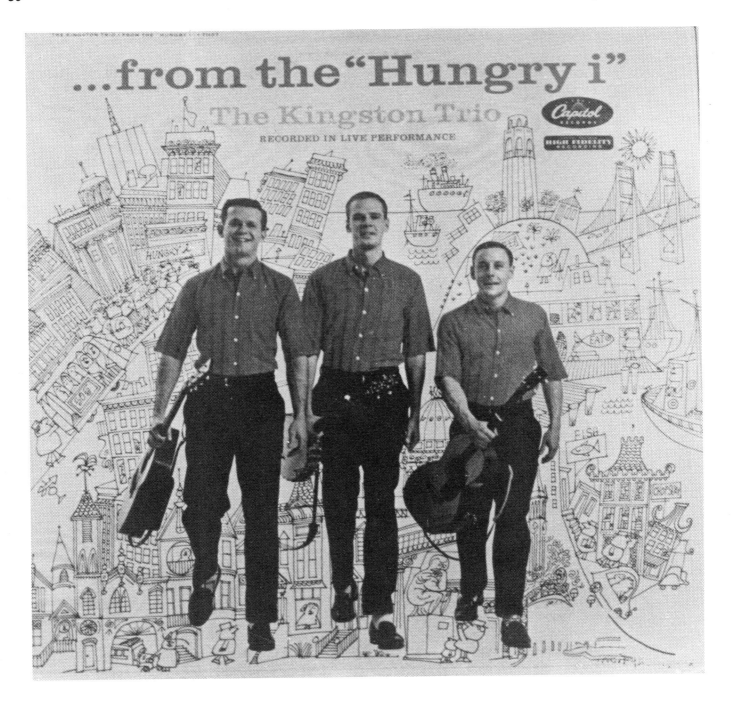

side one:

1　*Tic, Tic, Tic*
2　*Gue, Gue*
3　*Dorie*
4　*South Coast*
5　*Zombie Jamboree*
6　*Wimoweh*

side two:

1　*New York Girls*
2　*They Call The Wind Maria*
3　*The Merry Minuet*
4　*Shady Grove/Lonesome Traveler*
5　*When The Saints Go Marching In*

(hereafter referred to as an "EP") titled *M.T.A.*, with *Como Se Viene, Se Va* also eventually appearing as a 1961 single in Great Britain. The Denver session that produced *Raspberries, Strawberries* also yielded *Sally,* which was released as that single's B side. Both tracks were also issued on a 1959 EP titled *Raspberries, Strawberries,* along with *Scarlet Ribbons* and *Ruby Red.* It should be noted that of all these "stray tracks", only *Como Se Viene, Se Va* ever found its way onto an LP (A TRIBUTE TO THE KINGSTON TRIO, a 1966 release in Great Britain).

It is unfortunate that these early tracks were not recorded in stereo, because the technology existed. The industry in general was tentative about the sales potential of stereo discs by so-called "Popular" artists, as the medium had been created primarily for Classical music — or anything else requiring a fairly large orchestra. Young people, especially the more affluent college crowd, were buying stereo equipment to listen to Jazz, and when the Trio hit, many record distributors began receiving a steadily growing wave of requests for stereo versions of their albums. Shortly after the release of the *Raspberries, Strawberries* 45, Capitol geared-up to record all future KT records in both mono *and* stereo, but as it turned out the first stereo album by the Trio wasn't recorded by Capitol at all!

STEREO CONCERT, released by Capitol in March of 1959, was actually recorded without Capitol's knowledge at Liberty Hall in El Paso, Texas, on a single evening in late October of 1958. Between fifteen and seventeen songs were recorded on two-track stereo tape, reportedly by a Texas record dealer named Lee Morton. With Frank Werber's permission, Morton suspended a pair of microphones above the stage, in addition to the customary single floor mike, and a new phase in the recording career of the Kingston Trio was launched. Later, back in Hollywood, Gilmore and Capitol were no doubt as embarrassed as they were angry when the tape was offered to them for sale, but they culled ten tracks from it and released the album to appease the stereo seekers (the reason the clandestine recording had been made in the first place). The sound quality was remarkably good, differing from other live Trio recordings only in the muted volume of the audience's response. It should be remembered that the public was charged an extra dollar for stereo in those days, so this ten-band LP was not exactly a bargain. But it surprised Capitol by selling over 200,000 copies and helped establish the fact that Popular music could sell in stereo. It should also be noted that Voyle Gilmore was not too embarrassed to put his name on it as "producer".

In their rush to get it out, Capitol showed a lack of originality by using the same cover photo that appeared on the group's first LP and even forgot to leave separations between the bands on side one in early pressings. STEREO CONCERT was supposed to appeal to the stereo owners who had not bought the group's two mono albums, but it also coaxed a lot of the Trio's fans into buying stereo players, just so they could hear STEREO CONCERT! Even those who already owned the other LPs were getting a treat: new versions of nine KT favorites, plus the LP debut of the song *Raspberries, Strawberries.* Judging from the recording date, this live version is technically the Trio's *first* recording of the tune. This album's version of *They Call The Wind Maria* is even more rousing than that found on the previous live LP, showing the growth of the Trio as performers in a very short time. As a piece of musical history, this live version of *Tom Dooley* — recorded while the record was climbing the charts — is hard to top, and it remains the only released live recording of the song by Dave, Nick and Bob. One final note of interest is that this version of *When The Saints Go Marching In* lists Dave Guard as the writer, while Paul Campbell (an alias for The Weavers) received credit on FROM THE "HUNGRY i", or at least on later pressings of it. This song was the source of yet another lawsuit against the KT's publishing company.

Capitol's first *planned* stereo release by The Kingston Trio was an EP in April of 1959. On March 6, the Trio had released its third single, *The Tijuana Jail.* Voyle Gilmore had found the song for the Trio, and when Capitol caught wind of the rumor that Harry Belafonte wanted to record it they rushed the group into a New York studio (February 9) to cut it in a hurry. By May, the Trio had another top twenty hit, and the stereo EP was titled after it. Besides a stereo version of the hit, and its B side, *Oh, Cindy,* the EP also contained the STEREO CONCERT versions of *Coplas* and *Tom Dooley.* It is notable that *Oh, Cindy* (from the

side one:

1   Banua
2   Three Jolly Coachmen
3   South Coast
4   Coplas
5   They Call The Wind Maria

side two:

1   Zombie Jamboree
2   Tom Dooley
3   The Merry Minuet
4   Raspberries, Strawberries
5   When The Saints Go Marching In

John Wayne movie *Rio Bravo*) was the only KT record that ever gave even partial credit to Frank Werber as songwriter.

April 21 found the Trio back in Los Angeles recording *Tom Dooley* one more time for the soundtrack of a movie (*The Legend Of Tom Dooley,* starring Michael Landon) based on their million-seller. Next was an appearance at the first annual Grammy Awards on May 10, where they picked up the prize for "Best Country & Western Vocal Performance of 1958" (for *Tom Dooley,* which was also nominated in the "Best Performance by a Vocal Group" category). By the following year — because of what the Trio had started — a separate "Folk" catetory was established for the Grammys.

We should properly note that the rise of The Kingston Trio coincided with a period of profound change in the record industry. The late 1950s saw the flowering of the 12-inch LP album; the introduction of stereophonic sound; the formation of the Record Industry Association Of America (R.I.A.A.) as a watchdog to set quality guidelines for the manufacture of records, and to certify the sales of member companies' LPs and 45s (thus legitimizing the previously haphazard — and sometimes very questionable — awarding of gold records); and the beginning of the National Academy of Recording Arts & Sciences (N.A.R.A.S.), set up to honor both technical and performing excellence. The Trio and Capitol carved substantial inroads in all of these areas.

* * * * * * *

In June of 1959, Capitol released (in both mono and stereo versions) THE KINGSTON TRIO AT LARGE, the group's fourth album. The first two tracks, *M.T.A.* and *All My Sorrows,* were released as their fifth single on June 18. If master numbers are to be believed, *M.T.A.* was recorded before *The Tijuana Jail* (all of AT LARGE was recorded in New York City), perhaps making it the group's first stereo studio cut. Although no bigger a hit than *The Tijuana Jail, M.T.A.* quickly became (and still remains) the group's second most requested tune, and only *Tom Dooley* outranks it as the Trio's trademark. The song's popularity was no doubt helped by the fact that it became an instant favorite of DJs with its catchy lyrics about the doomed subway rider named Charlie. The group first heard the song from Will Holt.

AT LARGE (released as GOOD NEWS in some European countries) also included a newly-recorded version of *Scarlet Ribbons,* which offered further evidence of the group's improvement as vocalists over the past year. The Trio was obviously trying to find another *Tom Dooley,* judging from the subject matter of *Getaway John* and *The Long*

Bob Shane

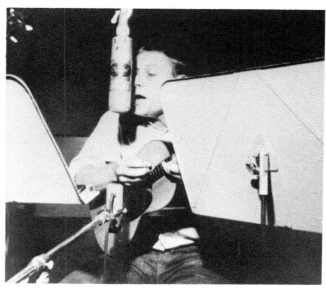

Nick Reynolds

Dave Guard   **Capitol Records Photos**

side one:

1 M.T.A.
2 All My Sorrows
3 Blow Ye Winds
4 Corey, Corey
5 The Seine
6 I Bawled

side two:

1 Good News
2 Getaway John
3 The Long Black Rifle
4 Early In The Mornin'
5 Scarlet Ribbons
6 Remember The Alamo

Black Rifle. The Seine is one of the most beautiful and best arranged of all Trio recordings. Tender and melancholy, the tune is handled with quiet understatement by Bob, who sings the lead. It was written especially for the Trio by Lord Irving Burgess. Burgess, Jane Bowers, and eventually John Stewart became known as the Trio "in-house" writers from 1959-1961. Bowers collaborated with Dave Guard on some of the group's finest songs.

Remember The Alamo, by Jane Bowers, was one of this album's most riveting tracks and was supposedly intended for release as the follow-up single to *M.T.A..* Legend has it that John Wayne was fond of the recording and made overtures about possibly using it in his epic film, *The Alamo* (under production at the time), so Capitol and the Trio decided to sit on the single until Wayne decided. Eventually he went with *The Green Leaves Of Summer* by Dimitri Tiomkin whom Wayne had hired to score the film, but he still wanted the Trio to record it for the movie. For reasons that remain clouded with the passage of time, Wayne and the Trio never got it together, and The Brothers Four (and Columbia Records) ended up with the memorable song, and all thoughts of releasing a 45 of *Remember The Alamo* were forgotten.

Dave, Nick and Bob claim authorship on AT LARGE of *All My Sorrows* and *Corey, Corey,* both traditional folk songs, with the latter beng almost a direct steal of The Weavers' *Darling Corey.* Dave takes the credit for *Blow Ye Winds* and *Getaway John,* while Bob gets his first solo acknowledgement as a writer for the forgettable *I Bawled.*

This album is filled with strong performances. It is Dave Guard's opinion that AT LARGE was the group's finest album, and many fans and music critics agree. It later won the group another Grammy (for "Best Folk Performance of 1959" — it was also nominated in the "Best Performance by a Vocal Group" category), held the number one spot on the charts for an astounding fifteen weeks, and went gold in 1960. AT LARGE sold almost a million copies, eventually being outdistanced only by 1962's THE BEST OF THE KINGSTON TRIO as the group's biggest-selling LP. It also proved to be the extra weight needed to propel Guard, Reynolds and Shane onto the August 3, 1959 cover of *Life.*

Three days later, Capitol issued the Trio's sixth single record, *A Worried Man/San Miguel.* The A side proved to be the original group's last top twenty hit, and it was one of their most rousing performances. *A Worried Man,* a fine example of the Trio's ability to combine wit and verve with ringing banjos, is loosely derived from the traditional *Worried Man Blues* and credited to Dave Guard and Tom Glazer. Dave's powerful solo

reading of Jane Bowers' *San Miguel* rivals *All My Sorrows* as the closest the KT ever got to scoring a two-sided hit, especially in Great Britain.

Both sides of the single were featured on the Trio's fifth LP, HERE WE GO AGAIN, released in October of 1959. This one established a statistical landmark right up front, as Capitol ordered an advance pressing of 250,000 copies — an all-time high in those pre-Beatle days. The company's expectations did not go unrewarded, as the album went on to sell over 900,000 units, again attaining the top chart position (remaining at number one for eight weeks) and earning gold status in 1960. HERE WE GO AGAIN garnered Grammy nominations for the Trio in the 1960 "Vocal Group" and "Folk" categories.

Recorded in California at Capitol's Studio B (where the vast majority of KT tracks were born), the album's selections are a fine continuance of the smooth mixture of sea chantys, banjo thumpers, folk blues and just plain good sound that made the group so popular with people of all age brackets. Haunting atmosphere is provided by such skillfully-handled tunes as *The Wanderer* (a bluesy solo by Nick), *Haul Away,* the aforementioned *San Miguel,* and even the darkly-rousing spiritual, *'Round About The Mountain* (from the pen of Limeliter Lou Gottlieb). The first line of *Molly Dee* gives this album its title and also marks the beginning of songwriter John Stewart's association with the Trio. *Across The Wide Missouri* is HERE WE GO AGAIN's harmonic high point. Actually a refurbished version of the folk standard *Shenandoah,* this track remains one of the group's all-time listening pleasures. Trio-owned songs are scarce on this LP, with Dave's name listed only on *Haul Away* and the Civil War relic *Goober Peas,* in addition to *A Worried Man.*

Since all of the group's major LPs (beginning with AT LARGE) were pressed in both mono and stereo versions, collectors may find it of considerable interest to note the minor differences in length of the cuts on mono and stereo releases. Two final master discs were always created from the master tapes (one to press mono LPs and one to press stereo LPs), and the discrepancy in length occurs only on tunes that "fade out" at the end, with the mixed stereo version usually having a longer fade. This was common on many Capitol releases, including those of The Beatles and The Beach Boys. For the Trio, perhaps the most obvious example is HERE WE GO AGAIN's *Rollin' Stone,* which actually comes to a halt on the stereo mix *before* the fade is completed.

Hot on the heels of HERE WE GO AGAIN, Capitol put out the KT's seventh 45 on October 9. The B side was a quiet, melancholy John Stewart

side one:

1 Molly Dee
2 Across The Wide Missouri
3 Haul Away
4 The Wanderer
5 'Round About The Mountain
6 Oleanna

side two:

1 The Unfortunate Miss Bailey
2 San Miguel
3 E Inu Tatou E
4 Rollin' Stone
5 Goober Peas
6 A Worried Man

composition called *Green Grasses* (it later ended up on the 1966 British collection, A TRIBUTE TO THE KINGSTON TRIO), and the A side was another story altogether, as Nick Reynolds will later detail. An apparant experiment in fusing rock, jazz and calypso, *Coo Coo-U* (co-written by David Wheat) was a commercial disaster and never appeared on an album. It is undoubtedly the strangest track ever recorded by The Kingston Trio.

* * * * * * *

The December 7, 1959 issue of *Billboard* listed four Trio albums among the top ten best sellers for that week, a feat that remains unsurpassed to this day. [For the record: HERE WE GO AGAIN was at position number two, AT LARGE was number four, THE KINGSTON TRIO was seventh and FROM THE "HUNGRY i" was eighth.] How were Dave, Nick and Bob able to achieve this incredible statistic? Good management, considerable talent, a classy image, exhaustive touring and heavy promotion certainly played a hand in it, but those credentials would also fit a great many other artists of their day. It is our theory that what was "in the grooves" kept the Kingston Trio at the top of the charts for so long, and when you get beyond natural talent

and clever arrangements, it is recording technique — producing, engineering and mixing — that make the difference.

Voyle Gilmore produced the group's records, which is to say that he worked a considerable amount of magic in often a very short time. Gilmore spent his first several years at Capitol in the sales department, not actually producing until he was forty. He worked with nearly every Capitol American recording artist of the Fifties and Sixties, but he was most lauded for his achievements with Frank Sinatra and The Kingston Trio. While producing The Four Preps and The Four Freshmen he invented what he called "double-tracking" (or "overdubbing"), the then-revolutionary technique of *adding* something to an already recorded track. The only drawback of overdubbing in those days was the "hiss" (extraneous noise and static) that increased in audibility with each additional mix of an added track. With the Trio, he first utilized this innovation on AT LARGE. Played with modern-day equipment, many of the cuts on that album have so much hiss that it sounds as though our boys were playing air conditioners as well as guitars! As Gilmore perfected the technique, such noise on future sessions became increasingly less evident.

Gilmore worked hand-in-hand with recording

The Kingston Trio, Bob Shane, Nick Reynolds and Dave Guard: On location for a photo session. Photo courtesy: Archives of Music Preservation.

engineer William D. "Pete" Abbot for the original sessions (engineer Curly Walters also assisted on the first LP), and then would re-mix the tapes with Rex Uptegraft. A typical KT LP would take Gilmore about three days to record and one day to re-mix. Beginning with AT LARGE, the recordings were usually done with seven microphones: standing mikes for the instruments (including bass) and hanging mikes for vocals. This enabled Gilmore to record each Trio member on a separate track; three tracks, with one voice and one instrument on each, and Wheat's bass on Nick's tenor guitar track for ease in equalization. Beginning with HERE WE GO AGAIN, Gilmore would tone *down* the vocals a bit when mixing and balancing. He would then playback the recording to Dave, Nick and Bob through earphones and have them sing their parts a *second* time over the original. This gave the Trio a much fuller sound, more than making up for the slightly diminished fidelity of stereophonic sound. The Trio did little or no instrumental overdubbing until late 1960 (on THE LAST MONTH OF THE YEAR), and although vocal *solos* were never overdubbed, from HERE WE GO AGAIN on we are hearing *six* voices ("double-voicing" as he called it) whenever the three sing together. The incredible "ringing" and color of the musical instruments was at least partially achieved by Capitol's echo chamber, which reportedly stretched-out like the Grand Canyon under a parking lot. We hope we have provided some clues as to why *your* group never sounded quite as good as The Kingston Trio: you should have recorded for Capitol Records!

Engineer Pete Abbot shared a few memories from the Capitol sessions with us:

"... The first albums just came so easy, because they'd go in there and do what they enjoyed doing ... We would go in and record four songs in three hours for three days running, and we would get an album all finished and ready to go ... I never got credit on any Capitol album, because Capitol Records did not give engineer credit ... Capitol always did two-track stereo, and then whatever the multi-channel recording that was 'in' at that time was the backup. So they always tried to get it right on two-track stereo the first time, which is the original generation, so you get a lot cleaner recording ... We *may* have done some overdubbing on two-track stereo, and some overdubbing on mono ... Overdubbing, at that time, meant that you laid a track down on tape and played that track back through the console and fed it to another tape machine, and then they sang ... A lot of times on the playbacks I used to think it was funny because they wouldn't all sit together and comment. Dave would go way down to the other end, Bobby's sort of sitting there, and Nick would go over on the other side ... Most of the time the sessions were closed ..."

Voyle Gilmore offers a suggestion to Dave, Nick and Bob. Bassist "Buck" Wheat stands at ready in the background. Photo courtesy: Capitol Records.

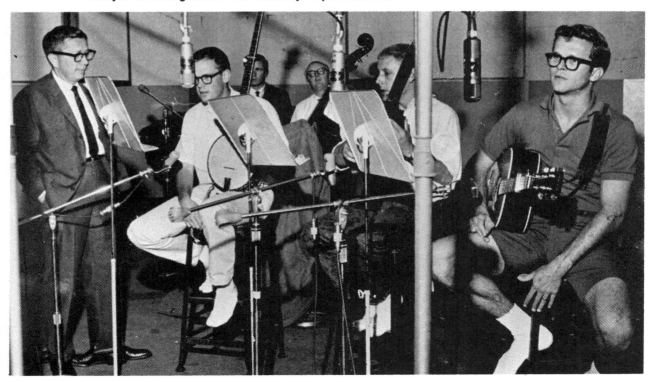

side one:

1 El Matador
2 The Mountains O'Mourne
3 Don't Cry Katie
4 Tanga Tika/Toerau
5 With Her Hand Tucked Underneath
    Her Arm
6 Carrier Pigeon

side two:

1 Bimini
2 Raspberries, Strawberries
3 Mangwani Mpulele
4 With You, My Johnny
5 The Hunter
6 Farewell Adelita

* * * * * * *

Getting back to the general sequence of events, Capitol followed the poor showing of *Coo Coo-U* with the recording of a new KT album in New York City in early February, 1960. Fans got their first taste of it on February 28, with the release of *El Matador* as a 45. This single eventually made a respectable top forty showing. The B side was *Home From The Hill* (from the film of the same title), and it has the distinction of being the first KT cut to feature a lush orchestral backing. Like *Coo Coo-U, Home From The Hill* was never included on an album and therefore never released to the record-buying public in stereo.

The new LP, SOLD OUT, was released in April. The KT's sixth album followed its older siblings to number one (where it spent twelve weeks), selling over 700,000 copies and earning the group (in 1961) its fifth gold album. The presence of an anonymous female model marked the first time anyone other than Dave, Nick and Bob had graced the front of a KT album cover.

Dave Guard has told us that SOLD OUT was the group's low point because of the sub-par quality of the material they had to work with. Familiar songs that they *all* liked were becoming scarce by this time, as evidenced by the appearance here of the *Tanga Tika/Toerau medley and Raspberries, Strawberries.* The former had left their repertoire some time earlier, having never been deemed quite worthy of inclusion on an album. The latter was a new recording of the old 45, which differs from that (and the STEREO CONCERT version) with its tighter arrangement, slightly slower tempo, an altered finish and a small change in the lyric (" . . . Paris air . . ." becomes ". . . air of France . . ."). This has become the definitive version of the song. Many of the group members have expressed dissatisfaction with the quantity of albums they had to grind ot every year, and lack of good new material was one of the key reasons for that dissatisfaction. Voyle Gilmore felt that three albums per year — outrageous by today's standards — was about right for the Trio, as he believed any less would allow the public to forget who they were!

Perhaps the nicest performance on SOLD OUT belongs to Nick Reynolds, whose voice is well-suited to the tender *The Mountains O'Mourne.* The guitar arrangement on this song is tastefully done, and the whole effect can best be experienced via stereo headphones. This listening method is recommended for most of the Trio's better-engineered stereo tracks. On this album those include *With Her Head Tucked Underneath Her Arm,* an amusing piece of English folklore nonsense, and *With You, My Johnny,* on which Dave Guard

handles the lead very well, and "Buck" Wheat's bass playing is a major part. Other examples of the album's better moments are: *Bimini,* where banjo and conga provide a fitting rhythm; *Farewell Adelita,* an uptempo ballad with a fine lead vocal by Bob Shane; *Mangwani Mpulele,* another

Bob Shane, Capitol recording session, 1959. Photo courtesy: Archives of Music Preservation.

nonsense tune (from folkster Theodore Bikel) on which the group really sounds like they are enjoying themselves.

Technically, this disc is hard to fault. Frequency response is excellent, surface noise and tape hiss very low. The Trio claims songwriter credit on SOLD OUT's final three tunes: *With You, My Johnny, The Hunter* and *Farewell Adelita.*

SOLD OUT was quickly followed by STRING ALONG, the Trio's seventh LP, released in July of 1960. Although this is one of the best albums the group ever recorded, the jacket suggests that Capitol rushed it out. The cover photo is one of the least imaginative of all the group's releases, and the liner notes (which began dwindling with the previous LP) are foregone completely in favor of a series of candid black & white snapshots. The title was a take-off on Mitch Miller's "Sing Along With Mitch" albums, which were sweeping the country and beginning to rival the Trio's in sales. Perhaps it is just the STRING ALONG title that gives rise to this opinion, but it seems the Trio (or perhaps Voyle Gilmore) gave more attention to the instrumental work here than they did on previous outings. Banjos ring in abundant clarity on the faster tracks, while melodic guitars nicely compliment the quieter tunes. One point of Trio trivia: this is the only album cover to feature Bob Shane holding a banjo.

Four tracks from side one were to become the group's next two singles: *Bad Man Blunder/The*

side one:

1. *Bad Man Blunder*
2. *The Escape Of Old John Webb*
3. *When I Was Young*
4. *Leave My Woman Alone*
5. *This Mornin', This Evenin', So Soon*
6. *Everglades*

side two:

1. *Buddy Better Get On Down The Line*
2. *South Wind*
3. *Who's Gonna Hold Her Hand*
4. *To Morrow*
5. *Colorado Trail*
6. *The Tattooed Lady*

Escape Of Old John Webb (released August 1), and *Everglades/This Mornin', This Evenin', So Soon* (released October 1). These two 45's mark the first time Capitol did any editing of the group's singles. The 45 version of *Bad Man Blunder* is minus Nick's famous last words ("Bang, you're dead!"), and the last half-minute or so is removed from *This Mornin', This Evenin', So Soon,* probably in hopes that the shorter length would invite more radio airplay (it didn't). *Bad Man Blunder,* a novelty tune in the tradition of *The Tijuana Jail,* was released as a single to generate more royalties for composer Cisco Houston, who was near death in a hospital at the time. It proved to be the last 45 by Dave, Nick and Bob to crack *Billboard's* top forty. *The Escape Of Old John Webb* was included on the album and the single for one specific reason: everybody was trying to persuade Capitol's parent company, E.M.I., to promote the KT in Great Britain. They felt that including a refurbished English folk tune here and there would soften-up the corporate difference (hence *The Hunter* and several others). *Everglades,* though not a best-seller as a single, proved to be one of the album's finer cuts. It somehow managed to be a dramatically well-paced murder ballad (complete with surprise-twist ending) and a delightful send-up of the Everly Brothers at the same time. Most of the guitar work on this track even parodies that of such Everly hits as *Wake Up Little Susie* and *Bird Dog.* As fate would have it, *Everglades* turned out to be the final chart single for the Trio during the years Dave Guard was a member.

STRING ALONG is graced with other memorable moments, as well. Among these are two of the prettiest tunes the group ever recorded, *Colorado Trail* (authories by poet Carl Sanburg and The Weavers' Lee Hays) and *When I Was Young* (another fine Dave Guard/Jane Bowers collaboration). Perhaps the most unusual song for the Trio here is the Ray Charles blueser *Leave My Woman Alone,* with its no-holds-barred lead vocal by Dave. Possibly the LP's very best track is *South Wind,* a haunting ballad of lonliness and lost love from the gifted pen of Travis Edmonson, which features vocals by Bob and Dave, while Nick is kept busy with the percussion chores. David Wheat, who by now also owned a California drum factory, had designed a special set of percussion instruments ("boo-bams") for Nick, which the group later took along on tour for the expressed purpose of performing *South Wind.*

STRING ALONG was the last KT album to go all the way to number one (a position it occupied for ten weeks), and the last *new* release to earn a gold record award (in 1962), eventually selling well over a half million copies. On this album, Bob is credited as co-writer of *Who's Gonna Hold Her*

Hand, Dave teams with Jane Bowers on *Buddy Better Get On Down The Line* (and the previously mentioned *When I Was Young*), and Nick, Dave and Bob all get a piece of the action with *The Tattooed Lady.*

The Kingston Trio spent what free time they had in the summer of 1960 working on a Christmas album, of all things. It was released in October as their eighth Capitol LP, titled THE LAST MONTH OF THE YEAR. With sales of just over 200,000 copies through the course of four Christmas seasons (it was deleted from the Capitol catalog after 1963), it remains one of the more elusive Trio releases for collectors to acquire (especially in stereo). It also sports the first LP cover where the group is pictured without their musical instruments. It happily marks a return to liner notes for the Trio, as well.

Of the ten albums recorded by Dave, Nick and Bob, this is probably the most interesting and certainly one of the best, with its diversified instrumentation and international flavor. It is to the Trio's credit that they did not just "grind out" a Christmas record, as was the norm for so many artists in those years. THE LAST MONTH OF THE YEAR reflects care and hard work on the part of its creators, and it stands up as one of the freshest holiday recordings ever hatched.

Somerset Gloucestershire Wassail and *Goodnight My Baby* were released from the LP as a single on October 20, 1960. The 45 released in England was *Bye Bye Thou Little Tiny Child/The White Snows Of Winter.* Neither sold well nor received a great deal of airplay.

The Trio supplemented their usual banjoes and guitars on this album with a celeste and a Bouzouki, the latter being a Greek mandolin fashioned especially for the group (according to the liner notes) by New Yorker George Atanasiou.

The group avoided the overdone popular carols of the day, digging instead into the holiday musical heritage of many lands for these twelve seldom-heard Yuletide tunes. They worked-up new arrangements for ten of the songs while tastefully maintaining an authentic flavor on all. The high points of THE LAST MONTH OF THE YEAR are many. Certainly *The White Snows Of Winter* is a beautiful song, with the lead vocal well handled by Bob Shane, who (along with Tom Drake) adapted the melody from Brahm's *First Symphony. Mary Mild* and *All Through The Night* are evocatively rendered, as well. On the "rousing" side, the title tune is a standout — akin to *When The Saints Go Marching In,* but the Trio manages to keep a restrained lid on this performance, and the resulting track is perhaps the most effective spiritual they ever set down.

side one:

1 *Bye Bye Thou Little Tiny Child*
2 *The White Snows Of Winter*
3 *We Wish You A Merry Christmas*
4 *All Through The Night*
5 *Goodnight My Baby*
6 *Go Where I Send Thee*

side two:

1 *Follow Now On Shepherds*
2 *Somerset Gloucestershire Wassail*
3 *Mary Mild*
4 *A Round About Christmas*
5 *Sing We Noel*
6 *The Last Month Of The Year*

For the first time, Nick Reynolds claims *solo* copyrights on three songs: *A Round About Christmas, Goodnight My Baby* and *All Through The Night.* In addition to *The White Snows Of Winter,* Bob Shane claims partial credit for *Mary Mild,* while Dave Guard claims all of *Sing We Noel* and *Bye Bye Thou Little Tiny Child,* and part of *Somerset Gloucestershire Wassail.* All three get a portion of *Go Where I Send Thee,* which incidentally became the last of the Trio's original Capitol demo songs to finally be re-recorded for an LP. "Buck" Wheat got praise for his bass playing on this track in the liner notes, marking the first time the Trio actually acknowledged his existance in print. In addition, much of the excellent guitar work heard on this LP is Wheat's.

* * * * * * *

Even before the release of THE LAST MONTH OF THE YEAR, the group was busy collecting songs (including several from Pete Seeger) for their *next* album, but perhaps this is a good place to pause and mention some of the Trio's other activities in 1960 that would be of special interest to audiophiles.

Three more records by the Trio were put out in 1960, although not released in the traditional manner. In January, the group kicked-off its fundraising efforts for the March of Dimes with a specially-pressed 45 that featured *Molly Dee* and *Haul Away* from HERE WE GO AGAIN. Royalties were waived by all concerned, and the proceeds (from sales of the record at fundraisers throughout the country) went directly to the March of Dimes. Later that year, the group endorsed both Welgrume Sportswear and Lion of Troy Shirts (men's clothing lines) with a giveaway single of *Farewell Adelita* and *Corey, Corey,* from SOLD OUT and AT LARGE, respectively.

Also under the heading of endorsements, around this time the Trio was well paid to promote the soft drink 7-Up in radio and TV commercials which consisted of familiar KT tunes with cleverly altered lyrics. A special EP was pressed as a promotional item for 7-Up called *Cool Cargo,* which contained the hits *Tom Dooley* and *A Worried Man,* plus *The Hunter* and *With You, My Johnny* from SOLD OUT. It should be stressed that the EP does *not* contain any of the Trio's special 7-Up versions of the four tunes. All three records were manufactured by Capitol on its special "Capitol Custom" label. A great many special promotional 45s and EPs by the KT were pressed for radio stations and jukeboxes over the years, but these are the only three we know of that were actually made

side one:

1. En El Agua
2. Come All You Fair And Tender Ladies
3. Jug Of Punch
4. Bonny Hielan' Laddie
5. Utawena
6. Hard Travelin'

side two:

1. Hangman
2. Speckled Roan
3. The River Is Wide
4. Oh, Yes, Oh!
5. Blow The Candle Out
6. Blue Eyed Gal

available (although not through the customary retail outlets) to the record buying public.

* * * * * *

1961 began for the Trio with the January release of MAKE WAY, their ninth LP. It climbed to number two on *Billboard's* chart and sold over 350,000 copies. Although it is a craftsman-like work, this record gets many votes as the least effective of Dave, Nick and Bob's outings. Perhaps it is just the brooding aura that the dark tones of the jacket convey, but this album seems to lack the spark of vibrant enthusiasm that made the Trio so endearing. No doubt the absence of any hard-driving tracks adds to that mood, although both *Hard Travelin'* and *Blue Eyed Gal* do their best to achieve some pep. The instrumentation seems almost subdued on even the more fast-paced numbers. Also, MAKE WAY (like STRING ALONG) is completely devoid of liner notes.

As one might expect on a "laid back" record like this one, it is the slow and melancholy tracks that are the most effective. *Come All You Fair And Tender Ladies* (with "sad" guitar providing a perfect counterpoint) and *The River Is Wide* are perfect examples of this, as is *Blow The Candle Out,* one of Bob Shane's finest solos and possibly the best track MAKE WAY has to offer.

Nine of the LP's songs list Trio members as writers, an all-time high. Dave claims a portion of *Oh, Yes, Oh, Come All You Fair And Tender Ladies* and *Bonny Hielan' Laddie.* Nick is given all of *The River Is Wide* and half of *Utawena* and *Hangman.* Bob gets part of *Blue Eyed Gal, Blow The Candle Out,* and all of *En El Agua,* the last of which was eventually the only side released from the LP as a single (and a B side, at that) on March 8.

As previously stated, words — and in some cases the music — of standard folk songs were changed enough to enable the Trio to claim royalties (occasionally under the group alias, "Jack Splittard"). Bob Shane relates a story about *En El Agua:* The Trio had known the song for years and assumed it was in the Public Domain, so they put Bob's name on it when the album and single were issued. After hearing it on the radio, a gentleman named Antonio Fernandez stepped forward and promptly sued Bob for a sizeable amount! It seems he had written the song in 1938 for a Mexican music festival and had actually bothered to have it copyrighted in the U.S.A.

January 19, 1961 · Four gold albums for Bob, Dave, Frank Werber, Voyle Gilmore and Nick.
Photo courtesy: Capitol Records.

side one:

1 You're Gonna Miss Me
2 Pastures Of Plenty
3 Coast Of California
4 It Was A Very Good Year
5 Guardo El Lobo
6 Razors In The Air

side two:

1 Billy Goat Hill
2 This Land Is Your Land
3 Run Molly, Run
4 Senora
5 Lemon Tree
6 You Don't Knock

Needless to say, when *En El Agua* reappeared many years later on one of the BEST OF albums, Mr. Fernandez was the credited writer.

The A side of the March 8 single (the group's twelfth) was *You're Gonna Miss Me*, a newly-recorded variation of the classic *Frankie and Johnny* folk staple. In England, *En El Agua* was released as the A side, with the KT oldie *Como Se Viene, Se Va* as the flip. This subtle change was the first solid indication that E.M.I. was beginning to show some selectivity and interest in what the Trio was peddling abroad.

You're Gonna Miss Me was recorded in Los Angeles at what were to be the last sessions for the original Kingston Trio: January 12-14, 1961. On January 19, Capitol officially presented them with gold album awards for AT LARGE, HERE WE GO AGAIN, FROM THE "HUNGRY i" and THE KINGSTON TRIO. The following day, Frank Werber and the group embarked on their first foreign tour, which lasted seven weeks and earned them lifetime fans in such diverse parts of the globe as Japan, The Phillipines, Tasmania, Australia and New Zealand. By the time they stopped in March to vacation in Tahiti, the group had collected several foreign arrangements for a proposed LP (working title: THE KINGSTON TRIO ON TOUR), and Werber had shot some seven thousand feet of color film for what was to have been a television special based on the tour. Both projects were scrapped when Dave Guard informed Werber, Reynolds and Shane of his intention to quit The Kingston Trio, giving them his six months' notice on May 11, 1961. All concerned, for obvious financial reasons, sought to silence the break-up rumors for as long as possible, but the national press was soon breaking the news to hundreds of thousands of shocked fans.

Why did The Kingston Trio break up? No question has been put to the members in years since more than that one, and several standard answers have emerged, all of them based in fact. The interviews in this book offer several reasons: too much touring away from their families, and too many hours together eventually made friendship a chore; being so close together in all aspects of their work, including endless traveling in a cramped private plane, caused them to eventually get on each other's nerves; growing criticism from the "purists" of the folk community about what they saw as the Trio's highly commercial disregard for authentic folk music began to get to Dave, while it was laughed off by Nick and Bob. Various other cumulative incidents led to an eventual "Nick and Bob vs. Dave" climax: on one or two occasions over the years, Nick and Bob had to do a show as "The Kingston Duo" when Dave became ill; when the group was invited to perform at President Ken-

nedy's Inaugural Ball, Dave vetoed the proposal.

All of these little things piled-up over a period of time, waiting for the proverbial straw to break the camel's back. That straw came to light in the June 9, 1961 *Life* story on the split: ". . . Another bone of contention is a $127,000 shortage in their jointly owned publishing subsidiary, High Ridge Music." Dave Guard elaborated further in an interview in the January, 1977 issue of *Peninsula Magazine* (a San Francisco area publication): "Some of our management was getting careless with money, and I was the only guy who was actively concerned about it. Our publisher actually embezzled $127,000." For whatever reasons, Dave had decided The Kingston Trio could not go on under the then-prevailing conditions and circumstances.

Amid all the squabbling and controversy, Capitol released GOIN' PLACES (from the January sessions) in June of 1961. It climbed to the number three chart spot and eventually sold almost 300,000 records. Musicologists generally agree that Guard's announced intention of departure was the roadblock that kept both GOIN' PLACES and MAKE WAY from reaching number one. An addiitonal note: GOIN' PLACES was also the first Trio album to feature photos of previous releases on the reverse.

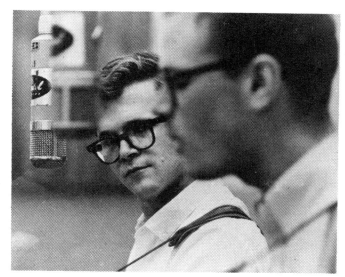

Bob listens to Dave at a Capitol session. Photo courtesy: Archives of Music Preservation.

Although the LP was recorded before their foreign tour, Bob, Dave and Nick's portion of the liner notes were composed upon their return. Taken out of context, their words offered ironic prophecy: ". . . We wanted to turn out some especially good tunes just in case the tour bogged down in Tahiti. Sort of a farewell album, you know, because you never can predict what might happen . . ."

And "good tunes" these are. Only a few tracks seem to retain the palor of the MAKE WAY sessions: *Lemon Tree* (later Peter, Paul & Mary's first top forty hit) and *Run Molly, Run* are rather uninspired performances, and the stringless *Guardo El Lobo* seems unsuited to the Trio's style.

You Don't Knock, a traditional spiritual with new arrangement credited to Dave, and the aforementioned *You're Gonna Miss Me* (also partially credited to Dave) are the movers and shakers of GOIN' PLACES. Woody Guthrie's *This Land Is Your Land* and *Pastures Of Plenty* are given properly

One of the last TV appearances of the Dave, Bob, Nick Trio on the Perry Como Show, January, 1961. From the collection of Maureen Wilson.

respectful readings by the group, and perhaps the LP's mock-serious squaredance number *Billy Goat Hill* ended up with the most airplay, but it is undoubtedly Bob Shane's classic version of *It Was A Very Good Year* (the Ervin Drake masterpiece that became a hit for Frank Sinatra years later) that is the album's finest cut. It also turned out to be the final track the Trio would cut with Dave Guard as a member. The other standout tracks are both collaborations by Jane Bowers and Dave Guard: the hauntingly historical *Coast Of California* and the liltingly lovely *Senora,* the latter boasting a fine vocal solo by Dave.

It is especially interesting to note that two of the album's selections were recorded much earlier at the sessions for 1960's STRING ALONG. Both *Coast Of California* and *This Land Is Your Land* were crowded out of that earlier LP but managed to find their way out of the vaults (no easy trick)

for inclusion on GOIN' PLACES, much to the delight of many fans.

GOIN' PLACES not only mentions Buck Wheat in the liner notes, but this time he's prominently featured on the cover. Although we were treated to the back of his head on the cover of MAKE WAY (in addition to various half-glimpses on the back of STRING ALONG and SOLD OUT), GOIN' PLACES gives us our first clear look at his countenance. This fact has led to speculation that Guard was attempting to establish Wheat as an individual per-

sonality before the eventual split of the Trio and the later formation of The Whiskeyhill Singers, of which both men were a part.

Although Dave had officially offered to fulfill all Trio commitments until November 12, 1961 (which would have included at least one more new album), his partners — having decided the group would *not* retire — decided it was best to seek a suitable replacement as soon as possible. The theory was that if a change had to be made, then the sooner the better, so that the furor could be dealt with and put behind them, and lucrative careers could continue. Understandably, the group's camaraderie in live performance was beginning to look forced, so a light schedule was maintained throughout that summer.

Sensing that it was now or never, Capitol put out an album designed to finish the job STEREO CONCERT had started two years earlier. KINGSTON TRIO ENCORES (released in July, 1961) offered six tracks each from THE KINGSTON TRIO and FROM THE "HUNGRY i" in the company's new "Duophonic Sound" process. This was an engineering idea designed to give a fuller dimension to early Capitol mono recordings. As Trio engineer Pete Abbot recalls: "That's where we took the mono recordings and electronically made them into stereo. That system was devised mainly by a person at Capitol named John Palladino, and it worked very well." This is hardly an essential disc for KT collectors, unless one happens to have a fondness for re-channeled "stereo". This album even shys away from originality on the *outside,* as the cover simply pictures the two old LPs and devotes more space to promoting "Duophonic Sound" than the Trio. KINGSTON TRIO ENCORES was not well received by record buyers, eventually selling less than 40,000 units, or about half of what stereo versions of GOIN' PLACES and MAKE WAY sold.

If ENCORES holds any value for Trio fans it is a sentimental one, as it turned out to be the last record the group released while Dave Guard was still a member. On August 19, 1961, Dave formally resigned his shares of "Kingston Trio, Inc." for a monetary settlement over a period of years.

For many fans, The Kingston Trio Story was effectively over. For others, it was just beginning.

* * * * * * *

Rock & Roll 55. THE KINGSTON TRIO. All in their early 20's Dave Guard and Bob Shane come from Hawaii and Nick Reynolds from Coronado, Cal.   Printed in U.S.A.

The Kingston Trio card from a collection of "Rock & Roll" cards. From the collection of Jean Ward.

The Kingston Trio at one of many of their club dates. Photo courtesy: Capitol Records.

SPRING FORECAST

DELTA ZETA

AND

TAU KAPPA EPSILON

PRESENT

THE THIRD ANNUAL

ALL COLLEGIATE FASHION SHOW

April 9, 1961

1:30 p.m. and 4:00 p.m.   TICKETS $1.00

SMALL BALLROOM — C S U STUDENT UNION BUILDING

"Come and see so others may hear"

"I am proud to be associated with you in this good cause."

Ronald Reagan

"We wish you success in your venture to raise funds for the University Speech and Hearing Center."

*Sincerely,
The Kingston Trio*

FASHIONS BY

Jo Ann Shoppe

AND

The Tannis Shop

FOR BENEFIT OF C S U
SPEECH AND HEARING CENTER

An unusual item from the collection of Allan Shaw: Testimonials from The Kingston Trio and Ronald Reagan for a benefit show for the Colorado State University Speech and Hearing Center, Fort Collins, Colorado.

Dave Guard, November 7, 1981. Photo by Jack Rubeck.

The Dave Guard Interview

by
Elizabeth Wilson

EW: Who influenced you, musically, when you were growing up?

DG: My heaviest influence was a guy named Gabby Pahinui, who's the best Hawaiian guitar player that ever lived.

EW: You produced an album by him.

DG: Yeah, I produced an album by him in 1979, and that got a Hawaiian Grammy, as a matter of fact. But he was — I'd never heard anybody play guitar so well. I still haven't, to tell you the truth, and I've heard Segovia in concert and all kinds of great jazz people, but the one that really spoke to me the most was Gabby Pahinui. And the Weavers were a very heavy influence, so I think those two would probably be my "kid influence" right there.

EW: Was there any musical background in your family? Were your parents musicians at all?

DG: My mother's family were all — my mother's mother was from a family of European composers. They travelled all over Europe and everybody in the family was a composer. My mother's mother was a piano teacher and my mother didn't have any instrument because she heard all these people coming in and doing piano lessons all day long, and didn't want anything to do with it. Actually, what she wanted to learn was accordian, and her mother wouldn't let her do it.

EW: So neither of your parents was a direct influence?

DG: No, they always liked to listen to the radio, though. They always had the radio on. They always liked tunes, and bought records, and didn't hold me back from it — they bought me my first guitar.

EW: What were you like when you were a kid? Were you a studious kid, or a troublemaker, or —

DG: Yes, to both.

EW: A studious troublemaker?

DG: Certainly. I was bored, you know. Bored. I hated school.

EW: But you did well in it, didn't you?

DG: Yeah, but I didn't like to sit there hour after hour and listen to somebody tell you what was going on. It seemed like the world of experience was much more interesting. So I was glad when school was over.

EW: Were you popular when you were in high school?

DG: I was not popular until track season, then I started winning races, and then all of a sudden, all the girls wanted to date me, like the next day. So I had a very good lesson in popularity. It was, you know, whatever —

EW: High school kids have deep, deep minds.

DG: Yeah, but the same thing happened in the music world, like in San Francisco when we first started out. None of the columnists would touch

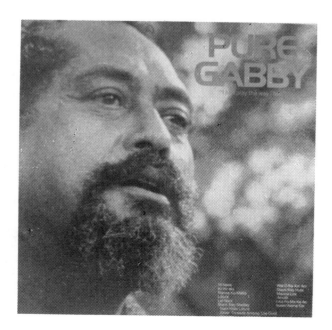

us. All the big important people said, "No, this is not even — it's disgusting. It's just a horrible sound." And then we came back and we'd be in the newspapers and stuff like that, and all the columnists would say — "San Francisco's own." So it's all a question of how you're doing, who's on top of the greased pole.

EW: How old were you when you first seriously thought about going into show business?

DG: Uh — 22.

EW: That late? What did you plan to be up until then?

DG: College, you know — college keeps you away from planning to be anything. I thought I would study until something came up that looked okay.

EW: But you didn't have any idea of being in show business before that?

DG: No, uh-uh. It was just a — you know, hobby. Something that we could do in school.

EW: If the Kingston Trio hadn't become successful, would you have pursued a career as a musician? Or do you think you would have fallen back on (laughter) economics, or whatever?

DG: Gee, I don't know. Whatever happened just happened, so — I don't know. What if I had joined the Japanese Air Force, would I have become a bomber pilot? (laughter)

EW: How was it decided that you were the leader of the Kingston Trio?

DG: Let's see — the original set-up was that Nick handled transportation, Bobby handled costumes and laundry, and I handled the music.

EW: (laughter) Really?

DG: Yeah, well, we all went to Judy Davis, who was a fine vocal coach, and she taught us our musicianship — you know, the key signatures and the scales and things like that. And we all took the lessons, but I was the one who was interested. I would stay up all night and write these things out. Bobby and Nick said that's just not the way they thought about music at all. They thought about the energy in it, the appeal, the drama or the — whatever you like, but certainly not in terms of any symbolic thing. Italian do-re-mis or Roman numerals or dots-and-stick notations — this was all alien to their feeling. So, I guess, then, somebody had to make sure that things were as musically correct as we could, because that's where the power is; otherwise, you get really slurry-sounding notes and stuff. But I certainly didn't know enough really about it — we just had a simple form. The thing about the "leader" was just

that I was the guy who was willing to sit down and write the music down and talk to the people who did know music about doing it the right way. It was never done in the — quote — "right way." It was just hunt-and-peck, really.

EW: The Kingston Trio started out as calypso, didn't they, and then changed to folk?

DG: Well, not me. First thing is, Bobby and I got together in Hawaii in the early fifties, and he knew how to play the guitar a little bit and I knew some Tahitian songs that he kinda was faking the words to.

EW: Did you really learn them from Polynesian travelers like it says on the albums?

DG: Well, sort of, yeah . . . 'cause we lived right there. I lived in Waikiki, for goodness sake. Bobby and I really loved the Tahitian music, 'cause it was wild. We put a couple of Tahitian songs on those albums, you know. Hawaiian stuff is very pleasant and everything, but it was just around, so we wanted the wild, eerie-sounding stuff so we learned that. But I didn't know how to play the guitar and Bobby didn't know the words to the Tahitian stuff. I would sit around and transcribe them off of records, and ask people what those words were and stuff. So we got together and he taught me a little guitar and I taught him the words to the songs, so we started off by —

EW: Bob taught you guitar?!!

DG: Yeah, he gave me my first guitar lesson. You know — "This is the C-chord and this is the D," and stuff. I mean, I had books but I didn't have somebody who would sit down and really reel it out for me. He gave me one lesson, basically, and then I was able to go on from there. But I had to see a real live human being sit down and say, "Look, put your hands like this. Play 'dang, dang'" — he did that. After awhile, everybody got okay with what they did. So then Bobby and I had a group. It was just sort of the two of us. We learned all kinds of funny routines from nightclub acts that were coming through town — little jokey things, you know, and the Tahitian music, both those things, and we'd sit out on the beach and play that and draw crowds of people. So then when we came to California to go to college, we were doing the same thing, but not so much Tahitian stuff; it was more like the jokey stuff. And then when Nick came up to Menlo to go to school with Bobby — I was going to Stanford and Nick was going to Menlo — we got our act together that way. Just sort of a funny thing. Whenever we would show up at parties, everybody would cluster around for some laughs. Eventually, we finally got

Dave reacts to a sour note at a Trio session. Photo courtesy: Archives of Music Preservation.

to singing — "groovy harmonies" is what we called them. You know, three voices sounding real smooth — smooth and groovy. So then when school was up, we decided — you know, how to make a living, so that was about the only thing that we really wanted to do for a living, 'cause people were already inviting us to do things like that. So rather than struggle and struggle and become businessmen or something that we weren't going to be very good at, why not do something that we were already naturally interested in?

EW: Are there any Kingston Trio albums that you thought were especially better than others?

DG: AT LARGE. I liked AT LARGE, to tell you the truth. I thought we achieved what we were trying to do in that situation.

EW: Which was?

DG: The blend and everything. It was representative of the way we were sounding at the time. The earlier albums — by the time that the records were released, we had improved our sound. Later albums — I didn't like the material as much, even though our technical ability was okay, the material wasn't what we were most interested in. The first four albums that we did — everybody kind of agreed that we liked the tunes. Just about halfway through HERE WE GO AGAIN was when we ran out of ideas, and then we had people come in and just lay tunes on us because we needed some material.

EW: At that point, you were pressured to just put out albums more, where before you were doing what you wanted to do.

DG: Yeah. Uh-huh. That's true.

EW: Why did you leave the Kingston Trio?

DG: To grow.

EW: In what way?

DG: In all the ways I've grown since.

EW: Why did you go right into another group situation?

DG: Capitol wouldn't let me go without signing into another group.

EW: You had to go with another group rather than . . . performing as a solo, where you wouldn't have the conflicts with, you know, different —

DG: I've never performed as a solo . . . because that's not my thing.

EW: (laughter) Do you like having other people around to share the blame?

DG: The blame — no, the harmony. I like harmony.

EW: Just from the standpoint of your personal satisfaction, do you consider the Whiskeyhill Singers a success? Were you doing the kind of music that you wanted to be doing?

DG: No, because it was the same as the other stuff was.

EW: What were you not doing with the Kingston Trio and the Whiskeyhill Singers that you wanted to be doing?

DG: Well, I didn't have a chance to really study my music as much as I wanted to do. I wanted to — I moved to Australia in '62 and then had my own TV show there, national TV show, and we did Chicago gospel music, like the Staple Singers basically. I wanted to study that, I wanted to do black music. Now I'm singing Indian music — Sanskrit — and that's been a great investigation. I've studied harmony and counterpoint and I've gotten myself so I can play good rhythm now. All those things I wanted to do which weren't possible in either of those formats. From the way I was, not from anybody else, it was just that I hadn't studied them and I didn't know about them or anything like that. Now I can do those things.

EW: When you started out with the Whiskeyhill Singers, did you think that they would catch on or were you not surprised by the fact that they didn't?

DG: Well, we never got the sound that we wanted, basically. I just got people that I thought would be real smart and fun to be with, and it never got a really satisfying musical sound because we had four different ideas of what the music was going to be.

EW: How much blame do you put on Capitol Records for the Whiskeyhill Singers not becoming successful?

DG: None. If the music was there, then they could have done something with it. We didn't really have a hit sound — a hit single or a hit sound out of that whole thing.

EW: You don't feel that they kind of, you know, tried to trash it a little because they were mad at

you for leaving a successful group? Wasn't there any resentment on their part?

DG: Maybe. You know, but how can I say? Everybody's dead in that situation. Except me, I guess. (laughter)

EW: How would you rate the album — the Whiskeyhill Singers album, say, in comparison to the Kingston Trio albums?

DG: Oh, it was about the same. Probably the same.

EW: This is just an idle question that I've always wondered about. You did the score for "How The West Was Won" and that got an Oscar. Did you actually get the Oscar or who got the — ?

DG: Alfred Newman got the Oscar for the soundtrack actually. It was the soundtrack of "How The West Was Won". The Whiskeyhill Singers did 27 folksongs on the soundtrack, but there were also sound effects like of a buffalo stampede and a train wreck and things like that, so all in all, for effect, which included the singing as well as the sounds, my feeling is that we were a great contributor to a successful effort.

EW: You know, a lot of groups start out and they don't do that well with their first album. It's usually not until a group's second album that people are starting to buy it. Do you think that maybe if you'd held the Whiskeyhill Singers together longer that maybe they would have caught on?

DG: Well, an album is a totality of influences. So, what you have is the right group at the right time with the right material. So many things are respon-

Capitol T/ST 1728, released April 1962; L to R: David Wheat, Dave Guard, Judy Henske, Cyrus Faryar.

sible for the success of one. It's not just the group because there's been a lot of great groups never selling. And it's not the record company; otherwise they'd have a hit with everything if they had a really good record company. And it's depending on a large number of forces. You know, is the country ready for it? Are the money people behind it? Every time you do a record you have to suppress another record. Not your own, but, say, when Elvis Presley hit with his stuff, they had to — all the record companies stopped printing the records they were into, and would start printing RCA Victor records because they had to keep up with the demand. So in our situation, when Capitol Records decided to get behind the Kingston Trio, they had to lay off promotion on other groups at the time, because you go with whatever's going rather than saying, "Well, all our artists are equally good and we're in love with them all." When someone's starting to move, then you go with that, so all those factors had to be present at the same time. That's a rare thing, you know — a success. I mean, someone is always successful but it's not always the same group or the same company.

EW: Well, what you said earlier, about the country being ready for it, do you think that the music you did with them was maybe ahead of its time? I mean, the Kingston Trio was like a simpler sound and maybe the times were simpler.

DG: The Whiskeyhill Singers? Yeah, it was almost trying to do rock 'n' roll in a non-rock 'n' roll atmosphere, basically. It was just starting to come in. There's always a big lag — the work gets done

and then people wake up to it, so the industry gears up to service it. Success on a large scale in a big country is something that takes a long time to gear up to, and by the time something has hit, maybe the original impulse has gone away, you know, so that's probably what happened.

EW: Was it difficult to decide to disband?

DG: For the Whiskeyhill Singers? Yeah, it was hard, because people had really worked very hard on the project and were quite deeply involved and everything. I just knew that the situation being what it was, we couldn't get what we wanted. It wouldn't yield our results, you know. My situation was my wife was pregnant with our third child and I was feeling a deep lack of family life, and I thought it was really important to get with my family. I sort of missed a lot of it traveling with the Trio and I saw it starting again. And there were — Capitol was not interested in the group whatsoever. When the Trio came by — even when we were small — we'd be met by representatives waiting there at the plane or the train or something like that, and they put ads in the newspaper and things like that. There was an absolute lack of that with the Whiskeyhill Singers, so I knew that behind the scenes, something wasn't happening. But what the reasons might be are only speculative, you know.

EW: Do you still have a strong interest in folk music?

DG: Oh, certainly. Oh, yeah — always.

EW: Would you consider that your favorite kind of music?

DG: Yeah, I would think so. All in all, top to bottom, and all the different ways. I admire a lot of rock 'n' roll, I admire classical music, I admire any kind of music that comes down the pike, but as a whole unit, what really gets me most of the time is the folk music thing, because it serves a lot of people's needs. It's a nutritious thing for large groups of people; otherwise, it wouldn't be folk music. You can have a folk-**styled** music and be phony with it. Imitation-sounding folk music.

EW: Some people accused the Kingston Trio of that.

DG: Everybody's going to accuse the Kingston Trio of everything, so we don't have to worry about that. That's their job. Our job was to do the music, their job was to do the criticism. If we had them doing the music and us doing the criticism, nothing would have happened. (laughter)

EW: How do you react to criticism? Can you just let it roll off your back, or do you get upset by it?

Dave at work in the studio, circa 1960. Photo courtesy: Archives of Music Preservation.

DG: Depends on who's doing it. Anybody can just throw a rock through a window, but if some teacher or something like that — somebody eminent whom you respect — comes along and gives you a word of decent advice, then you might not like it, but you're going to have to consider that. My father, when I had the Whiskeyhill Singers — he hated that sound. He liked the real smooth-sounding "ooh ooh ooh ooh" stuff that we did with the Kingston Trio. He was mad that we were making these awful, scratchy sounds. He was an engineer; he said, "If I built walls like you make music, they would fall down." (laughter) So I said,

"You son of a gun," but I took it to heart and it really made me study. It was something that I wasn't doing right; I needed more knowledge. In a four-part group, you need much more knowledge than a three-part group, just because of the mathematical complications . . . Mathematically, it's factorial three, which means that if you have three people, it's 3 times 2 times 1. That's like six different ways that you can arrange the combinations. But if you have four people, it's 4 times 3 times 2 times 1 — that makes twenty-four. So from adding one extra person, the complications increase four-fold. Musically, that's true, but politically things got a lot smoother with four people. Three people, it's always like two against one. (laughter) They're always working their way and they're always — one person feels like, "Boy, I'm really being left out." But four — there's always someone saying, "This is ridiculous." There's enough sense of humor in that kind of number of people that you don't get too crazy with it.

EW: You mentioned before, you moved to Australia right after that. Why Australia?

DG: Well, I'd been there on tour and found a place on the beach there, north of Sydney, that looked very — I wanted to get off the road because the phone was ringing all the time with all kinds of unnecessary things to my life. You find with most performers that have a busy life, they somehow insulate themselves — they move to the country or get answering services or something like that, because there's a lot of extraneous things which only interfere with your energy levels, so everybody walls themselves off to a certain extent, and I found that I had to do that by going to Australia.

EW: (laughter) You couldn't just go to Montana?

DG: Well, since I grew up in Hawaii, I always liked to go to the beach, and here was a place on the beach. In Hawaii, you can't really get on the beach — it costs so much money and it's just condos and hotels and stuff there. And since I was in the same — you know, one of the fifty states would still have those pressures. In Australia, I turned down jobs every day when I was there.

EW: Did you do recording there?

DG: Yeah, I was a studio musician and worked with about twenty-seven different albums there. And then I worked as an advisor on a show called "Jazz Meets Folk" where essentially I was the talent buyer or something like that. The groups would come in and audition and I would see if they were going to be acceptable — if they would look good on the show and what-have-you. And then the Australian Broadcasting Commission asked me to do a show out there so I had a national series called "Dave's Place", and we had American artists down there. The New Lost City Ramblers came down; Judy Henske actually came down from the U.S., and Sonny Terry and Brownie McGee; and we might have had more except there was sort of a political hassle between some promoters in Sydney and the guy that ran my show decided to join the boycott of the other promoter, and so it was a nonsense thing, but it stopped us from having some really nice artists on, like Josh White, Judy Collins, the Rooftop Singers, Lou Gottlieb —

EW: (laughter) I guess you can never get away from the hassles, can you?

DG: Well, sure, it's all — you know, a high-level business and there's always something going on like that.

EW: During the time you were in Australia, did you have any contact at all with Nick or Bob or John?

DG: Zero.

EW: None at all?

DG: None. I never heard any of their albums. I still haven't. I did hear one of their singles on the air — I think it was called *Ally Ally Oxen Free,* and the disc-jockey said, "Sounds like gibberish."

EW: Gibberish?!!

DG: They didn't know what "Ally Ally Oxen Free" meant. They don't use that in Australia.

EW: Oh, it's not an Australian expression?

DG: Yeah. So that's the — I just heard — I knew it was them and I heard about the last four bars of it and I heard what the disc-jockey said and I thought, "Okay," you know.

EW: What did you think of it when you heard it?

DG: Oh, it didn't sound terribly inspired. Why, was it an important record? I don't know.

EW: No, I don't think it was one of their biggies. So you really weren't aware of what they were doing as the Kingston Trio?

DG: Nothing whatsoever.

EW: And you didn't have any personal contact?

DG: No. No personal contact. It was better — you know, you have to leave those things behind if there's so much happening.

EW: Now, you wrote "Colour Guitar" while you were in Australia, didn't you?

DG: Just as I was finishing the Whiskeyhill Singers here, I got into a situation where I was studying musical theory, and one of the basic diagrams is to put the twelve notes of music in a circular thing like the face of a clock, and then I read a book called *The Art of Color* by Johannes Itten, and he had a diagram of twelve colors all laid out in a circle like the face of a clock, and I wondered if there would be any advantage in superimposing those systems. So that was my investigation, and in Australia I was able to work it up and I did that for the five years I was there, and then finished the book as far as the design, and then came up here and put the book together and then taught it for about seven years after that.

EW: You taught here, you didn't teach at all in Australia?

DG: No, I was just busy working it up, because if you just make that diagram, then they say, "Well, that's a great idea, but so what?" So you have to make charts and everything to show what chords look like — what a C-chord would look like in color, what an A-chord . . . Pete Seeger came down, though, on a tour and stayed over at our house, and we all had color instruments there. I was playing a mandolin, I gave Pete a Bouzouki — a Greek instrument — and then I had my four-year-old daughter Catherine playing a piano that we had colored up, so all the instruments were unfamiliar to us. We'd never played — I mean, her being four, me not being a mandolin player, and Pete not being a Bouzouki player. So we made a rule that we were just going to play the reds and the blues, you know, of the colors, and then we made music for twenty minutes between us, all three of us, and it sounded great, so I knew that — you know, somebody that knew the system, somebody who was too young, and somebody who might have been skeptical but a pretty good player . . . I mean, he's one of the best in the world . . . so we made, like I said, good music. Then we changed the rules — we played the yellows and the greens, leave the other colors out, and we made good music that way, so I knew that it was okay.

EW: When you taught the guitar, did you teach it in private lessons or in classes?

DG: Anywhere from individuals to groups of seventy. I wrote the method of **Colour Guitar** and I had a choice of doing it in kindergarten way or in a doctorate, dissertation way, so I figured that if I did it in a kindergarten way, people would say, "That's nice for kindergarten but you can't do anything good on it." And I knew that if I did it in a doctorate way, that people would say, "Oh, boy, that's very good if you understand music already, to see these demonstrations, but how can anybody learn to play that way?"

So I spent the basic time getting from — having done it in a doctorate, dissertation style, then I backtracked and for the seven years got the lessons up from absolute scratch for very young children. I think my youngest student was seven and the oldest was eighty-seven. I was teaching pop music and classical and color logic and things by patterns — design patterns . . . theoretical things, and eventually wound up with some people that could play. I think I probably ran through a thousand people, out of which a hundred could do it okay. I mean, they could play okay, and then ten probably wound up being very good at it.

EW: What does it take? Do you have any idea why some people pick it up and others don't? (laughter) Like me?

DG: It has to grab you, and it has to reinforce — it has to be something that leads you on deeper and deeper in spite of yourself. So that's, I think how people get to be musicians — I mean, 'cause it's a very large population in the world. My feeling is that ten percent — if you wanted to teach tennis or badminton or checkers, and you had a class of one hundred people, ten would wind up keeping that in their repertoire. They would remember their tennis. The rest of them would say, "Well, I tried and I can't." Then of those ten, one person would be a champ . . . would go on to make a career of it, life-long. So it's like a ten-percent sieve . . . because that's how you get your distribution of people — plumbers and architects and taxi drivers and stuff like that. A hundred will try, ten can do, and one must.

EW: Do you like teaching?

DG: Teaching is okay. Depends on what you're teaching. After I got the lessons all written . . . I wanted to have like a thousand pages of lessons. You know, classical music translated into this system and stuff like that. After that work was done, it was time to move on. It gets like baby-sitting — you know, you sit there and say, "This is how you make a C-chord. Look at my hand. Okay, can you do that? All right. Now let's play the C-chord. Okay. Now, what do you think? Is that the C-chord? By this time, their hand is tired. "Now make a C-chord" and they say, "I can't remember." I say, "Look at my hand. This is a C-chord." On and on, see? It's better done by machines. (laughter)

EW: Did you ever run into anybody who turned out to really be something? A real talent? That learned from you?

DG: Well, there's some professional musicians

now that learned that way . . . they didn't learn exclusively . . . a guy named John Nolan, for one. There's another guy in Seattle; my son Tom plays. Several others that I can't remember the names of, but they're players. They didn't stick with my system totally — they took what they needed out of it. There's certain things you can demonstrate that way. It's not long on rhythm and all sorts of things — you know, repertoire. I could only teach a certain kind of tune. I wasn't restricted by the kinds of tunes I could teach, but my taste meant that I was only teaching certain tunes and not others. So if they wanted other tunes, they'd have to go elsewhere to do that.

EW: Getting back to the chronological order of things, when did you come back to the United States?

DG: I came back in '66. I went to Sweden from Australia. I got a letter from George Russell, who is a jazz theoretician, and he was writing a book on composition and he had an idea of a concept called rhythmic gravity. I didn't know what that meant, so I wrote up a paper on that saying what I thought of it, and he wrote back saying, "That's really crazy, but it's one of the more fascinating things I've read, so why don't you try to come up to Sweden and we'll talk." So I went to Sweden and he read me his book on composition. He is an arranger and a composer — he's teaching at, I think, the Berklee School in Boston now. He'd been a drummer for Charlie Parker for a little while, and written some tunes that the Gil Evans Orchestra had used, and put out several albums on his own. I can remember being at his house when Miles Davis called him up to say — anyway, he was a great jazz man. Buck Wheat from the Kingston Trio, our bass player, introduced me to him, and he thought that because I had a way of explaining complicated things simply to a large number of people that I might be able to get what he got and maybe make it accessible. That was my feeling, anyway, so that's one of the reasons I got into the color music thing — I saw his theory and thought that if it could only be made available to kindergarten people, we could skip whole generations of learning that way.

So, anyway, I went to Sweden and studied composition with him, and then on the way back I went into Random House in New York with my **Colour Guitar** idea and gave the book to Christopher Cerf to look at, and he kept it for about six weeks and finally came back saying, "I'm not getting much out of this, but then again, I'm color-blind." (laughter) I gave him my guitar and the book, so I thought, "Naaa, I'm not going to sit around in publishers' offices, waiting to do this." So I decided that I would write the book on my own and publish it privately, and then go back and live in Australia. But after all the time it took to do the book, my wife was in Australia and felt that she was really isolated there and wanted to come back to the United States and be with her family and friends and stuff, so we moved the whole gang back. Came back in just the first part of 1968.

EW: What did you immediately get involved in? What kind of project?

DG: Oh, *The Whole Earth Catalog* was just going, and I'd moved very close to Menlo Park — I was in the next town, so I went in there and saw that they were doing some really important work, so I offered to review some books for them and stuff, and hung out there, and then about six months later they suddenly started selling a million copies of *The Whole Earth Catalog,* and it was just a little old dinky thing. I said, "This is going to really explode," and they had a feeling that it was, and it did. And then it became — it wasn't what it was in the beginning, so that they had to have all kinds of warehouse and new people and efficient organizations, and everybody came from all over the world because it was an important book. So I got more into my teaching of the guitar. By this time, also, I started picking up guitar students, so I was teaching from early morning to late night.

EW: So you weren't doing any performing?

DG: No, I didn't have any desire to do that. This was a chance for me to learn a lot of classical music — really formal things — and find out what the bare bones of all this was. You know — study. Study music.

EW: How long was it before you started performing again? I know you had several groups that you worked with.

DG: They had a "Great Folk Revival" show from a Long Island hockey rink in 1974, and they wanted the Limeliters, but Glenn Yarbrough was off on his yacht, and Lou was in India, but Alex Hassilev wanted to do the show, so he called myself and Mike Settle, and we rehearsed a little bit and did a few numbers and went and did the show, and then we liked it, and before the other Limeliters came back, we played a few places up and down the West Coast. "Hassilev, Settle and Guard" was the name of that, so that was a group there. Then I tried to get together with John and Nick in 1976, but it wasn't working out. I went up to see Nick, and John came up, but the way we tried to get a contract with the record company — remember that publisher that ripped us off? You know, that was the reason I left the group, because of that big rip-off and everything. By this time he was the president of a major record company — goes around ripping off all these companies (laughter) — so at this time, he was the president of a record company, and we thought that we could come in and say, "Now, Mr. So-and-so, you ripped us off before, how about — you owe us this big favor, why not do that?" So he said he would try. And what happened was that he couldn't really pull it off, because in order to get the budget to record us, he would have to actually steal from other people's budgets to get the money to do it, and people would say, "How come you're giving all this money to this group here?" And he would have to say really what the reason was, so he didn't want to get involved with that. Nick and John sat around Hollywood waiting for the guy to answer, and he never answered back.

So then I thought it was really difficult the way it was being done, so I went down to Hollywood and hung out with my old friends from — well, Cyrus Faryar had been in the Whiskeyhill Singers with me, so he was in a group this time called the Modern Folk Quartet, and Judy Henske from the Whiskeyhill Singers had married a man named Jerry Yester, and he was a member of the Modern Folk Quartet, and a couple of other guys from Honolulu were also in the group, so I started hanging out with them, and we worked together in 1977. They would be my back-up band in the beginning of the show. I would be the lead singer, then I would disappear and they would do their quartet number. So we did that for about a year, and that was limited too. It didn't really take off because, basically, one of the members was a professional photographer and didn't want to go on the road because it would mean that he —

EW: Henry Diltz.

DG: Yeah, Henry Diltz.

EW: He used to photograph the Monkees — I used to see his name in all my Tiger Beat magazines. (laughter)

Yeah, Chip (Douglas) Hatlelid was also the Monkees' producer — he was in the Modern Folk Quartet. But it would be like — we had a job in San Francisco to play the Great American Music Hall and Henry said, "I'd love to do it, but Paul McCartney is on his yacht in the Virgin Islands and *Rolling Stone* wants me to photograph the thing in color for the cover."

EW: Don't want to pass up that chance.

DG: He couldn't. So, Henry jumps out and I had my daughter Catherine come along and she played his parts. He plays the harmonica and the clarinet so I gave her a melodica and she just filled in for him.

But it would be like, can we go to Cleveland and play a gig with the Kingston Trio, and Henry would say, "Well, gee, how many nights are we going to do?" I'd say, "Well, three nights in Cleveland" and he'd say, "Yeah, but there's a day coming and a day going, that's really five." It got so it was really in conflict. The Modern Folk Quartet never was able to get going — not because of Henry, but, I mean, that was just one of the things that I could say. It would be other things that would come up. Jerry was a recording engineer in Hollywood, so that he had a fairly responsible position, so we weren't free like a band to go out and do stuff.

So then I started my own band in 1978 called "Dave Guard and the Expanding Band." And we had Brian Davies who'd played banjo for the Limeliters, and a couple of the ex-Sons Of Champlin had been there — guys that were in this big rock 'n' roll group — and Jackie Furman, also, had been the woman drummer for the Limeliters for awhile, so we had two ex-Limeliters and two Sons Of Champlin for awhile and it went on. But some of those people were living in L.A., so in order to get a band — most of my work was up here in the Bay Area, so I had to drive four hundred miles down, pick up the band, take the band up to the Bay Area, then take the band back to L.A., four hundred miles, and then go home again, so it was sixteen hundred miles' worth of traveling just to do a weekend's worth of work.

EW: (laughter) Is that where the name Expa-a-a-anding Band came from?

DG: They just needed a name for the marquee and I thought, "Oh-h, something ridiculous" — you know, the Expanding Band. So then that's '79, and then I went down and hung out with John — he was doing BOMBS AWAY DREAM BABIES and he was really — at the end, he was like $120,000 into it, and the company was saying, "Where's the album? Where's the album?" and he said, "I'm just finishing it," and they wouldn't give him any more money. So he was also working with Lindsey Buckingham, who was a pal of his, so I think Lindsey gave him enough money — loaned him enough money — just to finish the album. And I sat with John for the last piece of it, while it was all being put together, while he was in his deepest, darkest hour. (laughter) We were hanging out together and then the album worked out okay, so that worked out. And then my personal thing was when I came up here after working on the album, that my guru, Muktananda, who is a man that I had read for about three years and that I always wanted to meet — he had come to America again and I met him and started into playing Indian music. Not official, sitar-playing or anything like that, but the songs that we sing in the Indian tradition. So I've been working on that as well as writing tunes. And then what? Uh — this opportunity came for the Kingston Trio 25th anniversary.

EW: When did that first come up?

DG: It came up in probably 1980, I think. Yeah, JoAnn Young of Camera Three in New York wanted to have a project which involved the original members of the Kingston Trio — what they'd been doing, like a retrospective, and it was going to be — like, Bobby's group, the present group, was going to open up the show, like in a little concert hall, the Great American Music Hall in San Francisco, and then we were going to come out and do some numbers, and then they were going to flash into what we'd been doing in our private lives — you know, 10 minutes on me, 10 minutes on Nick, 10 minutes on Bobby. And I think that was totally rejected. (laughter)

EW: I don't know why — I think that would have been great.

DG: It would have been great but it was — Bobby's got a present group and everybody in the world would say, "Gee, why don't the original boys get back together?" Because I think that those are the records that they play on the air, basically, and that would defeat all the things that Bobby's been working for ever since. And so, when it finally came up, when we were able to get the show, it took the format of, "well, we'll just slip the original group into a little slot on the show, and do sort of a thing with Mary Travers and Tom Smothers and some things with John Stewart and Bobby's group" — so everything was just sort of a — I don't know what you would call it — a smorgasbord. So that's the way that show came out.

EW: What did you think of the whole thing when it happened? Did you sense any kind of the magic that all of us fans felt, of just getting back and singing with Bob and Nick again?

DG: Well, we had rehearsed a couple of times in hotel rooms and it was certainly magical there. It was overly magical — it sounded a lot better than we had sounded before, basically, and I think probably some people would take the viewpoint that it probably sounded better than the way the present group sounds. So that was unacceptable to the way things are set up nowadays.

Nick Reynolds, Bob Shane and Dave Guard perform "Zombie Jamboree" at the Reunion, November 7, 1981. Photo by Catherine Guard.

But in one of those rehearsals — we were in Laguna in a hotel, and John came by and then after we were through rehearsing, John said, "I'm putting together some music in a great recording studio," and asked Nick and myself to come on over and sing little choral parts on that. So that really sounded like music then — really the kind of sound we wanted to make, so from that came an idea that maybe we should work together, because Bobby's got his group very comfortably and it's very unlikely that Nick or John or I would be invited into any of those situations. So we thought, "Gee, that doesn't make any difference anyway because we like the way we sound a lot better than we could in such a situation," so right now we're really happily putting together a group called "Stewart, Reynolds and Guard." As soon as (laughter) the big money people come and say "yes." We've got the tunes and stuff.

EW: With the "Guard" represented by both you and your daughter Catherine.

DG: I hope that my daughter will be on the band, because she's gone through the California Institute of the Arts and knows music up and down and she can sight-sing and has a very beautiful voice. John asked her to sing on BOMBS AWAY DREAM BABIES so we actually had sung chorus there. I'd really like it if Cappy were on the band. We'll see how it works out.

EW: What kind of music would you do with Stewart, Reynolds and Guard? Would it fall into any category?

DG: Well, whatever categories would be — we'd really hope to use a lot of John Stewart numbers, the ones that would be most acceptable for group things, because I'm sure John will always be a single — not as a single, but I mean that he will always be a prolific composer, and therefore a lot of the tunes he will write will be just good for John to sing, or a lot of them will be things for this group, or things that neither John nor the group can handle but some other artist should have. But I think he would always have a lot of numbers available. I've written a few things that I kind of like, that I think would be good. And over the past twenty-five years, I've made a little collection of tunes that should be sung by some group sometime, that I would really like to hear, so those are all possible.

EW: Would most of the material come from you or John?

DG: I would think that we would try to get sort of a blend. Since John would be a third of the group, he would contribute maybe a third of the songs. I wouldn't want to have it any one way. The basis of the songs will be ones that the three of us would agree on unanimously, in order to get back to that Kingston thing like the first four albums, the albums that I thought were really representative of the best of our work — whether it was technically good or not, it was really heartfelt because we all liked the tunes.

EW: Sincere.

DG: Yeah. It stood for us, whatever that meant. There were all kinds of tunes there.

EW: Would there be any of those old Kingston Trio songs that you would do as Stewart, Reynolds and Guard?

DG: I don't think so. Immediately, we'd probably stay away from that, just to give everything some clarity. There's a lot of good material. The idea is that we would have the people and the feeling that the original group would represent. Like Bobby's doing, I think, a great service in making available to the public that fine repertoire that the original Kingston Trio had. I think he recognizes that's what his main contribution is. So since he's handling it, why should someone else?

EW: Would there be a leader? You or John or — ?

DG: I don't like the leader idea. Everybody has a different bag of skills. So in a sense, the leader would be the unanimity. That doesn't mean that we're gonna all say, "Yeah, yeah, yeah,' but I've been trying to think about that.

EW: Who would have the final say if you disagreed on something? Or would you just drop it?

DG: If it didn't — if we couldn't get unanimity, then that means that something was really bitter in there. I can visualize a situation where — I would hope — that most of our material, we'd all say, "Yes, all three of us want to do it," but then I'm always trying to figure out ways that would work out politically. I would say if we had a tune and voted on it and all three said yes, then it would be in. If two people wanted it, then we wouldn't have the unanimity, but it would have the capacity to be voted on again. We could say that it was eligible to be voted on. If it's only one person that wanted it, then let it slide. Okay, then we're in a situation where we still have — we've got, say, twelve tunes to do on an album, but we can only agree on nine or something like that, but we have three tunes that are two votes each. Then we could compromise — we'd have one that I hated, one that Nick hated, and one that John hated, but the other two liked. Then we could pop 'em in — you know, if two people like 'em, there's bound to be something in there about it. I don't know, the mechanics would probably allow for all kinds of ways.

EW: *What kind of music don't you like? Is there any specific kind that you just can't stand?*

DG: Oh, yeah, sure — I mean, I turn on the radio and turn it right back off.

EW: *What is it about it that you don't like?*

DG: Oh, if it's just — if it's not — if I can't feel that — let's see . . . oh my goodness, just ask me to focus on what just went down the toilet or something like that. (laughter)

EW: *(laughter) Close enough. What performers do you like?*

DG: Today? Like of the newer groups and stuff like that? I like Tom Petty and the Heartbreakers — I think it's really an interesting group. I like the Police. I think they're really funny. I think they're exceptionally good musicians, and funny. That's what I like of the new groups. My favorite folk groups were the Weavers and the Staple Singers. In rock 'n' roll, I liked the Beatles and the Kinks, I think, and an English group called the Audience. I like Bonnie Raitt. Of the sort of jazzy things, I like the Manhattan Transfer — they're very good friends of mine.

EW: *Yeah, you worked with them as a background —*

DG: Yeah, they let me play on a track that they were recording. They had Cyrus and myself come in. After Janis Seigel won the Grammy for the Best Jazz Arrangement of the Year for her arrangement of *Birdland,* then the next time I saw her, I came down and taught her George Russell's way of arranging. (laughter) It was really — it was just another way of looking at things. That was really funny, to go to somebody who'd already reached the pinnacle and start teaching them stuff . . . It was just another way to get a new direction or something. I like the music — I really do like the music that they have in my ashram. Muktananda — who's my guru — the music that they do, it's like hits that have been hits for thousands of years. So the music is deeply stirring, really very involving and very good.

EW: *It's sort of like folk music in a way. I mean, you're still getting back to that music that's endured through all the years.*

DG: Yes, exactly. It meets the needs. It's like food or something like that.

EW: *Yeah, you know it's gotta be good, 'cause twenty billion people can't be wrong.*

DG: They can be wrong, but I like it, too. (laughter)

And I like this cowboy singer, Joe Ely. He's really great. He has an album called MUSTA NOTTA GOTTA LOTTA. He's really great, and I like a lot of the things he does . . . There's another group that I like, the Steeleye Span, this British group that really sounds good . . . So, that's just a very small list. Like the Modern Folk Quartet — I liked them, I thought they were really nice harmonizers. And there are players and singers that I — I just can't mention them all at this time, but those are the ones that —

EW: *Yeah, put on the spot, it's hard to think of people.*

DG: Right. Yeah. I really admire those, but there're so many, like I say. Probably the all-time group is the Beatles, I would have to say. Yeah.

EW: *Do you think that the Kingston Trio played a part in the evolution of music through today's sound?*

DG: Yeah, they made a lot of things possible. They got a lot of people started because the form of the music was so simple. The lyrics weren't bubblegum lyrics, but the accessibility of the music was that you could just pick up your guitar, almost, while they were playing on the radio, and start playing along with it, and you'd have it. And then the fact that we were using tunes that were already popular; otherwise, they wouldn't have got to us. We didn't really originate too many tunes that made any impact, but the ones that we used — you know, people had been singing *Tom Dooley* for a hundred years before us, and *M.T.A.* was already a good song. And we used a lot of Weavers' songs and things like that. They were already out there with the people; we just sort of clustered them together in one place. That's what made a good show, sort of editorially.

EW: *Well, when the folk boom started — I mean, you started that kind of thing, and then it went into Bob Dylan and Joan Baez, that type of thing, and through — I mean, it seemed to me that what the Kingston Trio did is that they made music that young people liked to listen to that they didn't have to dance to. You know?*

DG: Yeah. They could play it themselves, is the thing. It gave people employment, is what it was. It started — it was the nucleus of a party. If you put on a Kingston Trio record, then everybody would start singing along with the record.

EW: *(laughter) My parents used to have whole parties where they just sat around listening to Kingston Trio records.*

DG: Yeah, but people weren't just listening, they

were singing. You know, they'd come to the concerts — I think even nowadays a good deal of the audience that goes to see the —

Dave signs autographs after a show during the Trio's heyday. Photo courtesy: Archives of Music Preservation.

EW: Yeah, you can't help but sing along.

DG: Yeah. It's in the right key, it's the right thing, you know. And it's all choruses. Every once in awhile, you'd sing a verse, but it's really chorus, and people would come in and do that.

EW: What do you feel about the kinds of gimmicks that a lot of the rock groups use, like the green hair or biting the heads off of bats (laughter) or that kind of thing, where it's a whole show?

DG: Well, the music world is really locked up. Every musician has heard about Miles Davis and Ella Fitzgerald and the great big bands. Those people are still doing it. All these monster talents and everything. The great talents of the past are still around, still doing it, so what's a kid gonna do that's starting out? If you want to get into folk music, they say, "Oh, well . . . " All these people are already in place, doing this thing, so there's no room for somebody new, so the only way to get a

job is to do music which is new in some way. Otherwise, people say, "We don't need you; we can always hire . . . "

EW: Sort of, "First, you get their attention"?

DG: Get their attention, and also then to make the kind of music that adults don't want to play. They say, "God, what is that scratchy, awful stuff?" and they say, "That's **our** music, and you can't have it." So that will always be coming up from that end of the age scale. It will always have people that will play music that sounds outrageous, you know — outlandish.

EW: With that kind of thing going on for young people, do you think that folk music could ever catch on with the younger people again?

DG: Well, the population grows to the extent that nothing is really lost, you know. I think there's more Dixieland players today than there ever were at the height of Dixieland, because there's a bigger population. There's more people playing Beethoven, there's more people playing Indian music, there's more people playing — you know, like when computer music comes in with these little tiny home computers, people are going to be making all kinds of music that way. Nothing is lost, though. Most of these folk singers that we are talking about are still working: Mary Travers and Tom Paxton and Bob Gibson and the Trio and the Limeliters . . . everybody, practically, who didn't die is still on the job.

EW: Is that a revival of the folk era or a continuation of it?

DG: A necessity to keep eating.

EW: (laughter) Well, yeah, but do you see any kind of revival — that maybe folk music is coming back into its own after having gone under with rock?

DG: The audience is still out there. Although rock came in and established itself very firmly, the people that like to listen to folk music are still there, so they want people to do that for them. They want to have somebody play the guitar for them while they sing in the audience. Those people are still alive, and I think there's a real feeling that it would be a contribution nowadays to have more of a sense of community; when everybody can sing together, then there's a feeling that we're a family. One of the emphasis things in rock 'n' roll or jazz is how great the musician is and how the audience should admire them, raher than how great the audience is. So the focus in folk music is on the audience, I would think.

EW: The Kingston Trio weren't known as ever being political to any degree. How do you feel about performers who advance their political ideas in —

DG: Well, if they honestly feel that that's the way it should be . . .

EW: Is that any direction that you would go?

DG: There's a big controversy about me being the guy that didn't want to do Jack Kennedy's inaugural ball. I turned that down. I was the guy that voted against it because . . . the purpose of the inaugural ball was to pay the campaign debts of the Democratic party. I thought that if it'd be one day later, I'd always be glad to play for any President of the United States, whether I liked him or not, but I didn't want to be on this party or that party, because you automatically make a bunch of people mad for no good reason. No matter what my — unless it's something that I have a really deep conviction about — but personally, I don't think you should mix the things. When people come for the music, they don't want to hear a lecture about how they should drink more milk, or "Buddha is the best" or something like that. That may be true, but that's not what you come for. When you get on an airplane, you just want to ride the plane, you don't want to hear a bunch of stuff about, you know, how "Your attitude is not correct" or "We have the right attitude" — you just want to go from here to there. But there are people who, in all honesty, feel that they must speak out on certain issues, and just because they happen to be famous, that's okay, too. They should lend their efforts no matter what, whether they're famous or not, to such things because non-famous people work for good causes. You can't forbid famous people from working for good causes.

EW: Yeah, except that they often have a platform afforded to them because of their celebrity status that a plumber — I mean, who will watch a plumber on *The Dick Cavett Show* saying, "Well, this is how I feel," and yet some performers can go on sometimes and use that —

DG: To get popular, do you think? Yeah, I guess . . . it cuts both ways, though. If you advocate a position and then maybe the other half of the world doesn't like that position, then you lose that audience that you might have had. So — I'm not sure exactly . . . it goes every shade of variation. I don't think there's a final answer on that. You're going to find people on every level, expressing themselves on every level, and with every result.

EW: But you, for the most part, try to stay away from that?

DG: If I had some really deep convictions, then I'm sure that I would do something like that. But then, everybody in the group would have to go along with that. We'd all have to — if we all felt that everybody should drink more milk, all three of us did, and thought that to not drink milk was something bad, then I would say, then, let's do a milk commercial. Really.

EW: Your daughter, Catherine, you mentioned before, sang on John's *BOMBS AWAY DREAM BABIES* album —

DG: Yeah.

EW: Well, let me ask you first — the whole world wants to know — where did the name *BOMBS AWAY DREAM BABIES* come from? He credited you with that title.

DG: Oh, I was working with the Modern Folk Quartet in the Ice House in Pasadena — like I said, I was the lead singer in the opening part of the show and they'd be the back-up band. So they are relaxed fellows, and some guy would be tying his shoes and somebody else would be looking for the plug, so in order to gently — instead of having a musical count-off like "1-2-3-4," I would say, "No-o-w, babies" (laughter) "Time to cluster our wits," you know, those things. I would say stuff like that, and — "Bombs away, dream babies." Henry Diltz wrote it down and showed it to John and John thought, "Isn't that off-the-wall?" (laughter) "That's really far-out." He wanted to have something that was — he thought up several titles, but nobody thought they were odd enough, so he used that. No one could get farther out than that at the time.

EW: Yeah, nobody knows what it means. Well, they do now.

DG: Yeah, that's what the use of it was.

EW: Okay. Getting back to Catherine — knowing the pitfalls of "show-biz" and all that, do you ever discourage her from pursuing a singing career?

DG: Well, if it's something you're really gifted at, I think you should go for it. She has a beautiful instrument, her voice, and she's bothering to learn all these styles. She sings in several European languages and sings lots of African music; she works with the African Ensemble from the California Institute of the Arts, and for a couple of years was the lead singer on the Indonesian Gamelan Band that they had. So she's studied all those things, so I think it's a mistake not to use that talent. She's working as a waitress, mainly, now, because she meets people and looks good in the place and everything, and that's a good way to make about fifty bucks a night or so, so that's what she's doing, but you wait for your chances, and then — she's singing studio things, too, as well, but to actually catch on and have steady employment — it takes a little commercial success to do that. Once people hear her, then they'll keep hiring her for the rest of the time on.

EW: How about your other kids? Are they interested in singing at all?

DG: Tom is a movie-maker. He's studying movie-making at the San Francisco Art Institute, so he's made several films and hopes to get into that. At the time of this interview, he's got either a semester or two left to go, depending on if he takes on extra units. Then he wants to get into serious movie-making. And my youngest daughter, Sally, is at Middlebury College in Vermont, and she's on the Dean's List and studies English and French and Italian. This summer she's working on *Sports Illustrated* magazine. Summer before that she helped restore a castle in France, one of those things . . . archeological . . . also a good way to keep your French up. She's a soccer player; she's on the soccer varsity there, so she has all those skills. I think her skill is writing. She'll be in literature of some sort. So we have music, literature, and movie-making.

EW: Wow. How did you become involved with the Muktananda study in the first place?

DG: Well, I read an article in *New York Magazine* by a lady named Sally Kempton, called "Hanging Out With The Guru," and she said a lot of things that were very interesting to me about the Indian way of studying. It's meditation and things like that. I remembered that the Beatles were meditators and they said a lot about that. And I thought that maybe that was a way to get out of the rut of liquor, drugs, and television and ballgames and stuff like that — you know, the same old stuff over and over again which only makes you a little tired, basically. I thought that this would be a good way to refresh myself, so I got a copy of Muktananda's book, which is called *Play of Consciousness,* and —

EW: What year was this?

DG: 1976, when I was going up to see Nick, to see if we could put that group together. And on the way to Oregon, I put the book on the car seat, and I found that I would have to stop and pull the car over and look into the book and get these very heavy electrical shocks in my body. So I thought something really odd was going on. I didn't know what it was but it seemed like there was some really heavy power there. So when I went to Nick's, I would get the book and — we'd talk to Nick for

awhile, and then I'd go down by the side of the river there and read the book and find myself passing out from these heavy electrical vibrations that were going through my body, so I figured it must have been something that was in the way that the book was talking, or something extra to the book — it wasn't just the words but some kind of heavy power. I read that for about three years and was doing meditation on my own, then when I went into Muktananda's ashram in Oakland, here, in California, I just sort of snuck in when nobody was looking. At the noon chant, they were chanting the mantra, "Om Namah Shivaya" and I found this heavy electrical thing was going through me for a solid half-hour. So I decided to stay and check it out, and it's been very nutritious ever since.

EW: Besides electricity, what has it done for you?

DG: It's gotten me away from all kinds of poisons — alcohol and joints and stuff like that are of no interest. And I think it's really stabilized my thought processes. I was really worried and nervous and everything before about the way things were going in the world, and thinking maybe all was doomed, or sitting around biting my lip about one issue or another. That slowed me down on just the basic living of my life. And now I'm able to stabilize my mental processes whenever I'm in distress — or even before I'm in distress, I can head that off at the pass, and just tune myself up mentally and physically. If that were the only thing, it would be worth it on its own, but there's a very profound knowledge that's come down, so I think I'll keep studying it. (laughter)

EW: You mentioned that you were writing out the sheet music for the Sanskrit tunes. Do you think that will have any influence on the kind of music that you do?

DG: Well, sure, I think everything will, all the learning that I —

EW: It all adds up?

DG: Yeah. We'll play, in the ashram — like once a month we'll play a song all night. In India, they play seven days in a row. Sometimes, on very, very special occasions, they play a month in a row, keep a song going for a month. There's one group called the Sikhs, way up in the Himalayas, that have kept the same song going for six hundred years. Somebody's always there on duty doing that; it's kind of like the phone company, it's always on. So, anyway, to play a song for twelve or fourteen hours takes a lot of stamina. Either that, or the tune itself is feeding you, so it's not wearing you out. It's cleaning the junk out of your system, so that adds a lot of strength and everything. I've been able to do that for a couple of years now . . . Of the fourteen hours, I'll play twelve; I'll take little breaks for half an hour to go get some fruit juice or something like that, then get back to it. But that's something really special to be able to do that. What else can you do for twelve hours at a time? Even driving . . .

EW: What other projects are you currently involved in?

DG: I'm designing some posters, which are based on the color music thing, but they just make really beautiful posters. My publishing house is interested in that. I've put out a couple of legends — books of legends. One of them was *Deirdre,* which is an Irish story from 2,000 years ago, and *Hale-Mano,* that's a Hawaiian legend from 400 years ago, and my publishers — we're in the second edition with those. And, what's some other — ? The Gabby Pahinui album I produced, which like I said, got a Hawaiian Grammy, and there was an off-shoot of that — it was included in some albums called THE BEST OF GABBY, so those are going on. And I've got a couple of other historical books now — not legends, but historical characters, one of which is Irish and the other one is a book about Alexander the Great's campaign in Central Asia, because he came into a very interesting area of the world there. The Horsemen, the wild Horsemen of the Steppes of Russia, and the Persians, and the Greeks, and the Indians all came together. So all those civilizations came into, like, a big clash. It was a melting point of all those ways and ideas and things like that, all wrapped up in Alexander's being there, so a lot of very, very interesting things happened between 329 and 327 B.C. (laughter)

EW: So let's end it off with real heavy, heavy question, okay? What do you want to be remembered for?

DG: Remembered for? For doing my best.

EW: And you always do that.

DG: Sometimes I do, but (laughter) I want to be remembered for doing my best — sometimes I don't do my best, but I want people to remember the best part. It's just that I see good things and I want to pass them on, basically. Like you would hip your friends to a good thing if you could, so I don't know if that's a service or not, but if I find something that I like, I want to tell people about it. I was able to do that musically, and with the books, too, and with this art or something like that. So — you know, just a . . . a pointer, I would say. Being a pointer to a good thing.

* * * * * * * * *

In the months since this interview was conducted, Muktananda passed away, and Dave Guard moved to an ashram in New York. The Stewart, Reynolds and Guard project went on, but without Guard. For the inside story on the recording of the Stewart/Reynolds project, see the upcoming chapter on REVENGE OF THE BUDGIE.

In January of 1986, Dave moved to Nashua, New Hampshire and began working up new material for

Scott Fisher and Steve Fiott, the White Mountain Singers, pick and sing with Dave Guard at an informal get-together in Nashua, New Hampshire in September, 1985. Photo by Dave Bellman.

Dave Guard, accompanied on electric bass by Chris Bonett at Dick Cerri's Twenty-fifth Anniversary Concert benefiting the World Folk Music Association, Washington, D.C., January 25, 1986. Photo by Kathryn Brown.

a tour. Also in the works is a new cassette. The music is folk-based, but more high-tech than the traditional Kingston Trio sound. The entertainment world has missed Dave Guard, and it seems that he's missed it just as much.

* * * * * * * * *

"Stewart, Reynolds & Guard", the trio that might-have-been but is yet-to-be, poses at Magic Mountain, near Los Angeles, California on November 7, 1981. Left to right: Nick Reynolds, Dave Guard and John Stewart.

The Capitol Years
Part Two (1961-1964)
by
Benjamin Blake & Jack Rubeck

The fact that 1961 was rough for The Kingston Trio is reflected by the statistical fact that no 45 by the group appeared on *Billboard's* singles chart during any of the fifty-two weeks of that year. A wait-and-see attitude had developed among the nation's DJs, as well as many of the Trio's fans. Could America's sweethearts pick up the pieces and carry on their high caliber careers without Dave Guard? It was quite literally a million dollar question.

Many candidates were reportedly considered for the position of filling Guard's shoes. Travis Edmonson, of the noted duo Bud & Travis, was a fine songwriter, vocalist and guitarist. Chip Douglas (real name: Douglas Hatlelid), later of The Modern Folk Quartet, was a trained musician and vocalist. John Phillips, of The Journeymen (he later went on to fame as the leader of The Mamas & The Papas), was an able singer, songwriter and guitarist. Mike Settle, later a founding member of The First Edition, was a noted songwriter, singer and instrumentalist. He had most recently joined The Cumberland Three, whose leader John Stewart was himself a gifted songwriter, singer and instrumentalist. Others no doubt "applied" for the job, but it was these five men who were most seriously evaluated by manager Frank Werber and surviving Trio members Nick Reynolds and Bob Shane. Age was the disqualifying factor for Douglas, who was too young to perform in nightclubs. The hiring of Edmonson or Phillips would have necessitated the presence of an additional sideman at concerts to play banjo, as neither were adept enough at that instrument. Werber and producer Voyle Gilmore also knew that choosing Phillips would mean the end of The Journeymen, a group that showed some promise of becoming Capitol's "Trio" of the future. Settle, although multi-talented in many areas, was thought to be too "low key" in the stage presence department. Whoever filled Guard's pivotal spot would have to make ready with wit, as well as harmony.

John Stewart fit the bill in every way. He was

tall, dark and handsome; adept at both guitar and five-string banjo, he could write and arrange songs; and he looked sharp in striped shirts. He also possessed the all-necessary, distinctively "different" voice that could (like Guard's) compliment the "smooth" stylings of Shane and the "enthusiastic" vocals of Reynolds. More importantly, they all *liked* each other. Stewart had been a fan, friend and contributor (*Molly Dee, Green Grasses*) to the Trio for several years. As Frank Werber has stated, it was as though John had been "waiting in the wings". Conveniently (and coincidentally?), he had resigned from The Cumberland Three on June 13, during the same week that *Life* announced the KT's intended break-up. John Stewart was paid five hundred dollars per week as a salaried employee of Kingston Trio, Inc. (Reynolds/Shane/Werber) for the duration of his membership in the group.

John performed for the first time publicly as a member of The Kingston Trio at a Boys Club fundraiser in Santa Rosa, California, on September 16, 1961, and shortly after that Nick, Bob and John put the finishing touches on the new group's first album, CLOSE-UP. The LP was released by Capitol in October, going on to equal the chart height of GOIN' PLACES (position number three), and eventually *surpassing* it in sales by more than 20,000 copies. CLOSE-UP earned the refurbished Trio a 1961 Grammy nomination for "Best Performance by a Vocal Group".

Before we get to what was in the grooves, there are a few things about the *package* of this particular album that deserve mention. Although John's picture and name appear several times, no specific mention was made of the fact that he was a *new* member. CLOSE-UP also marks the first time Capitol gave credit to the cover photographer (Ken Veeder). Depending on which pressing you may come across, various copies of this album *appeared* to contain different selections, this being an apparent result of poor communications in Capitol's graphics department.

Seven of the LP's twelve song titles suffered

side one:

1 *Coming From The Mountains*
2 *Oh, Sail Away*
3 *Take Her Out of Pity*
4 *Don't You Weep, Mary*
5 *The Whistling Gypsy*
6 *O Ken Karanga*

side two:

1 *Jesse James*
2 *Glorious Kingdom*
3 *When My Love Was Here*
4 *Karu*
5 *Weeping Willow*
6 *Reuben James*

either major or minor alterations from record label to jacket: *Coming From The Mountains* was listed on the jacket as *Wherever We May Go, Weeping Willow* became *Beneath The Willow, Glorious Kingdom* changed to *Baby Boy, The Whistling Gypsy* shifted to *The Gypsy Rover,* and *Oh, Sail Away* (which incidentally was released as the B side of a British 45) was shortened to just *Sail Away,* not to be confused with 1959's *Sail Away Ladies.* It should also be noted that whoever did the jacket was given incorrect spellings for *Reuben James* and *O Ken Karanga.*

A rare shot from the CLOSE-UP photo session. The covers of COLLEGE CONCERT and SEASONS IN THE SUN (European release) were also taken from this session. Photo courtesy: Capitol Records.

Two of the best performances on this album also proved to be the most popular: the hard-driving Woody Guthrie classic, *Reuben James,* and the tender, melodic *Take Her Out Of Pity* showed the group at its very best at both extremes of the folk performance spectrum. Bob's moving solo on John's sad-summertime composition, *When My Love Was Here,* is certainly the LP's beatific zenith, and Nick's infectious lead on *The Whistling Gypsy* provides another nice moment. Humor is provided by the tongue-in-cheek *Jesse James,* which incidentally was the first track recorded by the new group.

The Trio claims writing credit on six of the tunes: *Take Her Out Of Pity; Don't You Weep, Mary; Jesse James; Glorious Kingdom; Karu. Coming From The Mountains,* another Stewart composition, was released as Nick, Bob and John's first single on October 21. The B side, which has

yet to make an appearance on an LP, was *Nothing More To Look Forward To,* which the label tells us was from the Broadway production *Kwamina.* It featured a rather lifeless lead vocal by Bob, and Capitol master numbers indicate it was recorded at the same sessions that produced CLOSE-UP.

A mini-session in October produced another first for the group: a pair of songs (*Rocky* and *Old Kentucky Land*) sung in beginners' German for a single released exclusively in Germany later that year. English versions were never recorded.

October was also the month the Trio played Boston and first heard a group named Peter, Paul & Mary perform a new Pete Seeger tune, *Where Have All The Flowers Gone.* Knowing a great song when they heard it (and fearing P, P & M would beat them to it), the Kingstons rushed themselves to the same New York City studio that had produced the hits *M.T.A.* and *The Tijuana Jail,* and emerged six hours later with three minutes of tape that would become the new group's first top forty hit. *Where Have All The Flowers Gone* was released in December and reached number twenty-one on *Billboard's* hit list by February 1962. Voyle Gilmore always felt that the song, which had five verses, should have been trimmed to a length more easily programmable for radio stations (the theory being that more airplay equalled more sales). The integrity displayed by Nick, Bob and John in refusing to edit the 45 earned them some seldom heard kind words among the folk community. The single's B side was *O Ken Karanga* from CLOSE-UP.

Shortly before the studio single version was released, the Trio recorded *Where Have All The Flowers Gone* once more, this time live in concert at the University of California at Los Angeles. Voyle Gilmore and Pete Abbot actually taped *two* complete concerts (December 6 and 7) and then edited the best performances from each to construct the group's second Capitol outing, COLLEGE CONCERT, released in February of 1962. It peaked at number three on the charts and eventually sold nearly 400,000 copies. It proved to be Reynolds, Shane and Stewart's biggest LP, and a personal favorite of Gilmore's.

There are at least three reasons why COLLEGE CONCERT was the best selling KT album since STRING ALONG: 1) College campuses were still the strongholds of Trio fandom, so a live concert LP recorded at a major college was naturally popular with that crowd. 2) For the first time, the group re-recorded some tunes that were *already* proven favorites, like *M.T.A.,* an updated version of *Coplas,* and *O Ken Karanga,* Nick's percussive tour de force from the previous LP. 3) For the first time in years, here was a Trio album that boasted a song that people were hearing regularly on the radio. Although technically *not* the hit version, this

side one:

1 Little Light
2 Coplas Revisited
3 Chilly Winds
4 Oh, Miss Mary
5 Laredo?
6 O Ken Karanga

side two:

1 Roddy McCorley
2 M.T.A.
3 500 Miles
4 Ballad Of The Shape Of Things
5 Where Have All The Flowers Gone
6 Goin' Away For To Leave You

live track of *Where Have All The Flowers Gone* (with Nick's movingly-rendered intro) is equally admired by many fans.

In addition to *Coplas Revisited*, the album's humor is provided by a short spoof of the western hit *Laredo*, and *The Shape Of Things*, a new English madrigal by way of Broadway from the writer of *The Merry Minuet*, Sheldon Harnick. Other highlights include the rousing opener, *Little Light*, and a dramatic reading of The Clancy Brothers' *Roddy McCorley*.

If fans were to be polled on their favorite songs from COLLEGE CONCERT, it is assured that the third tracks on either side would be at or near the top of their lists. *Chilly Winds* and *500 Miles* are two of the most beautifully arranged tunes to ever grace a listener's ears. The latter (released as a 45 in Great Britain) was recorded by nearly every folk act of the era, surely keeping composer Hedy West in guitar picks for many years! The hauntingly memorable *Chilly Winds* is one of two John Stewart/John Phillips collaborations on the LP (the other being the infectious *Oh, Miss Mary*).

Another seldom-viewed shot from the photo session that produced the cover of COLLEGE CONCERT.
Photo courtesy: Capitol Records.

Reynolds, Shane and Stewart claim only three copyrights this time out: *Little Light, Laredo?,* and *Coplas Revisited.*

Technically, the sound on this record is something of an enigma. Everything is fine and state-of-the-art for the time *except* that it sounds as if Pete Abbot had used a filter which cut off everything below about 200 Hz. As a result, the music seems lacking in bass, with only occasional weak glimpses of what could have been in such places as the start of *Where Have All The Flowers Gone.* As for headphone listening, it can get a bit confusing as the voices jump from side to middle to side as the Trio members shift positions on stage. However, *500 Miles* and *Chilly Winds* are still good bets. *Chilly Winds,* incidentally, was reportedly one of Voyle Gilmore's all-time KT favorites, and it was released in Great Britain as a single (B side: *Roddy McCorley*).

COLLEGE CONCERT marked the last Capitol recording session in which David "Buck" Wheat participated as accompanist for the Trio. After fulfilling his contract with the group (which ran until the end of 1961), he hurried off to join Dave Guard & The Whiskeyhill Singers. He later joined Bud & Travis as arranger/accompanist, and wrote some memorable jazz-flavored songs in the early Sixties, including *Better Than Anything* (which later became a hit for Al Jarreau). It has been speculated that Wheat played a larger role in the sound of The Kingston Trio than he was ever given credit for, and that after COLLEGE CONCERT the group's arrangements were never quite as captivating.

* * * * * * *

The upward sales curve charted by CLOSE-UP and COLLEGE CONCERT was music to Capitol's ears. Here was a group that had lost its leader and peaked in popularity several albums earlier, now suddenly breathing fire again. All agreed it was time to assemble a "Greatest Hits" package, and it would be nice to have another "hit" to put on it.

To that attempted end, Capitol released its latest Kingston Trio single on March 28, 1962. It was unique in that it featured *both* versions of the Trio. The A side was *Scotch And Soda*, Bob Shane's trademark solo from the first Trio LP, a tune DJs had been clamoring for since the beginning. For an "old" song that almost a million fans already had, it made a respectable chart showing, reaching position eighty-one. The B side was a *new* song called *Jane, Jane, Jane,* which made KT history by being the first (and only) B side to chart, if only for one lonely week at the "height" of number ninety-three. *Jane, Jane, Jane* was recorded *before* the April 23-25 sessions that would yield the group's next *new* album, and this track would undergo some drastic changes before that LP's release three months later.

May, however, was the release month for THE BEST OF THE KINGSTON TRIO. *Scotch And Soda* was on the charts, *Where Have All The Flowers Gone* was still fresh in people's minds, *The Tijuana Jail* had never been on an LP before, and *M.T.A.* and *Tom Dooley* lived again. Although BEST

side one:

1 Tom Dooley
2 The Tijuana Jail
3 Scotch and Soda
4 Bad Man Blunder
5 Raspberries, Strawberries
6 Everglades

side two:

1 M.T.A.
2 The Merry Minuet
3 Where Have All The Flowers Gone
4 Billy Goat Hill
5 Take Her Out Of Pity
6 A Worried Man

OF only aspired to a chart spot of number seven, longevity proved to be its forte. It remained charted for over two years, the first KT LP since HERE WE GO AGAIN to roll up such a statistic. It was awarded a gold record (the group's seventh — and last) in 1964 and eventually tallied-up sales of over 1,000,000 units, making it The Kingston Trio's all-time best selling album.

Although eight of the Trio's chart singles are here (*Raspberries, Strawberries* is the SOLD OUT re-recording, and *not* the 45), there are also cuts from various LPs to round it out. Conspicuous in its absence is *El Matador,* a top forty hit that outperformed three of the singles that *are* here. Oddly, Capitol chose two tracks each from STRING ALONG and THE KINGSTON TRIO, while COLLEGE CONCERT, MAKE WAY, STEREO CONCERT and THE LAST MONTH OF THE YEAR were shut out completely.

Notes for collectors: nine of this albums twelve bands are in true stereo, while the original versions of *Tom Dooley, Scotch And Soda* and *The Merry Minuet* make their first appearance anywhere in re-channeled stereo ("Duophonic"). 45s of *The Tijuana Jail* and *Where Have All The Flowers Gone* — both stereo — make their LP debut here (although the liner notes would have you believe the latter is the COLLEGE CONCERT version, it is *not*). The back cover of the LP features photos of all thirteen previous KT albums, and very early copies featured them in color. The label is the black and silver Capitol "Star Line" series, while the very early copies were in gold.

Capitol chose to help launch its new line of seven-inch stereo 33⅓ r.p.m. singles with two selections from THE BEST OF, *Billy Goat Hill/Take Her Out Of Pity.* Neither side was ever released on a regular 45, and the new line of singles (called "Compact 33s") was short-lived.

The fact that the departed Mr. Guard appeared on ten of THE BEST OF THE KINGSTON TRIO's twelve cuts posed a bit of a packaging dilemma for Capitol. They solved the problem with a cover photo of the Trio taken from the rear during a concert performance. With Stewart's back dead center, he could easily be taken for Guard. Only Reynolds is given a full profile, and even at that his face is partially obscured by the neck of Stewart's banjo. It was clear that Capitol wanted an album cover that could withstand any *future* defections as well!

* * * * * * *

The Trio's next album provoked some angry fan letters. SOMETHING SPECIAL could have been more aptly titled "Something Strange", as it was as much a collaboration between Voyle Gilmore and arranger/conductor Jimmie Haskell as it was between Gilmore and the Trio. We quote from the anonymous liner notes: ". . . Their voices and instruments are set against larger-scaled backgrounds . . . The orchestrations are of two types — brass, woodwinds and strings forming the background on some of the tunes; just strings with rhythm on others — and a richly blended chorus is added on several selections." The earlier 45 release of *Jane, Jane, Jane* may hold the only clue as to what an untampered with version of this album *might* have sounded like.

Recorded in April, this blatantly commercial attempt at "Folk Music For Everyone" was released in July of 1962, right on the heels of THE BEST OF THE KINGSTON TRIO, and also reached the number seven chart position. Amazingly, it somehow managed a Grammy nomination in the "Best Folk Recording" category the following spring, and it eventually sold somewhat less than 300,000 copies. To say that SOMETHING SPECIAL suffered from overproduction on most of its tracks is letting everyone involved off easy. A totally unnecessary brass section and a particularly annoying tambourine make this an occasionally painful LP to listen to. Thankfully, it was the Trio's last attempt at this sort of nonsense.

The most offensive tracks on this record have to be *Tell It On The Mountain* and *Brown Mountain Light.* Awful arrangements aside, the former is simply not the Trio's style, and the latter — like many of the songs here — deserved better treatment on some other KT outing.

It should be said that *some* of the songs worked very well in this format (John Stewart reportedly offered helpful suggestions to Jimmie Haskell on a few of the string arrangements). *One More Town* (words and music by John, lead vocal by Nick) was actually complimented by the string background, as was *Pullin' Away. Jane, Jane, Jane* manages to *still* sound good amid the garnish, thanks to its innate gentleness and simplicity, although the single record version remains a cut above this augmented one. Two other tunes also stand out due to their simplicity of theme and lack of obtrusive orchestration. These are Mike Settle's *Little Boy* and John Stewart's *Portland Town,* complimented by effective solos by Nick and John. respectively. Bob's standout solo on the LP is Rodgers & Hart's *She Was Too Good To Me,* a bluesy show-stopper *so* crassly overproduced that it becomes endearingly memorable.

If there were awards for weirdness, one could certainly go to *Strange Day.* Co-written by Stewart as the LP's apparent moment of levity (boy meets-swine-at-the-dance?), it remains to this day the

side one:

1 Brown Mountain Light
2 One More Town
3 O Willow Waly
4 Tell It On The Mountain
5 Little Boy
6 Strange Day

side two:

1 Away Rio
2 Pullin' Away
3 She Was Too Good To Me
4 Jane, Jane, Jane
5 Portland Town
6 Old Joe Clark

ultimate four-minute KT enigma.

Reynolds, Shane and Stewart claim authorship on SOMETHING SPECIAL of *Tell It On The Mountain, Away Rio* and *Pullin' Away.* They have the decency to list *Old Joe Clark* as "traditional", with an arrangement by the group. This last track was released as the B side of their next single on July 25. The A side, *C'Mon Betty Home,* was never included on an LP and ranks just behind *Coo Coo-U* as the strangest side ever recorded by The Kingston Trio. Our heroes seem to be playing rinky-tink piano, harpsichord and bongos in an apparent attempt to fuse the styles of calypso and early Andy Williams! The song was written for the group by Peter Yarrow and Noel Paul Stookey (an act of sabotage, perhaps?), who had the good sense never to record it themselves. Master numbers indicate that *C'Mon Betty Home* was recorded *after* the SOMETHING SPECIAL sessions, and scarcity of this disc is readily attributed to its deservedly negligible sales figures (less than 3,000 copies). Not so for the final single from SOMETHING SPECIAL, *One More Town/She Was Too Good To Me,* released on October 5. The A side, easily the best cut on the LP, received considerable airplay and even charted for a few weeks.

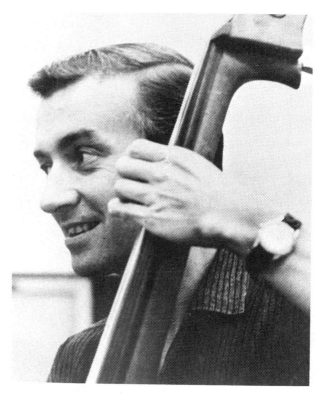

Dean Reilly, bassist extraordinaire. Photo courtesy: Archives of Music Preservation.

"Mr. Enthusiasm" · Nick Reynolds. Photo courtesy: Archives of Music Preservation.

Though hardly noticeable amid all the horns and strings, the Trio's new bass player made his debut with this album. Dean Reilly had known the group from his stint as house band leader at the *Hungry i* and had joined them at Lake Tahoe for a three-week trial in March of 1962. He was to remain with Nick, Bob and John for the remainder of the group's recording and performing career.

* * * * * * *

The Kingston Trio finished 1962 with another LP release in November. NEW FRONTIER took its title from the lone John Stewart composition on the record, *The New Frontier,* which in turn took its inspiration from the inaugural address of President John F. Kennedy. Judging from Stewart's liner notes, the Trio was caught-up in the whirl of Camelot, even dedicating the album to the volunteers of the Peace Corps. While the title song stirringly reflects this spirit, the album's other eleven cuts have little to do with current events. Incidentally, John lists NEW FRONTIER as his all-time favorite among the albums he recorded with the Trio.

NEW FRONTIER peaked at position sixteen on the album charts, making it the first major LP release by the Trio *not* to make the top ten list. It would be easy to blame fans' displeasure with SOMETHING SPECIAL for its follow-up's comparatively poor chart showing, but statistics can often be misleading. NEW FRONTIER actually *out-sold* its predecessor by more than 80,000 copies and became second only to COLLEGE CONCERT on the final sales list of albums by Nick, Bob and John. Why it fared so badly on *Billboard's* hit list remains a mystery.

Capitol went to great pains to mention in the non-Stewart portion of the liner notes that this was *not* another Jimmie Haskell collaboration, but the Trio "... singing lustily and providing their own ac-

side one:

1 Greenback Dollar
2 Some Fool Made A Soldier Of Me
3 To Be Redeemed
4 Honey, Are You Mad At Your Man
5 Adios Farewell
6 Poor Ellen Smith

side two:

1 My Lord What A Mornin'
2 Long Black Veil
3 Genny Glenn
4 The First Time
5 Dogie's Lament
6 The New Frontier

companiment . . ." While it is true that the old Trio verve is back, this album has more than its share of substandard material. *Dogie's Lament* and *Adios Farewell* are among the most easily disposable tracks ever recorded by the group.

But there are memorable moments here, too. Besides the invigorating *The New Frontier,* the KT performs well on several other tunes. *Long Black Veil* and *Poor Ellen Smith* both deal with murder in effectively different ways. The former (later covered by The Band) is a haunting, country-flavored account of a man who goes to the gallows rather than admit to an illicit love affair, while the latter tells its morbid tale with such high spirits that it's impossible to feel any sympathy for the murdered Miss Smith. *To Be Redeemed* marks the return of writer Jane Bowers with an unabashed evangelical spiritual.

In the mini-masterpiece department, Ewan MacColl's *The First Time* is tenderly harmonized here in one of the Trio's finest moments on record. One of the most beautiful love songs ever written, it has since been recorded by a great many artists, but never improved upon. Roberta Flack's million-selling version in 1972 earned *The First Time* and MacColl a Grammy for "Song Of The Year" a full decade later than it should have.

Reynolds, Shane and Stewart claim writing credit on NEW FRONTIER for five tunes: *Honey, Are You Mad At Your Man?; Poor Ellen Smith; My Lord What A Mornin'; Genny Glenn; Dogie's Lament.*

On January 12, 1963, Capitol released the only 45 from NEW FRONTIER, *Greenback Dollar/The New Frontier.* The A side was to become the song most associated with Nick, Bob and John, and it would equal the chart popularity of their earlier success, *Where Have All The Flowers Gone,* by peaking at position number twenty-one. *Greenback Dollar* marked Hoyt Axton's first success as a songwriter, and it also kicked-up its share of controversy over the word "damn" in the song's chorus. Recording engineer Pete Abbot remembers: "Voyle was very leery of that. He said, 'Oh, God, we can't put that out. They'll never buy it. We'd better make two versions.'" Gilmore left "damn" intact on the LP, but he brought in guitarist Jack Marshall to strum one chord over the naughty word on the single. It proved to be quite a gimmick and led to a lot of airplay. Gilmore did one other bit of tinkering with the 45 version, in that it fades out rather than concludes abruptly.

The finer moments on NEW FRONTIER showed the growing studio confidence of John Stewart. It

Voyle Gilmore and Frank Werber relax with the Trio during a break in a recording session at Capitol Records. Photo courtesy: Capitol Records.

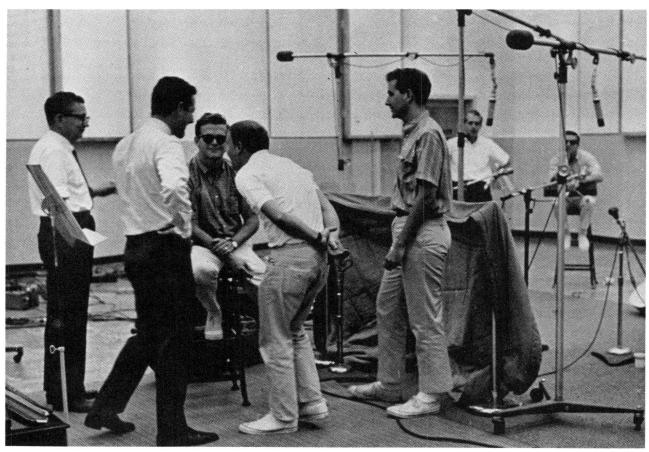

should also be noted that Jerry Walter (of The Gateway Singers) helped write some of the vocal charts for these sessions.

* * * * * * *

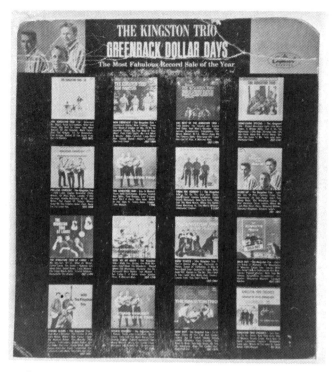

Record bin divider for the "Greenback Dollar Days" promotion. From the collection of Ben Blake.

In March of 1963, with *Greenback Dollar* peaking in the top forty, Capitol released THE KINGSTON TRIO #16. The jacket gives the impression of a rush-release, with its black and white photography and seemingly uninspired title, but the record inside showcased a rejuvenated Kingston Trio ready to be taken seriously once again after two fairly lack-luster LPs. Capitol chose the title to call attention to two items: 1) The longevity and popularity of the group (few artists ever lasted long enough to record sixteen albums); 2) The fact that there were fifteen *other* LPs that should be in every true fan's collection (#16 is actually number *seventeen,* but who's counting?). Capitol utilized #16 to kick-off a KT LP promotion called "Greenback Dollar Days", wherein retailers stocked massive quantities of Trio albums in special displays, offering a second Trio LP for one dollar to anyone who purchased one at the regular price. Needless to say, Capitol sold a lot of Kingston Trio records in 1963.

All of this was given an unexpected boost by a leftfield hit single from #16, *Reverend Mr. Black.* How it got released as a 45 in the first place is a story that rivals that of *Tom Dooley.* The song, basically a narrative written by Billy Edd Wheeler and Jed Peters around an ancient spiritual (*Lonesome Valley*), was given to Voyle Gilmore at a convention in Nashville. Although it became probably the most famous lead vocal John Stewart ever did with the Trio, it was not one that he

John, Bob and Nick in rehearsal for the live performance that produced the COLLEGE CONCERT album. Photo courtesy: Capitol Records.

side one:

1 Reverend Mr. Black
2 Road To Freedom
3 River Run Down
4 Big Ball In Town
5 One More Round
6 Oh Joe Hannah

side two:

1 Run The Ridges
2 Try To Remember
3 Mark Twain
4 Low Bridge
5 Ballad Of The Quiet Fighter
6 La Bamba

wanted to do. He did not care for the song, and he only agreed to sing it after Gilmore and the others badgered him into it. It was never intended to be a single, but a high school English teacher and his students were to change all that.

In Chicago, William R. Idol was having trouble trying to get a point across to his classes about the shaping of public opinion by "vocal minorities", raised in President Kennedy's *Profiles In Courage.* He finally decided to put it into terms they could relate to: the weekly "top ten" records. He wagered with his ninety-five students that *they* could make a top ten hit out of an obscure album cut that everyone there agreed was "the worst record" they'd ever heard, *Reverend Mr. Black,* from THE KINGSTON TRIO #16. The students began phoning Chicago's WLS on Monday, March 18, requesting that the station play the "great new record by The Kingston Trio". WLS requested the 45 from Capitol on March 19, and the company released it on March 20, having learned their lesson about foot-dragging with *Tom Dooley* almost five years earlier. *Reverend Mr. Black* eventually won the wager for teacher Idol by spending four weeks in Chicago's top ten, making it to number eight nationally by May, and eventually selling nearly 400,000 copies. This made it Nick, Bob and John's biggest hit, and second only to the phenomenal *Tom Dooley* as The Kingston Trio's most successful single, saleswise. All this brought about by less than a hundred phone calls from a handful of Chicago high school students who did not even *like* the record! If the Trio had not been touring England that April, they most certainly would have been touring Chicago.

The hit 45 helped boost #16 all the way to number four in *Billboard,* the best showing for the KT since COLLEGE CONCERT. #16 sold almost 350,000 records, several thousand *fewer* than NEW FRONTIER, contrary to popular opinion. It would be the *last* Trio LP to sell in excess of 200,000 units.

John Stewart wrote no less than four of the songs on #16. *Run The Ridges* and *Ballad Of The Quiet Fighter* stand as two of Stewart's best works. The latter proved to be the forerunner of John's many "introspective patriot" songs, and it can be argued that he has never really improved upon the spine-shivering simplicity of this near-perfect masterpiece. *Road To Freedom* shares a similar subject matter (Civil Rights), but with an uptempo assist from Nick and Bob. The fourth Stewart song, *Oh Joe Hannah,* is a repetitively simple mover about working on the river, one of several "river" songs on #16.

The album's other high points include Bob's beautiful solo on *Try To Remember,* from Broadway's *The Fantasticks,* yet another case of the Trio being the first to record a song that was later

John concentrates on his 12-string guitar during a Capitol recording session. Photo courtesy: Archives of Music Preservation.

popularized by everyone else. John's collaborative ballad, *River Run Down,* is given an evocative reading by Nick. *Big Ball In Town* marked the Trio's first return to Boston since *M.T.A.* (subject-wise), and in the process managed a few light-hearted pokes at the Kennedys. *One More Round* (the B side of *Reverend Mr. Black*) is a moody redressing of *Delia's Gone,* with minor verse changes. These last two arrangements, plus *Low Bridge* and *La Bamba,* are credited to Reynolds, Shane and Stewart.

Technically, the recorded sound on this album is outstanding, and Gilmore and the group took over-dubbing to new heights in these sessions. Songs such as *River Run Down* offered an effective means of demonstrating the frequency response and "punch" of any playback system. In fact, the sound on this record is *so* good that it is most worthwhile to listen to it in its entirety on both headphones and speakers so that all of its sonic highlights can be discovered and enjoyed.

We all know *Reverend Mr. Black* was one of the Trio's biggest hits, but was it one of their *best*? The overall sound of the record was something totally new (and very "*un*-Trio") for Nick, Bob and John, and the country flavor of Wheeler's lyrics placed Stewart in a "Johnny Cash sound-alike" quagmire that would take him years to live down. The Trio's arrangement of this song was one of the very few with dubbed-in background singers, and it is also interesting to note that the six-string banjo in the left channel was played not by John Stewart but by a pretty fair back-up player of the time named Glen Campbell. All of which backfired on the Trio when it became a hit, because it was virtually impossible to recreate the recorded sound in a concert situation.

* * * * * * *

Still, there is no quarreling with success. With *Reverend Mr. Black* still riding tall in the saddle, Capitol chose to ignore the many strong follow-up singles possibilities on #16, and instead sent Gilmore after additional Billy Edd Wheeler songs and whatever else they could scrape up to grind out a new LP. Released in July, SUNNY SIDE! was a rushed production, and it shows. For the first time, the filler outweighs the meat. Capitol skipped the photo session, opting for an uninspired artist's rendition of the group on the front cover, and a photo from #16 on the back. There are eleven songs rather than the customary twelve, with no cuts over three minutes and three of them under two minutes in length, with a total playing time of less than twenty-eight minutes. Cheap, cheap, cheap!

Each side starts off with a Wheeler song sung by John Stewart. *Jackson* later became a hit for Johnny Cash, of all people, and *Desert Pete* became the choice to follow the Reverend up the hallowed charts. Although it would only aspire to the number thirty-three spot, *Desert Pete* would actually outsell *Greenback Dollar* by several thousand copies. It would help propel SUNNY SIDE! to position number seven on the album chart, but it would also be the last top forty single for The Kingston Trio (and the last top ten LP).

There are so many low points on this album that it is difficult to know where to begin. The group sounds uninvolved and almost indifferent on *Blowin' In The Wind*. Already a chart hit for Peter, Paul & Mary when SUNNY SIDE! was released, the song's presence here is unnecessary, no matter how eager the Trio was to acknowledge the existance of Bob Dylan. Lifted from the songbag of The Tarriers, *Those Brown Eyes* is possibly the album's lowest moment. It is certainly a song the Trio should not have recorded, and one can almost hear them passing the bottle around just to get through it. Just *awful*.

There *are* a few good moments on this album. Although it may seem a bit heavy-handed two decades later, *Ballad Of The Thresher* (with a dramatic vocal by John) effectively captured the pathos of the moment from that year's nuclear submarine tragedy. As a B side of *Desert Pete*, it received respectable airplay during the summer of '63.

The high points of SUNNY SIDE! appear at the end. *Those Who Are Wise* is the LP's lone Stewart composition and is easily one of the best songs he has ever written. It shines here like a diamond in a manure pile, and it certainly deserved to be on a better album than this one. The drivingly executed *Rider* brings the album to a strong finish, with yet another lead vocal by Stewart. It is also the LP's lone writing credit for Bob and Nick (with Judy Henske).

So much concentration seems to have gone into making John's vocals predominant on SUNNY SIDE! (again, fallout from *Reverend Mr. Black*) that Nick and Bob are almost relegated to the status of back-up singers. Shane's one chance is with Rod McKuen's *Two-Ten, Six-Eighteen*, a fairly good song here given a fairly boring treatment. Aside from the energy he supplies to *Sing Out* (the LP's obligatory spiritual, written by John's brother Mike) and *Rider*, Reynolds might just as well have gone fishing. His only solo shot is Mike Settle's *Goo Ga Gee*, the album's required light touch that falls a bit short of its mark.

The album's foreign language item, *Marcelle Vahine*, had been in the Trio's songbag back in the early *Purple Onion* days, an indication of just how much barrel-scraping had been done for SUNNY SIDE!. It was later released as the B side of the KT's next single, on November 2. The A side was a gentle protest song by Rod McKuen titled *Ally Ally Oxen Free*, which the Trio had apparently seized upon as their attempt at appearing more serious (as indeed they were) about where music was heading after *Blowin' In The Wind* ushered-in the era of social consciousness. *Ally Ally Oxen Free* would be the last Kingston Trio 45 to appear on *Billboard's* "Hot 100" chart, peaking at number sixty-one. It first appeared on the chart dated the week of November 23, 1963, while Nick, Bob and John were in the process of recording their next LP. The single would become a part of that album (TIME TO THINK), which would be released in December.

On December 7, just prior to the appearance of TIME TO THINK, Capitol released the most amazing Kingston Trio LP ever to be recorded. SING A SONG WITH THE KINGSTON TRIO was unique because the Trio had nothing to do with it, aside from the fact that their pictures adorned the front of the jacket. To quote the cover: "Instrumental background re-creations of their biggest hits! . . . complete lyrics and chord symbols included for your sing-along, play-along pleasure." Produced by Kermit Walter and Voyle Gilmore, SING A SONG's instruments were manned by former Weavers member Frank Hamilton, although he was never publicly credited. The bogusly-titled LP would spend fourteen weeks on the charts, picking its

side one:

1   Desert Pete
2   Marcelle Vahine
3   Sing Out
4   Ballad Of The Thresher
5   Blowin' In The Wind
6   Goo Ga Gee

side two:

1   Jackson
2   Two-Ten, Six-Eighteen
3   Those Brown Eyes
4   Those Who Are Wise
5   Rider

way to number sixty-nine. Ironically, it would outsell many of the later albums by the *real* KT. To Hamilton's credit, several of the tracks stand on their own as decent instrumentals, most notably *The Sinking Of The Reuben James.*

* * * * * * * * *

It has already been decided by all concerned that TIME TO THINK would contain none of the fluffy ballads and carefree ditties of earlier works, since the month of October had seen Peter, Paul & Mary place all three of their LPs in the national top five. Folk For Fun was a thing of the past, and Folk With A Conscience was "in". The death of President Kennedy on November 22 would make TIME TO THINK's mood solemn, as well as serious. From the somber expressions in the cover photograph to the simple-yet-eloquent words on the back, the entire production did not look or sound like any other Trio release up to that time, and it met with mixed reviews and a moderate amount of apathy from record buyers. Many could not accept this dramatic change in a familiar product, while others no doubt felt that the group was trying to cash-in on the public's emotions at a trying time.

Those who have downplayed the importance of this LP over the years overlooked the fact that — emotions aside — this is a class production. Evidence abounds on every track of the time and care taken for each song. The material was easily the best of any Reynolds/Shane/Stewart album; the sound was tight, and the performances were more than professional. And if it can be said that the "messages" in these songs were apropos in 1963, listening to them today shows that the times have not changed much at all.

Recorded in San Francisco, TIME TO THINK stands today as quite possibly the finest studio

half hour of the folk era. Sadly, its sales popularity did not approach its heights of class. The twenty-one weeks it spent on the charts were dominated by The Beatles and all that they inspired, and the big money days of commercial folk music were drawing to an end. TIME TO THINK climbed as high as position eighteen and managed to sell slightly more than 100,000 copies.

A total of five tracks from TIME TO THINK were released on 45s, an all-time record for the Trio on Capitol. After *Ally Ally Oxen Free* had run its course, two of the album's finest tracks were released as a single on February 5, 1964. The LP's closing cut, Ed McCurdy's poignant anti-war anthem, *Last Night I Had The Strangest Dream,* and Billy Behen's Irish folk tune, *The Patriot Game,* which opens the album, form the A and B sides of one of the group's most powerful singles. The 45 version of *The Patriot Game* is yet another oddity for collectors. Although it *is* the same take that appears on TIME TO THINK, the song was re-mixed so that John's spoken verse — which appears near the end of the track on the LP — actually opens the single. The record is effective either way, and it is unclear why such tinkering occured in the first place. On April 12, *If You Don't Look Around/Seasons In The Sun* became the final single release from the album, and it turned out to be the last new Capitol 45 by Nick, Bob and John. The A side, written by Stewart, pretty well sums up the anger and frustration of 1963 America, but *Seasons In The Sun,* easily the finest of all Rod McKuen/Jaques Brel collaborations, actually received more airplay.

It is difficult to single out any one song as being the high point on this album. Several of them were later recorded by other artists, most notably *Seasons In The Sun,* a million seller for Terry Jacks in 1974. As presented here, the song has one of the Trio's most unusual and atmospheric arrangements (a sort of cross between *Raspberries, Strawberries* and *Greenback Dollar*), with the lead vocal handled admirably by Bob Shane. With its spare instrumentation, air of moody sadness, changes of tempo and abrupt ending, *Seasons* ranks as one of Voyle Gilmore's most ambitious productions.

Nick Reynolds is the featured vocalist on two of the album's finest cuts, *Hobo's Lullaby* and *No One To Talk My Troubles To.* The lilting guitar work of session sideman John Staubard is showcased on these tunes. *Hobo's Lullaby* in particular (a personal favorite of Nick's) is often cited as an example of just how powerful the Trio could be when they put their minds to it. It is certainly one of the very best of all KT recordings. This album's Billy Edd Wheeler composition, *Coal Tattoo,* is a driving, atmospheric study of the

side one:

1 The Patriot Game
2 Coal Tattoo
3 Hobo's Lullaby
4 Seasons In The Sun
5 These Seven Men
6 Ally Ally Oxen Free

side two:

1 Deportee
2 No One To Talk My Troubles To
3 If You Don't Look Around
4 Turn Around
5 Song For A Friend
6 Last Night I Had The Strangest Dream

A serious moment in the Capitol studio. Photo courtesy: Capitol Records.

darkness of the mines, with a pulsating lead vocal by John, and the group at its echo-chambered best on the chorus. *Turn Around* and *Deportee* are two more of the memorable and well-arranged performances to be found here.

Certainly one of TIME TO THINK's most moving moments is supplied by John's *Song For A Friend.* John's involvement with JFK's New Frontier theology made the pain at the loss of his President (and hero) even more intense. Written hours after the assassination and recorded on the day of Kennedy's funeral, *Song For A Friend* is a true folk song, mirroring the emotions of a devastating event, and John's broken vocal is *still* capable of whisking the listener back to that pivotal weekend in history. Master numbers suggest this was also the final studio track the group recorded for Capitol.

TIME TO THINK was the first KT album to feature song timings on the jacket, and also the first in many years to feature *no* songwriting credits for Shane or Reynolds.

* * * * * *

The Kingston Trio's seven-year contract with Capitol Records expired on February 15, 1964. Had this occured a year earlier, the group might well have remained signed to the label of their birth, but Capitol was understandably preoccupied with promoting The Beatles, so the Trio's contract renewal became a very secondary matter. From Capitol's standpoint, the group's slumping sales gave Frank Werber very little leverage for bargaining any increases in the contract. From Werber's standpoint, the Trio had accounted for approximately twenty per cent of Capitol's gross for several years and deserved a fat bonus. In addition, the group was receiving tantalizing financial offers from Decca Records. So it can be fairly said that although both Capitol and The Kingston Trio would have *preferred* to remain together, neither side felt it a great loss to part company.

The Trio still owed Capitol one new LP, so Voyle Gilmore and Pete Abbot once again packed their equipment off to the *Hungry i* in San Francisco for another live Trio recording. From March 23rd to 31st, 1964, Nick, Bob and John recorded their final Capitol tracks. The best moments from these performances would be edited and released in June on an album titled BACK IN TOWN.

side one:

1   *Georgia Stockade*
2   *Ann*
3   *Ah, Woe, Ah, Me*
4   *Walkin' This Road To My Town*
5   *World I Used To Know*
6   *Salty Dog*

side two:

1   *Let's Get Together*
2   *Isle In The Water*
3   *Farewell Captain*
4   *Tom Dooley*
5   *Them Poems*
6   *So Hi*

A publicity shot for the Trio's final Capitol sessions, from the series of photos that produced the BEST OF THE KINGSTON TRIO VOL. 2 cover. Photo courtesy: Capitol Records.

The new directions pointed to on TIME TO THINK seem to have fallen by the wayside in this weak offering, which is easily the Trio's most forgettable live recording. Selections like *Farewell Captain, Georgia Stockade* and a rehash of *Tom Dooley* (worst version on record) all vie for the dubious honor of weakest cut on the LP, and most of the other songs here do not even qualify as good filler. We can't even point to a saving composition by John, as Mr. Stewart was wise enough not to waste one on this set. The presence of Glen Campbell *on stage* as a back-up guitarist and the way the members occasionally misread the lyrics lend creedence to the belief that this group of songs was "learned in a hurry" by the Trio for the sole purpose of satisfying their contract obligations.

But even this mess has its moments. *Let's Get Together* is a powerful song which might have done well for the Trio as a single (as it later did for We Five and The Youngbloods) if it had been released. John's vocal work gives considerable power to the reflective lyrics of *Walkin' This Road To My Town*. Both of these songs deserved studio production and would have been more at home on TIME TO THINK. Perhaps the most harmlessly enjoyable track on BACK IN TOWN is Billy Edd Wheeler's *Ann,* on which John's voice dominates the group vocal. The main problem with *World I Used To Know* (another Rod McKuen tune) is that Bob can't seem to decide if this is a serious solo or a light-hearted throwaway. Whatever its qualities, it received some airplay in the summer of '64. Jimmie Rodgers trotted out a cover version when Capitol failed to single the Trio's.

Since BACK IN TOWN was recorded and released after the Trio had left the label, it is understandable why Capitol failed to move on 45 requests from DJs. Despite the company's indifference to this LP, it managed to stay charted for nearly five months and reached a height of number twenty-two, actually outselling TIME TO THINK by a few thousand copies.

We wish we could tell you that The Kingston Trio's final Capitol cut was a real classic, but in truth the master numbers indicate that Mason Williams' *Them Poems* was the last chosen track from the March *Hungry i* sessions.

A rare shot from the photo session that produced the BACK IN TOWN cover photo. Photo courtesy: Capitol Records.

* * * * * * *

In July, *Variety* reported the official news that Decca was interested in signing the Trio. Signatures were affixed to the finalized document on October 13, 1964.

Since the group's first Decca LP was not due until December, Capitol sought to fill the six-month void between releases with a three-record anthology, THE FOLK ERA. The people at Capitol exhibited an unusual amount of creativity by compiling a set that covered the Trio's seven-year history remarkably well. Its main shortcoming is that the powers-that-be missed a golden opportunity to squeeze in a few of the non-LP singles or unreleased items. Since eight of the selections are in rechanneled Duophonic stereo anyway, how nice it would have been to have the original versions of *Scarlet Ribbons* and *Raspberries, Strawberries,* or the censored take of *Greenback Dollar.*

The album contains thirty-three songs, although the cover lists only thirty-two (they somehow misplaced *Reverend Mr. Black*), with nineteen of these recorded with Dave Guard and fourteen with John Stewart. With the exception of STEREO CONCERT and THE LAST MONTH OF THE YEAR, all of the Trio's albums are represented.

Cloth-bound, THE FOLK ERA featured an eight-page "deluxe illustrated booklet", including nine photos of the group and a short history of the rise to fame of Guard, Reynolds, Shane and Stewart. The anonymous annotator (on the final page are the words "Capitol wishes to express its thanks to Dr. Lou Gottlieb for his technical advice") goes to considerable pains to group the songs into three specific categories: "Traditional" (sides one and two), "New Words To Old Melodies & Folk Destination" (sides three and four), "Contemporary" (sides five and six). It should be noted that record one contains sides one and six, record two contains sides two and five, and record three contains sides three and four. Of passing interest to Triophiles is the selection *Ann,* here given a more polished echo chamber ending, althouth this *is* the same live track from BACK IN TOWN.

THE FOLK ERA failed to chart, due no doubt to its high list price and the lack of anything rare or new in its contents. Capitol hardly noticed, turning full attention to The Beatles and The Beach Boys for the remainder of the decade. The Kingston Trio moved on to their new label with high expectations, but the years at the top — as well as the hit records — were now behind them.

John, Bob and Nick, sans striped shirts, pose for the camera. From the collection of Maureen Wilson.

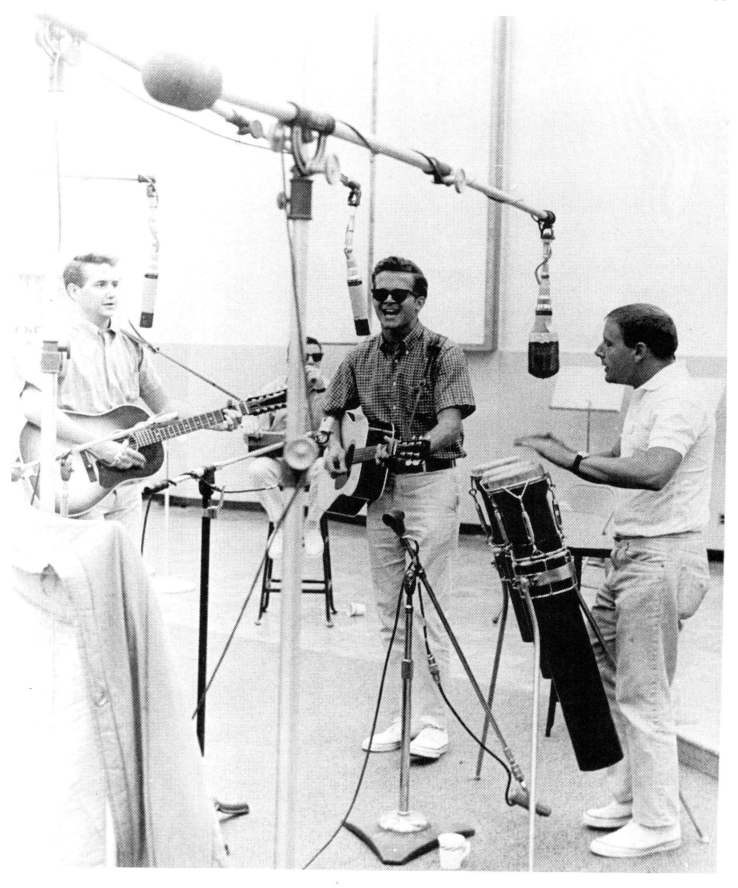

The Trio in the Capitol studio during a recording session. Photo courtesy: Capitol Records.

Nick Reynolds, November 7, 1981. Photo by Jack Rubeck.

The Nick Reynolds Interview

by
Jack Rubeck

JR: *Where did you guys get the songs that you recorded?*

NR: In the beginning, we were big fans of The Weavers, Harry Belafonte, Theodore Bikel, The Gateway Singers — these were the people that were motivating us, who we went to see or listened to their records. So you see we had a cross-influence of all that. A lot of the material . . . I imagine the first couple of albums were from those first four or five people who I mentioned, who were where we'd heard them. It was a very democratic process. People would bring in, or we'd have favorite songs, and the first few albums were things that we just put in the act. We all had to decide on — no one said, "Okay, we're going to sing this", because everyone would look around and say, "Oh yeah?" (laughs) It wasn't just Dave. Dave was pretty much the musical coordinator in the beginning, and we'd all make up head arrangements . . . Sit around and say, "Okay, we're gonna sing this song; you're gonna sing this verse". We'd more or less decide on a song all the way through, even when John was writing the material. He wrote a lot of songs that we didn't sing, but the ones that he did write — we didn't take a vote or hold up our hands, but we'd say, "Hey, yeah, that's all right, that's neat", and we'd just go along with it. There was never very much argument about what songs we were going to sing, ever.

JR: *How long would it take to do an album?*

NR: Oh, as I say, the first ones we knew all the songs down pat. We'd take longer as we had to do more albums, produce more albums, rehearse on the road. So we didn't have the songs down pat. We weren't singing them in the show. They had to be new songs. So it would take, oh, three . . . four . . . five days, I would say. A week at the most.

JR: *Back then it wasn't the big thing it is now with the overdubbing and multi-track?*

NR: That's what fascinated me so. I went into a studio with John and did a couple of demos with him when I was in Los Angeles a few years ago, and I saw the size of the tapes — twenty-four track or something — and I said, "God, John, I can remember when we were using one microphone", for the first Kingston Trio album and the HUNGRY i album before there was even any stereo. And we had "two-track", and that was *amazing* that we could put the bass on another track or something. That was magic to us. . . . That's one of the things I think the Trio *did* have . . . Everybody talks about overproduction. Looking back, if we had a year to make an album under the groovy circumstances which they do now, things could have been really beautiful. They may not have had the same *feeling*, though. That's why it is okay that we were rushed and had to put so many albums out . . . We would just get them and sing them because we liked them . . . And it would be just the three of us and bass player Dean Reilly or Buck Wheat or whoever it was — and it was up to the guy in the studio to mix two, three or four track, and that was all. And that's why I think there was a lot of sincerity in that.

JR: *So you just all sort of got your heads together on everything?*

NR: Yeah, we just got together and banged the songs out. We'd just go in there and put our heads together and sing 'em . . . "Okay, you sing this harmony". I could harmonize pretty well, and David was a great harmonizer. We used to have to tell Bobby what to sing. "Bobby, you sing this", and he'd nod his head and his glasses would fall off. (laughs) He was perfect. Bobby is the most majestic performer of all time! He was the main key in the whole thing.

JR: *Is it true that only John and Dave could read music?*

NR: John couldn't read music at all when he was with us. He was just starting to tamper with it. Dave was self-taught; he could teach himself to do anything in about three days. He's a brilliant man and real sensitive — a sweetheart. . . . Like, we had our differences, but , boy, they are not there anymore.

JR: Could you or Bob read music?

NR: No. That was one of the hassles we had with
David. David wanted us all to read music . . . but
we wouldn't go for that . . . which is a real elitist
attitude, because I'd really love to read music, but
I'm too non-disciplined to do it. David is a student;
he can do anything he wants to, and rightfully so. I
was just too damned lazy, and the fact that he
said it (laughs) — I wasn't gonna go for it anyway!

***JR: We'd always wondered — when we first heard
that not all of you could read music — about playing the instruments for the accompaniments.***

NR: We would sit there and Dave would say — or
at a later time John would say — "Play this
chord", and after awhile I got to know which chord
to play. I could hear it; I've got a good ear and I
can harmonize. I'd say, "I'll put my part in later",
or David would say he'd put his part in later —

meaning he'd sing it at the session, or we'd try it
out . . . try different little things at rehearsal — but
it got to be real easy after awhile. John knew the
chords and the names of the chords, but he would
call them "cowboy" or "Tahitian" . . . several different names we had so that we didn't have to do
anything with C, D or E, because Bobby wouldn't
go for that. Bobby would just clam up! (laughs) He
was so funny . . . the sweetest guy that I know in
the world. I was so lucky to be involved with these
three madmen, and they're all absolutely crazy,
and I know they think I'm crazy, but they were all
crazy, and I can tell you a lot of different things . . .
If you ever look in their eyes, any one of them,
you'll know they're crazy. That's why it worked,
because we had too good a time and it was infectious, and it spooked people, and it made people
get off their ass and start playing their own
guitars. They couldn't quite understand it. They

**Nick sings out during a recording session with Dave and Bob. Photo courtesy: Capitol
Records.**

said, "Goddamn, they're only playing three chords." "Yeah, but they're having a real good time playing three chords!" (laughs)

JR: Which album do you feel was the best or most satisfying?

NR: My favorite one was the TIME TO THINK . . . in some ways, and in other ways the Christmas album was my favorite. THE LAST MONTH OF THE YEAR. Both of those stand out in my mind more than any. I don't think that TIME TO THINK is the best, maybe, or the most invigorating, but it was really a very curious time in our career, because John was still new with us and President Kennedy was killed, and stuff like that. We were doing it in rehearsal and writing it during the turmoil of the Kennedy thing, and we were all very emotional. *Song For A Friend* . . . that was just awful tough. That was just . . . John just sat down and sang that.

JR: The mood of the Trio seemed to change from then on.

NR: Well, the whole mood of the country was changing.

JR: What were your favorite songs?

NR: *Hobo's Lullaby* was maybe my favorite song of all time. It was not just because I sang it, but we only performed it once . . . on stage. God, it was a killer! It was just too heavy. . . . *Where Have All The Flowers Gone* and *I'm Going Home* . . . those were two of my favorites . . . and *Reverend Mr. Black* was fun to sing, too. I really liked the shouters, you know, get the big chorus going . . . got really exciting. *Midnight Special* was great. We used to warm-up with that backstage . . . we used to do that and *Sloop John B*, even though we didn't sing them in the show.

JR: Getting back to the actual recording of the songs, what would be the sequence of events in learning and recording a song, such as No One To Talk My Troubles To, for example?

NR: Okay. We would have a tape of the song. Who wrote that? I know. Dick Weissman, a great banjo player. Fantastic banjo player. Really sensitive, and a really nice guy and really talented. He's one of the few good banjo players I've ever heard, and there aren't more than five . . . in the world. (laughs) I think banjo players, at best, are terrible. First of all, they can't keep 'em in tune. It's impossible to keep a five-string banjo player playing in tune. I mean, I'm exaggerating when I say that, 'cause I'm sure that throughout the South and . . . there are many unknown fantastic banjo players. Dick Weissman was one of the greatest . . . we just loved the tune.

So we'd get a tape of the tune, get the lyrics and . . . all these people were thrilled to have us do their tunes. My God, they'd make a hundred, two

hundred thousand dollars, you know, just in writing royalties. And we'd sit down and listen to the tape. We all had good ears. Bobby Shane has a perfect ear, I have a very good ear. I can remember songs. Somebody'd mention one, I could sing it. I couldn't remember the lyrics unless they were in front of me, but the tune . . . We'd sit down and say, "Okay, you wanna sing the lead on this?" Like, say I brought the tune in. I'm not sure exactly about *this* case. I'd say, "You wanna sing it?" They'd say, "Yeah, we like this song." And then we'd sit down and figure out the chords. John or Dave or whoever was the one who could really figure 'em out would show us the chords. And I'd start singing the melody, say, "Bobby, you sing this part." John, who does not have a great ear, but has got great talent . . . we'd say, "Okay, you sing this, John." (laughs) And a lot of it would be worked out in the studio, too. But we'd work on it for about an hour and then go into the studio with five or six songs that we had worked on.

JR: Do you recall who wrote the few lines on the back of TIME TO THINK?

NR: Yeah. Frank, and John, Bobby and I got together at Frank's house in Marin County and said, "We gotta say something", and wrote it out, all four of us, ourselves. And edited it. It was a very poignant time.

JR: This was one of the very first, would you say, "protest" albums? Popular songs that were making social comments?

NR: Well, we didn't really start it out or anything . . . We never tried to be political. We sang some things that later became, possibly, political . . . Dave was very adamant against taking a side of any kind. Bobby was apathetic; he didn't care one way or another. John was very adamant about the "New Frontier", etc., and I was more along with him. I think TIME TO THINK might have been more of a turning point in our career. And how we felt about current situations, possibly. It so happened that the President was assassinated while we were doing the album. We didn't go in and say, "Okay, we're gonna make a soulful or protest album because of this particular historical event."

JR: But it seemed like after this time more and more people came out with songs of protest.

NR: Oh yeah, yeah. Everybody was yelling and screaming. Dylan, Peter, Paul & Mary, and God knows who. Listen to the early Clancy Brothers' records if you want to hear some protest albums. They've been protesting for years.

JR: But they weren't that much in the public eye. It wasn't stuff that you were hearing on the radio all the time. Then, after TIME TO THINK, you were hearing it all the time. You were saying that this

was a turning point?

NR: It might have been, I don't know. I can't say for sure. So nebulous, all this thing. We were rehearsing, recording what songs we were gonna do. You just had to come up with so many . . . ones you liked even if . . . you tried not to do songs you didn't like. There were several that were semi-forced on us just because we knew the people and . . . you know . . . they needed some help, etc.

JR: One thing that stands out on most of the earlier albums is that they contained older folk tunes "modernized" a bit.

NR: Yeah, right. Yes, we modernized them because that's what we liked. We sat around and sang 'em in bars and stuff like that. That's what we had in the act, so that's what we went in and recorded. And they were standards, pretty much. A lot of them were very well known. And then it came to a point where we were . . . John was writing a lot of stuff, and we were meeting a lot more people who would give us material. Like *I'm Going Home* . . . the only true hobo I ever met. What was his name? . . . Fred Geis . . . he's been through my town. Stopped here for dinner one night. Called me one time. He was being sued because they said it was . . . too close to another song. He was one of the funniest guys I ever met. We sat and drank coffee and beer 'til about three in the morning and (laughs) he coughed and said, "Can you lend me a dollar?" And I know he had about five hundred on him, but he wasn't gonna let me get away with it, right? 'Cause he was a true hobo; he just traveled around the country.

JR: Did you know that many Kingston Trio compilations are still being sold around the world?

NR: I guess they are . . . still get royalties once in awhile for some song I stole. (laughs) That's another funny thing . . . we've been put down for stealing songs, plagarizing, right? Publishing money is just B.S. anyway . . . it's fine if it comes in, but we had more lawsuits — we had to give back ninety percent of the things we claimed to be writers of anyway.

JR: Such as?

NR: *Tom Dooley.* We claimed *Tom Dooley!*

JR: How about some of the other traditional ones you changed around?

NR: We split up some of those . . . *When The Saints Go Marching In* — we used one of The Weavers' verses, so we blew that one, right? Freddy Hellerman and Pete Seeger came down on us real hard . . . (laughs) They said, "Boys, we stole it first!" And they knew what they were talking about, and they didn't "steal" it, it's Public Domain. So that's why I couldn't get serious about the publishing end of it, although there was a lot

Nick solos at a Trio recording session. Photo courtesy: Capitol Records.

of money in it.

JR: So that was the main reason for changing some of the Public Domain songs, just to get the action? It wasn't necessarily because you didn't like the way it was in the first place?

NR: No, it was strictly monetary. We were in the business and we loved doing the singing and doing what we were doing, but if we could change a verse and make another hundred thousand dollars, far out, too . . . why not? Who owns it? It's in the Public Domain. There were a lot of people that condemned us for it, because of the thing we created — the revival and such, with all the clubs that opened and all the people who were making a fortune . . .

JR: You certainly weren't the only ones who were doing it, or still are.

NR: All those old folkies did it when they made their records; they changed a verse, too. They never got quite as much feedback, but that never bothered my anyway.

JR: Did both Capitol and Decca give you guys complete control over what you did?

NR: Capitol never knew what we were doing in the first place. Voyle Gilmore — . . . one of the sweetest guys — was a great producer . . . Sinatra, Nat King Cole, Beach Boys, you name it, all the way down the line. And he just said, "Do what you're doing. You're doing it real well, whatever it is." When we made our first album we all kind of looked at each other and said, "Oh, God, how boring!" (laughs) "Let's put it out and see what happens, because we don't have anything else going this month. And something *did* happen, so they just kind of let us go ahead, and Voyle would just work the knobs. As I said, it was just like two-track in those days, and it wasn't really hard. And we'd do some overdubbing, and that was the hardest thing to do, which is real easy to do now. And we didn't do any overdubbing in the first two or three albums, I'm sure, but they just said, "Go ahead and do whatever you want to do." And we'd do about sixteen tunes for an album, so there are probably a bunch of tunes that aren't released in those old tapes . . . I'd be fascinated to know what they even *are*. (laughs) I have no idea . . . There were a lot of outtakes and a lot of silly stuff. I know that we recorded the last week's work that we did at the *Hungry i* . . . Those tapes haven't been released. They would probably be interesting, because I know there were a lot of remarks made . . . It was a pretty emotional time . . .

JR: One thing that shows on the later albums, especially the Decca ones, is that there were hardly any "traditional" folk songs.

NR: Well, there were some pretty new writers. Mason Williams, Rod McKuen, Gordon Lightfoot. All these people were coming out with these great songs that we really liked. We'd gone through a lot of the standards that we wanted to do. We were not 'folkies"; we didn't . . . we weren't trying to propagate folk music as such.

JR: That was the label you had.

NR: Well, they called us that because they called everybody else that afterwards.

JR: What did you think of the SOMETHING SPECIAL album?

NR: I kind of liked it. You know, you kind of sit back and your ego starts going and you say, "God! Strings, cellos, voices — behind *me*? (laughs) "God, how far out! That's neat!" I think it was probably Capitol's idea . . . We were really under pressure to put out a lot of albums. I think this SOMETHING SPECIAL deal was some kind of media hype . . . The other was the sing-along album that we didn't even play or sing on. We got *money* . . . it was still under our name . . . We really didn't pay much attention to business, because Frank took care of most of that, and we were on the road all the time.

JR: Why did you switch from Capitol to Decca?

NR: Decca made us an offer we couldn't refuse, and Capitol had The Beatles coming up — which you can translate any way you want to! (laughs) We knew we were on the decline as far as record sales were concerned, and Capitol had the hottest thing in the world on their hands, and Decca made us a tremendous offer because they were . . . MCA or one of the big conglomerates owned Decca, and

they wanted some prestige people to sign with them so they could draw other artists to their company, so they made us a real good offer. So we asked Capitol, "Do you want to match this offer?" And they didn't even come close, so we said, "Okay, bye!" Because record sales were going downhill, and it was certainly a business transaction. Although Capitol was great to us, they also made a tremendous amount of money. I mean, if you want to read the record contract compared to what they are today, we got nothing for the first eight albums, and then they finally gave us another one percent or something as a bonus one year. Really nice! (laughs) But they were great! If it hadn't been for Capitol, we would never have done anything. There are no hard feelings at all.

JR: What did you think of the Decca albums?

NR: Well, I didn't think too much of them. For one thing, we produced 'em ourselves. There were some great songs. Absolutely fantastic songs, but they just came out muddled and . . . crappy! . . . If we could do 'em over again, if we could have done 'em with Voyle Gilmore and Pete Abbot down in Capitol's studios with one goddamn piece of tape, it would have come out a hundred times better.

JR: Which one do you think was the best, artistically?

NR: I can't think of any of them that were any good. But you know, that's my personal opinion. Name one or two.

JR: How about the first one, NICK-BOB-JOHN?

NR: Yeah, that was a pretty good album. There was an old studio in the building, the Columbus Tower in San Francisco, and it was a terrible studio. You just couldn't get any sound out of it, no matter what you did. We had bad over-dubbing facilities, we had a bad . . . echo system, you know, where you'd throw a little echo in here and there to smooth things out. CHILDREN OF THE MORNING was my most disappointing album. And it had the best songs.

JR: Why was it disappointing? Just because of the sound?

NR: It was disappointing just because of the quality of the recording. The *Children Of The Morning* song itself was such a beautiful song, and I was so disappointed when I heard the final results four months later after being on the road. There was just no blend; there was no harmony. Whoever was singing the verse would not be brought up enough to cover anything else.

JR: How about some other Decca songs, like Lei Pakalana?

NR: Aha, yeah, Bobby and I'd been singing that for fifteen years. We wouldn't let John sing on that (laughs) 'cause we'd been doing it for so long. He couldn't get the harmony right, because there is a certain thing, and Bobby and I — we finally told John . . . I said, "You just go out, and I'll sing your part. Go out and get a hamburger." He was so pissed off! (laughs) He's probably *still* pissed off! I remember that vividly. . . . I'm a big fan of John's, by the way . . . I've got his complete collection . . . CALIFORNIA BLOODLINES was my favorite album of all time.

JR: How about Long Time Blues, by Mason Williams?

NR: Good song! Mason sang so good, and he played so good. You know, you get around a guy like that, you say, "Oh boy, I want to sing *that* song." But you can't sing it as good as he can. And three people. I've always been terribly . . . adverse to the idea of a trio when you get into personal songs. 'Cause how can three people . . . express the feeling of something that personal? When you get three guys harmonizing, no matter how much you try to put into it, it's . . . It invalidates the song by having more than one person sing it, in many cases. With the big rousers, fine! *Midnight Special, I'm Going Home* . . . but when you get into a real personal song it's really hard. Like, that's why *Scotch and Soda* was such a . . . smash. That's why it was a killer. What if we'd been singing harmony behind Bobby on *Scotch and Soda*?

JR: How was the Trio treated by the critics?

NR: Sometimes great, sometimes terribly. It always hurt me because, being who I am, if I got a bad review I felt bad. But it didn't really make any difference, 'cause I knew that the audience had an absolute ball. And the critics would usually say that. "There were twenty thousand people there last night, and they all were shouting and screaming, but I thought it was just crap." I'd say, "Oh, gee, I'm sorry! They didn't have any fun, did they?"

JR: Was there anything to the supposed feud between The Kingston Trio and The Limeliters?

NR. We didn't have any feud at all! I could tell you some stories!

JR: Go ahead!

NR: No, they're not printable! They would not be printable. But let me tell you that the Trio had a lot more fun than The Limeliters, and when we got together we made The Limeliters have more fun than they thought they were capable of having.

JR: When did you guys get together?

NR: We used to get together all the time . . . Chicago was the meeting place . . . the center of the folk culture — as people think New York was, right? But as far as the groups, there were a couple of real good clubs in Chicago that we'd play.

Nick "hams it up" at a Capitol rehearsal while John looks on in amusement. Photo courtesy: Archives of Music Preservation.

And The Clancys were either always in town, or The Limeliters, or we would be in town, and there'd be two or three local groups in town. And so you'd get in town and you'd find out who was there, and then you'd get together and have some parties that you wouldn't believe. We burnt down a hotel, almost, one time (laughs) in Chicago with The Limeliters and The Clancy Brothers. And the priests that came along. The Clancy Brothers arrived from their concert in a fire engine in a snowstorm with two priests. One of those big fire engines. Riding in the back, steering in the back. Good Lord! They were such naughty boys! We'd get in town, we'd find out where they were staying, we'd go over to their place and get a bottle of tequila or something like that and just get 'em so messed up before their show. And then The Limeliters would show up and we'd show them too good a time. They'd . . . we'd scare them . . . but we would show them a lot of fun.

JR: Sounds like you had a good time, anyway.

Oh yeah, we had a great time. But there were no feuds at all. I mean, I think Peter, Paul & Mary might have been a little bit above it all, if you want to quote me. You know, they were a little holier than thou after they became famous. But they were the only group that would do that. The

Weavers were the most kind, gentle, helpful people. And they were the best of all folk groups. And they'd scare you, boy. They'd turn your hair right up on your neck. They were so powerful. Freddy Hellerman, he arranged the back song of *Tom Dooley* — which is a little sidelight. It was called *Ruby Red*. Well, Capitol said, "You want a percentage, Fred, or do you want to be paid a hundred bucks?" Fred said, "I think I'll take the hundred bucks." (laughs) He could've had a percentage. He's been screaming ever since!

JR: What about the songs the Trio did for various movies?

NR: Ahh, I know they did a thing on *Tom Dooley*. I once got a check for $198 for some kind of thing that . . . I have no idea what it was for. It was something that had been held up since 1962. The California State Comptroller said, "I have some residual money here. I don't know where to send it. Who are you?" (laughs) My wife, Linda wrote 'em, and they sent me 198 bucks. Didn't say what it was for, just residuals. So, I really don't know. I know we turned one down, and it became really big. Dimitri Tiomkin — we got in a media hassle with him and The Brothers Four . . . (over *The Green Leaves Of Summer*) . . . We were supposed to do it with Tiomkin and immediately got off on the wrong foot and refused to do it.

JR: Can you think of any other songs that people shoved at you that you didn't do that later turned out to be hits?

NR: Okay. I found the tape for a letter; in fact, I still have it. Albert Grossman sent me a letter, and I have it framed somewhere, and it says: "Dear Nick: I'm submitting this tape of a new artist I just signed by the name of Bob Dylan. I hope you like some of the songs." Well, they were all of the new songs, and I never heard the tape! They were all the great ones that Peter, Paul & Mary did later on. Not that we would have done them anyway, but it just kinda seemed funny.

JR: What about the striped shirts?

NR: The striped shirts were actually all our idea. We were playing where we first started. We'd wanted to buy three shirts alike and wear Levi's or khakis or whatever was the style in those days. So we went in and got three striped shirts, and it just held. "Let's buy three more", you know. So we had three, two pairs apiece so one wouldn't be dirty. (laughs) And then it got to be kind of a trademark. And then we cut off the sleeves three-quarters, because we couldn't play the guitars with the full thing, and the short sleeves we didn't want to do. So we'd buy long-sleeved shirts and cut 'em off to three quarter length. There was nothing exciting about it. We just went into a store, got three shirts that were the same and that looked like they wouldn't get dirty fast.

JR: If either of the original Trios had gone on, what kind of direction do you think the music would have taken?

NR: Really, it was going on. You saw where it had progressed from the TIME TO THINK days. Paxton, Dylan . . . things, we would have gone along with that. Plus what John, or whoever current writers were writing. There was no tack we were on. Looking for the best material and the stuff you like. It wouldn't have gone electric . . . David Guard, by the way, is the first person — and I'm putting this on record — that said we should go electrical. And I remember very well, because we went back to Cape Cod when John first joined the group, and played there, and The Whiskeyhill Singers were there, and David was playing electric guitar. And he was the first one I know of the "folk" people — before The Byrds, before everybody else — that ever wanted to go electrical. He was right on as far as where the music was going to go. That was years before The Beatles . . . I never would have wanted to go that way. It's hard enough getting my ass out of bed, much less an amplifier!

JR: Is it true that Dave was big on enunciation when you were recording?

NR: (laughs) Yeah! He was very good at that. And he used to stress rhythm. (laughs) Buck Wheat, who was one of the finest musicians I've ever met in my life, said, "God, Nick, don't ever let Dave change your rhythm, 'cause he has none at all!" (laughs) You can't have any rhythm on a banjo. Buck Wheat said, "Just shake your ass and have a good time. Let the rhythm happen."

JR: What was the real reason that the group disbanded in '67?

NR: The real reason was . . . primarily John and I had gotten together and talked . . . Bobby wanted to keep on going forever, and still is! Frank Werber had other interests, etc. But John wanted to do his own thing, and I was trying to encourage him to *do* it, because I wanted to get out, too. John definitely wanted to be on his own. He was very dissatisfied, and rightfully so. If he had been able to freelance after a couple of years with us he could have made it a lot sooner. He saw people rising around him, and to a talented songwriter and performer it was very frustrating to be stuck in the position that he was in. *Very* frustrating . . .

When I talk about the ending of the thing, it became evident to me that I was going out on the road and paying more people at the office . . . than it was really bringing back to me, emotionally and everything else. It just wasn't worth it, and it just wasn't going to get any bigger at that time, so we sat down a year before we quit — Frank and Bobby and John and I, and our accountant and

•A most unusual moment in the history of pop music: four members of the Kingston Trio and two of Fleetwood Mac. Left to right: Lindsey Buckingham, Dave Guard, Nick Reynolds, Bob Shane, John Stewart and Mick Fleetwood. Photo taken at a rehearsal for the "Kingston Trio & Friends Reunion", November, 1981. Photo by Henry Diltz.

lawyer — and said, "This is pretty much how we want it to go down," and our accountant said, "Well, work real hard next year, and it can go down that way." And it was planned a year in advance. There was no sudden cut-off, break-up, fist fights (laughs) . . . We knew exactly what we were doing at the time . . . I found myself more and more feeling that after playing to two or three generations of college kids, and having seen it all go through and go down and stuff — it was like doing a parody of yourself after awhile. And doing the gruelling thing of getting there — we didn't have jet planes to fly us around like The Rolling Stones do — we were flying in charter planes or private planes like DC-3s or something. It wasn't the romance that it is today where you have the huge entourage, and playing for five hundred thousand people. It's really hard to go to some obscure place, put a lot of effort out and not have any freedom for creativity or self-expression, really. Fans were very adamant about having their happiness reaffirmed. That's fine, but that's what records are for. We'd get irate fans coming up and saying, "Why didn't you sing this song?" . . . But it was never that I got tired of singing with Bobby and John, or Bobby and Dave or whoever. That was *always* a kick.

JR: *A few questions about the recent Trio Reunion concert. How did you feel after it was all over?*

NR: Exhausted. Drained, emotionally and physically. It was quite an experience, Jack. You know, what can I say? I don't know *how* I felt, really. I wish I could give you a concrete answer. I talked to John Stewart . . . and he said he went home and cried for three days! (laughs) And I said, "Well, I'm glad someone else felt that way." I wasn't sure if I was gonna cry or laugh, or be thankful it was over, or sorry that it had begun, or what . . . It was a very heavy trip.

JR: *How did it turn out compared to what you thought it was going to be?*

NR: I had no idea. It turned out really well, I think.

JR: *It was magic.*

NR: It was . . . it really was . . . It was pretty exciting for everybody. I know I was like in a daze — it all went by so fast, you know. Especially like when we were on stage it just seemed like it was gone in a flash. You know, I was just gettin' warmed up! . . . I don't know if it was more than I expected, less than I expected — just whatever it was, it *was.*

JR: *No regrets?*

NR: Absolutely no regrets. No, I'm just very relieved. I've had a procession over the past few years of nightmares of walking on stage somewhere and forgetting all the lyrics, you know? Absolute terrible nightmares; waking up in a cold sweat. I'm

Nick, Bob and Dave perform "Zombie Jamboree" at the "Kingston Trio & Friends Reunion", November 7, 1981. Photo courtesy of Camera Three Productions.

sure I won't have those anymore.

JR: Well, it didn't look like any problem out there.

NR: It was very healthy for everybody. John's got a new humility about what's goin' on. (laughs) He's been down there, you know, in that "show biz" thing, and to see us just come out — and including *him,* when he came out — and just *do* it and have all those good vibes and stuff, it really makes a lot of sense. When we were rehearsing, Lindsey said — when Dave and Bobby and John and I were rehearsing one night at Larrabee Studios, and Lindsey was sitting-in on the bass — Fleetwood Mac was doing some mastering next door, and Lindsey said, "Here are all these guys next door trying to make it happen, and here you guys are just sitting over here *doing* it." And I know what he means by that, and he was just kind of shaking his head. He was almost in tears, you know . . . He works so hard to get the sound just right . . . and it's pretty natural — what *we* did — for better or worse.

Do you think you could ever go through it again?

NR: Oh, sure. If the right time and the right place . . . who knows? . . . When all six of us were

on stage singing, that was *heavy duty.* I'd like to see more of *that,* really . . . Personally, what I'd like to see is a chorale album, like The Beach Boys . . . more voices, more parts, with the Trio now, and John and Dave and I, too . . . I'm talking about a recording situation with new material, 'cause these guys are talented boys — Roger and George — and with the recording techniques they have today, we could make some pretty scary albums.

JR: Well, it looked great, and it sounded great, and we're hoping to hear more.

NR: Nothing that magical *dies,* you know. It lays dormant for awhile, maybe. (laughs) Gotta come out and hit 'em on the head once in awhile! . . . I loved it.

* * * * * * *

Since this interview was conducted, Nick Reynolds has busied himself with a return to recording (see the upcoming chapter on REVENGE OF THE BUDGIE), and he has also renovated and re-opened a fifty-year-old movie theater in Gold Beach, Oregon, where he plans to offer the local folks a return to "family" entertainment.

JOHN STEWART   NICK REYNOLDS   BOB SHANE

THE KINGSTON TRIO

PERENCHIO/ARTISTS' REPRESENTATIVES,
434 NORTH RODEO DRIVE
BEVERLY HILLS, CALIFORNIA

The Kingston Trio, 1965. Photo courtesy: Archives of Music Preservation.

The Decca Years, and Beyond (1964-1973)

by
Benjamin Blake & Jack Rubeck

According to the Decca files at MCA, The Kingston Trio actually recorded ten tracks on October 13, 1964 — the very day the recording contract was signed. All four of their Decca albums would be recorded in the basement of the Trio's Columbus Tower Office Building in San Francisco, where the group had built its own Columbus Recording Studio earlier in 1964 (no recordings for Capitol were done there). They returned to that studio the following day to record the two songs that would be released as their first Decca single on November 9, Tom Paxton's *My Ramblin' Boy* and John Stewart's *Hope You Understand.* They had cut their first version of *My Ramblin' Boy* the previous day, and although all were impressed with the playback, it was deemed too lengthy (3:42) for a single. The version recorded on October 14 was a streamlined 2:40, but it still received little airplay (*Hope You Understand* actually fared better as the B side), so when the first LP was readied a month later, the original, longer version was utilized.

On November 21, Reynolds, Shane and Stewart waxed two final tracks for the LP, titled THE KINGSTON TRIO: NICK-BOB-JOHN, which was released on December 7. The two tracks, *I'm Going Home* and *Little Play Soldiers,* would be released as their second Decca 45 on January 11, 1965. Although *none* of the group's eight Decca singles would ever crack *Billboard's* "Hot 100", *I'm Going Home* is considered by many to be the best track the group recorded after leaving Capitol, and it was one of only a few that the Trio liked enough to add to their stage performances. Written by real-life hobo Fred Geis, and performed with the time-honored KT gusto, *I'm Going Home* is the rousing high point of NICK-BOB-JOHN.

Other fine moments are provided by Bob's vocals on *My Ramblin' Boy* and Rod McKuen's *Love's Been Good To Me.* The latter is another example of a tune that was originally sung by Bob Shane and later turned into a hit for Frank Sinatra. The aforementioned *Hope You Understand,* the LP's lone Stewart composition, is also one of the best tracks on this LP. Good harmony, good picking and a simple-yet-eloquent message make for a winning combination. In the album's other better moments, John gives an effective rough-edged vocal to Ian Tyson's *Some Day Soon* (later a hit for Judy Collins), and Nick gives a thoughtful reading to the sensitive lyrics of *Poverty Hill.*

The LP's only attempt at humor can be found in Mason Williams' *More Poems.* Apparently the Trio's way of providing continuity for their fans during the label transition, this batch proves a weak sequel to *Them Poems* from BACK IN TOWN. It is apparent that this brand of whimsy was more effective before a live audience (preferably plastered!), so *Them Sand Pickers, Dog Kickers* and *Tummy Gummers* falls a bit short of the intended mark here, despite Mr. Shane's humorous vocal.

Also on the debit side is Bob Dylan's *Farewell,* a fine song given a substandard treatment by the Trio. Rough edges abound, and the key chosen has Nick's voice jumping around like an excited puppy. This and several of the other tracks indicate how much the group would come to miss the expertise

side one:

1 Midnight Special
2 Love's Been Good To Me
3 Poverty Hill
4 Some Day Soon
5 Gotta Travel On
6 Hope You Understand

side two:

1 Little Play Soldiers
2 Love Comes A Trickling Down
3 My Ramblin' Boy
4 More Poems
5 Farewell
6 I'm Going Home

of Voyle Gilmore. Soundwise, the entire album can best be described as being rather "thin". The mid-range and highs are here, but the low end is weak, and this would prove to be characteristic of all the Trio's Decca recordings. Frank Werber was an outstanding manager and innovative business partner for the KT, but as a producer he was an obvious amateur. Many of Gilmore's secrets of re-mixing and overdubbing remained with him at Capitol Records, and what is lacking in the Trio's Decca outings clearly proves that he was not just "a guy who turned the knobs", but a true creative genius in his field. Werber would later reportedly admit to Gilmore that he never realized how much of The Kingston Trio's sound was Gilmore's doing.

Statistically, NICK-BOB-JOHN was a chart weakling, but its thirteen week "life" and height of number fifty-three would place it head and shoulders over those that would follow.

The Decca albums also differed from Capitol's in that songwriter credit was assigned to the jacket instead of the label.

* * * * * * *

The one thing Decca did for the Trio, at least at the beginning, was to *promote* their recordings. The first album was given a major push by the sales staff, and the result was more reviews in various media than the group had received in several years. Capitol took advantage of the free publicity and threw together THE BEST OF THE KINGSTON TRIO, VOLUME TWO, released in February of 1965. This album is of little interest to Trio collectors, as it contains nothing different or new. It is not known who was responsible for choosing the songs for this album, but it seems to have started out as a well-intentioned sampler of the Reynolds/Shane/Stewart years (their photos are on the cover), but then someone apparently felt that the years with Dave Guard should be represented, so we end up with three tracks that seem a bit out of place (*Coplas, Scarlet Ribbons, Across The Wide Missouri*). The most glaring omission here is *One More Town,* and the most ridiculous choice (along with *Coplas*) has to be *Blowin' In The Wind.*

Another of Capitol's eleven-band jobs, and the first by the group to spot the company's laughable "New improved Full Dimensional Stereo" logo (*Coplas* is in Duophonic, by the way!), THE BEST OF THE KINGSTON TRIO, VOLUME TWO deservedly failed to chart.

* * * * * *

As with NICK-BOB-JOHN, Decca's artist cards show the Trio recording the songs for STAY AWHILE in a very short amount of time. In this case, one day: March 29, 1965. This seemingly impossible feat, as well as Mason Williams' liner notes (which indicate at least three of the songs were recorded in early January), tend to lead us to the conclusion that Decca's "recording dates" are *probably* the dates the final *mixing* on the master tapes was done. In any case, STAY AWHILE (the Trio's second album for Decca) was released on May 17, 1965, and spent only ten weeks on *Billboard's* album chart. It aspired to position number one hundred and twenty-six, a very dismal showing for a group as well established as the KT, and it was the last of their Decca LPs to even appear on a chart.

Despite the shortcomings of poor production, there are some fine songs on STAY AWHILE that manage to shine through here and there. Rod McKuen's *Rusting In The Rain* is given an effectively understated lead vocal by John Stewart, whose only solo credit as a writer on the LP is *Stories Of Old* (not one of his better tunes). *Where I'm Bound* is one of two Tom Paxton songs on the album and is well-suited to the group's style. The title track is a Reynolds/Shane/Stewart original, complete with Clancy Brothers accents, and it provides a rousing finish to the album's stronger side. Probably *I'm Going Home* (from the previous LP) and *Stay Awhile* are the two Decca tracks that come closest to capturing the patented Gilmore/KT sound.

Perhaps for many this LP is best remembered as "the Mason Williams album". The up-and-coming writer/performer, who provided the witty liner notes (he's also given a small write-up and photo on the reverse of the jacket), was a great favorite with the Trio, who had previously popularized his *Them Poems.* On STAY AWHILE they serve-up three of his more serious offerings, including one of Nick's personal favorites, *Three Song.* The simple, yet emotionally effective *If I Had A Ship* closes out

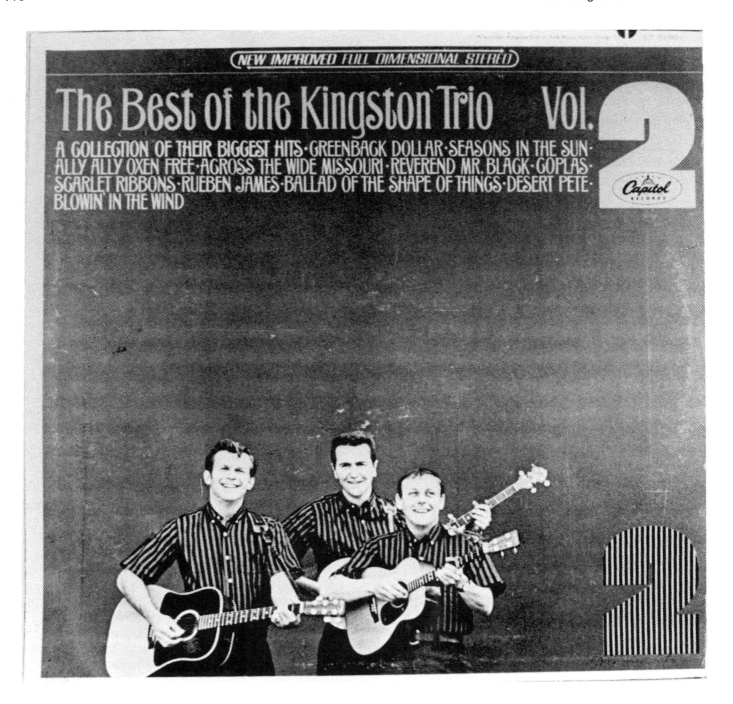

side one:

1 Reverend Mr. Black
2 Ally Ally Oxen Free
3 Coplas
4 Seasons In The Sun
5 Scarlet Ribbons
6 Greenback Dollar

side two:

1 Blowin' In The Wind
2 Desert Pete
3 Ballad Of The Shape Of Things
4 Across The Wide Missouri
5 Reuben James

side one:

1　Hanna Lee
2　Three Song
3　Gonna Go Down The River
4　Rusting In The Rain
5　Dooley
6　If I Had A Ship

side two:

1　Yes I Can Feel It
2　Bottle Of Wine
3　Stories Of Old
4　Where I'm Bound
5　If You See Me Go
6　Stay Awhile

side one and is probably that side's strongest track. *Yes I Can Feel It* is a beautiful love song that features Bob on lead vocal. This last Williams track was everybody's choice for a single, but all concerned felt it needed a little something extra, so the Trio cut it again on May 4. The LP was already being pressed, so the original version is the one that appears there. The single, released on June 14 (*Stay Awhile* was the B side), is about thirty seconds shorter and features an anonymous female voice providing background counterpoint vocal.

* * * * * * *

By the summer of 1965, the influence of the British invasion had reached commercial folk music, transforming it —through Dylan and The Byrds — into "folk-rock". The Kingston Trio's slumping album sales, as well as their collective desire to not be left behind in the dust of others' creativity, led to the recording (August 30) of twelve tracks that would be released on November 15 as the group's third Decca LP, SOMETHIN' ELSE. This, the group's only attempt at "electric" music, was an almost total financial and artistic failure. It was the group's first major new LP release that failed to make a chart appearance.

The album earns its title in several ways, including liner credit to the sidemen: Dean Reilly, Randy Steirling, Jerry Granelli, Andrew Belling, David Wheat, John Chambers, Rex Larsen. If you noticed a familiar name in there, you correctly identified David "Buck" Wheat's return as guitarist on this LP. Randy Steirling played twelve-string guitar (as well as other instruments), had a hand in composing three of the tunes, as well as arranging all of the tunes on SOMETHIN' ELSE. The Trio hedged their bet with the cover photo: no amplified instruments, but no banjo either. The front cover also broke new ground by listing the titles of several of the songs, actually *misspelling* one.

Dick Nolan of the *San Francisco Examiner* managed to sound genuinely excited about the record in his liner notes, but he only dared single-out *Go Tell Roger*, John's whimsical look back at childhood, which *is* one of the album's few good moments. In most cases, the songs that work here are the ones with the sparsest instrumentation. Mason Williams' *They Are Gone* and *Long Time Blues,* and the Williams/Stewart collaboration *Dancing Distance* shine above the rest of the mess.

Two of the worst offenders were released as a single, in advance of the LP, on November 8. *Parchment Farm Blues* (listed as just *Parchment Farm* on the 45 and the front of the album) is actually embarrassing to listen to in *any* year, as the group is so obviously uncomfortable with the vocals (". . . a-huh-huh. . ."), and *Runaway Song* (the B side) has to be *the* most abrasive recording of any Stewart song to date. Just plain awful is the best way to describe *Verandah Of Millium August,* a John Stewart/Randy Cierly (Steirling) composition that has since been revealed to be an intended satire of Bob Dylan. It may be of some comfort to the listener to know that it was *supposed* to sound awful, besides giving obscure lyrics a new birthright.

Stewart also penned the album's *Where Are You Going Little Boy,* and all three members (under their alias of Jack Splittard) shared royalties with Steirling on the arrangements of *Parchment Farm Blues* and *Red River Shore.* It may be of some interest to note that *Parchment Farm Blues* was the last KT 45 to dent any chart, spending six weeks on *Billboard's* "Easy Listening" lists, reaching a height of number thirty.

* * * * * * *

1966 proved to be a pivotal year in the career of The Kingston Trio. On February 18, Nick, Bob and John delivered to Decca the first two tracks of what would be their final studio LP, CHILDREN OF THE MORNING. Those tracks comprised the Trio's first single release of the year, *Norwegian Wood/Put Your Money Away,* on March 14. Decca lists the delivery date for most of the album as March 25, but there is evidence that songs were being added as late as April 13. A second single, *The Spinnin' Of The World/A Little Soul Is Born,* was issued on May 23, followed by the album on May 30. A third 45 was released on September 5, *Lock All The Windows/Hit And Run.* The album and singles were all commercial flops, much to the displeasure of Decca Records.

CHILDREN OF THE MORNING featured a whopping *eight* John Stewart compositions, making it a sought-after disc for his many post-Trio fans. Although his talent as a writer was spread a little

side one:

1 Parchment Farm
2 Early Morning Rain
3 Where Are You Going Little Boy
4 Interchangeable Love
5 Last Thing On My Mind
6 Go Tell Roger

side two:

1 Red River Shore
2 Verandah Of Millium August
3 They Are Gone
4 Long Time Blues
5 Dancing Distance
6 Runaway Song

side one:

1 Children Of The Morning
2 Hit And Run
3 When You've Been Away For A Long Time
4 Lei Pakalana
5 Gaze On Other Heavens
6 A Taste Of Honey

side two:

1 Norwe
2 Put Y
3 Lock
4 Les
5 The
6 A

thin on this LP, some of the songs have acquired a "classic" feel to them over the years since they were recorded, most notably *Hit And Run, Lock All The Windows* and the title song.

Ironically, two of the album's most appealing tracks were non-John. *Less Of Me,* one of Glen Campbell's rare compositions, is a sincere, easygoing performance that doesn't suffer from the frenzied we're-singing-as-hard-as-we-can vocals that much of this album indulges in. The same can be said of *Lei Pakalana,* a beautiful Hawaiian ballad (here credited to Samuel F. Omar) that is one of the highlights of side one. *Lei Pakalana* is also one of two duets on the LP, as John took a walk while Bob and Nick cut this track.

Bob is the absent member on *Norwegian Wood.* John goes into detail in the liner notes as to how they had become great admirers of Lennon & McCartney, and the thrill he and Nick got out of recording the track late one evening. Although they sang their hearts out, this attempted fusion of folk and English pop fell a bit short, and the single of the song sank from sight amidst several other cover versions of Beatles tunes that year.

Even though this LP was a deliberate step back from the experimentation of SOMETHIN' ELSE, even at this late date the Trio was not beyond trying another new twist. Dean Reilly plays Flugelhorn on *A Taste Of Honey,* another song previously recorded by The Beatles. It is one of the Trio's shortest tracks, and also one of the oddest.

The strained vocals referred to earlier are best exemplified by *Gaze On Other Heavens* and *The Spinnin' Of The World.* The patented Trio harmony seems to be missing on these tracks, and everyone sounds like they had sore throats.

It should also be noted that the Trio gave their new recording engineer (Hank McGill) credit for the first time on the jacket of CHILDREN OF THE MORNING.

Even *prior* to the release of CHILDREN, Reynolds, Shane, Stewart and Werber had mutually agreed on a termination date for the career of The Kingston Trio. In April they had decided to work as hard as possible for one more year, squeezing-in as many concerts as they could. A formal announcement would not be made until January 30, 1967, after which a "farewell album" and tour would be launched.

Many good reasons have been given for the decision to disband. John Stewart felt trapped within the confines of a group that was fast becoming a parody of itself, and he wanted his new songs to be *heard.* All three members felt stifled by fans that wished only to hear the KT standards and not new material. Nick Reynolds was tired of "show biz" and wanted to retire. The

failure of SOMETHIN' ELSE, and the fact that the Trio could no longer count on filling large concert halls to capacity (it was "back-to-the-clubs" time) made them all see the writing on the wall. The group was no longer at the top of its profession, artistically or financially, and recording had ceased to be a source of fulfillment. Indeed, the final straw may have been listening to the playback of CHILDREN OF THE MORNING in their Columbus Recording Studio in the spring of 1966. As John said in the liner notes: "... Those three big speakers that play back note for note, mistake for mistake, the sound of your ideas. An artist has his canvas; to a musician, it's a half-inch of tape that never lies."

* * * * * * *

The Kingston Trio did not wish to bow out with a weak album. Dismayed with the sound of their recent studio tracks, the group decided that their parting shot would be a live recording. During a three week engagement (July 1-22, 1966) at the Sahara Tahoe Hotel at Lake Tahoe, Nevada, Nick, Bob and John recorded their last LP, intended to be a two-record live set for Decca. But Decca began to balk at the expense of such an elaborate package after CHILDREN OF THE MORNING had failed to turn a profit, and Werber and the Trio suddenly found themselves up the proverbial creek with three weeks' worth of tapes and no way to release them.

Ironically, the group's last release for Decca was a 45 that is generally considered to be the worst recording ever made by The Kingston Trio. *Texas Across The River,* from the movie of the same name, was written by the noted team of Sammy Cahn & James Van Heusen, and the Trio's performance of it gives new shades of meaning to the word pathetic. Almost as awful, the B side —

side one:

1 Lemon Tree
2 El Matador
3 Jane, Jane, Jane
4 San Miguel
5 This Land Is Your Land
6 En El Agua

side two:

1 It Was A Very Good Year
2 Three Jolly Coachmen
3 They Call The Wind Maria
4 500 Miles
5 Hangman

Babe, You've Been On My Mind — is one of several Bob Dylan tunes the group had recently added to their repertoire. The two tracks were delivered to Decca on September 27, 1966, and released on October 31. Decca master numbers indicate that *Babe, You've Been On My Mind* was the last track recorded in a studio by Nick, Bob and John.

* * * * * * *

November of 1966 saw the release of BEST OF THE KINGSTON TRIO, VOLUME THREE. If Capitol knew the group was about to retire, there is no hint of it anywhere on this package. It was more likely released to cash-in on the popularity of Sinatra's version of *It Was A Very Good Year,* as BEST OF VOLUME THREE sported an outside sticker proclaiming the "original" version. Since Capitol had missed the boat by not releasing it as a single in 1961, they were now trying to make up for lost time. *Lemon Tree* had once more been covered (this time by Trini Lopez), therefore earning it a spot on this LP for similar reasons.

Considering when the album was released, the most amazing thing about it was the fact that nine of the eleven bands hail from the Guard years, and the group pictured on the cover was Guard/Reynolds/Shane (Capitol must have had to dig for an old photo, because two of the three faces are out of focus!). Only *Jane, Jane, Jane* and *500 Miles* represent what was then the current group of Reynolds/Shane/Stewart, and Capitol again misses a chance to offer a rarity by using the standard SOMETHING SPECIAL version of *Jane, Jane, Jane* rather than the 45. Everything here is stereo except *Three Jolly Coachmen,* since the powers-that-be showed the rare good taste to dish-up the superior STEREO CONCERT rendition of *They Call The Wind Maria.*

In Great Britain, E. M. I. chose not to release the album, instead packaging their own version. Released early in 1967, A TRIBUTE TO THE KINGSTON TRIO is just what the title implies, complete with fine liner notes (by Dave Travis) and cover photos of *both* Trios (unique to date). The notes even refer to the group's pending retirement in June. E. M. I. gave its customers not only fourteen tracks, but three songs previously unavailable on LPs: *Oh Cindy; Green Grasses; Como Se Viene, Se Va.* This last track, incidentally, is the only one here that is not in stereo. A TRIBUTE TO THE KINGSTON TRIO has only four selections in common with its American counterpart (*San Miguel, El Matador, This Land Is Your Land, 500 Miles*), and it also leans heavily toward the Guard years, with on-ly *One More Round, 500 Miles* and *If You Don't Look Around* featuring John Stewart's participation. Sadly, this fine LP was never released in the United States.

* * * * * * *

Meanwhile, back in California, Frank Werber got the official word from Decca at the end of 1966 that the Sahara Tahoe album was *not* going to become a reality. In fact, Werber and the Trio were asked to refund part of the advance payment they had received on CHILDREN OF THE MORNING to help cover the LP's losses. Werber promptly offered the new album to Voyle Gilmore at Capitol for a substantial sum, apparently *too* substantial, as the deal was never completed.

Frustrated but resigned, the Trio launched into its final six months of performing, culminating in a final two-week stand (June 5-17, 1967) at the *Hungry i,* which Frank Werber taped for posterity. The final evening's show was reportedly sold out four months in advance, and featured an audience filled with old friends and fellow stars. It must have been quite an evening, if for no other reason than that bassist Dean Reilly played the entire set dressed in a red chicken costume!

* * * * * * *

And then it was time for new beginnings. Nick Reynolds hung up the guitar and congas and settled down with his family (after a stint at car racing) on a ranch in Oregon to live the peaceful life. John Stewart began writing songs fulltime, and by the end of the year The Monkees had made a million seller out of his *Daydream Believer.* He formed a duo with singer Buffy Ford and returned to Capitol Records to begin recording again, and he and Buffy then signed-on as campaign aides for Robert Kennedy. John's colorful post-Trio recording career is detailed later on in this volume. Frank Werber turned his attention to managing the Trio's many business interests, most specifically the Trident Restaurant. He and Hank McGill would spend a good part of the next year editing and mastering the tapes of the Sahara Tahoe sessions, still hopeful that a major label would be interested in them.

Bob Shane remained signed with Decca Records as a solo artist, returning to the studio on November 17, 1967, to record his first solo single, *Simple Gifts/Weeping Annaleah* (released December 18), which failed to attract any attention. On January 30, 1968, he would record two tunes by

Capital EMI

A tribute
to the
Kingston
Trio

A THIRD COLLECTION
OF SOME OF THEIR
GREATEST RECORDINGS

side one:

1 You're Gonna Miss Me
2 One More Round
3 The Escape Of Old John Webb
4 Buddy Better Get On Down The Line
5 San Miguel
6 This Mornin', This Evenin', So Soon
7 You Don't Knock

side two:

1 Oh Cindy
2 Green Grasses
3 El Matador
4 This Land Is Your Land
5 Como Se Viene, Se Va
6 500 Miles
7 If You Don't Look Around

Decca single 32275:
Honey by Bobby Russell. Master # L14,846.
I Don't Think Of You Anymore by Bobby
Russell. Master # L14,847.

* * * * * * *

Bob Shane had been the one dissenting member
when the final vote came to disband the Trio. Ten
years of group work had left its mark, and he
found he did not enjoy performing as a solo. After
severing relations with Decca, he formed a duo
called Shane & Travis with old chum Travis Edmonson, a union which did not prove to be
durable. It was about a year after The Kingston
Trio retired that Bob decided it was time to resurrect it. He approached business partner Frank
Werber with the idea of starting a new group with
Bob at the helm. Werber was no longer interested
in managing such a venture, but he agreed (with
Nick Reynolds' consent) to lease Bob the name
"New Kingston Trio" if Shane could come up with
a group worthy to bear the title.

Bob returned to his home in Georgia and began
a talent search that stretched to Nashville, audi-
tioning dozens of young men eager to be a part of
the next step in a musical legend. He settled on
Mike Heard (banjo) and Dave Peel (guitar), and the
three hit the road to polish up the act for Werber's
approval. This group was variously known as The
Shane Gang or Bob Shane & Friends, and made no
recordings that we know of. By the time The New
Kingston Trio became a legal reality in early 1969,
Heard and Peel had been replaced by superstar
banjoist Jim Connor and talented guitarist Pat
Horine (formerly of Richard & Jim and Pat & Barbara, respectively).

Bobby Russell, *Honey* and *I Don't Think Of You
Anymore.* Released as a single on February 26,
Honey would sell like hotcakes (100,000 copies in
two weeks) in two test markets, but for unknown
reasons Decca chose not to release it on a national basis. A dejected Russell then gave the
song to Bobby Goldsboro, who soon had the biggest hit of his career with it. Russell then offered
Shane *Little Green Apples,* but Bob declined
because he felt Decca would just give it the *Honey*
treatment, and O.C. Smith ended up with the hit.

All four of Bob Shane's Decca tracks were also
produced by Bobby Russell, and since they are
technically not Kingston Trio recordings, we will
list the pertinent information on them at this point,
rather than in our chapters on the Trio song
listings and discography.

Decca single 32239:
Simple Gifts by Rod McKuen. Master
119,608.
Weeping Annaleah by Mickey Newbury & Dan
Dolger, Master #119,607.

* * * * * * *

In the meantime, Frank Werber had found a
home for the Sahara Tahoe album on Bill Cosby's
newly-formed Tetragrammaton Records. Werber
and engineer George Horn did a re-mix of the old
tapes from January through March, and the double
LP set was released at last in June of 1969. ONCE
UPON A TIME proved to be a well crafted farewell
package, containing twenty songs and a book-type
jacket with an extra page of rare photos (including
a 12-inch by 20-inch collage of fascinating artifacts
from the group's colorful history), plus intelligent
liner notes by someone named Joaquin
Bandersnatch. Sound quality, considering the club
environment, was very good, and the stereo image

record one, side one:

1   *Hard Travelin'*
2   *Early Morning Rain*
3   *M.T.A.*
4   *Tomorrow Is A Long Time*
5   *Rovin' Gambler/This Train*

record two, side two:

1   *Police Brutality (comedy)*
2   *One Too Many Mornings*
3   *Colours*
4   *A Day In Our Room (comedy)*
5   *Wimoweh*
6   *Tom Dooley*
7   *Goodnight Irene*

record one, side four:

1   *Tijuana Jail*
2   *Silicone Bust (comedy)*
3   *I'm Going Home*
4   *Where Have All The Flowers Gone*
5   *Scotch And Soda*
6   *Blind Date (comedy)*
7   *When The Saints Go Marching In*

record two, side three:

1   *Hard, Ain't It Hard*
2   *Getaway John*
3   *Ballad Of The Shape Of Things*
4   *Greenback Dollar*
5   *Babe, You've Been On My Mind*

was excellent. It was also the final Trio LP to chart, making it as high as position one hundred and sixty-three during its six-week run in the summer of '69.

Loose is the word for the performances on this album, both in the singing and in the stage talk. This made for a relaxed atmosphere in which everyone seemed to have a good time (a Trio trademark), and this comes across quite plainly to the listener. This is most blatantly evident in the performance of *Greenback Dollar,* where Nick, Bob and John have to halt the song more than once to recover from fits of laughter! This is not to say that there are not some professional performances on ONCE UPON A TIME, because there are. Dylan's *Tomorrow Is A Long Time* and Donovan's *Colours* are handled with appropriate sensitivity. Dylan's influence on the Trio's later years is well represented here by a total of three songs, including *Babe, You've Been On My Mind,* which fares better here than it did on the 1966 Decca single (which was actually a *later* recording). Other previously unrecorded songs include the *Rovin' Gambler/This Train* medley, The Weavers' classic *Goodnight Irene* and Dylan's *One Too Many Mornings.*

One of the extra treats of listening to this album is hearing Reynolds, Shane and Stewart resurrect several tunes previously heard on record only by the original Trio, including *Getaway John; Hard Travelin'; Wimoweh; The Tijuana Jail; Hard, Ain't It Hard* and *When The Saints Go Marching In.*

Goodnight Irene and *Where Have All The Flowers Gone* prove to be the emotional high spots of the album, followed closely by *Scotch And Soda* and *I'm Going Home. Silicone Bust, Blind Date, Police Brutality* and *A Day In Our Room* demonstrate the glib tongue of John Stewart and provide comic relief between songs. It should be noted that these four selections are comedy routines and *not* song titles, although listing them as bands on the album gave John the same royalties he would have earned from musical compositions. It is not known whether any Stewart songs were recorded during the three weeks of taping that became ONCE UPON A TIME, but the fact that John was earnestly involved in trying to establish a solo career (devoid of any association with The Kingston Trio) at the time of its release may have had something to do with his total absence as a songwriter on these four sides.

This album's only real weakness is the club's orchestra, which insists on striking up an off-key version of *Tom Dooley* whenever the KT enters or exits. Mercifully, they remain silent during the group's performances.

The last of Nick, Bob and John's 45s was released

ed from this LP in July of 1969, with *One Too Many Mornings* on one side and the venerable *Scotch And Soda* on the other. The single and album were warmly received by the critics, but they might have fared better in sales at an even *later* date. ONCE UPON A TIME was a genuine exercise in nostalgia, and it is more enjoyable to listen to with each passing year.

* * * * * * *

Concurrently, Bob Shane, Jim Connor and Pat Horine had been polishing their performances all around the world as The New Kingston Trio. A 1970 stop in Tokyo, Japan, afforded them an opportunity to make their first recordings. We know little about the sessions except that they produced an album (actual producer unknown) that was released only in that country (on the "World Popular Collection" of Birdree Records). Titled simply THE NEW KINGSTON TRIO, the album contained twelve tracks, including three new titles: *I'm Going Up Cripple Creek, Turkey In The Straw* and *Way Back Home. Turkey* is the familiar American square dance reel, but the other two are credited to Jim Connor. While some of the re-recordings seem unnecessary, they are well performed. A new twist is given to *Wimoweh* by Bob's spoken introduction over a bevy of bird calls and jungle sounds ("How could the lion sleep through this?"), and a new verse for *Sloop John B* ("Well, the stewardess she got stewed/Ran 'round the poop deck nude . . .") livens things up a bit.

This record shows Jim Connor to be a fine banjo picker and Pat Horine to be a fine vocalist. It also showcases the group's first electric bassist, Stan Kaess, who would remain the heart and soul of Bob Shane's back-up band through 1985. A harmonica is featured on a few tracks, and conga and bongos are ably played on several by percussionist Frank Sanchez. It is not known how long Frank remained with the New KT.

side one:

1 Try To Remember
2 I'm Going Up Cripple Creek
3 Tom Dooley
4 Turkey In The Straw
5 Way Back Home
6 Sloop John B

side two:

1 Where Have All The Flowers Gone
2 I'm Going Home
3 Early Morning Rain
4 Wimoweh
5 Scotch And Soda
6 This Land Is Your Land

The New Kingston Trio

A posed publicity shot for the New Kingston Trio. Left to right: Pat Horine, Bob Shane, Frank Sanchez (Percussion), Stan Kaess (Bass), Jim Connor.

Since no one connected with the group that made the album has yet to even acknowledge its existence, it is possible that it never got beyond the test pressing stage and was never formally released. Lending credence to this idea is the fact that the cover is very much of a "home made" affair. The jacket is basically a plain white one with a cover from the Trio's Japanese tour book (labelled as "The Kingston Trio" despite the fact that the group was the "New Kingston Trio") pasted on the front, and clippings from publicity photos pasted on the back along with hand-written title and date and personnel information. (*We learned of this album as this book was going to press, so as and when additional information about this album and the sessions that produced it become known, we will provide details in the Kingston Korner Newsletter.*)

Spring of 1971 found them back in Atlanta, Georgia, recording what was intended to be their debut LP for Capitol Records, but the only tracks that ever surfaced were on a Capitol 45, released in July of that year. The A side, *Windy Wakefield,* was written by The Addrisi Brothers, who had done some big hits for The Association (including *Never My Love*). Pat's haunting vocal, and the arrangement and production (Lari Goss and Don Carroll, respectively) were so un-Kingston that most listeners would think this *was* The Association. The flip side, *Tell The Riverboat Captain,* had Bob Shane doing the lead on the Bob Morrison composition and sounding much more like the KT of old. The label says this side was produced and arranged by The New Kingston Trio. This single was issued in stereo and has never been included on an album. Jim Connor remembers that they all thought *Windy Wakefield* was going to be a smash, especially after *Billboard* listed it as a "Hit Pick Of The Week." But nothing happened, the album was never completed, and the group left Capitol shortly after that.

The group's sound continued to evolve as they kept up a heavy touring schedule. By the time they again settled into a recording studio (this time in Nashville), it was early 1973, and their music had drifted away from the commercial folk bag to more of a country sound. The results of the Nashville sessions caught the attention of the people at Vanguard Records, who were especially interested and impressed with a track titled *The World Needs A Melody,* which everyone felt had the makings of a hit. A recording contract was drawn-up and preparations made for the release of a single and LP, but the group was off on a tour of Japan, so the actual contract signing was postponed. In that fateful interval, a rumor began circulating through music industry circles that Johnny Cash was going to record the same song. Vanguard got cold feet in

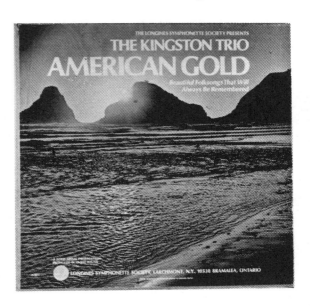

a hurry, and when Bob, Jim and Pat returned from their tour, the contract had been torn-up.

Fate stepped in again, as the mail-order Longines Symphonette Society was about to issue a six-LP set (culled from the old Capitol KT albums) titled AMERICAN GOLD, and they were looking for a bonus record that would serve as a "giveaway" enticement to potential customers. The idea of an LP by The New Kingston Trio, composed of all new recordings, fit the bill perfectly. And so it came to pass that THE WORLD NEEDS A MELODY found its way into the mailboxes of several thousand Trio fans in April of 1973 as a free companion volume to the elaborate Longines anthology.

AMERICAN GOLD contained sixty songs that covered the Guard/Reynolds/Shane/Stewart Capitol years, and as such makes it the most ambitious KT collection prepared to date. However, as in past collections, there is nothing contained therein to warrant its purchase in terms of rare releases or forgotten singles. There are a few oddities, however: *Tom Dooley* is the second-rate BACK IN TOWN version; *Reuben James* is the non-KT instrumental from SING A SONG WITH THE KINGSTON TRIO; and Will Holt's *Little Boy* has acquired the parenthetical subtitle, (*A Rose*). Produced by Longines Symphonette Society Divisional Vice President Eugene Lowell, AMERICAN GOLD was pressed in both mono and stereo versions, yet another oddity for 1973.

"Ten Songs Heralding A New Folksong Era," proclaimed the cover of THE WORLD NEEDS A MELODY, and that was about all the information we were given, as the reverse was devoted to "The secret of Longines Symphonette 'Living Sound' Gold Medal Recordings — made with such meticulous care . . ." It has been a piece of detective work just discovering who wrote the songs,

side one:

1 The World Needs A Melody
2 Grandma's Feather Bed
3 In Tall Buildings
4 Riley's Medicine Show
5 Blue Skies And Teardrops

side two:

1 Jug Town
2 Lovin' You Again
3 Come The Morning
4 Roll Your Own, Cowboys
5 Nellie

Blue Skies And Teardrops was written by Mike Williams. The recorded sound on this album is first rate, but we remain in the dark as to who produced it.

Shane/Connor/Horine disbanded in late 1973. Pat Horine returned to Lexington, Kentucky, playing local clubs and doing occasional recording. He reunited with Barbara King in 1984 and Pat and Barbara (based in Atlanta) are a popular duo once more. Jim Connor went off on a solo career and earned acclaim as one of this country's finest banjo pickers. John Denver's 1974 recording of *Grandma's Feather Bed* made Connor a pile of loot, as well as leading him to producer Milt Okun. Okun decided Jim was worthy of a solo LP, so JIM CONNOR, PERSONAL FRIEND OF ARTHUR KUYKENDALL, MONK DANIEL AND CLUNY RAKESTRAW (RCA Victor APL1-0874) was released in the spring of 1975. Jim played banjo on Denver's tour that year, and in a sort of "KT banjo reunion," joined voices with John Stewart on *Sweet Surrender* from Denver's BACK HOME AGAIN album. Today, Jim Connor continues to tour the South, performing excerpts from his work-in-progress, *Sand Mountain Symphony.*

and composers of four of them remain unknown. Jim Connor was able to fill in only a few of the gaps for us: John Hartford wrote *In Tall Buildings,* Billy Edd Wheeler wrote *Jugtown,* and *Nellie* was composed by Barry Etris. Connor himself penned *Grandma's Feather Bed,* later to be immortalized by John Denver. This version by the New Trio does not have to take a backseat to Denver's, however. The title song is a rousingly effective piece of work woven around a medley of old spirituals (including *Old Time Religion*), and we have since learned it is credited to "J. Slate/L. Hinley/H. Delaughter." We have recently discovered that

Bob Shane wasted no time in forming *another* New Kingston Trio with another two talented individuals, and his most recent decade at the helm of an American institution is the subject of our next chapter.

* * * * * * * * *

"Pat and Barbara"

Pat & Barbara Publicity Photo

THE NEW KINGSTON TRIO

PUBLIC RELATIONS:
SALTMAN- MIRISCH, INC.
8831 SUNSET BLVD.
LOS ANGELES 657-8680

The New Kingston Trio, Circa 1970. From the collection of Maureen Wilson.

The **Kingston Trio**

An early promotional drawing of (top to bottom) Roger Gambill, George Grove and Bob Shane, The Kingston Trio, 1976-1985.

Out With The "New" And In With — The Kingston Trio (1973-1986)

by

Allan Shaw

Although Bob Shane usually refuses to talk about the Shane/Connor/Horine aggregation other than a curt, "It was wrong," it is generally believed that what Bob felt was wrong was that the group had strayed too far from the original concept of the Kingston Trio. While Bob was tired of singing *Tom Dooley* and *M.T.A.,* the demands of audiences for the old favorites had convinced him that if he was going to use the Kingston Trio name, he was going to have to do the songs that were associated with the name and not the slicker, more highly produced and refined songs that were currently in vogue. He more or less acknowledged this in a 1983 interview with Mary Campbell, which was carried on the Associated Press service, when he said:

> "I was doing a solo about nine months in 1968. I didn't like it. I realized I enjoyed singing with a group. Then I started The New Kingston Trio with a couple of other fellows. We made one single record for Capitol. It was horrible. I don't remember what it is. Basically we were doing bars, hardly any concerts at all. We couldn't get any better jobs. We were singing mostly new material. If I was going to keep the name, I was going to have to do the old material, because of the amount of people we had sold records to. It took four or five years before that sank in with me."

So, although he was still committed to taking the Trio in new directions, Bob also realized that the sounds were inseparable from the name, and he set out to find two other singers whom he felt could re-create the old songs and the old sound while still bringing to the group the ability to do some songs out of the established mold. One of the two he found was 31 year-old Roger Gambill.

Roger, originally from North Carolina, began to study voice at the age of five, the only formal musical education he received. In an interview on Dick Cerri's *Music Americana,* Roger described his family background and musical training:

> "Well, I'd studied voice for fourteen years. I was raised in a little community that had a little Baptist church. I grew up and my mother and father sang. My dad played the piano and organ by ear. My uncles played mandolin and guitar and fiddle. We had a battery-powered radio so the *Grand Ole Opry* was a big event every year there on the farm. I was raised with my grandparents, great-grandparents, Mom and Dad, and music was just a constant source of entertaining ourselves. We sang together, we sang at church. We sang at weddings and funerals and corn-shuckin's and molasses makin's and the whole nine yards. Sounds like Walton's Mountain, but it's not quite that.
>
> "The church choir had raised some money to hire a professional teacher to come out and teach this little country choir some more fundamentals of music. I'd gone with Mom and Dad — walked about five or six miles with them to choir practice that night when that lady was helping them. During a break this lady heard me singing, Mother told me. I was about five years old at the time, and she asked where my parents were. And Mother and Dad came over and she says, 'I want to teach this man. I want to teach this young man.' And she drove out in the country and gave me free lessons every other Wednesday.

"And then my mother went to work in a hosiery mill and worked for twenty years and never missed a day — to pay for her boy's voice lessons. So if you want to make an audience real tough for me, put my Mom in it. I'll get nervous. Put the King and the Queen and the President there and I'm not shakin'. But put Mom in the front row and I get a little uptight."

Following high school graduation, Roger went to Wake Forest College, but quickly lost interest in pursuing academics. Although music was his first love, after leaving college he tried a number of jobs, but knew that if he wanted to realize his ambition of a career in music and entertaining, he was going to have to go out and find it — it wasn't going to come to him. So in 1968 he quit his job and went to Nashville where he teamed up with a friend, Larry Moore, and formed a duo called Gamble(sic) & Moore. They released one album, called simply GAMBLE MOORE (A&M 103).

Of particular interest is the fact that the lead-off song is *Remember The Alamo,* a song written by Jane Bowers for The Kingston Trio, which appeared on the Trio's 1959 album THE KINGSTON TRIO AT LARGE. While it cannot be said that the Gamble-Moore version is a copy of The Kingston

Trio version, the handling of the song by Gamble-Moore, particularly Roger's harmonies, is strikingly indicative of the contribution that Roger would later make to The Kingston Trio sound.

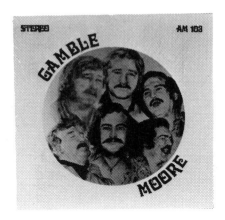

Between 1968 and 1973, Gamble & Moore played extensively throughout the area east of the Mississippi River including Sugar Mountain, North Carolina. On one of their appearances there, Bob Shane's wife, Louise, heard them perform. Knowing that Bob was working on putting together a new Trio, she told Bob of the show she had seen and that she thought one member of the duo was an entertainer in whom Bob would be interested. It

The New Kingston Trio: Bill Zorn, Bob Shane, Roger Gambill, circa 1974. Promotional photo.

The New Kingston Trio, circa 1974. Promotional photo autographed for the Chicago Guitar Gallery. Photo courtesy of the Chicago Guitar Gallery.

wasn't long before Bob was on the 'phone looking for Roger and, after a number of calls, caught up with him in Spokane, Washington. After introducing himself (as if an introduction was needed), he invited Roger down to Sea Island, Georgia to talk things over and audition.

At the same time, Bob was looking at other singers too, and among those in whom he was interested was Bill Zorn, then 26 years old, and originally from Phoenix, Arizona. Bill had just finished up a tour of duty as a singer and banjo player with the New Christy Minstrels. Like Roger, Bill was intrigued with the idea of becoming a member of The New Kingston Trio, so in late 1973 Bob, Roger and Bill became the second "New" Kingston Trio. Determined to avoid the mistakes he had made with the previous group, Bob originally handled everything himself, right down to the bookings. As Bill Zorn put it less than a year later, "We've had club dates all over and played military bases in Officers' and NCO clubs, and we've just finished a tour of Japan. Bob had so many contacts from the old days, we haven't even signed with an agent yet."

And this time, Bob pulled another trick from his "old days hat," and got the group some valuable national exposure by negotiating appearances on national television. The first, and perhaps most significant of these, was an ABC-TV's Wide World of Entertainment show called "The Great Folk Revival," which was broadcast on Wednesday, February 6, 1974, only three months after this configuration of the Trio first got together. Featuring other notable folk acts including the Highwaymen, the Tarriers, and a trio composed of Dave Guard, Alex Hassilev (of the Limeliters) and Mike Settle, The New Kingston Trio received top billing, opening the show with their medley of *M.T.A./Tom Dooley.* They also sang, *Hard Ain't It Hard* and the title song from the prior configuration's LP, *The World Needs A Melody.* To many fans, this was the first notice that there was a "new" Kingston Trio.

Adroitly using his contacts, Bob followed up the ABC-TV show with a national tour that garnered considerable press as the print media was delighted to feature stories on a fondly remembered group that was making what was perceived to be its first appearances in over five years. Bob also garnered for the group an appearance on Dinah Shore's show which was broadcast on October 15, 1974. Opening with a rousing version of *Hard Travelin'*, the second number, *Little White Cloud In A Lonesome Summer Sky*, featured Bill Zorn on the solos and showcased his strong, smooth tenor voice as well as his versatile banjo playing.

Unfortunately, and as far as we know, these two television appearances are the only "recordings" ever made by this configuration of the Trio. Certainly they were never in the recording studio, or if they were, the product of any such sessions has never and probably will never be made known. But the memories of those who saw this Trio in concert, refreshed by surreptitiously made recordings of live performances, are those of a group with a very pleasant sound and a delightful mixture of The Kingston Trio "standards" and contemporary songs of the era including John Stewart's *July, You're A Woman* and Hoyt Axton's *Lion In The Winter*.

But again, unfortunately, the relatively high proportion of "new" songs, which gave this New Kingston Trio an appeal to many devoted Trio fans also seemed to hasten its demise and cause Bob to regard it as sharing the problems he perceived the Shane/Connor/Horine group as having. In a 1982 interview with Lee Grant of the Los Angeles Times, Bob lumped the entire 1968-1975 era of the "New" Kingston Trios together and said about them, collectively, "I don't like to talk about that period. It became simply a job, a way to make a living and keep my kids in private schools. It was wrong and I had to make a move."

Part of that move was replacing Bill Zorn with George Grove in December of 1976. But, unlike the break-up of the earlier New Kingston Trio, which reportedly was Bob's unilateral decision over the protests of the other members, Bill Zorn's departure was strictly his own decision. But it came at an opportune time and facilitated making the changes that Bob thought were needed. George Grove expressed it well a couple of years later when, in response to being asked why Bill Zorn left the Trio, replied:

"I think personalities; not so much Bob, Roger and Bill together, but the fact that Bill got married after he was a member of The Kingston Trio, and marriage sometimes does not work well with business, and I think this had something to do with his losing interest in the group. Bill is a very talented man, and a very sincere and honest person. I like him very much. But he saw that he was losing interest in the group and he felt that that was not good for the conti-

nuance of the Trio. So it was a mutual understanding — all very totally above board and totally loving and honest. He decided to go to London where he has a brother in the record business and work in some industry there. So it was a fitting time, especially with the record people starting to knock on the door seriously. If there should be a change, it should be done right away, and they decided to go ahead and make the change."

And thus did that Trio become history.

* * * * * * * * *

Even as Bill Zorn expressed his desire to leave The New Kingston Trio, Bob was continuing to wrestle with the seemingly ever-present dilemmas that were presented by having the "new" in front of the Kingston Trio name. It was becoming increasingly obvious that the audiences wanted to hear the old Trio hits, but that word "new" was causing them to wonder what it was they were going to get. Bob himself expressed it well in a 1978 interview done by Arnie Amber of radio station WPQR-FM in Pennsylvania, when he said:

"I then went to work and leased the name "New Kingston Trio" from our own corporation, because I wanted to do new music and not pull the wool over anybody's eyes and wanted them to know there were two new members. And that got us jobs working in a lot of clubs but very few concert situations, so when I finally got wise to the whole thing with the group throughout the years, I just decided: if I could buy the name . . . so I did a stock trade on it with them."

The "them," of course, was Nick Reynolds and Frank Werber, the remaining two owners, along with Bob, of The Kingston Trio, Inc. Ably assisted by Russ Gary of Fuji Productions, Inc., by then the Trio's booking agent, Bob was able to trade his interest in the corporation, along with an undisclosed amount of cash, for the name "Kingston Trio", totally unfettered from that troublesome "new". In answer to the charge that it was wrong to call the group THE Kingston Trio when only he of the original three remained, Bob later said, in an interview broadcast in Sweden:

"In early '69 I started a new group called The New Kingston Trio. And I now own the name outright, so that we're now the Kingston Trio again. The original Kingston Trio was myself with Dave Guard and Nick Reynolds. Now, it still

The Kingston Trio, circa 1977. Promotional photo.

stayed the Kingston Trio when Dave Guard left and John Stewart took his place. We just think of this as the same thing. So John Stewart and Nick Reynolds left — we got two other fellows. As long as you have one of the original members of a group, you can still retain the same feeling."

So with the name secured and the license constraints no longer holding him back, Bob began to search for a replacement for Bill Zorn, ultimately finding 28 year-old George Grove.

George, another native of North Carolina, began showing his musical instincts and abilities at such an early age that he jokes about having been born, "with a trumpet in my hand." George's parents wanted him to become a doctor, but he had no such inclinations himself. "I couldn't stand to be in the lab six hours a day and I just couldn't get in enough practice on the piano and guitar," he says. So in college he majored in piano and trumpet which, Bob jokingly notes on stage, "has been a great help to us."

After leaving college, George enlisted in the Army and spent his tour of duty with the Army band.

Following his stint in the service he moved to Hampton, Virginia where he teamed up with a singer named Judy Ward whom he calls, "a natural talent, like Bob Shane, someone you learn from just by being around." But his career wasn't going in the direction he wanted, so he headed for Nashville where he worked as a studio musician and became acquainted with Roger Gambill. "I loved Nashville," he said, "and I really learned my chops there, but I found out the hard way how fractionalized and politicized the music business can be. I just had to get out." So George returned to Norfolk, Virginia and became music director of a recording studio. He summarized his situation by saying, "Professionally I had risen with a great deal of luck and with a great deal of hard work to become music director of a recording studio. I had no worries financially; I had no worries as far as what I was going to be doing for the next fifty years if my health held out."

But as Bob and Roger mulled over a replacement for Bill Zorn, George Grove was the person that kept coming into Roger's mind. The story of how George auditioned for and came to join the Trio is best told by George himself:

"When the time came to replace Bill Zorn, Roger remembered me and asked if I would be interested. I went down to Atlanta where both Bob and Roger live and just sat down in front of the fireplace, had some beer, picked a few songs and had a lot more beer, set the instruments down and had some more beers and sang and talked and realized that we all enjoyed each other . . . I joined the group in Chicago at the Mill Run Theatre. It was the first time with the group and I listened for several weeks to what Bill Zorn was playing with the group and the approach the group had towards performing, and the first of December (1976) was the first concert. It was in Louisville, Kentucky . . . a private party, and that was the first show that I actually did on stage with them."

Another reason that the timing of Bill's departure and George's arrival was fortuitous was the fact that the Trio's efforts to obtain recording contracts, after two years of work, were just beginning to pay off. They felt that it was best that the group going into the recording studios be the group that would be performing the songs on stage in the future. And so it was that the first recording session of this latest Kingston Trio occurred shortly after George joined the group. Three songs were recorded at what became known as the K-Tel session: *Tom Dooley, Greenback Dollar* and *Where Have All The Flowers Gone.* There were apparently no residual royalties from the session, with the Trio just being paid a fee for the session in exchange for releasing all control over the songs. It may have been a decision for later regrets, as it appears to be a recording session that the Trio would just as soon forget ever happened.

First of all, the performances were weak. Although the musicianship was fine, George had just joined the Trio, and it showed. But Bob and Roger did no better. The recordings sound to be exactly what they are, a "one-night-stand" for a quick buck. But no matter, The Kingston Trio (not the "New" Kingston Trio) was back in the recording studio for the first time in nearly a decade and could truthfully tell appreciative live audiences they were recording again. Besides which, it appeared that K-Tel promised that the recordings would only be used in foreign markets, and with no foreign tours in the offing, who cared what might be sold overseas?

Initially there appeared to be no problem as none of the K-Tel recordings were heard in the U.S. In 1978, K-Tel even came out with an LP of folk music titled GOODTIME MUSIC, which featured the Kingston Trio singing those three songs, but the cuts used were the old original tracks licensed from Capitol, with Capitol being credited on the jacket. But strangely, the European release of the same LP, which was released a year earlier, had only two of the three songs on it, with *Where Have All The Flowers Gone* missing from it, and the other two tracks being those from the K-Tel session. Credits on the European version are given to S.J. Productions, Inc. Why the difference? Probably because of some quirk in the license agreement with Capitol in the U.S. Where the no-additional-licesne-or-royalty K-Tel tracks could be legally used, they were, but this didn't explain the exclusion of *Where Have All The Flowers Gone* from the non-U.S. version of this LP.

But this version of *Where Have All The Flowers Gone* was certainly not overlooked in other respects, and next appeared as the B side of a single released on the Rebound label in Vancouver, B.C., Canada. The K-Tel *Tom Dooley* was the A side of this release, and both sides of this disc were noted to have been manufactured "by Total Records, 549 Homer, Vancouver, Canada by agreement with Key Seven Music."

Interestingly too, the K-Tel version of *Where Have All The Flowers Gone* was the first, and so far the only one of the K-Tel tracks to appear on a domestically released LP. As of this writing, it has appeared on three various artists compilations, LOOKIN' BACK (Columbia House), THE AMERICAN DREAM (Imperial House) and 24 GREAT HEARTBREAKERS & TEARJERKERS (Excelsior). Strangely too, although S.J. Productions is given publisher credits on LOOKIN' BACK, it is Imperial Music, Inc., that gets the publisher credits on THE AMERICAN DREAM. And who are Rebound, Total and Key Seven Music? Who knows? Who cares?

But what may be the most distressing use of these three songs is their inclusion on the Italian produced LP LA GRANDE STORIA DEL ROCK (LEGENDS OF ROCK). In additon to these three K-Tel tracks, the balance of that album is an abridged version of the first record from ONCE UPON A TIME. (See, "Re-issued, Rumored & Unreleased" for additional details.) Perhaps needless to say, this mixing of the works of these two very different Trios without any apparent attempt at explanation, unless it is somewhere there in the Italian liner notes, can only be an irritant and an affront to both Trios.

As an interesting aside, the K-Tel track of *Greenback Dollar,* has the "damn" replaced with a guitar stroke, not in the same fashion, but with the same effect as in the original Capitol 45. Why this was done fifteen years after the original controversy over the word is indeed strange, particularly with the Trio today using memories of that earlier censorship as one of their standard joke lines. But for the devoted collector, it certainly provides another oddity.

But while the Trio's K-Tel session may have produced the Trio's worst recordings, the next session, this one for Mountain Creek Records in Louisville, Kentucky, produced some of the best. Unfortunately, it appears that one of these tracks, *Aspen Gold,* may be forever lost, and the other two, *Big Ship Glory* and *Johnson Party Of 4* are available only on an obscure 45 of which only promotional (DJ) copies were ever made. Although two of the three songs (*Aspen Gold* and *Big Ship Glory*) were later recorded elsewhere, the sound and sparkle of *Big Ship Glory* when compared with its later appearance on LOOKING FOR THE SUN-SHINE, indicates that *Aspen Gold* must have been a real treasure (pun intended!) and that stereo versions of the other two would also have been outstanding. The reason? There are probably several, but one stands out head and shoulders above any others: these songs were produced by Voyle Gilmore, the master from Capitol Records who produced all of the Trio's recordings on that label. Gilmore's contributions to the Kingston Trio's Capitol recordings did so much for them, and the further taste we are given on the Mountain Creek 45 is so tantalizing, that the thought of never hearing his stereo mixes of these songs is sad indeed. This may well have been Gilmore's (who was already retired) last season, as he died in 1979.

So what happened to these tracks? *Aspen Gold,* of course, was never released, and was subsequently lost in the debacle that overcame the other two. In the 1978 Bob Shane interview by Arnie Amber, Bob commented briefly in response to a question about recordings:

> "Well, we're sort of in limbo. We had a really nice single that came out about four months ago, and the company that we were with, Mountain Creek, as we understand it, is going bankrupt! And it had gotten really nice airplay at middle-of-the-road and light-country stations, and we are very, very happy with the play that it got. In fact, we've had a lot of people ask for the song, so we know it was being played."

A few months later, in commenting upon the Trio's recording plans, George Grove revealed a great deal about the fate of the 45. Some of George's comments on the subjects are as follows:

George Grove, Bob Shane and Roger Gambill. The Kingston Trio in concert, Kansas City, Missouri, July 9, 1979. Photo by Frank Wright.

side one:

1 A Worried Man
2 Greenback Dollar
3 Reuben James
4 Hard, Ain't It Hard
5 California (I'm Going Home)

side two:

1 Aspen Gold
2 Early Morning Rain
3 Scotch And Soda
4 M.T.A./Tom Dooley
5 Longest Beer Of The Night

"Okay, well let me talk about recording 'contracts' in which we've been involved in the last couple of years. We started getting a lot of inquiries from different record companies. We recorded a few songs for K-Tel and we had other inquiries from other people who do the same kind of recording that K-Tel does; then we started getting the new record companies. Some had intelligent comments to make and worthwhile things to offer, but they couldn't back it with money, and that's very important. You have to have production, you know, everything these days is expensive.

So we finally signed a contract with a company called Mountain Creek Records, and we recorded three songs in Los Angeles in September of '77, and we're very proud of all three of them. From those three songs a single was released. There was no 'A' side listed on the record because we felt this was a projection into the community of disc jockeys, and we would see what they chose and what the people who listened to the record would choose as the popular song. Well, it turned out that turned against us, because both sides were popular in different market areas and in order for some of the trade magazines to report a song as being on the top list or Top 100, they have to have a certain number of reports on a certain side. Well, they were getting twice the number of reports that they needed as far as the record was concerned, but just not quite enough reports on one particular side to put that side in the Top 100. We made the *Gavin Report,* which is a trade magazine out of California. I think we were also a 'pick hit of the week' in *Billboard* one time.

But the company which owned Mountain Creek Records went bankrupt because their initial money came from insurance and there was a big strike in a certain segment of our industrialized nation, and it took the company's money because it was corporate insurance. So now, in the last few months we have been negotiating with Nautilus, and they are a financially sound company. They are approaching us regarding doing a 'direct disc recording.' The first time will be like 'The Best Of,' it will include a lot of the most popular songs that the Trio recorded. We have not sat down and definitely decided what these songs will be yet."

So with those words George takes us from the Mountain Creek story into the Nautilus story, Nautilus being the label on which the Kingston Trio's next album, ASPEN GOLD, was recorded on January 25 and 26, 1979 at Kendun Recorders in Burbank, California. Released in May, 1979 in a spectacularly beautiful jacket, ASPEN GOLD was digitally recorded and mastered (rather than direct-disc), the latest in state-of-the-art recording techniques. As George had predicted, it was pretty much of a "Best Of" album with eight of the ten songs (or 9 of 11 if the *M.T.A./Tom Dooley medley is counted as two songs) being old Trio favorites. But the two new songs (Aspen Gold* and *The Longest Beer Of The Night*) were real stunners and Gordon Lightfoot's *Early Morning Rain* was re-done in a style totally different from the Trio's earlier recordings of the song on SOMETHIN' ELSE and ONCE UPON A TIME. Coming from a Trio that specialized in note-for-note copies of the renditions of the earlier Trios, this change, along with the two new songs, was a real treat for the devoted fans looking for something new. And yet the predominance of faithful reproductions of some of the Trio's big hits of the past offered something to the casual fan of the past looking for the songs remembered from the past.

Technically, the recording was without parallel, with the digital recording process amply demonstrating the fidelity it offered. And Nautilus did a masterful job in explaining the recording process, as well as providing a detailed insert describing just about everything that went on in the studio while the disc was being recorded. Since that insert is being reproduced here, we'll not attempt to explain or expand upon it.

Demonstrating what over three years of singing together had done for the Trio members, the vocals and instrumentals on this album are those of the Kingston Trio at its best. Although some fans may prefer the original recordings of the original Trios, the musicianship of the Trio members on this recording cannot be faulted. The inclusion of the two new songs (*The Longest Beer Of The Night* being a solo by George Grove) and the re-done version of *Early Morning Rain* enabled the Trio to show that it was adept at handling new material as well as faithfully reproducing the very recognizable Kingston Trio sounds of the past.

The album was not without negatives though, the most glaring one being the back-up instruments of electric bass, drums, and electric fiddle and mandolin played respectively by Stan Kaess, Tom Green and Ben Schubert. There was nothing wrong with their playing. Technically it was well done, and effectively complemented the Trio. However, it wasn't needed, and to add insult to injury, it was too loud, nearly drowning out the

A CLOSER LOOK

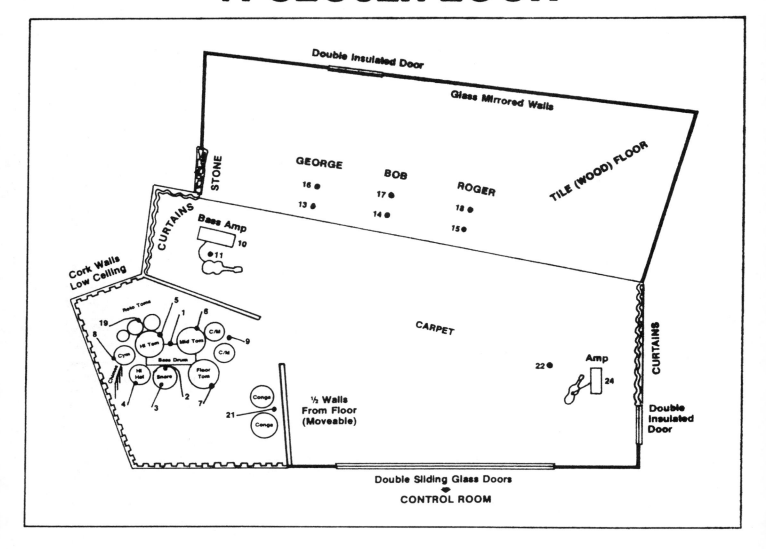

TECHNICAL INFORMATION

This album, featuring the Kingston Trio, marks a significant achievement in the recording industry. The Trio, of
course, is historical in its contribution to our musical heritage.
It is only appropriate that the Trio has chosen to introduce its
new music by using the finest recording technology and
equipment known to date. The studio was Kendun Recorders'
new $1.2 million "super" studio featuring an SSLL (Solid State
Labs Limited) board from England. This board is the only one
in the United States and has a price tag at over $250,000. It is
completely automated by computer with a noise floor at over

(continued on back)

INPUT SPECIFICATIONS

Inputs to the board were as follows:
1 - Bass drum (Sony C-500)
2 - Snare drum (Shure SM-57)
3 - Under snare drum (Shure SM-57)
4 - Hi-hat (Sony C-55P)
5 - Hi-tom (AKG 452EB)
6 - Mid-tom (AKG 452EB)
7 - Lo-tom (AKG 452EB)
8 - Overhead left (chimes) (AKG 414) ·

(continued on back)

TECHNICAL INFORMATION

-87 dB. It is one of the quietest and most accurate recording consoles in the United States.

The console was fed directly into the Soundstream Digital recording system at +10 input with a noise floor at over -93 dB. The Soundstream tape drive system uses 1″ Ampex 460 Digital Audio Tape, and two of Soundstream's four available tracks were utilized to make this recording. Digital recording converts the continuous, or sine wave, energy of an analog audio signal into a series of pulses. These signals (audio wave forms) are sampled at over 50,000 times per second by the Soundstream computer and are converted into either "on" or "off" information. This accuracy accounts for the ability of the recording system to capture literally a flat response from 0 Hz (DC) to beyond 20 kHz. Tape wow and flutter and print-through are completely eliminated. The result is an *exact* recording of what went on in the studio.

24 of the SSLL's 40 inputs were used, 11 on the drums and percussion instruments and the remaining 13 on the Trio members and two other back-up artists.

There is still the Kingston Trio technique and "sound" in each of the songs, but the music is more "today", even in the older numbers that made the Trio famous.

INPUT SPECIFICATIONS

9- Overhead right (cymbals) (AKG 414)
10- Bass Amplifier
11- Bass (ElectroVoice EV RE-20)
12- Bass (direct-feed)
13- Banjo, acoustic guitar (George Grove) (Sony C-55P)
14- Acoustic guitar (Bob Shane) (Sony C-55P)
15- Acoustic guitar (Roger Gambill) (Sony C-55P)
16- Vocal (George) (AKG H-17)
17- Vocal (Bob) (AKG H-17)
18- Vocal (Roger) (AKG H-17)
19- Roto-toms (AKG 452EB)
20- Not used
21- Percussion (congas) (AKG 452EB)
22- Fiddle (live) (Neumann KM-861)
23- Not used
24- Electric mandolin (direct-feed)

George, Bob and Roger rehearse for the ASPEN GOLD album, January 1979. Photo courtesy: Nautilus Records.

The contract is inked for ASPEN GOLD. Standing, left to right: Roger Rohrs, (Nautilus), Russ Gary, (Kingston Trio manager), Steve Krauss (Nautilus). Seated, left to right: Bob Shane, Roger Gambill, George Grove. Photo courtesy Nautilus Records.

Trio members themselves in some instances. It is one thing to see the Trio in live performance, usually in a somewhat noisy club where the back-up musicians are substantially drowned out by the noise of the audience and, in some instances, assist the Trio in overcoming unwelcome audience noise. In the recording studio, however, they are totally redundant except for some of the bass, although there are many fans who miss the acoustic stand-up bass to the point that they find the electric bass obtrusive. Regardless, prior to ASPEN GOLD, most of the Trio's recordings were unaccompanied except for the Trio members' instruments and the acoustic bass. That is what the record listener has come to expect on a Trio recording, but on ASPEN GOLD, is not what one gets. But for Trio fans who had been awaiting the reappearance of the Kingston Trio on an LP, ASPEN GOLD was indeed welcome.

There was also a 45 from ASPEN GOLD, the two new songs, *Aspen Gold/Longest Beer Of The Night*. Although not identified on the label as being a promotional record, there appears to have been no other reason to release a 45, particularly when it was of the two new songs that wouldn't generally be identified with the Kingston Trio

anyway. Certainly to a non-follower of the Trio, George's solo on *Longest Beer Of The Night* has no identification with the Trio, and *Aspen Gold* has little more. Was this an attempt to showcase this "new" group? Of all the possible explanations, this seems to be the most likely, but still doesn't really make sense.

ASPEN GOLD was also released in an analog version on the 51 West (Division of Columbia) label, apparently in hopes that additional sales would be generated. Although it isn't known how successful this was, it was obvious from the start that the digital version would have a very limited market. Although digital discs could be played on analog phonographs, the premium price of a digital disc was a strong deterrent for all except devoted Trio fans, of whom there were very few who were even aware of the disc's existence, and high-fidelity buffs, many of whom would be more inclined to classical discs rather than Kingston Trio product. However, distribution of the analog disc was not particularly good, although this appeared to be more the result of lack of interest from the stores rather than lack of effort on the part of the label to get the disc out. Regardless, the promotion and distribution was minimal so that most buyers of the record were those who knew of it and searched it out rather than "discovering" it while browsing in a record store.

Also, the jacket of the analog disc was not particularly attractive, with a small portion of the digital disc's colorful cover photo being reproduced in the upper right hand corner of the analog disc's jacket and black-and-white photos of the Trio members across the bottom. But to devoted Trio fans, it was gratifying to know that the Kingston Trio was back in the recording studio. Unfortunately, the relative lack of promotion and distribution probably resulted in many fans not being aware of the existence of the record. But that was a problem not unique to the Kingston Trio, as it is one shared by all except a very few superstars. Although neither Nautilus nor 51 West can probably be faulted for the degree of promotion and distribution they gave ASPEN GOLD, the question remains of how much better the album might have sold if there had been more promotion and better distribution. But subsequent events indicate that it may not have made a great deal of difference, at least not as a practical matter. In the late 1970's and early 1980's, there was not a great deal of interest in "Kingston Trio type" music, and

it is questionable how well an album would sell even if heavily promoted and well distributed. It is said that everything has its time, and that just did not seem to be the time for this kind of music.

George, Bob and Roger in the studio recording ASPEN GOLD. Photo courtesy Nautilus Records.

George, Bob and Roger rehearsing for the ASPEN GOLD recording sessions. Photo courtesy Nautilus Records.

There was also a production run of cassettes of the analog version. They apparently did not sell well either, as they quickly became unavailable except for a few cassette cut-out bins.

The Trio's next recording venture is not only a recording session, but a video appearance, as well. Whether this will ever appear on a phonograph record or audio tape is doubtful, and since it is the intent of this book to deal primarily with audio recordings, we won't cover this venture in great detail.

The item we speak of is a live performance released in 1981 by Pioneer Artists on a laser video disc entitled THERE'S A MEETIN' HERE TONIGHT. The disc consists of opening and closing narrations by Mary Travers of Peter, Paul & Mary, and concert performances by the Limeliters and the Kingston Trio. There are 14 songs done by the Kingston Trio; in order, *Greenback Dollar, Hard Ain't It Hard, The First Time* (the somewhat rank song dealing with fornication rather than the classic recorded for NEW FRONTIER), *Longest Beer Of The Night, Chilly Winds, Lover's, Columbus Stockade, Scotch And Soda, Worried Man, MTA/Tom Dooley, Early Morning Rain, Merry*

Minuet, Zombie Jamboree and *California* (formerly *I'm Goin' Home*). The performances here are certainly adequate, and since this is the only opportunity to hear a number of these songs performed by this configuration of the Trio, or in some cases any configuration of the Trio at all, this disc is an absolute must for a complete Trio collection. Recorded exclusively for the laser disc release, this show was not made available on the far more popular video cassette format. There are many Trio fans hoping for it's ultimate release in that mode, but as of this writing, there have been no indications that such will ever happen.

Chronologically, the next event of historical importance for the group is the famous "Kingston Trio & Friends: Reunion" Show, held and filmed at the Six Flags Over California amusement park near Los Angeles on November 7, 1981, and subsequently shown on Public Television. For Trio devotees it was an event of monumental impact as it produced the first appearance together of Dave Guard, Bob Shane and Nick Reynolds since 1961, and the first appearance together of John Stewart, Bob Shane and Nick Reynolds since 1967. It was also the first, and has since become the only occasion on which every man who ever sang with the

Kingston Trio (as opposed to the New Kingston Trio) appeared together. On the show (which aired in March of 1982), Guard, Reynolds and Shane sang *Hard, Ain't It Hard, Zombie Jamboree* and *Tom Dooley;* Stewart, Reynolds and Shane sang *Reuben James, Chilly Winds* and *Greenback Dollar;* Grove, Gambill and Shane sang *Three Jolly Coachmen, Early Morning Rain, Scotch And Soda, Hard Travelin'* and *Where Have All The Flowers Gone?;* and all six together sang *Sloop John B, Worried Man* and *MTA*. It was a night to remember, and a more detailed account and some fine photos may be found in our next chapter, "A Night On Magic Mountain."

But this is a book about records, and the Kingston Trio's next record album was recorded in studios in Sharon, Vermont and Hollywood, California in late 1981. Produced by Mike Settle and entitled 25 YEARS NON-STOP, this album could well have been called "Greatest Hits of the Kingston Trio," for that is, in essence, what it is. Every one of the Trio's biggest hits of the glory days is faithfully reproduced on this album.

For those wanting to hear again the Trio's biggest hits, and not caring that it was not the original group, this album fit the bill to a "T". The group had been together for over five years and the renditions of the songs were about as tight and well done as anything ever done by the Kingston Trio. The Trio's accompanists of Stan Kaess (bass), Ben Schubert (electric fiddle/tenor guitar) and Tom Green (drums) backed them ably and, although the accompanying instruments are clearly present, they are not as overly obtrusive as they were on ASPEN GOLD. Lest there had been any doubt, this album proved beyond doubt that the Kingston Trio could ably and competently reproduce the Trio's past hits such that only the most discerning listener could recognize the changes in voices and instrumental styles. Nick Heyl, the album's executive producer described it well when he said that it was "not just another nostalgic golden oldie recording," but rather an "invitation to experience the artistic growth and development of one of the founding groups in contemporary folk music." It appeared that Bob Shane had finally succeeded in doing what he had claimed to want to do for so long — assemble a group that could present the songs and sounds associated with the Kingston Trio name by the public at large, while still having only one of the original three members in the group.

The album was released on the Xeres label, a division of the Chnito Productions owned by Nick and Jane Heyl. It came out in January of 1982 and

The Kingston Trio, circa 1982. Promotional photo.

side one:

1   M.T.A.
2   Tijuana Jail
3   Tom Dooley
4   Greenback Dollar
5   The Merry Minuet
6   Reverend Mr. Black

side two:

1   Scotch And Soda
2   Hard Travelin'
3   Sloop John B
4   Zombie Jamboree
5   They Call The Wind Maria
6   Where Have All The Flowers Gone
7   A Worried Man

was promoted on late night television with an 800 telephone number. Although the promotional flyer stated that 8-tracks as well as LPs and cassettes were available, it appears that the 8-tracks were never produced.

Although everyone involved is very tight-lipped about the success of the promotion and the sales of the record, reading between the lines one arrives at a conclusion that the promotion was a disaster and that sales were next to nil. There appears to have been a feeling that the Kingston Trio name would be a big draw and that the records would practically hop off the shelves. But this doesn't appear to have been the case.

So what went wrong? Had the Kingston Trio lost its appeal? Did the record-buying public want new songs? Or did they maybe want the old songs but wanted them done by the original artists? Was there something wrong with the promotion or did it just not reach the right audience? There's probably an element of truth to each of these and a great deal more besides. But whatever, 25 YEARS NON-STOP appears to have been a great disappointment to everyone who was concerned with bringing it out.

But faith in the Kingston Trio and optimism for the future remained at Xeres and it was decided to try again, but this time with an album of new songs, LOOKING FOR THE SUNSHINE.

Actually, LOOKING FOR THE SUNSHINE had been in the works for as long as had 25 YEARS NON-STOP, but it had been decided that the Trio should be re-introduced with an album of their big hits of the past rather than with new material. So although 25 YEARS NON-STOP was produced and released first, LOOKING FOR THE SUNSHINE was more of a sister than a child and was released just over a year later in January of 1983. The recording was done at the Wizard Recording Studio in Hollywood, California and at the Eddy Offord Studio in Atlanta, Georgia. Exact recording dates are not known, but all the songs were recorded in 1982. Mike Settle was again the producer, and Nick and Jane Heyl's Xeres was again the label. Stan Kaess, Ben Schubert and Tom Green again accompanied the Trio, but were joined by other musicians on a number of songs, most notably John Sebastian of the Lovin' Spoonful on autoharp and harmonica.

Although generally described as an "all new" album, this was a slight misnomer as four of the twelve songs had previously been recorded and released by the Trio. However, the arrangements on LOOKING FOR THE SUNSHINE were so new and refreshing, or the previous recordings had been so little known, that even these four songs were new and refreshing.

Probably the best known of the four was Bob Shane's solo on *A Rolling Stone*, which previously appeared on the Trio's 1959 album, HERE WE GO AGAIN. However, this time out it wasn't strictly a solo, and George's and Roger's accompanying harmonies gave it a completely new feel and sound. It was a welcome return of an old friend. Similarly, *The Long Black Veil* had been recorded by the Trio in 1963 for NEW FRONTIER. But like *Early Morning Rain* on ASPEN GOLD, the arrangement here was so fresh and new that it may as well have been a completely new song.

The other two "repeaters," *The World Needs A Melody*, from THE WORLD NEEDS A MELODY LP, and *Big Ship Glory*, from the Mountain Creek 45, had been heard little enough by most Trio fans that they were generally regarded as new songs. And the other eight songs on the album had previously been heard only in concert, so most fans regarded LOOKING FOR THE SUNSHINE as a totally new album.

Most also regarded it as a real treat, with the general feeling being one of delight and the question, "Why did it take so long for this album to be released?" was asked by many. Several Trio devotees, including some normally critical of the Grove/Gambill/Shane group, conceded this album to rank in quality and listenability with some of the Trio greats of the past. But it also illustrated again that old bugaboo — the devoted Trio fans, many of whom had purchased every Trio album to come along, were overjoyed to have this new material, but the much larger number of casual fans, many of whom had forgotten about the Trio for many years, still preferred the big hits and apparently couldn't have cared less about the new stuff.

Perhaps it was this dichotomy that Xeres had in mind when they decided to promote both albums together, which they did with an expensive ad in *TV Guide* magazine shortly after LOOKING FOR THE SUNSHINE debuted. That ad featured both albums together for the single price of $10.00. Although Xeres subsequently accommodated those who already had 25 YEARS NON-STOP by selling LOOKING FOR THE SUNSHINE separately, for those who wanted only one or the other of the albums, from the *TV Guide* ad it appeared that this couldn't be done — one either bought both albums or neither album. Whether this caused any lost sales cannot be determined, but it certainly angered and frustrated those fans who had already bought 25 YEARS NON-STOP and were now being asked to spend another $10.00 (or $5.00 apiece) for LOOKING FOR THE SUNSHINE and a second copy of 25 YEARS NON-STOP. Clearly the promotional thrust in the *TV Guide* ad seemed to have been a mistake, but whether Xeres was trying to unload some excess inventory of 25 YEARS NON-STOP, or

side one:

1 Looking For The Sunshine
2 Hawaiian Nights
3 I Like To Hear The Rain
4 Big Ship Glory
5 Sometimes Love Is Better When
    It's Gone
6 I'm A Rake And Ramblin' Boy

side two:

1 The World Needs A Melody
2 Long Black Veil
3 Will You Love Me If I Don't Do Coke
4 Cortelia Clark
5 Rollin' Stone
6 Easy To Arrange

whether they felt a double-barreled promotion would be an effective marketing tool is not known. Regardless, there were apparently a disappointingly few albums sold.

The problems were not limited to those resulting from the marketing plans, however, as once again, the fates appeared to have deserted the Trio. Having learned that late night TV watchers didn't buy many Kingston Trio records, Xeres contracted to buy the spot in *TV Guide* to coincide with a variety show on which the Trio was to make an appearance. But with one of the many slips between the cup and the lip, the TV show was moved around after the *TV Guide* ad was locked in so that the hoped-for and planned tie-in between the ad and the show was lost. Whether or not this mattered in the long haul is debatable, but it certainly epitomized the frustrations of the Trio and its backers in seeing well-laid plans go amok.

Both 25 YEARS NON-STOP and LOOKING FOR THE SUNSHINE subsequently appeared in a number of record stores around the country, but without any promotion they usually languished in the stacks until someone happened to chance upon one. Whether it was the *TV Guide* promotion or something else that was the "straw that broke the camel's back" is hard to say, but after the lackluster sales performance of both albums, Xeres seemed to lose heart for any further promotions. And because of the practical and financial difficulties of carrying albums around with them, even the Trio members found it difficult to promote the albums in their personal appearances. The Trio members couldn't sing and sell records, and what good did it do to send fans to record stores that didn't have the records anyway? Consequently, the feeling was that everyone involved lost all taste for promoting the albums further. Although there was fairly good store distribution, with no promotional efforts, the albums generally languished in the bins waiting to be discovered, and few were. Would a continued promotional effort have made any difference? That is hard to say. But whether or not Xeres efforts were the correct ones, at least at first they were substantial, and the results were disappointing for all concerned.

There were also two 45s produced by Xeres, and the handling of them is also somewhat puzzling. The first, for public consumption, combined *Reverend Mr. Black* from 25 YEARS NON-STOP with *Looking For The Sunshine* from LOOKING FOR THE SUNSHINE. Apparently it was hoped that this coupling of one of the Trio's past big hits, which was identified only with the Trio, and also one that wasn't as widely available as *Tom Dooley* or *MTA*, would attract old Trio fans as well as call their attention to the song that was then regarded as the Trio's best effort for commercial success

with a new song. But as far as we know, although this 45 was pressed, it was never released, at least not in the sense that we normally think of a record being released. We are not aware of it's ever having been available in any stores, nor was it ever listed in catalogues of in-print 45s. Perhaps the high hopes for it were dashed by the failure of the efforts to realize big sales of the albums.

The second 45 is somewhat of an enigma too, as it was a double-sided (mono/stereo) record of *Looking For The Sunshine*. Planned for distribution to radio station disc jockeys, this 45 further illustrated the extent of Xeres commitment to help the Kingston Trio get a hit with a new song. The curious thing about the record though, is that the record was in a picture sleeve, whereas the release intended for public consumption was in a plain sleeve. This is exactly the opposite of what is normally done and, except for the fact that the picture sleeve makes no mention of *Reverend Mr. Black,* one might well guess that the picture sleeves just got put on the wrong records.

The sleeve itself is nicely done, although it doesn't contain a picture of the Trio. Perhaps it was felt that the attractive sleeve would inspire disc jockeys to play the record. Whatever, it is certainly another of the curiosities of the Kingston Trio's records. It also gives the Grove/Gambill/Shane Trio the unique distinction of having five different 45s (have you been counting as you read this?), all of which for one reason or another top the list of least distributed and probably scarcest Kingston Trio records. While this hasn't given any of them any unusual value, it is the sort of thing that can drive many collectors to distraction.

There is another curiosity about the three albums of the Grove/Gambill/Shane Trio, and that is the low visibility of the Trio members themselves. Only on 25 YEARS NON-STOP did a picture of the Trio appear on the front cover, and even in that picture the Trio members were hard to identify. Although the analog version of ASPEN GOLD had black-and-white photos of the members on the cover, they were photos taken from the inner cover of the digital disc and were of the three individually rather than of the Trio. The same was true of the photos on the back of LOOKING FOR THE SUNSHINE. While they were all good photos and all taken at the same time and place, they were three separate photos of the Trio members rather than a photo of the Trio itself. Several photographers have commented upon the difficulty of getting a photo of the Trio singing since they stand apart at three separate microphones, and this may explain the individual photos. But it doesn't explain the relative absence of photos from the fronts of the jackets. Was it a deliberate attempt to play down the fact that this is not the same Kingston Trio of two decades earlier, or is it merely coincidental? More than a few Trio fans have debated this question, and we will probably never know for sure.

After LOOKING FOR THE SUNSHINE, there were no new recordings in two years. Xeres was not about to produce another Trio record and the Trio wasn't able to line up another label, although there is no indication that there were any serious attempts to do so. In response to questions about a new record, Bob Shane generally expressed a disinclination to return to the studio while George and Roger merely said they would love to record, but without a label, weren't able to consider doing such. In late 1984, George mentioned that the Trio had learned (or re-learned) 40 songs which were either totally new or had been resurrected from old Trio albums, giving hope that a new album, whenever, would contain some real treats. Then disaster struck.

While visiting with his family in North Wilkesboro, North Carolina on March 2, 1985, Roger experienced some chest pains. He went to the hospital and there suffered a massive heart attack. Initially it was feared that he wouldn't survive at all, but after the critical first few days had passed, he seemed to rally and was able to be transferred to Atlanta with a prognosis of being able to return to the Trio in six months. However, a few days later he suffered a massive stroke and subsequently died on March 20 at the age of 42. The eulogies poured in from around the world, but perhaps the most moving came from Roger's wife Catherine who said, "A lot of people, from throughout the world, have said how happy Roger made them. He was incredible and I'll be eternally grateful for the thirteen years I had with him. It was most remarkable." But the best words were some which had been spoken by Roger himself, in an interview with Dick Cerri on "Music Americana." In what was probably the best eulogy that he could possibly have had, Roger said, "I've got a lot of dear friends that I love, and my family, and if I can in some way through my music and my God-given talents, if I can go on stage and give my audience the same thing my friends and my family give me — if I can do it musically, I will have done one hell of a job!"

When Roger was first stricken on March 2nd and appeared to be facing a six-month recovery period, Bob and George went looking for a capable fill-in performer to meet their already-scheduled concert commitments. Although they considered cancelling the dates and taking the time off, they quickly realized that they not only had obligations to the dates they were booked to play, but to their fans as well.

The first person they thought of was Bob Haworth of the Brothers Four, a gifted singer and instrumentalist whom they had known for many years. Bob Shane was quoted in the New York Times as saying, "Roger's illness came out of nowhere during the first week in March. We weren't prepared for it at all. But I had asked Bob Haworth about five years ago if he could sub if anything happened to anyone in our group and he said he probably could. He was the first person I called when Roger had a heart attack. He'd never sung with us but he admits he learned how to play rhythm guitar by listening to our stuff."

As soon as the decision was made to keep going, Bob Shane was on the phone to Bob Haworth, and by Tuesday afternoon, only three days later, Bob and George were on a plane to Seattle, near where Bob Haworth lives on Vashon Island, Washington. Two days of working together and getting to know each other's musical styles were followed by a flight to Los Angeles on Thursday where the Trio met with their sidemen for one day of rehearsing before their first show on Friday — less than a week after Roger was stricken.

In the days that followed, Bob Haworth quickly and competently worked his way into the Trio, despite the fact that he was still obligated to fulfill Brothers Four concerts. Fortunately, the Brothers Four concerts and the Trio shows meshed together such that neither group missed a show while Bob was performing with both of them.

Even though Roger's condition had been deteriorating to the point that his death was not unexpected, when the tragic news came on March 20th, it was still hard to take. But in the two weeks that Bob Haworth had been with the Trio, and with the rapidity with which he had become a part of the group, there was no doubt to whom the invitation to become a permanent member would go. Bob Haworth expressed it as follows:

"I was 12 years old and had been playing guitar for a year and a half when *Tom Dooley* hit. I was enamored of the Kingston Trio and hoped to some day know them, and it was exciting when I finally got to know them and associate with them later. But I never dreamed of being part of the group. I never thought there would be a change, and even thought I had agreed to sub if I was ever needed, until Bob called, it never occured to me that I might ever be part of the Kingston Trio.

"When it became obvious that Roger would not return and I realized that I might be asked to stay on, it was a bit of a dilemma for me. Both as a solo act and

George Grove, Bob Shane and Bob Haworth. The Kingston Trio, 1985. Promotional photo.

as a member of the Brothers Four I had reached the level of professionalism I had always aspired to and felt I had found my performing niche. But as I got into it with the Trio, found out how well I worked with Bob and George and felt the love and enthusiasm of Trio audiences, my dilemma was quickly resolved. When the invitation was given, it was a thrill to accept it."

But still, Roger's death was a shock. The Associated Press quoted Bob Shane as saying, "It's pretty hard to take, but you go on and do the best you can under the circumstances." And under the circumstances, some changes were inevitable, as Roger's solos were very much his own. Bob Shane was quoted in the previously mentioned New York Times story as saying, "We do individualistic things as soloists. We've just dropped the songs that Roger sang and we'll go on to things that Bobby Haworth does. We've had no chance to rehearse anything yet. We've just tried to keep the show going. What we really miss about Roger was his humor. He was such a fine humorist."

After playing with the Kingston Trio in Green Bay, Wisconsin on April 19th, Bob Haworth flew to Seattle to fulfill his last concert commitment with the Brothers Four on April 20th. Then it was permanently back to the Kingston Trio.

From his earliest remembrances Bob Haworth had a fondness for music which led to his beginning to learn the guitar at age 10 and, after finishing high school, enrolling at UCLA as a music major where he sang with the UCLA Chorale under the direction of Robert Wagner. Weekend evenings were spent performing in clubs.

After two years at UCLA, in 1967 Bob moved to Oregon where he attended the University of Oregon and continued his musical education. But he had done enough live entertaining that it was in his blood, and he soon left school to pursue a career as an entertainer. After a short stint as a solo act, he joined the New Yorkers (a group that later became the Hudson Brothers) and recorded with them for Decca and Sceptre for two years, leaving in 1969 to resume his solo career. A chance meeting with a business partner of the Brothers Four led him to join that group in 1971 as a replacement for Mark Pearson, and he can be heard on all of their records since that time. During off times from the Brothers Four he continued to work as a single under the name "Bo Mooney", as well as perform and record as part of a duet with his wife Mardi under the name "Mooney & Starz."

As Bob Haworth gained confidence as a member of the Kingston Trio, the group quickly learned more than the "obligatory, include in every show" Trio favorites. Not only was Bob featured as a solo in each show, but as summer turned into fall, audiences were again treated to long lost Trio favorites such as *Raspberries, Stawberries*. George Grove took on an increasing portion of the between song humorous monologues and the traditional striped shirts re-appeared, albeit with full-length rather than three quarter-length sleeves. Although Roger Gambill was sorely missed, Bob Haworth conclusively reconfirmed what John Stewart, Pat Horine, Jim Connor, Bill Zorn, Roger Gambill and George Grove had already amply demonstrated — that capable, talented performers could ably fill the shoes of their predecessors and keep going what has become an institution, The Kingston Trio.

Although Roger's death dealt a severe blow to all recording plans then in process, as this book went to press, it appeared that that obstacle too was on it's way to being overcome. Both George Grove and Bob Shane reported that arrangements for the Kingston Trio to do a CD (Compact Disc) were underway, and that such a disc might be released as early as mid-summer, 1986. Nothing has yet been said as to whether such a disc might be of new songs or old favorites or a combination of the two, but whatever, Trio fans are looking forward to this first Trio recording on a new audio medium.

But at the same time as this exciting news began to surface, another tragedy befell the Kingston Trio "family" with the death of Stan Kaess, the Trio's bass player for 16 years, of cancer, on March 14, 1986 at the age of 40. Having started with the Trio in the early days of the Shane/Connor/Horine configuration, Stan had been an active part of the Trio for longer than anyone else except Bob Shane. Although Stan's death and replacement by Carey Black (of Seattle, Washington) received less fanfare than had Roger's a year earlier, the general feeling among Triophiles was that Stan's musical contributions to the Trio sound were of much greater significance than most fans will ever realize.

In his initial column in the Kingston Korner Newsletter, George Grove wrote his words of farewell to Stan. Since they so well expressed the

sentiments of so many of Stan's friends, and since this chapter ends the "Kingston Trio Story" to the degree that this book has attempted to tell it, George's words about Stan seem to be an appropriate way to end this part of that story.

"Stan was a unique man. He was a musician who not only played his instrument well but played it well enough and thoughtfully enough to have developed *style*. He was also a gifted accompanist — he knew what and when to play (and not to play) in order to allow the instrument or voice he was accompanying to sound better. Stan was my tennis partner. Many of you knew him as a large man — he was a fine athlete. Whether it was tennis, golf, skiing, hiking, camping or whatever, Stan was always doing and doing well, usually with his family. And therein lies the most important quality of Stan Kaess: he was family oriented. Everything he enjoyed doing he enjoyed more because he included his family. He would drive all night long and thousands of extra miles during some of the Trio's tours so that he could include his family — Ruthie and their four children. There were times when he would play a concert, get in his van and drive all night and all day in order to arrive barely in time to get on stage and play another concert without sleep or rest, all in order to include his family. And the Trio never worried since Stan was always there and always dependable — musically, professionally and personally. We shall all miss him."

* * * * * * * * *

Coincidentally, at about the same time that we first learned that Stan Kaess was dying of cancer, we belatedly learned of the death from a heart attack of David "Buck" Wheat, the Kingston Trio's bass player from 1958-1961, on July 15, 1985, at age 63 in Los Angeles, California. And so, on the next page we pause for a moment to remember these four men who each, in their own unique ways, contributed so much to The Kingston Trio.

DAVID "BUCK" WHEAT
1942 - 1985

ROGER GAMBILL,
1942 - 1985

STAN KAESS
1945 - 1986

VOYLE GILMORE
1912 - 1979

PAST AND PRESENT -- The original Kingston Trio (on top, left to right)
Nick Reynolds, Bob Shane, and Dave Guard, and the current Kingston Trio
(below, left to right) George Grove, Shane and Roger Gambill, appear
together for the first time in THE KINGSTON TRIO AND FRIENDS: REUNION, a
special celebratory broadcast to be seen at 9:00 PM, ET, on Friday,
March 12 on the Public Broadcasting Service (PBS). Shane, Grove, and
Gambill today continue the Kingston Trio's brilliant folk music in
concerts throughout the nation. (Editors: Please check your local
schedule for area date and time of the broadcast.) (KCET photo by
Mitzie Trumbo.)

Promotional photos for the PBS TV showing of "The Kingston Trio & Friends Reunion."

A Night On Magic Mountain: November 7, 1981

by
Benjamin Blake

Camera 3 producer JoAnn Young made good on her promise to make the Kingston Korner contingent feel like honored guests. Not only did we have an assurance of choice concert seats and passes to the "wrap party", but she now informed us that the nationally syndicated "Entertainment Tonight" television program wanted to interview us as the trio of fans who had come a collective five thousand miles to see tonight's reunion of *the* Trio.

. . . Allan Shaw had flown in from Illinois and Jack Rubeck had flown in from Oregon. Together, we three had chronicled the past and present doings of our heroes for three years in the pages of *Goldmine* Magazine, but not until earlier that afternoon at the Los Angeles bus depot had we actually met face to face. Fear of flying and a severe case of *emptyus pocketbookus* had sent me on a seventy-four hour bus trip from Connecticut to California with only four hours of sleep en route, but a quick shave and shower at our hotel in Valencia got my energy reserve working. It was difficult for any of us to believe it was finally Saturday evening, November the Seventh, 1981, and the Heart Of The Dream was at hand . . .

We were grouped just outside the open ampitheatre at Six Flags Magic Mountain Park, and suddenly it was my turn to have that bright light stabbing my tired eyes, and a pleasant lady with a microphone asking me why I had traveled almost three thousand miles on a bus to witness the taping of the Kingston Trio's Reunion Concert. I replied something about "magic" and how I wished to see that magic firsthand. Then she wanted to know what made the Trio so special to so many. Any of us could have easily written a lengthy book in answer to that one, but faced with an optimum of thirty seconds I found myself mumbling something about the increase in domestic and international guitar sales since 1958, and in my final seconds in the Hollywood spotlight I let loose and credited the Kingstons with everything from the Beatles to a cure for the common cold! And all I

had intended to say was "hello" to the folks back home.

The final rehearsal had just finished up inside, and we got to give a hurried handshake and greeting to Nick Reynolds and Bob Shane as they emerged into the waning West Coast sunset, respectively searching for a clean shirt and something to eat. We mortals decided to wolf down some burgers and fries and then lined up at the "V.I.P." gate with several hundred other invitees. JoAnn had informed us upon our arrival that enough V.I.P. tickets had been issued to fill the entire ampitheatre, so they had decided to do another show immediately following the first to accommodate the regular Park patrons. But as the concert was scheduled to begin at half past six (it was already after seven) and the Park closed at eight, it began to look like the performances would both have to be quite brief!

The seats saved for us were third row center, and we found ourselves rubbing elbows with Trio family members: Catherine Guard, Buffy Ford Stewart, Linda Reynolds and youngsters. The place was filled to capacity by the time Supervising and Executive Producer Chuck Simon came out to instruct everyone to please remain seated during the taping and to refrain from taking flash photos. After testing several sections of the audience for applause noise levels, Chuck surrendered the stage to our host for the evening, comedian Tom Smothers.

After a few chuckles to warm up the crowd, Tom introduced the Kingston Trio: Bob Shane, Roger Gambill and George Grove. George had five years in the Trio under his belt, Roger had eight and Bob had them all. They looked great and sounded even better as they launched into *Three Jolly Coachmen* and *Early Morning Rain,* tunes from 1958 and 1965, respectively. On a projection screen at the rear of the stage the first of many slides of album covers and group photos were being presented. The boys were warmly received by a most appreciative audience, but the director came out yelling "stop

Nick, Bob and Dave rehearse for "The Kingston Trio and Friends Reunion". Photo by Henry Diltz.

John, Nick and Bob rehearse for "The Kingston Trio & Friends Reunion". Photo by Henry Diltz.

tape!'' There had been a buzzing noise captured on the soundtrack and the two songs would have to be performed again. The Trio obliged, and we all loved it even more the second time. He emerged again to say they still didn't get an acceptable tape of *Coachmen,* and at this point Bob looked up into the sound booth and said "Whoever you are up there, get it right this time or go fish, and I mean it."

After a perfect third rendition of *Jolly,* the group introduced a new tune, *Looking For The Sunshine.* Then Bob finished the set with another fine performance of his hallmark, *Scotch And Soda,* and the Trio exited to rousing applause. This was the first time I had seen them perform in person, and I was pleasantly surprised at just how professional and *good* they were. Roger came across with a fine, robust voice and pleasing personality, and George lived up to reports that he was perhaps the finest instrumentalist that had ever graced the group. And though his voice had taken on a rough timbre that balanced the silver in his hair, Bob Shane was still Bob Shane.

As we stared at a darkened stage for several quiet moments, we were again reminded of the fact that we were witnessing the making of a television show and not a regular concert. Los Angeles' KCET-TV (a Public Broadcasting Service affiliate), New York's Camera 3 Productions and California's One Up Productions were combining forces and resources (underwritten by a grant from Atlantic Richfield Corporation) to produce a special titled "Kingston Trio And Friends: Reunion". We had no doubt that when it finally aired over the PBS-TV Network (sometime in the "Pledge Drive" period from February 21st to March 6th, 1982) all the bugs would be edited out and only the highlights would remain.

It was about eight when a spotlight shone once more on Tom Smothers, as he introduced — "playing together for the first time in twenty years" — Dave Guard, Nick Reynolds and Bob Shane, the original Kingston Trio. It was questionable for a moment or two whether or not the audience was going to let them perform, so deafening and unabating was the applause. They stood there and waited for the crowd to clap away the years: Bob, stoicly center stage; Dave, grinning ear-to-ear and not having aged a day; Nick, with non-Trio mustache and thinning hair, looking just a bit nervous and overwhelmed by it all. The rear screen held a shot of their first album.

At last they were allowed to begin with *Hard, Ain't It Hard,* and suddenly it was '58 or '59 all over again: Dave's driving five-string banjo, Bob's steady six-string guitar, and Nick's overgrown four-string ukelele, melded with that patented soaring harmony and raucous good humor. When they

finished the number on the applause meter went up another notch on the scale. The earphoned director made another stage appearance — something about a camera flash on Nick's glasses — and we were all treated to another round of the Woody Guthrie classic. At this point I was hoping they would do *everything* twice. History was being reaffirmed here this night, and that magic I had speculated about earlier was unleashing itself on that stage before our eyes and ears. About this time I noticed a gentleman watching the show very intently from the wings at stage right. It was John Stewart.

Tommy stepped out again to say a few words about the group's biggest record, and then they did it: *Tom Dooley.* And it didn't sound like a song we were all sick of hearing, that they had slogged through countless times; it sounded real, and alive. It was shocking to discover Bob playing the banjo on this one, after assuming all these years it was Dave. When the crowd finally calmed itself after that one, Dave took the liberty of introducing some of the celebrities in the audience — Mike Settle of the First Edition, Alex Hassilev and Lou Gottlieb of the Limeliters, Larry Ramos of the Association, and Dick Smothers. Dave then delivered one of his droll song intros, much to the delight of everyone. I can't remember a word he said, but I loved every minute of it.

In the meantime, Nick had shed his uke and rolled his tall conga drum into place near the microphone. When Dave had finished, they took off with *Zombie Jamboree* and never came down. It was Dave's song all the way, just like in the old days, and he was enjoying every minute of it. The audience response was deafening as they turned to exit, but I could just manage to hear John shouting "sneak in a couple more, Dave!" He was applauding just as hard as we were. Twenty years was a long time to wait, but it had been worth it.

As the hour grew later on Magic Mountain and the temperature plummeted, the chances of getting in a second show disappeared, and anyone outside the amphitheatre had long since departed when the Amusement Park shut down for the night. We again warmed our hands by applauding as Bob, Roger and George reclaimed the stage. Bob introduced Mary Travers, and they all sang a Pete Seeger song the Trio had lifted from Peter, Paul & Mary almost twenty years earlier, *Where Have All The Flowers Gone.* George remained to accompany Mary on two John Denver compositions, *Leaving On A Jet Plane* and *Rhymes And Reasons.* She left the stage to enthusiastic applause.

Mr. Smothers then introduced "the second generation of the Kingston Trio" — Nick Reynolds, Bob Shane and John Stewart. Although their performance wasn't quite as well polished as that of the evening's other Trios, it was every bit as enthusiastic and well received. John attacked the banjo as they began their set with the rousing *Reuben James,* one of the first songs they recorded in 1961. They had not been on a stage together in over fourteen years, but they still sounded great (although John cursed himself for a couple of mistakes on the banjo). John introduced the striped-shirted bass player at stage left who turned out to be Trio fanatic Lindsey Buckingham from the supergroup Fleetwood Mac. They then performed their classic *Chilly Winds,* reminding everyone what a fine way with a ballad the second Trio always had. About halfway through the song Tom Smothers strolled out with his guitar and joined in. Then Nick, Bob and John closed out their part of the show with one of their biggest hits, *Greenback Dollar.* They exited to shouts of "more, more!"

A brief intermission gave us an opportunity to rest our hands and stretch our legs. Soon a small band took their places on stage and struck up a rock/jazz instrumental. It went on for several minutes, and in the background we could make out Dave Guard and Lindsey Buckingham dancing together behind one of the curtains. Then John Stewart reappeared with electric guitar and two young ladies, and they all turned in a rocking performance of his 1979 smash *Gold.* Tom then came

out and officially introduced John's performance, and John then introduced his back-up group, the Jukebox Commandoes. He dedicated the next song to Dave, Nick and Bob — one of his best from 1973's THE PHOENIX CONCERTS album, *Kansas.* Then, with a shot of his popular album BOMBS AWAY DREAM BABIES on the screen, John introduced the man who had helped him make it a reality, Lindsey Buckingham. They performed an exciting version of that album's acoustical duet, *The Spinnin' Of The World,* which John pointed out was originally featured on the Trio's last studio album in 1966. They left the stage to warm applause.

Bob, Roger and George returned to the stage after a short break in the program, and they turned in a spirited rendition of *I'm Going Home.* They then performed an enchanting ballad they had yet to record titled *Hawaiian Nights* and then broke a string or two on the robust Trio standard *Hard Travelin'.* Bob then brought Dave, Nick and John back on stage and all six of them wowed the capacity crowd with *Sloop John B.* Despite instructions to the contrary, it was standing ovation time at Magic Mountain for a full five minutes. Next up was *A Worried Man,* with a quick change of instruments and positions we were treated to the once-in-a-lifetime sight of Dave, John and George all playing banjos together at the microphone at

Nick, Bob and John rehearse "Reuben James" for "The Kingston Trio & Friends Reunion" show.

Rehearsal for the finale of "The Kingston Trio & Friends Reunion" show. Left to right: Roger, Nick, Tommy Smothers, Mary Travers, Bob, Dave, George and John.

stage right. Nick and Roger worked from stage left and Bob held center as they enjoyed another standing ovation and then let loose with *M.T.A.*, with Nick and Roger trading verses. Bob called Mary and Tom out to join in halfway through the song, and Lindsey and the Commandoes also reappeared. It was a rousing finish to a great evening of entertainment, and everyone on stage seemed honestly overwhelmed by the warm and loving reaction of the audience. They all took a bow and left the stage, and we clapped and cheered until it became obvious they were not coming back for an encore.

It was half past ten on Magic Mountain as we made our way to the wrap party at Timbermill Restaurant next door, where we met and congratulated our heroes, and then joined them in laughing at old tapes of early Trio appearances on various TV shows of the Fifties and Sixties. Bob told us he was enthusiastic about the way the evening went, and he felt that if the PBS broadcast stirred enough interest he might consider taking the whole troupe on the road in the Spring. Nick was anxious to get his family back to Oregon but said he would like to make a Reunion album or get together like this again if anyone was interested.

Dave and John sat together downstairs staring at the ancient videotapes until Saturday became Sunday on Magic Mountain.

The finale of "The Kingston Trio & Friends Reunion" show.

(A NIGHT ON MAGIC MOUNTAIN is reprinted with permission from *Omaha Rainbow* #29.)

The Kingston Trio: Their Instruments

By William J. Bush

Perhaps no other group in the history of American music has done more to popularize the acoustic guitar and 5-string banjo than the Kingston Trio. In the original Trio, as with all the Trios to follow, the Martin guitar remained the staple instrument for concerts and recording.

Bob Shane's first instrument was a Martin ukulele, graduating to a Sears Silvertone 4-string tenor guitar sold to him by George Archer, a popular writer of Tahitian music. Although Shane is pictured holding a Martin 000-28 on the cover of the Trio's first album, he never owned or played one with the group. His main instrument was the Martin D-28, the first of which he purchased from Bergstrom Music in Honolulu for $180 in 1956. All other D-28s, and there were many ("If I broke a guitar, we'd give it away in radio station contests," he says), were purchased from Harmon Satterlee of Satterlee-Chapin Music in San Francisco and Sid Hiller of Columbia Music, also in San Francisco.

In 1963, Harmon Satterlee, who did virtually all the repair work on the Trio's instruments, affixed two large, black pickguards to one of Shane's original D-28s, making it a Shane trademark of sorts among Trio fans. When asked what was the idea behind the procedure, Bob laughingly says "a lot of scarred wood." Shane had picked up the idea from Stan Wilson, another San Francisco folk singer (who had picked it up from Josh White), as a way of preventing a complete wearing through of the top through heavy usage.

Satterlee was also to build a custom 12-string guitar for Shane featuring a large Guild-like body, wide neck, and a mother-of-pearl bat with ruby eyes. This guitar, which Shane refers to as "The Bat Wing Guitar", is owned by a private collector in San Francisco; his original D-28 with the wide pickguards is owned by his brother-in-law.

In 1966, Shane purchased one of the first Martin D-35's, an instrument virtually identical in size to the D-28, but featuring a 3-piece back, bound fingerboard and extra wide body binding. Shane's D-35 was one of the few to feature pearl-button Grover Rotomatic tuning machines.

Bob played this guitar until the group disbanded in 1967. Throughout most of the years of the first two Trios, Shane used heavy gauge D'Angelico bronze strings. He also played a Vega "Folklore" long-neck, 5-string banjo in the Trio.

Nick Reynolds was also raised in the Martin tradition, owning Martin ukuleles from childhood. "Martin was **the** ukulele," says Reynolds. "In my family, it was the epitome, and they were pretty serious players. My father always had Martin guitars, old ones; in fact he had an old New York Martin (pre-1898 vintage) that I still have. In the Trio, we considered Martins to be real tough workhorses, like the Porsche; they just don't break down. And the way we used to beat 'em and thrash 'em, there was no delicacy involved."

"Reynolds first played a Martin 0-17T mahogany-bodied (top, back & sides) tenor guitar in the Trio, which was then replaced by a 2-18T tenor purchased from Harmon Satterlee. This guitar, serial #38023, was built in 1929 and was used by Reynolds on many of the early Trio albums.

In 1961, Reynolds had it converted to an 8-string tenor model by Harmon Satterlee who replaced the neck, removed the pickguard and refinished the body. Beginning in 1959, Reynolds added a Martin 0-18T to his road and recording instrument collection, although he continued to use the 2-18T occasionally. Nick presently has two 0-18Ts, one of which has also been converted to an 8-string model; the other, serial #191378 (1963) remains stock with the exception of Grover Rotomatic machines. Reynolds used a thick felt ukulele pick for playing the 4-string tenor, and a flexible plastic pick for the 8-string. Nick also played bongos, conga, and "boo-bams", a series of tuned, cylindrical plastic tubes of varying lengths designed by David "Buck" Wheat, the Trio's bassist. (Nick's drum solo on *O Ken Karanga* from the Trio's CLOSE-UP and COLLEGE CONCERT albums is played on Wheat's "boo-bams".)

Dave Guard's first guitar was a Martin as well, a small mahogany-bodied 6-string model (most likely an 0-15 or 0-17 model) purchased when he was 16. For his guitar work in the Trio, Guard used a Martin 00-21. He also owned and played a Velasquez classical made for him in New York. While Guard is high in his praise for Martin ("nothing else came close"), he is equally quick to praise Gibson, owning both a Gibson 12-string guitar and a 5-string Mastertone banjo.

"We were playing on a show with the Everly Brothers," he recalls, "and I really liked those jumbo Gibsons they were playing (Gibson J-200s), so I asked Gibson to make me a jumbo 12-string, using the same body as the 6-string model the Everlys were playing. I think it's the first Gibson 12-string made because the neck was way off. I had Harmon Satterlee re-make the neck and it's been just a terrific guitar since then; you can play it 10 hours a day and it stays perfectly in tune."

On the first Kingston Trio album, Guard is pictured playing a Stewart banjo. This was given to him by Nick Reynolds' father, and remained Guard's recording and concert banjo until late 1958 when he purchased a Vega Pete Seeger Long Neck, 5-string model directly from the factory. Guard says the change to the Vega long neck was because he wanted to play in lower keys. When he first began playing banjo in the Trio, Guard used only a thumb pick and his fingers; he later switched to two metal finger picks. On guitar work he used both flat and thumb picks.

Like Dave Guard before him, John Stewart played a Martin 00-21, a Martin D-28, a Gibson 12-string (B-25) and a Vega Pete Seeger Long Neck 5-string banjo. In 1962, Stewart briefly switched to a Gibson RB-5 Long Neck Banjo ("I just wanted to try something different," he says, "it didn't cut nearly as well as the Vega"), switching back to the Vega as his main concert and recording banjo.

Bob, Dave and Nick in a posed publicity photo prominently showing their favorite concert and recording studio instruments. Bob is holding his Martin D-28 guitar, Dave his "Pete Seeger" model Vega long-neck 5-string banjo and Nick his Martin 0-18T Tenor guitar. Photo courtesy of the University of Wisconsin-Milwaukee.

Nick, John and Bob, in a posed publicity photo with their favorite concert and recording studio instruments. Nick is again holding a Martin 0-18T Tenor guitar, but note the Grover Rotomatic keys. John, like Dave Guard before him, used a "Pete Seeger" model Vega long-neck 5-string banjo. Bob is again holding his Martin D-28 guitar, but this time sporting the Harmon Satterlee pick-guards which gave the guitar its "bat-wing" nickname. Photo by Jay Thompson.

"The long neck Seeger banjos just looked *so great,*" John recalls, "and they sounded good and they cut, and they were just the good workhouse folk banjo. You could do Scruggs, frailing, the basic Pete Seeger double-thumbing strum. They were light, too, and had the extra three frets so you could play in an open F key. Such standbys! Martin was making the best guitars then, very durable, and they sounded terrific. The action was always off when you got a new one, so you had to take them in and have them adjusted, but other than that they were just fine. I played the 00-21 as a matter of EQ. Bobby played that big dreadnaught D-28, and in order to cut through Bobby's rhythm, my guitar had to have a different EQ; I would've gotten lost if I played a big guitar, too. The 00-21 was a *very* good finger picking guitar; it wasn't really suited for rhythm. I stuck with Martins up till the 70s and then switched to Ovations, which I play exclusively. (In the Trio) they (Ovation) brought us the first Ovation made and it was bad — tight, stiff; but they were nice people and wanted to please. I stayed in touch with them and they kept

working on their guitars, and now I wouldn't play anything else."

In the later years of the Stewart Trio, John used a maple-bodied Guild 12-string guitar, as well as a custom classic made for him by a San Francisco luthier (which Stewart had converted into a guitar-dulcimer). John used light-gauge bronze strings and National fingerpicks exclusively.

With the formation of the New Kingston Trio in 1969, the instrumental format of the Trio changed to include drums and electric bass. Shane and Pat Horine continued to play acoustic guitars, Martin D-35's, and Jim Connor played a Vega Pete Seeger Long Neck 5-string banjo. Bob Shane has owned and played many guitars over the years since 1967, and it is difficult to document all of them.

The third Kingston Trio, which included George Grove and the late Roger Gambill, used the following instrumentation:

Bob Shane played a Martin D-37K2, a guitar identical in size to the D-28, but featuring flamed Hawaiian Koa wood top, back and sides. Bob also owns a Martin D-37K, which features a spruce top, abalone inlay around the sound-hole, and Koa wood back and sides. In addition, he owns a Mossman D-size guitar with custom inlay work and an Aria Pro II Dreadnaught a Japanese copy of the Martin D-28, but with "Tree of Life" pearl inlay on the fingerboard.

George Grove, the Trio's major instrumentalist plays 3 Gibson Mastertone 5-string banjos (2 RB-800s & 1 RB-250), 4 Martin guitars (1978 D-45, 1965 D-28, 1955 D-18, 1962 00-21), a 1974 Guild F5-12 12-string, and an Aria Pro II with custom sunburst finish.

Roger Gambill played a Martin D-25K, a koa-bodied (spruce top) "miniature dreadnaught" guitar.

It is interesting to note that despite the enormous visibility given Martin guitars by the Trio in its 30-year history, none of the Trio members were ever given complimentary guitars by the company or asked to endorse Martin in any manner.

"We owe those boys a lot," says Mike Longworth, Martin's Consumer Relations Manager, "and I know that people around here are especially proud that the Trio played our guitars because they *wanted* to; they were never given guitars or asked to endorse Martin, which makes it all that much more special."

The New Kingston Trio, circa 1970. Left to right: Pat Horine, Jim Connor and Bob Shane. Pat and Bob are both holding Martin D-35s, while Jim Connor is holding his "Pete Seeger" model Vega long-neck 5-string banjo. This is rather unusual as later pictures of Jim usually showed him playing a short-neck banjo as did Bill Zorn and George Grove who followed him. Photo from the collection of Maureen Wilson.

The Kingston Trio: A Discography

by
Benjamin Blake,
Jack Rubeck
and Allan Shaw

Introductory note: What follows is a comprehensive listing of all known U.S.A. disc appearances by the Kingston Trio. We have also attempted to include as many foreign releases as possible, especially in cases where the content differs from domestic versions. Where a variation exists (different title, number, cover, etc.) on a non-U.S.A. release, but the *content* remains the same, we have elected *not* to include it in the listings. For example, World Record Club, the Music For Pleasure label, and just about all Japanese releases were given new covers, but none of the inside tracks were changed. To cut down on repetition, we have not listed these, although several are pictured where the photos are rare or unusual. There are undoubtedly many non-U.S.A. releases that we have no knowledge of; Japan, in particular, was noted for releasing a great many extra singles and collection LPs that we have very little accurate information about.

Many of the Capitol and Decca LPs were also issued on reel tapes. Several of the more recent releases were also issued on eight-track cartridges and/or four-track cassettes. We have listed tape releases only in those instances where they are in some way unique.

Tom Dooley, M.T.A. and *A Worried Man* (and possibly others) were released on 78 r.p.m. records in Canada and possibly in some other countries. The numbers and B sides were the same as the American 45s, so we have not included a special "78" section.

By dividing the Discography into several sections, we hope we have made the going a bit easier for the general Trio fan. Only those who are so inclined need delve into the sections regarding radio station promos and the group's appearances on "various artists" collections.

There have been many times over the past few years when we thought this listing was "complete", only to have a formerly unknown item crop up. We welcome any and all additions and corrections.

Section One: Domestic Long Play (LP) Album releases

(12 inch, 33⅓ r.p.m. records, original issues only; for re-issues and collections see Section Two)

1. THE KINGSTON TRIO, Capitol T 996, released June 1958
2. . . . FROM THE "HUNGRY i", Capitol T 1107, January 1959
3. STEREO CONCERT, Capitol ST 1183, March 1959
4. THE KINGSTON TRIO AT LARGE, Capitol T/ST 1199, June 1959
5. HERE WE GO AGAIN, Capitol T/ST 1258, October 1959
6. SOLD OUT, Capitol T/ST 1352, April 1960
7. STRING ALONG, Capitol T/ST 1407, July 1960
8. THE LAST MONTH OF THE YEAR, Capitol T/ST 1446, October 1960
9. MAKE WAY, Capitol T/ST 1474, January 1961
10. GOIN' PLACES, Capitol T/ST 1564, June 1961
11. CLOSE-UP, Capitol T/ST 1642, October 1961
12. COLLEGE CONCERT, Capitol T/ST 1658, February 1962
13. SOMETHING SPECIAL, Capitol T/ST 1747, July 1962
14. NEW FRONTIER, Capitol T/ST 1809, November 1962
15. #16, Capitol T/ST 1871, March 1963
16. SUNNY SIDE, Capitol T/ST 1935, July 1963
17. TIME TO THINK, Capitol T/ST 2011, December 1963
18. BACK IN TOWN, Capitol T/ST 2081, June 1964
19. THE KINGSTON TRIO: NICK-BOB-JOHN, Decca DL4613/74613, December 1964
20. STAY AWHILE, Decca DL4656/74656, May 1965

21. SOMETHIN' ELSE, Decca DL4694/74694, November 1965
22. CHILDREN OF THE MORNING, Decca DL4758/74758, May 1966
23. ONCE UPON A TIME, Tetragrammaton TD-5101, June 1969 (2-record set)
24. THE WORLD NEEDS A MELODY, Longines Symphonette SYS 5607, April 1973 (New KT)
25. ASPEN GOLD, Nautilus NR-2, May 1979 (a digital recording)
26. 25 YEARS NON-STOP, Xeres SCH 1-10001, January 1982
27. LOOKING FOR THE SUNSHINE, Xeres SCH 1-10006, April 1983
28. REDISCOVER, Folk Era FE 2001, August 1985 (previously unreleased 1958-63 Capitol tracks)

Section One-A: Foreign LP Releases (original issues)

1. THE NEW KINGSTON TRIO, Birdree PLS-107, 1970, Japan

Section Two: Domestic LPs & Cassettes — Re-issues & Collections

1. ENCORES, Capitol DT 1612, July 1961 (re-channeled selections from Capitol T 996 and T 1107)
2. THE BEST OF THE KINGSTON TRIO, Capitol T/ST 1705, May 1962
3. SING A SONG WITH THE KINGSTON TRIO, Capitol KAO/SKAO 2005, December 1963 (instrumental versions of Trio tunes played by Frank Hamilton)
4. THE FOLK ERA, Capitol TCL/STCL 2180, October 1964 (3-record set)
5. THE BEST OF THE KINGSTON TRIO VOLUME 2, Capitol T/ST 2280, February 1965
6. BEST OF THE KINGSTON TRIO VOL. 3, Capitol T/ST 2614 (later changed to SM 2614), November 1966
7. THE KINGSTON TRIO, Capitol DT996, 1969 (re-channeled Capitol T 996)
8. TOM DOOLEY, Capitol DF-514 (later changed to N-16185), July 1970 (edited re-issue of Capitol DT 996)
9. SCARLET RIBBONS, Capitol SF-515 (later changed to SN-16186), July 1970 (edited re-issue of Captiol ST 1199)
10. TOM DOOLEY, Pickwick/33 SPC-3260, January 1971 (re-issues from Capitol)
11. THE BEST OF THE KINGSTON TRIO, Capitol ST 1705 (later changed to SM 1705 and SN-16138), November 1971 (edited re-issue of *original* Capitol ST 1705)
12. THE BEST OF THE KINGSTON TRIO VOLUME 2, Capitol ST 2280 (later changed to SM 2280 and SN-16184), November 1971 (edited re-issue of *original* Capitol ST 2280)

13. THE PATRIOT GAME, Pickwick/33 SPC-3297, February 1972 (re-issues from Capitol)
14. WHERE HAVE ALL THE FLOWERS GONE, Pickwick/33 SPC-3323, September 1972 (re-issues from Capitol)
15. AMERICAN GOLD, Longines Symphonette SYS 5569-5574, April 1973 (re-issues from Capitol; 6-record set)
16. THE HISTORIC RECORDINGS OF THE KINGSTON TRIO, Candlelite Music/Capitol SLB-6971, 1975 (re-issues from Capitol; 2-record set)
17. . . . FROM THE "HUNGRY i", Capitol M-11968, July 1979 (re-issue of T 1107)
18. ASPEN GOLD, 51 West Q16116 (later changed to P18116), May 1981 (non-digital re-issue of Nautilus NR-2)
19. IN CONCERT, Stack-O-Hits AG 9031, 1981 (edited re-issue of record 1 of Tetragrammaton TD-5101)
20. GOIN' PLACES, Mobile Fidelity MFSL C-046, April 1984 (Original Master Recording high fidelity *cassette* re-issue of Capitol ST 1564)
21. WE CAME TO SING, Capitol Special Markets 4XL-9026, May 1984 (*cassette;* re-issues from Capitol)
22. EARLY AMERICAN HEROES, Pair PDL 2-1067 (Capitol Special Markets PLB-72057), 1984 (re-issues from Capitol; 2-record set)
23. THE KINGSTON TRIO, Romulus R-6053, (year unknown) (edited re-issue of Tetragrammaton TD-5105)
24. THE TIJUANA JAIL AND OTHER HITS, Capitol Special Markets 4XL-9176, May 1985 (*cassette;* re-issues from Capitol)
25. SOME OF OUR FAVORITES, Capitol Special Markets 4XL-9208, May 1985 (*cassette;* re-issues from Capitol)
26. MORE GREAT HITS, Star SC-1090 (Capitol Special Markets 4XL-9251), May 1985 (*cassette* identical to #24; re-issues from Capitol)

Section Three: Foreign LPs — Collections

1. A TRIBUTE TO THE KINGSTON TRIO, Capitol/EMI T/ST 20922, 1967, Europe
2. WHERE HAVE ALL THE FLOWERS GONE, Capitol CP-7077 (year unknown), Japan
3. POPULAR SUPER GOLD 2000-BEST OF THE KINGSTON TRIO, Capitol ECS-60015, (year unknown), Japan
4. HITS OF THE KINGSTON TRIO, Liming LN-2020, (year unknown), Taiwan (re-issues from Capitol)
5. BEST OF THE KINGSTON TRIO, VOL. 1, Song Jwu SAL-7029, (year unknown), Taiwan (re-issues from Capitol)

6. BEST OF THE KINGSTON TRIO, VOL. 2, Song Jwu SAL-7030, (year unknown), Taiwan (re-issues from Capitol)

7. SEASONS IN THE SUN, Capitol/EMI OU 2040, (year unknown) Europe

8. MIDNIGHT SPECIAL, MCA/Coral 6848, 1973, Europe (re-issues from Decca)

9. 1958-1963 THE GOLDEN YEARS, TeeVee/Capitol Of Canada SLB-6971, 1975, Canada

   (2-record set; same as Candelite collection in Section Two)

10. THE BEST OF JOHN STEWART WITH THE KINGSTON TRIO, Australian World Record Club, WRC.R.02377, 1975, Australia (re-issues from Capitol)

11. LA GRANDE STORIA DEL ROCK (LEGENDS OF ROCK) #67: THE KINGSTON TRIO, Curcio/Valentine, R/MC-67, 1983, Italy (edited re-issue of record 2 of Tetragrammaton TD-5101, plus three 1978 K-Tel tracks)

12. TOM DOOLEY, Astan F40116, (year unknown), Germany (edited re-issue of record 2 of Tetragrammaton TD-5101)

Section Four: Domestic Singles

(7-inch, 45 r.p.m. records, original issues only; for re-issues and promotional 45s see Section Five; European release numbers — where known — are listed in parentheses)

1. *Scarlet Ribbons/Three Jolly Coachmen,* Capitol F3970 (CL14918), May 1958

2. *Tom Dooley/Ruby Red,* Capitol F4049 (CL14951), September 1958

3. *Raspberries, Strawberries/Sally,* Capitol F4114 (CL14985), December 1958

4. *The Tijuana Jail/Oh, Cindy,* Capitol F4167 (CL15002), March 1959

5. *M.T.A./All My Sorrows,* Capitol F4221 (CL15040), June 1959

6. *A Worried Man/San Miguel,* Capitol 4271 (CL15073), September 1959

7. *Coo Coo-U/Green Grasses,* Capitol 4303 (CL15113), November 1959

8. *El Matador/Home From The Hill,* Capitol 4338 (CL15119), January 1960

9. *Bad Man Blunder/The Escape Of Old John Webb,* Capitol 4379 (CL15138), May 1960

10. *Everglades/This Mornin', This Evenin', So Soon,* Capitol 4441 (CL15161), September 1960

11. *Somerset Gloustershire Wassail/Goodnight My Baby,* Capitol 4475, November 1960

12. *You're Gonna Miss Me/En El Agua,* Capitol 4536, March 1961

13. *Coming From The Mountains/Nothing More To Look Forward To,* Capitol 4642, October 1961

14. *Where Have All The Flowers Gone/O Ken Karanga,* Capitol 4671 (CL15242), December 1961

15. *Scotch And Soda/Jane, Jane, Jane,* Capitol 4740, April 1962

16. *C'Mon Betty Home/Old Joe Clark,* Capitol 4808, July 1962

17. *One More Town/She Was Too Good To Me,* Capitol 4842, September 1962

18. *Greenback Dollar/The New Frontier,* Capitol 4898 (CL15287), December 1962

19. *Reverend Mr. Black/One More Round,* Capitol 4951 (CL15298), April 1963

20. *Desert Pete/Ballad Of The Thresher,* Capitol 5005 (CL15318), July 1963
21. *Ally Ally Oxen Free/Marcelle Vahine,* Capitol 5078 (CL15327), November 1963
22. *Last Night I Had The Strangest Dream/The Patriot Game,* Capitol 5132 (CL15341), February 1964
23. *Seasons In The Sun/If You Don't Look Around,* Capitol 5166 (CL15355), April 1964
24. *My Rambling Boy/Hope You Understand,* Decca 31702, November 1964

25. *I'm Going Home/Little Play Soldiers,* Decca 31730, January 1965
26. *Yes I Can Feel It/Stay Awhile,* Decca 31790, June 1965
27. *Parchment Farm Blues/Runaway Song,* Decca 31860, November 1965
28. *Norwegian Wood/Put Your Money Away,* Decca 31922, March 1966
29. *The Spinnin' Of The World/A Little Soul Is Born,* Decca 31961, May 1966
30. *Lock All The Windows/Hit And Run,* Decca 32010, September 1966
31. *Texas Across The River/Babe, You've Been On My Mind,* Decca 32040, October 1966
32. *One Too Many Mornings/Scotch And Soda,* Tetragrammaton T-1526, July 1969
33. *Tell The Riverboat Captain/Windy Wakefield,* Capitol 3149, July 1971 (New KT)
34. *Looking For The Sunshine/Reverend Mr. Black,* Xeres SCH 1-10004, July 1982

Section Five: Domestic Singles — Re-issues & Promotional

1. *The Merry Minuet/Tic, Tic, Tic,* Capitol PRO 856, 1959 (radio station promo)
2. *Molly Dee/Haul Away,* Capitol Custom JB 2782/2783, 1959 (March Of Dimes promo)

3. *A Worried Man/*(B side by Sonny James), USAF 79/80, 1959 (Air Force radio public service promo)
4. *El Matador/*(B side by Dinah Shore), USAF 103/104, 1960 (Air Force radio public service promo)
5. *Farewell Adelita/Corey, Corey,* Capitol Custom WLP-2006/NLB-2007, 1960 (promo for menswear lines)
6. *Everglades/*(B side by Four Preps), USAF 129/130, 1960 (Air Force radio public service promo)
7. *Tom Dooley/M.T.A.,* Capitol Star Line 4514, February 1961 (re-issue)
8. *Tom Dooley/M.T.A.,* Capitol Star Line 6002, January 1962 (re-issue)
9. *A Worried Man/Scotch And Soda,* Capitol Star Line 6046, April 1964 (re-issue)
10. *Greenback Dollar/Reverend Mr. Black,* Capitol Star Line 6071, August 1965 (re-issue)
11. *Big Ship Glory/Johnson Party Of 4,* Mountain Creek MCR 301/302, September 1977 (radio station promo)
12. *Aspen Gold/Longest Beer Of The Night,* Nautilus NR2-45, May 1979 (a digital recording; radio station promo)

Section Six: Foreign Singles

1. *Rollin' Stone/Across The Wide Missouri,* Capitol 7P-183, 1959 (Japan)
2. *En El Agua/Como Se Viene, Se Va,* Capitol CL15192, 1960 (Europe)
3. *Bye Bye Thou Little Tiny Child/The White Snows Of Winter,* Capitol CL15228, 1960 (Europe)
4. *Rocky/Old Kentucky Land,* Capitol K 22442, 1961 (Germany)
5. *Where Have All The Flowers Gone/En El Agua,* Capitol 7P-259, 1961 (Japan)
6. *500 Miles/Oh, Sail Away,* Capitol CL15275, 1962 (Europe)
7. *Chilly Winds/Roddy McCorley,* Capitol CL15367, 1962 (Europe)
8. *500 Miles/500 Miles instrumental,* Capitol CR-1137, year unknown (Japan)
9. *Chilly Winds/Portland Town,* Capitol CR-1602, year unknown (Japan)
10. *Last Night I Had The Strangest Dream/Two-Ten, Six-Eighteen,* Capitol 4F193, 1964 (Europe)
11. *Runaway Song/Red River Shore,* Decca DS-422, 1965 (Japan)
12. *Tom Dooley/Where Have All The Flowers Gone,* Rebound RB238, year unknown (Canada)

Section Seven: Domestic Extended Play (EP) Albums

(7-inch, 45 r.p.m. records; for promotional EPs see Section Eight)

1. *The Kingston Trio*, Capitol EAP1-996, June 1958
   Three Jolly Coachmen/Sloop John B/Bay Of Mexico/Saro Jane
2. *M.T.A.*, Capitol EAP1-1119, July 1959
   M.T.A./Como Se Viene, Se Va/All My Sorrows/Sail Away Ladies
3. *Tijuana Jail*, Capitol SEP1-1129 (stereo), April 1959
   The Tijuana Jail/Oh Cindy/Coplas/Tom Dooley
4. *Tom Dooley*, Capitol EAP1-1136, October 1958
   Tom Dooley/Coplas/Banua/Santy Anno
5. *Raspberries, Strawberries*, Capitol EAP1-1182, February 1959
   Raspberries, Strawberries/Ruby Red/Sally/Scarlet Ribbons
6. *The Kingston Trio At Large, Part 1*, Capitol EAP1-1199, June 1959
   M.T.A./All My Sorrows/Scarlet Ribbons/Remember The Alamo
7. *The Kingston Trio At Large, Part 2*, Capitol EAP2-1199, June 1959
   Blow Ye Winds/Corey, Corey/The Long Black Rifle/Early In The Mornin'
8. *The Kingston Trio At Large, Part 3*, Capitol EAP3-1199, June 1959
   The Seine/I Bawled/Good News/Getaway John
9. *Here We Go Again, Part 1*, Capitol EAP1-1258, October 1959
   Molly Dee/Across The Wide Missouri/Goober Peas/A Worried Man
10. *Here We Go Again, Part 2*, Capitol EAP2-1258, October 1959
    Haul Away/The Wanderer/E Inu Tatou E/Rollin' Stone
11. *Here We Go Again, Part 3*, Capitol EAP3-1258, October 1959
    'Round About The Mountain/Oleanna/The Unfortunate Miss Bailey/San Miguel
12. *A Worried Man*, Capitol EAP1-1322, March 1960
    A Worried Man/Molly Dee/San Miguel/Oleanna
13. *Sold Out, Part 1*, Capitol EAP1-1352, April 1960
    El Matador/The Mountains O'Mourne/The Hunter/Farewell Adelita
14. *Sold Out, Part 2*, Capitol EAP2-1352, April 1960
    Don't Cry Katie/Tanga Tika; Toerau/Mangwani Mpulele/With You My Johnny
15. *Sold Out, Part 3*, Capitol EAP3-1352, April 1960
    With Her Head Tucked Underneath Her Arm/Carrier Pigeon/Bimini/Raspberries, Strawberries
16. *String Along, Part 1*, Capitol EAP1-1407, July 1960
    Bad Man Blunder/The Escape Of Old John Webb/Colorado Trail/The Tattooed Lady

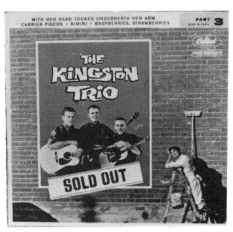

20. *The Last Month Of The Year, Part 2,* Capitol
    EAP2-1446, October 1960
    *We Wish You A Merry Christmas/All Through
    The Night/Mary Mild/A Round About
    Christmas*
21. *The Last Month Of The Year, Part 3,* Capitol
    EAP3-1446, October 1960
    *Goodnight My Baby/Go Where I Send
    Thee/Follow Now, Oh Shepherds/Somerset
    Glucestershire Wassail*

17. *String Along, Part 2,* Capitol EAP2-1407, July
    1960
    *When I Was Young/Leave My Woman
    Alone/Who's Gonna Hold Her Hand/To Morrow*
18. *String Along, Part 3,* Capitol EAP3-1407, July
    1960
    *This Mornin', This Evenin', So
    Soon/Everglades/Buddy Better Get On Down
    The Line/South Wind*
19. *The Last Month Of The Year, Part 1,* Capitol
    EAP1-1446, October 1960
    *Bye Bye Thou Little Tiny Child/The White
    Snows Of Winter/Sing We Noel/The Last
    Month Of The Year*

22. *Make Way, Part 1,* Capitol EAP1-1474, January 1961
    En El Agua/Come All You Fair And Tender Ladies/Blow The Candle Out/Blue Eyed Gal
23. *Make Way, Part 2,* Capitol EAP2-1474, January 1961
    The Jug Of Punch/Bonny Hielan' Laddie/The River Is Wide/Oh, Yes, Oh
24. *Make Way, Part 3,* Capitol EAP3-1474, January 1961
    Utawena/Hard Travelin'/Hangman/Speckled Roan
25. Close-Up, Part 1, Capitol EAP1-1642, October 1961
    Coming From The Mountains/Oh, Sail Away/Weeping Willow/Reuben James
26. *Close-Up Part 2,* Capitol EAP2-1642, October 1961
    Take Her Out Of Pity/Don't You Weep, Mary/When My Love Was Here/Karu
27. *Close-Up, Part 3,* Capitol EAP3-1642, October 1961
    The Whistling Gypsy/O Ken Karanga/Jesse James/Glorious Kingdom

Section Eight: Domestic EPs · Promotional

1. *Selections From The Kingston Trio's Three Hit Albums,* Capitol PRO 1211/1212, 1959 (radio station promo)
   M.T.A./The Long Black Rifle/Tic, Tic, Tic/Bay Of Mexico
2. *Cool Cargo,* Capitol Custom NKB-2670/2671, 1960 (promo for 7-Up)
   Tom Dooley/A Worried Man/The Hunter/With You My Johnny
3. *Minute Masters,* Capitol (number unknown), 1960 (radio station promo; various artists)
   Don't Cry Katie
4. *Kingston Trio: New Frontier/Frank Sinatra: Sings Rodgers & Hart,* Capitol PRO 2230, 1962 (record/appliance store promo)
   The New Frontier/Some Fool Made A Soldier Of Me
5. *From Time To Think,* Capitol PRO 2529/2530, 1963 (radio station promo)
   Coal Tattoo/Seasons In The Sun/If You Don't Look Around/Last Night I Had The Strangest Dream

Section Nine: Foreign EPs

1. *Where Have All The Flowers Gone,* Capitol EAP1-20358, year unknown (France)
   Where Have All The Flowers Gone/Razors In The Air/O Ken Karanga/You Don't Knock
2. no title, Capitol EAP 20386, year unknown (Europe)
   Where Have All The Flowers Gone/O Ken Karanga/Jane, Jane, Jane/Scotch And Soda
3. no title, Capitol EAP 20412, year unknown (Europe)
   C'Mon Betty Home/Old Joe Clark/One More Town/She Was Too Good To Me
4. *Greenback Dollar,* Capitol EAP1-20460, 1963 (Europe)
   Greenback Dollar/Where Have All The Flowers Gone/One More Town/Little Boy
5. no title, Capitol EAP 20477, year unknown (Europe)
   Greenback Dollar/The New Frontier/Jesse James/500 Miles
6. *Biggest Hits,* Capitol EAP 20592, year unknown (Europe)
   Where Have All The Flowers Gone/Greenback Dollar/Tom Dooley/La Bamba
7. no title, Capitol EAP 20595, year unknown (Europe)
   Try To Remember/Bad Man Blunder/One More Town/Lemon Tree
8. *Lemon Tree,* Capitol EAP1-20655, year unknown (Europe)
   Lemon Tree/It Was A Very Good Year/Take Her Out Of Pity/Scotch And Soda
9. *Time To Think,* Capitol EAP4-2011, 1964, (Europe)
   Turn Around/Deportee/Hobo's Lullaby/Coal Tattoo
10. *The Kingston Trio,* Brunswick OE 9511, 1964 (Europe)
    I'm Going Home/Farewell/My Ramblin' Boy/Little Play Soldiers
11. *Parchment Farm Blues + 3,* Decca 60007, year unknown (France)
    contents unknown

Section Ten: Domestic "Compact 33" Singles
(7-inch, 33⅓ r.p.m. stereo records; Sets of these records were accompanied by juke box title strips and, in the case of NEW FRONTIER, mini pictures of the LP cover, indicating that these records were produced for juke box play rather than retail sale.)

1. *When I Was Young/Leave My Woman Alone,* Capitol X1-1407, July 1960
2. *This Mornin', This Evenin', So Soon/Everglades,* Capitol X2-1407, July 1960
3. *Buddy Better Get On Down The Line/South Wind,* Capitol X3-1407, July 1960
4. *Who's Gonna Hold Her Hand/To Morrow,* Capitol X4-1407, July 1960
5. *Colorado Trail/The Tattooed Lady,* Capitol X5-1407, July 1960
6. *We Wish You A Merry Christmas/The Last Month Of The Year,* Capitol XE1-1446, October 1960
7. *Sing We Noel/Go Where I Send Thee,* Capitol XE2-1446, October 1960
8. *The White Snows Of Winter/All Through The Night,* Capitol XE3-1446, October 1960
9. *Follow Now, Oh Shepherds/Somerset Gloucestershire Wassail,* Capitol XE4-1446, October 1960
10. *Bye Bye Thou Little Tiny Child/Mary Mild,* Capitol XE5-1446, October 1960
11. *Some Fool Made A Soldier Of Me/To Be Redeemed,* Capitol SXE-1-1809, March 1963
12. *Honey, Are You Mad At Your Man/Adios Farewell,* Capitol SXE-2-1809, March 1963
13. *Poor Ellen Smith/My Lord What A Mornin',* Capitol SXE-3-1809, March 1963
14. *Long Black Veil/Genny Glenn,* Capitol SXE-4-1809, March 1963
15. *The First Time/Dogie's Lament,* Capitol SXE-5-1809, March 1963
16. *Billy Goat Hill/Take Her Out Of Pity,* Capitol SM-1705, July 1963

Section Eleven: Domestic & Foreign "Compact 33" EPS

(for promotional see Section Twelve)

1. *The Kingston Trio,* Capitol MA1-1577 (mono), February 1961
   The Tijuana Jail/A Worried Man/Bad Man Blunder/Raspberries, Strawberries
2. no title, Capitol CP-4031 (stereo), (year unknown), (Japan)
   500 Miles/Blowin' In The Wind/Last Night I Had The Strangest Dream/Lemon Tree
3. no title, Capitol CP-4107 (stereo), (year unknown), (Japan)
   Greenback Dollar/This Land Is Your Land/Scarlet Ribbons/Ally Ally Oxen Free
4. no title, Capitol CP-4182 (stereo), (year unknown), (Japan)
   Try To Remember/Bay Of Mexico/Scotch And Soda/Turn Around

Section Twelve: Domestic "Compact 33" Stereo EPs — Promotional & Juke Box

1. *All Together Now,* Capitol Custom SNLB-2537/2538, 1961 (appliance store promo for General Electric)
   Molly Dee/(plus tracks by Stan Kenton, Gordon Macrae, June Christy, Jonah Jones and George Shearing)
2. *New Frontier,* Capitol SXA-1809, 1963 (juke box)
   The New Frontier/Honey, Are You Mad At Your Man/Greenback Dollar/The First Time/Dogie's Lament/Adios Farewell
3. *#16,* Capitol SXA-1871, 1963 (juke box)
   Reverend Mr. Black/Road To Freedom/One More Round/Ballad Of The Quiet Fighter/Big Ball In Town/Run The Ridges

Section Thirteen: Flexidisc Soundsheets — Promotional/Magazine

(7-inch, 33⅓ r.p.m., one-sided)

1. *Echo Magazine,* Volume One, Number Three, 1960
   Coo Coo-U (plus other artists)
2. *A Surprise Gift From The Beatles, The Beach Boys and The Kingston Trio,* Evatone 8464, 1964 (Capitol Record Club promo)
   When The Saints Go Marching In/(plus tracks by the Beatles and Beach Boys)
3. *A Medley Of Exerpts From American Gold,* Longines Symphonette LYN 2592, 1973 (Longines mail promo; featuring comments by Bob Shane)

Section Fourteen: Domestic Appearances by The Kingston Trio on "Various Artists" LPs

(collections featuring several artists; for promotional see Section Fifteen)

1. GREAT SMASH HITS, Capitol T/ST 1488, February 1961
   Tom Dooley
2. CHARTBUSTERS, VOL. 1, Capitol T/ST 1837, December 1962
   Where Have All The Flowers Gone
3. CHARTBUSTERS, VOL. 2, Capitol T/ST 1945, August 1963
   Reverend Mr. Black/Greenback Dollar
4. CHARTBUSTERS, VOL. 3, Capitol T/ST 2006, November 1963
   Desert Pete
5. CHARTBUSTERS, VOL. 4, Capitol T/ST 2094, June 1964
   Ally Ally Oxen Free
6. SUPER OLDIES, VOL. 5, Capitol STBB-216 (year unknown)
   Where Have All The Flowers Gone
7. BEST OF FOLK-COUNTRY SONGS, Capitol SL-6599 (year unknown)
   Lemon Tree

8. THE GREAT FOLK-COUNTRY HITS, Capitol SL-6647 (year unknown)
   Where Have All The Flowers Gone
9. POP HITS OF THE 50s, Capitol SL-8006 (year unknown)
   Tom Dooley
10. GOOD TIME MUSIC, K-Tel 9268, 1978
    Tom Dooley/Greenback Dollar/Where Have All The Flowers Gone
11. MONSTER HITS, Pickwick/Star Trax PDA 064, 1979
    Tom Dooley
12. 24 GREAT HEARTBREAKERS & TEARJERKERS, Excelsior 2XMP-4405, 1980
    Where Have All The Flowers Gone
13. THE AMERICAN DREAM, Imperial House NU9790, 1981
    Where Have All The Flowers Gone

14. CAPITOL CLASSICS 1942-1958, Capitol (number unknown), December 1984
Tom Dooley

15. WE'LL TAKE ROMANCE, Intermedia S-5051, 1985
Colours

16. PLAZA HOUSE PRESENTS: THE GREATEST HITS OF THE 50'S & 60'S, Capitol SLB-6718 (year unknown)
selections unknown

17. LOOKIN' BACK, Columbia House 1P 69752 (year unknown)
Where Have All The Flowers Gone

18. BABY BOOMER CLASSICS: FOLK SIXTIES, JCI JCI-3109, 1985
Where Have All The Flowers Gone

Section Fifteen: Various Artists LP Appearances — Promotional/Public Service/Commercials

1. WHAT'S NEW, VOL. 2, Capitol SN2, 1959 (radio station promo)
M.T.A.

2. U.S. MARINE CORPS SOUNDS OF SOLID GOLD, (number unknown), 1959 (radio public service promo)
M.T.A.

3. JOURNEY INTO MUSIC, Capitol PRO-1519/1520, April 1960 (radio promo)
Bimini/Don't Cry Katie

4. SING FOR 7-UP, 7-Up 13734, 1960 (radio commercials)
six 60-second commercials

5. SING FOR 7-UP, 7-Up 14169, 1960 (radio commercials)
six 60-second commercials

6. GOIN' PLACES WITH CAPITOL!-MINUTE MASTERS, Capitol PRO-1834/1835, 1961 (radio promo)
You Don't Knock

7. WHO'S NEWS?, Capitol NP1, 1962 (radio promo)
Where Have All The Flowers Gone

8. FULL DIMENSIONAL SOUNDS, Capitol PRO-2081/2082, 1962 (radio promo)
Raspberries, Strawberries

9. GREAT NEW RELEASES FROM THE SOUND CAPITOL OF THE WORLD, Capitol PRO-2125/2126, August 1962 (radio promo)
Brown Mountain Light/One More Town/Old Joe Clark

10. HIRE DISABLED VETS, Veterans Administration Program No. 734, (year unknown), (radio public service promo)
selections unknown

11. NEW ADP SET UP, Veterans Administration Program No. 834, (year unknown), (radio public service promo)
selections unknown

12. HERE'S TO VETERANS, Veterans Administration Program No. 983, August 1962 (radio public service promo)
Tell It On The Mountain/Portland Town/Jane, Jane, Jane/Away Rio

13. SOUND TRACK FIVE, Veterans Administration Program No. 130, (year unknown) (radio public service promo)
Portland Town

14. GUARD SESSION, National Guard Shows No. 57/58, 1963 (radio public service promo)
Reuben James/Where Have All The Flowers Gone/Greenback Dollar/Tom Dooley

15. GUARD SESSION, National Guard Shows No. 59/60 (with Jonah Jones), 1963 (radio public service promo)
Poor Ellen Smith/Honey, Are You Mad At Your Man/One More Town/The New Frontier

16. GUARD SESSION, National Guard Shows No. 75/76, (year unknown) (radio public service promo)
selections unknown

17. INSTANT MUSIC — MARCH MINUTE MASTERS, Capitol PRO-2292/2293, March 1963 (radio promo)
Road To Freedom/Oh Joe Hannah/Mark Twain/Low Bridge

18. GREAT NEW RELEASES FROM THE SOUND CAPITOL OF THE WORLD, Capitol PRO-2304/2305, March 1963 (radio promo)
Reverend Mr. Black/Run The Ridges

19. GREAT NEW RELEASES FROM THE SOUND CAPITOL OF THE WORLD, Capitol PRO-2414/2415, August 1963 (radio promo)
Desert Pete/Marcelle Vahine

20. CHRISTMAS HOLIDAY FAVORITES, Spots For The Guard XPD-1212, October 1963 (radio public service promo)
Glorious Kingdom

21. CHRISTMAS SEAL CAMPAIGN 1963, Decca M6 79606, 1963 (radio public service promo)
Tom Dooley/Take Her Out Of Pity

22. SOUND TRACK FIVE, Veterans Administration Program No. 138, 1963 (radio public service promo)
Reverend Mr. Black

23. SILVER PLATTER SERVICE, Capitol #87/88, 1963 (radio promo)
Ally Ally Oxen Free

24. BALANCED FOR BROADCAST, Capitol PRO 2519, January 1964 (radio promo)
Ally Ally Oxen Free

25. SILVER PLATTER SERVICE, Capitol #111/112, 1964 (radio promo)
Walkin' This Road To My Town

26. THE KINGSTON TRIO SHOW, Peace Corps
    (number unknown), 1964 (radio public service
    promo)
    *Walkin' This Road To My Town/Ann/Let's Get
    Together/The New Frontier/Salty Dog/World I
    Used To Know/Farewell Captain*
27. GREAT NEW RELEASES FROM THE SOUND
    CAPITOL OF THE WORLD, Capitol
    PRO-2614/2615, May 1964 (radio promo)
    Let's Get Together/Ann
28. BALANCED FOR BROADCAST, Capitol PRO
    2808, March 1965 (radio promo)
    Reverend Mr. Black
29. THE YOUNG MAN FROM BOSTON — A
    TRIBUTE TO JOHN F. KENNEDY, WR-4546,
    May 1965 (one-sided radio promo for KABC-TV
    special)
    The Kingston Trio performs song excerpts from
    the television documentary.

Section Sixteen: Videodiscs
(12-inch video/audio laserdisc)

1. THERE'S A MEETIN' HERE TONIGHT, Pioneer
   Artists LaserDisc PA-81-004, 1981 (also featur-
   ing 13 tracks by Glenn Yarbrough & The
   Limeliters)

* * * * * * * * *

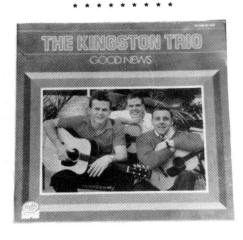

**Unusual and interesting alternate covers from
foreign releases. (GOOD NEWS is a European release
of AT LARGE.)**

Re-Issued, Rumored
& Unreleased

by
Benjamin Blake

Advanced audiophiles are a peculiar breed. They seek out and acquire — often at great expense — every known release (as well as every *variation* of said release) by a particular artist, and then they just naturally start digging for the *unknown.* Among this group are an ever-growing number of Kingston Trio fans, and it is to them that we respectfully dedicate this chapter. Only those who suffer from the most acute form of this affliction could possibly find the subject of re-issues worth wallowing in, so we recommend that

the rest of you go directly to "Episode Two".

For the sake of the fanatical collectors, we have done our best to leave no stone unturned. Collecting is part hobby and part obsession, and your authors try to keep their feet squarely planted on the "hobby" side of the line. Incidentally, would the lady who claims to have the training wheels from Bob Shane's first bicycle please write to us again? We have the check ready, but we seem to have misplaced your address.

* * * * * * * * *

Episode One: "Romancing The Re-Issues"

An apocryphal account:

'Tis a bleak but pivotal incident in Trio history we must now relate. It is written that in a time known as the "Early Seventies" (later recognized by most musicologists as the beginning of the New Dark Ages), the Great Keeper of the Capitol Non-Current Inventory Catalog went fishing, and during his absence a power surge in the compuuter caused the circuits of sanity to be wiped clean of all but rock and roll. With the exception of the three BEST OF albums, the entire Kingston Trio LP inventory was remaindered (cut-out, discontinued, banished from *Schwann,* etc.), and by this unfortunate act Capitol gained immediate notoriety as the first major label to cut R.I.A.A. — certified gold albums from its catalog. Thus began the need for re-issues.

Actually, the first KT re-issue dated back to February of 1961, when Capitol pressed a "Star Line" 45 with *Tom Dooley* and *M.T.A.* back-to-back. Then came the Duophonic nonsense of the EN-CORES album (see "The Capitol Years, Part 1") in July of that year. Both of these discs are now long out-of-print. *Tom Dooley* and *M.T.A.* were re-issued *again* on the Capitol Star Line label in January of

1962, and that version is still available. The same is true of the Trio's other two Star Line re-issues, *A Worried Man/Scotch And Soda* and *Greenback Dollar/Reverend Mr. Black* (April of 1964 and August of 1965, respectively).

In 1969, the year the industry went "total stereo", Capitol deleted those mono perennials THE KINGSTON TRIO and FROM THE "HUNGRY i", re-issuing the former in a new Duophonic pressing. When the above-mentioned catalog purge occurred, even *that* re-issue was remaindered. It was brought back (sort of) in 1970 as half of one of the first re-issues in a really silly series called "Double Play", where each release consisted of two edited albums by the same artist, taped together and sold for one "low" price. The Trio's entries in this series were ten-band LPs titled TOM DOOLEY and SCARLET RIBBONS. The former was THE KINGSTON TRIO minus *Banua* and *Santy Anno,* while the latter was AT LARGE without *The Seine* and *The Long Black Rifle.* Both were given new jackets as well. Amazingly, both of these re-issues are individually still in print, although the Double Play series is long gone.

The next Trio re-issue was either a deliberate attempt to confuse future discographers (like us), or

a simple case of one hand not knowing what the other hand was doing. Yet another album titled TOM DOOLEY was released in January of 1971, this time by Pickwick International (on its "Pickwick/33" budget label), consisting of nine tracks leased from Capitol. To compound the confusion of having two LPs with the same title out at the same time, Pickwick's TOM DOOLEY confounds us even further by offering seven tracks from AT LARGE, six of which had just been re-issued on SCARLET RIBBONS! Besides being an

TOM DOOLEY
(Pickwick)

Tom Dooley
Seasons In The Sun
Corey, Corey
Blow Ye Winds
Early In The Mornin'

M.T.A.
Scarlet Ribbons
The Seine
All My Sorrows

THE PATRIOT GAME

The Patriot Game
Tell It On The Mountain
Blow The Candle Out
Go Where I Send Thee
La Bamba

M.T.A.
The Whistling Gypsy
Farewell Captain
The World I Used To Know

WHERE HAVE ALL THE FLOWERS GONE
(Pickwick)

Where Have All The Flowers Gone
Coplas Revisited
Chilly Winds
Isle In The Water

500 Miles
Try To Remember
The Long Black Rifle
Turn Around
O Ken Karanga

inferior pressing on poor vinyl, this LP also ticked a few folks off by including the hideous BACK IN TOWN version of *Tom Dooley* as its lead track. What *Seasons In The Sun* is doing on this disc is anyone's guess.

Pickwick was to put out two more collections of Capitol KT re-issues, THE PATRIOT GAME (February, 1972) and WHERE HAVE ALL THE FLOWERS GONE (September, 1972). Both showed considerably more creativity in their song selections, drawing tracks from nine different LPs. Pickwick pulled one additional boner, however, by putting *M.T.A.* on THE PATRIOT GAME when they had already included it on TOM DOOLEY, and all this while Capitol still had it available on SCARLET RIBBONS and THE BEST OF THE KINGSTON TRIO. All of the Pickwick KT LPs are now out-of-print.

Both THE BEST OF and THE BEST OF, VOLUME 2 underwent a major change in November of 1971, when they took on their present ten-band form. *Everglades* and *Billy Goat Hill* were cut from the first set, and *Scarlet Ribbons* was sent packing from VOLUME 2. For reasons unknown, VOLUME 3 has been allowed to retain all of its original eleven bands to this very day. Its British counterpart, A TRIBUTE TO THE KINGSTON TRIO, also escaped such editing, as did Capitol's KT anthology, THE FOLK ERA, but both are now banished from their respective catalogs. A TRIBUTE TO was detailed in "The Decca Years" chapter; the track listings for THE FOLK ERA are as follows: *Tom Dooley, Bay of Mexico, Three Jolly Coachmen, Hangman, Getaway John, Saro Jane, Blowin' In The Wind, Some Fool Made A Soldier Of Me, Two-Ten, Six-Eighteen, Song For A Friend, Greenback Dollar, Corey, Corey, The Unfortunate Miss Bailey, Old Joe Clark, Little Maggie, When The Saints Go Marching In, Where Have All The Flowers Gone, Ann, Last Night I Had The Strangest Dream, Turn Around, The Merry Minuet, Reverend Mr. Black, M.T.A., Scarlet Ribbons, They Call The Wind Maria, Reuben James, Deportee, Leave My Woman Alone, Ballad Of The Shape Of Things, Lemon Tree, The Tijuana Jail, Raspberries, Strawberries, A Worried Man.* For more about THE FOLK ERA, see "The Capitol Years, Part 2."

Capitol never did assemble a BEST OF, VOLUME 4. Indeed, the company seemed to nearly forget about the Trio for over a decade. In Europe, E. M. I. eventually assembled a sixteen-band compilation LP titled SEASONS IN THE SUN, which apparently is still in print. With eleven of the songs available through the BEST OF series, and with such questionable additions as *Salty Dog* and *Ah, Woe, Ah, Me,* we have to wonder what the E. M. I. folks were taking in their tea at the time.

In Japan, the Capitol affiliate was busy compil-

ing two KT collections. WHERE HAVE ALL THE FLOWERS GONE, with its hilariously disguised cover from SOMETHING SPECIAL, sported fourteen tracks, including some seldom re-issued tunes like *Jesse James* and *Run Molly, Run.* Weighing in with sixteen tracks was the awkwardly titled POPULAR SUPER GOLD 2000 — BEST OF THE KINGSTON TRIO, the songs being the following: *500 Miles, Blowin' In The Wind, Where Have All The Flowers Gone, Greenback Dollar, Try To Remember, Lemon Tree, Last Night I Had The Strangest Dream, Across The Wide Missouri, Sloop John B, Tom Dooley, Scarlet Ribbons, Reverend Mr. Black, Chilly Winds, Two-Ten, Six-Eighteen, This Land Is Your Land, The Tijuana Jail.*

We know of three unique compilations to emerge from Taiwan. HITS OF THE KINGSTON TRIO was on the Liming label and contained the following songs: *Greenback Dollar, Tell It On The Mountain, Chilly Winds, Turn Around, Blowin' In The Wind, Salty Dog, 500 Miles, Georgia Stockade, Ally Ally Oxen Free, Last Night I Had The Strangest Dream, Ann, Two-Ten, Six-Eighteen, Across The Wide Missouri, This Land Is Your Land.* The Song Jwu label accounted for BEST OF THE KINGSTON TRIO, in two fourteen-song volumes. VOL. 1 contained: *500 Miles, Greenback Dollar, Blowin' In The Wind, Two-Ten, Six-Eighteen, Turn Around, Portland Town, Try To Remember, Where Have All The Flowers Gone, Tell It On The Mountain, Ally Ally Oxen Free, Old Joe Clark, Pastures Of Plenty, Reuben James, Last Night I Had The Strangest Dream.* VOL. 2 contained: *Tom Dooley, Bay Of Mexico, Sloop John B, Lemon Tree, Hard Travelin', Chilly Winds, This Land Is Your Land, Across The Wide Missouri, Scotch And Soda, Jesse James, Scarlet Ribbons, Raspberries, Strawberries, The Tijuana Jail, When The Saints Go Marching In.*

MCA never released any kind of BEST OF Trio package in the United States, but twelve of its Decca tracks were re-issued in Europe in 1973 on the MCA/Coral label. The album was titled MIDNIGHT SPECIAL, and it contained the following selections: *Midnight Special, If I Had A Ship, Children Of The Morning, Farewell, Stories Of Old, Dooley, Bottle Of Wine, Where I'm Bound, Early Morning Rain, Last Thing On My Mind, Hanna Lee, Gotta Travel On.* Fully half of the contents of MIDNIGHT SPECIAL were drawn from Decca's STAY AWHILE album, and it even featured the same cover photo. All of The Kingston Trio's recordings for MCA (Decca) are now out-of-print worldwide, and the conglomerate shows no interest in re-issuing or leasing them to other manufacturers. It has been speculated that the original masters are no longer at MCA, and that ownership reverted to Kingston Trio, Inc. when the Trio's contract with Decca expired.

SEASONS IN THE SUN

Seasons In The Sun
Sloop John B
500 Miles
Raspberries, Strawberries
Ally Ally Oxen Free
Greenback Dollar
World I Used To Know
Ah, Woe, Ah, Me

Tom Dooley
It Was A Very Good Year
M.T.A.
Reverend Mr. Black
Where Have All The Flowers Gone
O Ken Karanga
This Land Is Your Land
Salty Dog

WHERE HAVE ALL THE FLOWERS GONE
(Japan)

Where Have All The Flowers Gone
Blowin' In The Wind
Hard Travelin'
Jesse James
Pastures Of Plenty
Corey, Corey
When The Saints Go Marching In

Tom Dooley
Reuben James
Run Molly, Run
This Land Is Your Land
Across The Wide Missouri
Little Maggie
Come All You Fair And Tender Ladies

THE HISTORIC RECORDINGS OF
THE KINGSTON TRIO

Tom Dooley
This Land Is Your Land
Scarlet Ribbons
The Merry Minuet
500 Miles
El Matador
Reverend Mr. Black

A Worried Man
Blowin' In The Wind
Sloop John B
Seasons In The Sun
Reuben James
Last Night I Had The
    Strangest Dream
The Tijuana Jail

Where Have All The
    Flowers Gone
Let's Get Together
Lemon Tree
All My Sorrows
Raspberries, Strawberries
Greenback Dollar

M.T.A.
They Call The Wind Maria
Desert Pete
Bad Man Blunder
Everglades
Scotch and Soda

Leasing was another matter at Capitol. During the decade that they "forgot" the Trio, the folks at Capitol were only too happy to oblige when other labels came bearing dollars to the door. Hot on the heels of Pickwick International came the Longines Symphonette Society, which dipped into Capitol's Trio treasure trove and assembled 1973's AMERICAN GOLD set, the contents of which are as follows: *Tom Dooley, La Bamba, Raspberries, Strawberries, They Call The Wind Maria, Everglades, Wimoweh, Mark Twain, This Land Is Your Land, The Tijuana Jail, Reverend Mr. Black, Lemon Tree, 500 Miles, Reuben James, Let's Get Together, Old Joe Clark, Three Jolly Coachmen, Fast Freight, Blow The Candle Out, Rider, The First Time, Early In The Mornin', Molly Dee, Blue Eyed Gal, She Was Too Good To Me, Salty Dog, Tic, Tic, Tic, With Her Head Tucked Underneath Her Arm, To Be Redeemed, Run The Ridges, Last Night I Had The Strangest Dream, It Was A Very Good Year, Zombie Jamboree, You Don't Knock, Poor Ellen Smith, Dogie's Lament, Sloop John B, Bad Man's Blunder, Hard Travelin', Little Maggie, Oh Joe Hannah, Goober Peas, A Worried Man, The Escape Of Old John Webb, Come All You Fair And Tender Ladies, The River Is Wide, Scotch And Soda, The Merry Minuet, Pastures Of Plenty, Senora, Road To Freedom, M.T.A., Scarlet Ribbons, The Tattooed Lady, Little Boy, Where Have All The Flowers Gone, Blowin' In The Wind, Try To Remember, Guardo El Lobo, Georgia Stockade, When The Saints Go Marching In.* For more about AMERICAN GOLD, see "The Decca Years".

1975 saw Candlelite Music hawking the Trio on television with their two-record set (pressed by Capitol) titled THE HISTORIC RECORDINGS OF THE KINGSTON TRIO. The twenty-six selections were well-chosen, and it's nice to see a normally overlooked title like *Let's Get Together* included among the hardy regulars. This set had a twin in Canada titled 1958-1963 THE GOLDEN YEARS on TeeVee Records (pressed by Capitol of Canada). The same year saw a KT compilation LP offered to members of the Australian World Record Club. It was titled THE BEST OF JOHN STEWART WITH THE KINGSTON TRIO, and it contained thirteen selections. Capitol even loaned them the cover photo from John's CALIFORNIA BLOODLINES for the back of the jacket.

All of those Capitol-leased compilations are now unavailable, but Capitol itself has recently stepped back into the Kingston business. The company re-issued FROM THE "HUNGRY i" in 1979, *intact*. Happily, they also seem to have gotten away from their Duophonic madness, as this one is pressed in its original mono.

The recent Trio of Shane, Gambill and Grove has also had the honor of being re-issued. ASPEN

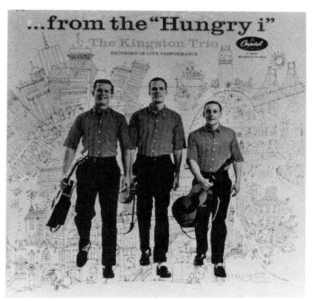

THE BEST OF JOHN STEWART WITH THE KINGSTON TRIO

Song For A Friend
Reverend Mr. Black
Some Fool Made A Soldier Of Me
Ballad Of The Quiet Fighter
Desert Pete
Those Who Are Wise

Dogie's Lament
Ballad Of The Thresher
Jackson
Take Her Out Of Pity
Weeping Willow
Deportee
These Seven Men

IN CONCERT

Hard Travelin'
Early Morning Rain
M.T.A.
Tomorrow Is A Long Time
Rovin' Gambler/This Train

The Tijuana Jail
I'm Going Home
Where Have All The Flowers Gone
Scotch And Soda
When The Saints Go Marching In

EARLY AMERICAN HEROES

Tom Dooley
The Tijuana Jail
Across The Wide Missouri
Where Have All The Flowers Gone

Saro Jane
Blowin' In The Wind
South Coast
Coplas

M.T.A.
A Worried Man
Greenback Dollar
Sloop John B

All My Sorrows
Hard, Ain't It Hard
Scotch And Soda
They Call The Wind Maria

LA GRANDE STORIA DEL ROCK

Tom Dooley
Greenback Dollar
Where Have All The Flowers Gone
Hard, Ain't It Hard
Getaway John

Wimoweh
Babe, You've Been On My Mind
One Too Many Mornings
Colours
Goodnight Irene
Ballad Of The Shape Of Things

TOM DOOLEY
(Germany)

Hard, Ain't It Hard
Greenback Dollar
One Too Many Mornings
Tom Dooley
Ballad Of The Shape Of Things

Getaway John
Babe, You've Been On My Mind
Colours
Goodnight Irene
Wimoweh

THE KINGSTON TRIO
(Romulus)

Early Morning Rain
Tomorrow Is A Long Time
I'm Going Home
Scotch And Soda
Hard Travelin'
M.T.A.
Rovin' Gambler/This Train
The Tijuana Jail
Where Have All The Flowers Gone
When The Saints Go Marching In

Getaway John
Babe, You've Been On My Mind
Colours
Goodnight Irene
Wimoweh
Hard, Ain't It Hard
Greenback Dollar
One Too Many Mornings
Tom Dooley
Ballad Of The Shape Of Things

GOLD, originally released by Nautilus as an expensive digital "Superdisc", was re-issued as a regular analog LP in 1981 by 51 West Records. The Nautilus disc is now out of print, due to the demise of the label.

1981 was also the year that ONCE UPON A TIME began to resurface, sporting a variety of disguises. A KT release called IN CONCERT on Stack-O-Hits Records, poorly mastered and deceptively packaged, turned out to be a re-issue of Record One of the Tetragrammaton classic, minus all of the comedy routines and between-song patter. Legal issues were raised by various parties concerning the misrepresentation of the likenesses in the cover art (the drawing is from photo of Nick, Bob and *Dave* that appeared on the reverse of SOLD OUT), and the proper licensing of the masters. Whether everything was settled and substantiated to the satisfaction of all concerned remains unknown, but IN CONCERT is now out of print, and Stack-O-Hits has vanished from our planet.

Most of Record Two of ONCE UPON A TIME was re-issued in Italy in 1983 as part of a series called LA GRANDE STORIA DEL ROCK (Legends of Rock) on Curcio/Valentine Records. What makes this re-issue extraordinary is the fact that its first three tracks are the 1978 K-Tel sessions by Shane/Gambill/Grove! This makes LEGENDS OF ROCK the only known release to feature both that group and one of the earlier Trios. A photo of Reynolds/Shane/Stewart was utilized on the cover of this album.

All ten songs from ONCE UPON A TIME's second record cropped up in Germany on the Astan label. The title of the LP is TOM DOOLEY (hardly original), but what makes *this* album unique is the cover photo of the *New* KT of Bob Shane, Roger Gambill and Bill Zorn! Since the group never released a record with Zorn as a member, this one is especially puzzling, and it is the only release we know of with this configuration of the Trio pictured on the jacket.

But the most enterprising of all the legally questionable "re-issues" of ONCE UPON A TIME appeared in the United States on Romulus Records. Titled simply THE KINGSTON TRIO, and sporting no photos at all, this album managed to cram all twenty songs onto one record. While we can't verify the current status of the Italian or German items, we can report that Romulus (like Stack-O-Hits) has moved, leaving "no forwarding address."

All of these variations (and there may be more) of the original Tetragrammaton album seem to have been taken from what is known as a "ghost" master — an extra master that is kept just in case the original, polished version (from which ONCE UPON A TIME was made) is ever lost. A reliable

source informed us that the "ghost" was unaccountably missing for several months in 1981, before re-appearing just as mysteriously. It obviously passed through many hands! Oddly enough, only IN CONCERT adheres to the track sequence of the original album.

1984 saw the release of the most exciting KT re-issue yet. Mobile Fidelity Sound Lab leased GOIN' PLACES from Capitol and put it out as a superb-sounding Original Master Recording High Fidelity *Cassette.* We were assured that their next Trio re-issue would be an LP if the sales of this cassette warranted it, but the sound on the GOIN' PLACES cassette is so good that we would have been delighted to see an entire series of KT cassette re-issues. Most Mobile Fidelity releases are strictly "limited editions", so we were not surprised when this welcome reprise of a Trio classic did not appear in their 1986 catalog. One thing learned from this worthy experiment was that, for the most part, Trio collectors are not great fans of cassettes. Sadly, there have been no further KT releases from Mobile Fidelity.

Capitol released a Trio cassette of its own in 1984, under its "Capitol Special Markets" logo. WE CAME TO SING offered a re-issue of nine songs, most of which were already available elsewhere (three are even from GOIN' PLACES). Only *The First Time* and the COLLEGE CONCERT version of *Where Have All The Flowers Gone* are dusted off anew.

1984's final KT re-issue package was a 2-record set pressed by Capitol Special Markets for Pair

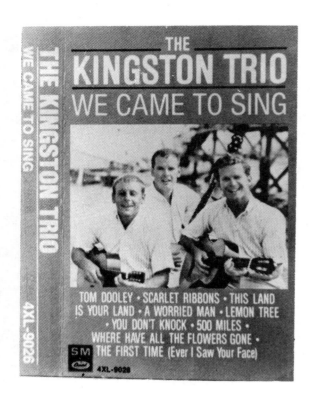

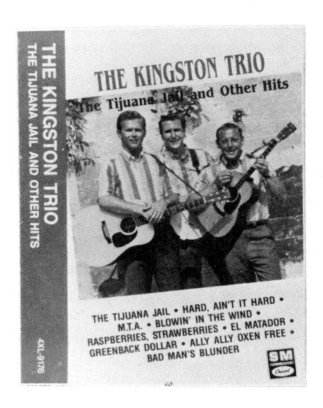

Re-issues on Cassettes From Capitol Special Markets

Records. Titled EARLY AMERICAN HEROES, it featured sixteen tracks which were already available on other current re-issues. The only bonus of this set was the great cover photo of the Reynolds/Shane/Stewart Trio, although this was perhaps a bit deceptive, since that group was only featured on three of the selections.

Capitol Special Markets was busy once again in the budget cassette field in 1985, with another nine-song re-issue titled THE TIJUANA JAIL AND OTHER HITS. Again, nothing was included that was not already available. The identical cassette was licensed to Star Records under the title MORE GREAT HITS, and the only other difference between the two is in the photo of the Trio: the former features Nick/Bob/John, while the latter sports the likenesses of Dave/Nick/Bob. 1985 also saw Special Markets producing an *eight*-song re-issue, SOME OF OUR FAVORITES, which strangely apes

TIJUANA JAIL in content (four songs in common), but redeems itself by bringing *Turn Around* out of the cobwebs. The song sequence on SOME OF OUR FAVORITES is as follows: *The Tijuana Jail, Turn Around, M.T.A., Reuben James, Greenback Dollar, It Was A Very Good Year, Raspberries, Strawberries, Scotch And Soda.*

Public interest (translated: sales) will determine the Trio re-issue schedule for the future. Certainly any fan's dream would have been Capitol and Mobile Fidelity working hand-in-hand to bring back *all* of the classic LPs, sounding even better than they did in the Fifties and Sixties. But KT collectors have considerably more to seek out than just the famous albums, various re-issues and compilations. There is a body of recorded work that has never been re-issued or compiled (or even released, in some cases), and it is the subject of the next leg of our audiophilic odyssey.

* * * * * * * * *

Episode Two: "Raiders Of The Lost Masters"

Deep in the Los Angeles vaults of Capitol Records, in some dark, catacombed corner where musicologists seldom sift, mislaid, misfiled and all-but-forgotten in shuffled stacks amidst the leavings of Al Martino, Mrs. Miller and Buck Owens & His Buckaroos, rest dust-covered tape cannisters inscribed with such magic-markered holy titles as *Golden Spike, Old Kentucky Land* and *Sea Fever.* Not unlike the attic-exiled relics of some Christmas past that birthed too many shiny toys, the fabled, previously unreleased masters of the legendary Kingston Trio have patiently awaited their day in the sun, hoping persistent fans would persuade indifferent executives of their historical and potentially commercial value, before the fickle Fault of San Andreas pulled the plug on the matter for eternity. Collections of "rarities" are not a priority at Capitol. In recent years they had issued such volumes by The Beatles and Beach Boys, but only after import sales of foreign versions inspired them to do it.

In 1985, Trio fans Steve Fiott (of the White Mountain Singers) and Allan Shaw (of Kingston Korner, Inc.) decided to take matters into their own hands.

In the Kingston Trio's twenty-eight year recording history, dozens of titles fell by the wayside for one reason or another. Many "takes" were usually required before a song passed muster, and in most instances the substandard takes were destroyed or erased. Some recorded songs were not considered "good enough" (often in comparison with what

else was currently up for consideration) to be included on a certain album, but still worthy of salvation. (Some of these got out of their cans because a B side was needed to be sacrificed for the latest 45, or to round out an EP, but after that brief glimpse of daylight they were once again relegated to "the shelf" with their even less fortunate kin. More about these later.) The vast majority of unreleased Trio tracks were recorded for Capitol. Armed with a list of these unreleased titles and their respective master numbers (assembled by various forces in KT fandom over the years, thanks to opportune "leaks" in the Capitol files), Steve and Allan approached Jack Reynolds, Director of Special Markets at Capitol Records, with the idea of leasing the tapes for release on a new label they were forming, "Folk Era". As might have been expected, there were a few disappointments and dead ends during their search of the hallowed vaults. *Just Once Around The Clock* (from the SOLD OUT sessions) and *Mary Was Pretty* (from the GOIN' PLACES sessions) were two titles that simply vanished during the two decades since the Trio left Capitol. Alternate, earlier versions of *When The Saints Go Marching In* (a studio take from the *Ruby Red* session) and *The Hunter* (from the HERE WE GO AGAIN sessions) had apparently met a similar fate. A master titled *Gleanora* turned out to be the finished, familiar version of *Oleanna* from HERE WE GO AGAIN, and a title listed as *Don't Knock* proved to be (you guessed it) *You Don't Knock* from GOIN' PLACES. One of the two vault versions of *Four*

Strong Winds was marked "unreleasable". Why it was saved if it was not for potential, eventual release is something we may never know. The other version of the song (from the TIME TO THINK sessions) was left in an "unfinished" state, with only Bob Shane's vocal and guitar and Dean Reilly's bass present.

But when the dust settled, Steve and Allan settled down to glean twelve titles from the pleasant pile and assemble an album they titled REDISCOVER, which was released by Folk Era in August of 1985. Nick Reynolds was an active supporter of the project and contributed the liner notes. Besides his obvious financial contribution, Steve Fiott also had the pleasure and responsibility of mixing the raw master tapes to make them suitable for release. Assisted by Jay Ranellucci, an engineer who had assisted Pete Abbot and Voyle Gilmore on some of the Trio's sessions, Steve put Studio A's old three-track equipment and under-the-parking-lot echo chambers to good use. And he had his work cut out for him: of the twelve tracks that appear on REDISCOVER, only two had been given what could be called Gilmore's "final polish", *Rocky* and *Old Kentucky Land,* which had been released in Germany on a 45 (see "The Capitol Years, Part Two"); and even these two had never been mixed into stereo before. But let us dissect side one first.

Blue Tattoo posed a problem, being the oldest of the twelve and the only one that had not been recorded in stereo. Says Steve: "There wasn't much we could do with *Blue Tattoo,* so we used a bit of EQ, and the new synthetic stereo unit that Capitol has to replace the old Duophonic one, and livened up the tune. This is done by taking frequencies and spreading them out, or panning them to create a stereo image." This track was apparently recorded in the studio at about the same time the Trio was recording the live FROM THE "HUNGRY i" album. The title had led us to believe it might be an earlier version of *Coal Tattoo,* but it proved to be an entirely different song. Bob Shane does the lead vocal on this rousing, nearly rocking tune, which may have been originally intended for release as a single. *Blue Tattoo* leads off REDISCOVER's first side, a collection of six songs by the original Guard/Reynolds/Shane Trio.

Steve was limited in what he could do with the five remaining songs from the Guard era, as the original three-track masters had been lost. Says Steve of the two-track tapes he had to work with: "The mixing here was just a re-mix, cleaning up the vocals in parts that were questionable, using EQs to bring out the clarity of vocals and instruments and generally taking Gilmore's mix and enhancing it with today's technology."

Sea Fever and *Oh Mary* date from the MAKE WAY sessions of 1960. The former is a haunting Jane Bowers song, done softly and with sparse instrumentation by the Trio, and it is one of REDISCOVER's high points. *Oh Mary* is an earlier version (with different lyrics) of what would later be re-worked into *Don't You Weep, Mary* (CLOSE-UP) by the Stewart Trio. A slightly slower tempo and added emphasis on enunciation make this earlier track an interesting find.

Three fine songs from the 1961 GOIN' PLACES sessions account for the rest of side one. Both *Wines Of Madiera* and *Adieu To My Island* were originally intended to be on that album, according to an ad for the LP which appeared on the reverse of a promotional record titled *All Together Now* (see Discography), but they never survived the final cut. *Wines Of Madiera* is a sort of cross-pollination of *Raspberries, Strawberries* and *Jug Of Punch,* if one can imagine such a hybrid. *Adieu To My Island,* from the pen of Travis Edmunson (he later incorporated part of this song into *Haiti* on the Bud & Travis album NATURALLY), is a lilting, Belafonte-ish performance that ranks among the best of all Trio tracks, and how it could have been left behind when GOIN' PLACES was released is something quite beyond the scope of your resident *Kingston historians. Golden Spike* features a riveting-if-unorthodox banjo performance by Dave Guard, and it is another of REDISCOVER's better tracks. When interviewed for this book several years ago, before any list of unreleased songs was known of, *Golden Spike* was the only rare title that remained in engineer Pete Abbot's memory:

> "I distinctly recall one song. It was called *The Golden Spike,* and it was about the transcontinental railroad — when they finally put in the golden spike and connected up the continent by railroad. And it was a good song. And we just had worked so many hours and days and nights on that thing, and they just stuck it away and never released it. A few years ago they had the hundredth anniversary of that golden spike ceremony up in Utah or Wyoming or somewhere, and I thought what a great idea to release that record now. I called someone at Capitol and mentioned it, and they said yeah, they'd look into it, but the Trio not being on Capitol anymore, and all departed — not being together — they just figured it would be a lost cause."

Well, Pete, thanks to Folk Era Productions, *Golden Spike* has finally been heard.

So those are the six "Guard era" cuts on REDISCOVER. Still resting in the vaults by that

side one:

1. Blue Tattoo
2. Adieu To My Island
3. Sea Fever
4. Oh Mary
5. Wines Of Madeira
6. Golden Spike

side two:

1. Rocky
2. Old Kentucky Land
3. Love Has Gone
4. Allentown Jail
5. Green Grasses
6. Folksinger's Song

Trio are early mono alternatives of *Tanga Tika Toerau* and *Dorie,* both recorded at the sessions for the first KT album. The latter is listed as *Dodi Lii* and is apparently the same song before it was given an English translation.

Side two of REDISCOVER is the domain of Reynolds/Shane/Stewart, and it leads off with the afore-mentioned *Rocky* and *Old Kentucky Land,* which are sung in German. These date from the group's earliest 1961 sessions (CLOSE-UP).

The "Stewart era" masters had all survived in their original three-track form, giving Steve, Jay and Allan a bit more room to work. The third track on side two is *Love Has Gone,* a rather sappy leftover from the 1963 sessions for #16, featuring Bob Shane on lead vocal.

The title jogged Allan Shaw's memories of the mixing session in Studio A: "We walked into the control room and looked out into the studio itself. Except for the fact that there was no one in there, it was the HERE WE GO AGAIN cover laid out before us. The wooden-looking panels on the walls, the stools, the recording equipment — it was as though time had stood still for twenty-five years. The first tape to be mixed was *Love Has Gone,* and as the voices and guitar notes began to pour from the speakers, I had only to close my eyes and see the Trio members sitting there on the other side of the glass. But we were not there for dreaming, and the mixing controls were working their magic. We were able to do what I had always wanted to do at home: listen to each channel separately to hear what each of the Trio members was singing and playing, while not hearing the other two. It was helpful to be able to hear who hit a sour note that could be toned down or who had a particularly good line that could be toned up. As Steve and Jay played with the knobs, and I offered my opinions, the pleasant but somewhat mediocre sounds became tight harmonies, excellent phrasing and great instrumentation. 'What a genius Voyle Gilmore was', I thought, and my thoughts were immediately vocalized by Steve."

Next up is *Allentown Jail,* which dates from the "experimental" 1962 mini-session that produced the *C'Mon Betty Home* 45. What sounded like a harpsichord on the single sounds more like a mandolin here, but John Stewart swears it is really his twelve-string guitar! Despite an exuberant performance by the Trio, *Allentown Jail* is one of REDISCOVER's weakest cuts.

Green Grasses was a real find for Stewart devotees, as it turned out to be John's 1961 *audition* tape for joining the Trio. For reasons unknown (even to John), it was added to the Captiol master list during the 1962 recording session for NEW FRONTIER. *Green Grasses,* thanks to its simplicity

and Stewart's low-key vocal, works very well, making it *the* stand-out track on side two, and in some ways superior to the single by the original group. Adds Steve Fiott: "I love the song, and this version had only John's banjo on tracks one and three and only his vocal on track two, with no other instrumentation or vocal. This was my favorite mix. I worked hard on the EQ and played around for what seemed forever getting the echo to make the banjo sound as though it was in the swamp fog of the storyline. I'm delighted with the results."

Ending REDISCOVER is a Mike Settle ditty titled *Folksinger's Song,* which is also the "newest" track on the LP, having been recorded in 1963. If you have always wondered what became of the twelfth track on SUNNY SIDE, wonder no more. By the standards of then and now, the lyrics are in poor taste, although it was obviously intended as satire, something that is not carried off easily. As Allan Shaw points out: "It was the old story of the joke that bombed. It just wasn't funny. On the other hand, the vocals were strong, and there were some great twelve-string guitar runs by John. In short, the weaknesses were in the message and not the medium. The sound was that of the Trio members at their best, and they sounded as though they were enjoying themselves singing. So in it stayed."

If *Folksinger's Song, Allentown Jail* and *Love Has Gone* made the final cut, what was left by Nick, Bob and John that did not? We mentioned *Four Strong Winds* earlier, and that could not be used because it was never completed. There was a fine alternate version of *Ann* from the TIME TO THINK sessions, but it was not considered quite unique enough for a project like REDISCOVER. *Water Boy,* from the CLOSE-UP sessions, can most kindly be described as "strange", going so far as to include a jazzy piano (pianist unknown). Says Allan: "The vocals were weak and not very impressive. In short, it wasn't a song well suited to the Trio, and they didn't sound comfortable with it." Another leftover from the #16 sessions, *Softly As I Leave You* suffered from a double-tracked vocal by John that just couldn't be re-mixed to anyone's (including John's) satisfaction.

In addition to the "regular" edition of REDISCOVER, Folk Era also issued a limited, numbered edition (500) with a special insert of additional liner notes and photos. Nick Reynolds personally signed each of the 500 inserts.

With a strong first side and a so-so second side, REDISCOVER (on balance) emerges as just what we all would have hoped for: a typical Kingston Trio album. And in case anyone has forgotten the formula for a typical KT LP, it goes like this: two or three classic cuts, three or four "very good" tracks, some "filler" and a couple of clunkers. We Trio fans owe Allan and Steve a vote of thanks, and the good word is that they are only just beginning.

* * * * * * * * *

You will recall an earlier mention of some Capitol Trio tracks that fall into a category we will dub "Released, But Still Rare". You may have compiled your own list as you waded through "The Capitol Years" chapters or the Discography. Various scratchy 45 flip sides, EP cuts and the like have long been the bane of KT collectors who hoped they might eventually be assembled on an LP. The good news is that the wait is just about over. Folk Era Productions plans a 1986 album release that is tentatively titled THE "B" SIDES. How many and which songs would be on the album was undecided as "The Kingston Trio On Record" went to press.

Some seemingly obvious candidates from the Dave Guard era would be: *Como Se Viene, Se Va, Ruby Red, Sally, Oh Cindy, Sail Away Ladies, Coo Coo-U, Home From The Hill.* A formerly obvious choice would have been *Green Grasses,* but with the alternate version already out on REDISCOVER, this one is probably now relegated to the "possible contender" category, a space it shares with the early 45 versions of *Scarlet Ribbons* and *Raspberries, Strawberries.*

The John Stewart era choices would appear simpler: *Nothing More To Look Forward To* and *C'Mon Betty Home.* The 45 version of *Jane, Jane, Jane* may be a candidate for inclusion if a stereo mix still exists sans orchestration. And completists might argue on behalf of the censored *Greenback Dollar* or re-arranged *The Patriot Game* 45s.

And let us not rule out some of those unreleased alternates that would not fit on REDISCOVER, and there may be even more of those. A relative of one of the original Trio members has in her collection an unreleased EP that contains studio versions of *Gue, Gue* and *New York Girls.* (The release of FROM THE "HUNGRY i", wherein those songs are done live, apparently scotched the plans for the EP. *Gue, Gue* is the studio track that augmented the live cut on FROM THE "HUNGRY i". For the completists among you, the other two cuts on the EP would have been *Ruby Red* and *Como Se Viene, Se Va.*) From a collector's standpoint, it would be really nice if THE "B"SIDES turned out to be a double album.

* * * * * * * * *

And let us hope our Raiders of the Lost Masters don't stop there.

Nick, Bob and John's unreleased list at Decca contains *Come Gather The Time* and an alternate take of *Long Time Blues.* Released non-LP tracks include: *My Ramblin' Boy, Yes I Can Feel It, Texas Across The River, Babe, You've Been On My Mind.* Decca also lists an unreleased "short version" of Bob Shane's *Honey* (master #119,819).

Returning to Capitol, the Shane/Connor/Horine group left these five unreleased titles in the vaults: *Peace-Loving Gentlemen, I'll Find You, Friends Forever, Bitter Green, To My Guitar.* Released, but never on an LP: *Windy Wakefield, Tell The Riverboat Captain.* (How about *these* on THE "B" SIDES, Folk Era?) The same group's THE WORLD NEEDS A MELODY sessions produced five additional tracks, but it is unclear where they now reside. They are: *Fourth Avenue New Hope Mission, You're The One, Sold American;* plus alternate takes of *Riley's Medicine Show* and *Nellie.*

The Shane/Gambill/Zorn group reportedly recorded a live LP that was never released (because of Zorn's departure). It is not known what became of the tapes.

The Shane/Gambill/Grove Trio's Mountain Creek session produced one unreleased side, *Aspen Gold.* Also from that session, but never included on an album, were *Big Ship Glory* and *Johnson Party of 4.* The same group's session for K-Tel yielded a version of *Greenback Dollar* which has yet to be released in the United States. Their Nautilus sessions produced at least one unreleased cut, *Run The Ridges.* Their Xeres work includes unreleased renditions of *Last Thing On My Mind* and *Everybody's Talking,* plus an alternate take of *Will You Love Me If I Don't Do Coke.*

* * * * * * * * *

Not only unreleased, but *non-existent* department: THE KINGSTON TRIO ON TOUR, a working title for a 1961 album that never got off the ground because of Dave Guard's departure. SONGS TO SING AFTER A DAY SKIING was to have been a 1962 album, but it never got beyond the photo session, and THE BEST OF THE KINGSTON TRIO was assembled instead.

The only known instance of last-minute tampering with a Trio LP cover concerns COLLEGE CONCERT. Don't bother steaming off your cover photos, however, as the intended cover (which we are pleased to present to the public for the first time) was never released. Apparently the expressions were considered too stern for the Trio's

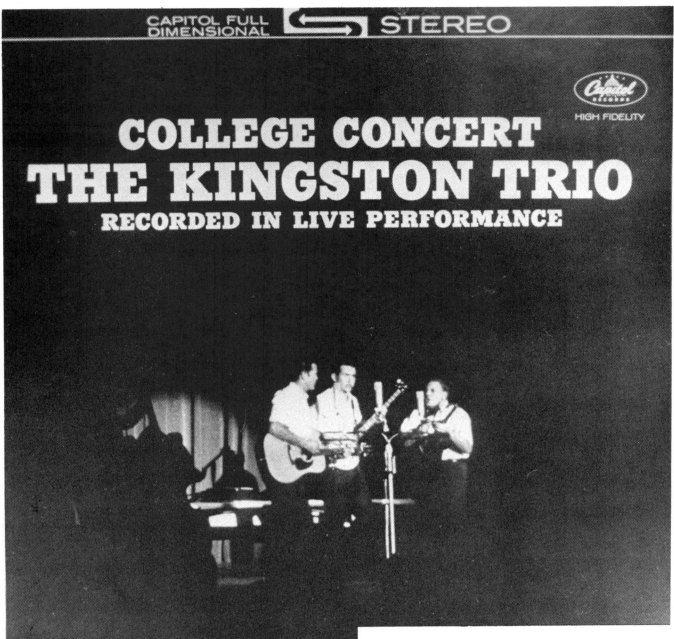

CAPITOL FULL DIMENSIONAL STEREO

COLLEGE CONCERT
THE KINGSTON TRIO
RECORDED IN LIVE PERFORMANCE

Capitol Records HIGH FIDELITY

The original, never released cover for COLLEGE CONCERT. The only known instance of a last minute change in a Kingston Trio album cover. Courtesy of the Archives of Music Preservation.

"good time" image. It is unfortunate, because it would have made for a much more impressive package. A similar pose was released on the picture sleeve of the Japanese single of *Chilly Winds* in 1962.

In our attempt to be all-inclusive, we should also mention that there were somewhere between five and seven songs that were taped for, but not included on, STEREO CONCERT. The titles are unknown to us, and it seems unlikely that they are in Capitol's possession. While on the subject of Trio concerts recorded by someone other than their producers, we would be remiss to not include those taped right from the "house" sound system

One of the "Guard" Trio's many television appearances, "The Perry Como Music Hall", with guests Steve Lawrence and Juliet Prowse. This show was broadcast in January, 1961, and was one of the last television appearances of the Trio with Dave Guard. Note the full-length shirt sleeves rather than the usual three-quarter length for which the Trio was known. From the collection of Maureen Wilson.

(perhaps by the proprietors, and no doubt in dubious quality mono) at the Santa Monica Civic Auditorium (April 21, 1961 with surprise guest Pat Boone joining in on _You're Gonna Miss Me)_ and the Hollywood Bowl (June 23, 1962), as well as at the University of California At Berkely (November 20, 1962), and the University of Kentucky in Lexington (October 4, 1963). Nothing from any of these shows has ever been released.

The Kingston Trio has made dozens of television appearances, almost always as musical guests on some variety or comedy program, with occasional rare dramatic roles (_Playhouse 90, Convoy_). But there are at least three TV programs that are _dominated_ by the group, and many fans would love to see these released on video-cassettes or discs. The first is a sixty-minute pilot for CBS titled _Young Men In A Hurry,_ filmed in January of 1962. It was to have aired in March of that year, but somehow never did. Reportedly a comedy/drama with songs (the boys played struggling young executives who let off steam by singing together), this show has been described by one anonymous Trio member as "painful". The group performed specially recorded (non-Capitol) versions of _Oh Miss Mary_ and the title song (written by John Stewart) during the program. A second delight to acquire would be an August 27, 1962 concert, videotaped in Owings Mills, Maryland. It aired three times in September of that year on a Hartford, Connecticut "Pay TV" station, to a total of seven hundred homes. It was one of the first concerts ever taped for this early ancestor of cable television. It is not known who owns the rights to these first two programs, but our chances of eventually owning a third video Trio treat look much better. _The Kingston Trio & Friends: Reunion_ was videotaped at Valencia, California on November 7, 1981, and was first aired on PBS in March of 1982. It will no doubt eventually be commercially released, hopefully with some of the extra songs that were cut from the telecast. The concert (see the "Out With The New . . ." and "Night On Magic Mountain" chapters for details) was recorded in stereo, so hopefully it will be released that way.

Getting back to unreleased _audio_ recordings, perhaps the time capsule contents every Trio devotee hopes most anxiously to find are the long-overdue final _Hungry i_ recordings of the Reynolds/Shane/Stewart KT. That two weeks' worth of tape from June of 1967 is rumored to include the only known professional live recording of _Reverend Mr. Black,_ as well as at least one song the group had not previously recorded, Eric Andersen's _Thirsty Boots._

* * * * * * * * *

So there you have the lost leftovers of twenty-eight years of KT recordings. Although enough to fill several albums, some of these items are perhaps best left to the decomposition processes of eternity. Some KT alumni would tell you they'd just as soon let them remain on the shelf, but as REDISCOVER has proven, there are more gems in the various vaults and broom closets than we might have expected. Thanks to Folk Era Productions, we keepers of the Kingston flame have taken heart, and now eagerly await the release of THE "B" SIDES and whatever other surprises may yet follow from our "Raiders Of The Lost Masters".

A 3" x 5" four-color postcard produced to promote "The Kingston Trio & Friends Reunion" show on PBS. Courtesy of Camera Three Productions.

The Kingston Trio: Song-By-Song

by
Benjamin Blake

What follows is a comprehensive, alphabetical listing of some 407 versions of 319 songs, give or take a tune here or there, recorded by the Kingston Trio, in all of its many configurations.

Following any given song title will be (where known) the name of the writer, the record company's master number, year of recording and release, and the various forms of release (LP, EP, 45, etc.). Where we felt this last bit of information became cumbersome, or of a "minor"nature (not of interest to the general reader), we have tied it in to the "Discography" chapter. By referring to the specific section and number listed, the ultra-serious Trio collector may ascertain (for example) just which of the five versions of *Greenback Dollar* appears on the various artists GOOD TIME MUSIC album.

It should be noted that the "Song-By-Song" listings do *not* include a variety of recordings done exclusively for video presentations, such as "The Kingston Trio & Friends: Reunion", "The Folk Music Reunion", "The Young Man From Boston", "There's A Meetin' Here Tonight" or any of the guest TV appearances the Trio has made (except in cases where said recordings were actually released).

While we *have* included unreleased masters listed in the various studio files, we have *not* included any of the privately-recorded Trio concerts' contents, including the *"Hungry i"* recordings of June 5-17, 1967, the contents of which are (at this time) subject to much speculation and conjecture.

Also noted herein are the many candidates for the 1986 Folk Era collection, tentatively titled THE "B" SIDES (see "Re-issued, Rumored & Unreleased" chapter), the final line-up of which was still in the planning stages at press time.

Scattered throughout, you will find photos of the Trio's many song folios and even a few sheet music covers.

Everybody's favorite Kingston Trio song is here, somewhere. We hope you enjoy seeking out your own.

Across The Wide Missouri by Jimmy Shirl & Ervin M. Drake. Capitol master #31750, recorded and released in 1959 on HERE WE GO AGAIN and in Japan on Capitol single 7P-183. Later included on BEST OF VOL. 2. Also, see "Discography" chapter: Section Two (#12, 22); Three (#2, 3, 4, 6); Seven (#9).

Adieu To My Island by Travis Edmunson. Capitol master #35209, recorded in 1961 at the GOIN' PLACES sessions, and finally released in 1985 on REDISCOVER.

Adios Farewell by Terry Gilkyson. Capitol master#38403, recorded and released in 1962 on NEW FRONTIER. Also: Section Ten (#12); Twelve (#2).

Ah, Woe, Ah, Me by Reynolds-Shane-Stewart. Capitol master #51755, recorded live in 1964 for BACK IN TOWN. Also: Section Three (#7).

Allentown Jail by I. Gordon. Capitol master #37857, recorded in 1962 (at the same mini-session that produced the single *C'Mon Betty Home*), and released in 1985 on REDISCOVER.

All My Sorrows by Guard-Shane-Reynolds. Capitol master #22601, recorded in 1959 for AT LARGE, and issued as the B side of *M.T.A.* Also: Section Two (#9, 10, 16, 22); Three (#9); Seven (#2, 6).

All Through The Night by Nick Reynolds. Capitol master #33990, recorded in 1960 for THE LAST MONTH OF THE YEAR. Also: Section Seven (#20); Ten (#8).

Ally Ally Oxen Free by Rod McKuen & Steven Yates. Capitol master #50466, issued as single 5078 and on TIME TO THINK in 1963. It was later included on BEST OF VOL. 2. Also: Section Two (#12, 24, 26); Three (#4, 5, 7); Eleven (#3); Fourteen (#5); Fifteen (#23, 24).

Ann by Billy Edd Wheeler. Recorded twice: (1) Unreleased Capitol master #50907 from the 1963 TIME TO THINK studio sessions; (2) Capitol master #51754, recorded live in 1964 for BACK IN TOWN

and also included on THE FOLK ERA. Also: Section Three (#4); Fifteen (#26, 27).

Aspen Gold by Harold Payne. Recorded twice: (1) Unreleased 1977 Mountain Creek master (# unknown) from the same session that produced the single record version of *Big Ship Glory*. (2) Title track from the 1979 Nautilus album, recorded digitally (master # unknown). Also: Section Two (#18); Five (#12).

Away Rio by Reynolds-Shane-Stewart. Capitol master #37552, recorded in 1962 for SOMETHING SPECIAL. Also: Section Fifteen (#12).

Babe, You've Been On My Mind by Bob Dylan. Recorded twice: (1) Decca master #14,211, released in 1966 as B side of *Texas Across The River*. (2) Recorded live in 1966, and later released in 1969 on ONCE UPON A TIME (master # unknown). Also: Section Two (#23); Three (#11, 12).

Baby Boy (see *Glorious Kingdom*).

Bad Man Blunder by Cisco Houston & Lee Hays. Capitol master #33628, recorded and released in 1960 on single 4379 and the album STRING ALONG. Later chosen for a spot on THE BEST OF. The single ends a few seconds earlier than the album version does. Also: Section Two (#11, 15, 16, 24, 26); Three (#9); Seven (#16); Nine (#7); Eleven (#1).

Ballad Of The Quiet Fighter by John Stewart. Capitol master #38997, released in 1963 on #16. Also: Section Three (#10); Twelve (#3).

Ballad Of The Shape Of Things, by Sheldon Har-

nick. Recorded twice: (1) Capitol master #36919, recorded live in 1961 for release on 1962's COLLEGE CONCERT, and later included on THE BEST OF VOL. 2 and THE FOLK ERA. (2) ONCE UPON A TIME. Also: Section Two (#12, 13); Three (#11, 12).

Ballad Of The Thresher by Allen-Nielsen-Donald. Capitol master #39969, done in 1963 for the B side of *Desert Pete* and the LP SUNNY SIDE. Also: Section Three (#10).

Banua, adapted by Dave Guard. Recorded twice: (1) Capitol master #18399, mono only, for THE KINGSTON TRIO (1958). Also: Section Two (#7); Seven (#4). (2) Recorded in 1958 in stereo for what became STEREO CONCERT (1959), a live recording with no assigned master #s.

Bay of Mexico, adapted by Dave Guard. Capitol master #18398, recorded and released in mono only on 1958's THE KINGSTON TRIO. Re-issued in "Duophonic" on ENCORES and THE FOLK ERA. Also: Section Two (#7, 8); Three (#6); Seven (#1); Eight (#1); Eleven (#4).

Beneath The Willow (see *Weeping Willow*).

Big Ball In Town by Reynolds-Shane-Stewart. Capitol master #39030, released in 1963 on #16. Also: Section Twelve (#3).

Big Ship Glory by Charlie Merriam. Recorded twice: (1) 1977 Mountain Creek single (no master # known). (2) Recorded in 1982 for the 1983 Xeres album LOOKING FOR THE SUNSHINE.

Billy Goat Hill by Jim Day & George Arno. Capitol master #35203, recorded and released in

1961 on GOIN' PLACES. Later included on THE BEST OF. Also: Section Two (#20); Ten (#16).

Bimini by Bill Olofson & Mark McIntyre. Capitol master #22994, recorded for SOLD OUT in 1960. Also: Section Seven (#15); Fifteen (#3).

Bitter Green by Gordon Lightfoot. Unreleased 1971 Capitol master (# unknown) by the New Kingston Trio, recorded at the same sessions that produced the *Windy Wakefield* single.

Blowin' In The Wind by Bob Dylan. Capitol master #39936, recorded in 1963 for SUNNY SIDE, and later included on THE FOLK ERA and THE BEST OF VOL. 2. Also: Section Two (#12, 15, 16, 22, 24, 26); Three (#2, 3, 4, 5, 9); Eleven (#2). An instrumental version was done by Frank Hamilton for the SING A SONG WITH THE KINGSTON TRIO album.

Blow The Candle Out by Bob Shane & Tom Drake. Capitol master #34622, done in 1960 for 1961's MAKE WAY album. Also: Section Two (#13, 15); Seven (#22).

Blow Ye Winds by Dave Guard. Capitol master #22562, recorded in 1959 for AT LARGE. Also: Section Two (#9, 10); Seven (#7). First stereo studio track by the Kingston Trio.

Blue Eyed Gal by Bob Shane, Tom Drake & Miriam Stafford. Capitol master #34624, recorded in 1960 for MAKE WAY, released in 1961. Also: Section Two (#15); Seven (#22).

Blue Skies And Teardrops by Mike Williams. Recorded and released in 1973 on THE WORLD NEEDS A MELODY, an album for which no master #s are on record.

Blue Tattoo by A. Clancy. Capitol mono master #18539 (1958), released in 1985 on REDISCOVER.

Bonnie Hielan' Laddie by Joe Hickerson & Dave Guard. Capitol master #34641, recorded in 1960 and released in 1961 on MAKE WAY. Also: Section Seven (#23).

Bottle Of Wine by Tom Paxton. Decca master #13,675, recorded and released in 1965 on STAY AWHILE. Also: Section Three (#8).

Brown Mountain Light by Scott Wiseman. Capitol master #37555, recorded and released in 1962 on SOMETHING SPECIAL. Also: Section Fifteen (#9).

Buddy Better Get On Down The Line by Jane Bowers & Dave Guard. Capitol master #33669, recorded and released in 1960 on STRING ALONG, and later collected in Europe on A TRIBUTE TO THE KINGSTON TRIO. Also: Section Seven (#18); Ten (#3).

Bye Bye Thou Little Tiny Child by Dave Guard. Capitol master #33988, done in 1960 for THE LAST MONTH OF THE YEAR and released in Europe as

single CL15228. Also: Section Seven (#19); Ten (#10).

California (see *I'm Going Home*).

Carrier Pigeon by Jules Fox & Sam Freedman. Capitol master #23004, recorded for SOLD OUT (1960). Also: Section Seven (#15).

Children Of The Morning by John Stewart. Decca master #L14023, recorded for the 1966 LP of the same name. Also: Section Three (#8).

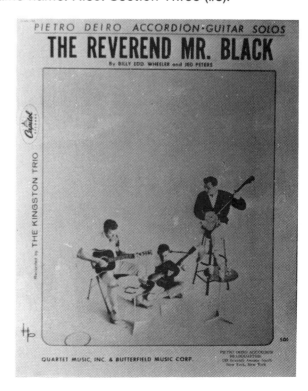

Chilly Winds by John Phillips & John Stewart. Capitol master #36911, done live in 1961 and released in 1962 on COLLEGE CONCERT, in Europe on single CL15367, and in Japan on single CR-1602. Also: Section Two (#14); Three (#3, 4, 6). SING A SONG WITH THE KINGSTON TRIO featured an instrumental version of the song by Frank Hamilton.

C'Mon Betty Home by Paul Stookey & Peter Yarrow. Capitol master #37856, recorded and released in 1962 on single 4808. Also: Section Nine (#3). *C'Mon Betty Home* is a very definite candidate for THE "B" SIDES, a planned 1986 album on the Folk Era label.

Coal Tattoo by Billy Edd Wheeler. Capitol master #50928, recorded in 1963 for TIME TO THINK. Also: Section Nine (#9); Eight (#5).

Coast Of California by Jane Bowers & Dave Guard. Capitol master #33666, recorded in 1960 at the STRING ALONG sessions and released in 1961 on GOIN' PLACES. Also: Section Two (#20).

Colorado Trail by Carl Sandburg & Lee Hays. Capitol master #33670, recorded and released in 1960 on STRING ALONG. Also: Section Seven (#16); Ten (#5).

Colours by Donovan. Recorded live in 1966 and released in 1969 on ONCE UPON A TIME. No master # is available. Also: Section Two (#23); Three (#11, 12); Fourteen (#15).

Come All You Fair and Tender Ladies by Dave Guard & Gretchen Guard. Capitol master #34623, recorded in 1960 and released in 1961 on MAKE WAY. Also: Section Two (#15); Three (#2); Seven (#22).

Come Gather The Time by John Stewart. Unreleased Decca master #14,033, recorded at the 1966 sessions that produced CHILDREN OF THE MORNING.

Come The Morning (writer unknown). Recorded and released in 1973 by the New Kingston Trio on THE WORLD NEEDS A MELODY.

Coming From The Mountains by John Stewart. Capitol master #36383, recorded and released in 1961 on CLOSE-UP and single 4642. Also: Section Seven (#25).

Como Se Viene, Se Va by Herscher & Dupree. Capitol mono master #19852, recorded in 1958 at the same session that produced *Ruby Red*. Released in 1959 on the *M.T.A.* EP, and in 1960 in Europe as the B side of single CL15192; later in Duophonic on A TRIBUTE TO THE KINGSTON TRIO. It could see its first U.S.A. LP release in 1986 on THE "B" SIDES.

Coo Coo-U by David Wheat & Bill Loughborough. Capitol master #32418, recorded in 1959 for single 4303. A stereo version of the single was released to some FM radio stations. Additionally, *Coo Coo-U* is the only known Trio track to be released in a magazine: *Echo Magazine* ("The Magazine You Play On Your Phonograph"), Vol. 1, No. 3 (1960). A prime contender for THE "B" SIDES album.

Coplas, adapted by Dave Guard. Recorded twice: (1) Capitol mono master #18392, recorded in 1958 for THE KINGSTON TRIO, and later issued in

later collected on THE FOLK ERA. Also: Section Two (#9, 10); Three (#2); Seven (#7). Instrumental: SING A SONG.

Cortelia Clark by Mickey Newbury. LOOKING FOR THE SUNSHINE (1983).

Dancing Distance by Mason Williams & John Stewart. Decca master #13,870, recorded and released in 1965 on SOMETHIN' ELSE.

Deportee by Woody Guthrie & Martin Hoffman. Capitol master #50911, for 1963's TIME TO THINK. Later included on THE FOLK ERA. Also: Section Three (#10); Nine (#9).

Desert Pete by Billy Edd Wheeler. Capitol master #39934, recorded in 1963 for SUNNY SIDE and single 5005, and later included on THE BEST OF VOL. 2. Also: Section Two (#12, 16); Three (#9, 10); Fourteen (#4); Fifteen (#19).

Dodi Lii (writer unknown). Unreleased Capitol mono master #18403 from the 1958 sessions that produced THE KINGSTON TRIO. An earlier, non-English language version of *Dorie*.

Dogie's Lament by Shane-Reynolds-Stewart. Capitol master #38415, recorded in 1962 for NEW FRONTIER. Also: Section Two (#15); Three (#10); Ten (#15); Twelve (#2).

Don't Cry Katie by Dick Glasser. Capitol master #22999, recorded in 1960 for SOLD OUT. Also: Section Seven (#14); Eight (#3); Fifteen (#3).

Don't You Weep, Mary. Recorded twice: (1) (see *Oh Mary*); (2) by Shane-Reynolds-Stewart; Capitol master #36380, included on 1961's CLOSE-UP. Also: Section Seven (#26).

Dooley by Mitchell Jayne & Rodney Dillard. Decca master #13,678 from 1965's STAY AWHILE. Also: Section Three (#8).

Dorie by Guard-Reynolds-Shane. Capitol mono master #30202, recorded live in 1958 for FROM THE "HUNGRY i" (1959), and later released in Duophonic on ENCORES. Also: Section Two (#17).

Early In The Mornin' by Randy Starr & Dick Wolf. Capitol master #22596, recorded in 1959 for AT LARGE. Also: Section Two (#9, 10, 15); Seven (#7). Also known as *Early Mornin'*.

Early Morning Rain by Gordon Lightfoot. Recorded four times: (1) Decca master #13, 861 for SOMETHIN' ELSE in 1965. Also: Section Three (#8). (2) In 1966 for 1969's ONCE UPON A TIME. Also: Section Two (#19, 23). (3) Recorded and released in Japan in 1970 on THE NEW KINGSTON TRIO, an album for which no master #s are known. (4) In 1979 for ASPEN GOLD. Also: Section Two (#18).

Easy To Arrange by Jak Kelly. LOOKING FOR THE SUNSHINE (1983).

E Inu Tatou E by George Archer. Capitol master

Duophonic on THE BEST OF VOL. 2. Also: Section Two (#7, 8, 12, 22); Seven (#4). (2) STEREO CONCERT. Also: Section Seven (#3).

Coplas Revisited by Reynolds-Shane-Stewart. Capitol master #36910, recorded live in 1961 for 1962's COLLEGE CONCERT. Also: Section Two (#14).

Corey, Corey by Guard-Shane-Reynolds. Capitol master #22600, recorded in 1959 for AT LARGE, and also issued on a special endorsement promo single for the group's line of menswear. It was

#31772 from 1959's HERE WE GO AGAIN. Also: Section Seven (#10).

El Matador by Jane Bowers & Irving Burgess. Capitol master #22996, recorded in 1960 for SOLD OUT and single 4338. Collected on BEST OF VOL. 3 and A TRIBUTE TO. Also: Section Two (#16, 24, 26); Section Three (#9); Five (#4); Seven (#13).

En El Agua by Antonio Fernandez. Capitol master #34639 from the 1960 sessions that produced MAKE WAY (1961). Also released as the B side of single 4536, in Japan as the B side of single 7P-259, and in Europe as single CL15192. Later included on BEST OF VOL. 3. Also: Section Seven (#22).

The Escape Of Old John Webb by Tom Drake. Capitol master #33625 from 1960's STRING ALONG, also released as the B side of single 4379. Later included on A TRIBUTE TO. Also: Section Two (#15); Seven (#16).

Everybody's Talking by Fred Neil. Unreleased Xeres master from the 1982 LOOKING FOR THE SUNSHINE sessions.

Everglades by Harlan Howard. Capitol master #33624, recorded and released in 1960 on STRING ALONG and single 4441. Later included on THE BEST OF. Also: Section Two (#15, 16); Three (#9); Five (#6); Seven (#18); Ten (#2).

Farewell by Bob Dylan. Decca master #13,548, recorded in 1964 for NICK-BOB-JOHN. Also: Section Three (#8); Nine (#10).

Farewell Adelita by Shane-Reynolds-Guard. Capitol master #22990, released in 1960 on SOLD

OUT, and also issued on the Trio's menswear promo single. Also: Section Seven (#13).

Farewell Captain by Mike Stewart. Capitol master #51751, recorded live in 1964 for BACK IN TOWN. Also: Section Two (#13); Fifteen (#26).

Fast Freight by Terry Gilkyson. Capitol mono master #18397, recorded in 1958 for THE KINGSTON TRIO. Also: Section Two (#7, 8, 15).

The First Time (Ever I Saw Your Face) by Ewan MacColl. Capitol master #38416, released in 1962 on NEW FRONTIER. Also: Section Two (#15, 21); Twelve (#2).

500 Miles by Hedy West. Capitol master #36917, recorded live in 1961 and released in 1962 on COLLEGE CONCERT, in Europe on single CL15275, and in Japan on single CR-1137. It was later included on BEST OF VOL. 3 and A TRIBUTE TO. Also: Section Two (#14, 15, 16, 21); Three (#3, 4, 5, 7, 9); Nine (#5); Eleven (#2). An instrumental version by Frank Hamilton (master #50704) appears on SING A SONG, and on the B side of Japanese single CR-1137.

Folksinger's Song by Mike Settle. Capitol master #39994, recorded at the 1963 SUNNY SIDE sessions, and released in 1985 on REDISCOVER.

Follow Now Oh Shepherds by Gretchen Guard. Capitol master #33992, recorded in 1960 for THE LAST MONTH OF THE YEAR. Also: Section Seven (#21); Ten (#9).

Four Strong Winds by Ian Tyson. Recorded twice: (1) Unreleased Capitol master #50467 (marked "not releasable" in the files), recorded in 1963 at the same session that produced the *Ally Ally*

Oxen Free single; (2) Unreleased Capitol master #50912, recorded later in 1963 at the sessions that produced the balance of TIME TO THINK.

Fourth Avenue New Hope Mission (writer unknown). Unreleased master from the 1973 sessions that produced THE WORLD NEEDS A MELODY.

Friends Forever (writer unknown). Unreleased Capitol master from the 1971 sessions that produced the New Kingston Trio single *Windy Wakefield*.

Gaze On Other Heavens by John Stewart. Decca master #L14027, recorded in 1966 for CHILDREN OF THE MORNING.

Genny Glenn by Shane-Reynolds-Stewart. Capitol master #38401, recorded in 1962 for NEW FRONTIER. Also: Section Ten (#14).

Georgia Stockade by Reynolds-Shane-Stewart. Capitol master #51758, recorded live in 1964 for BACK IN TOWN. Also: Section Two (#15); Three (#4).

Getaway John by Dave Guard. Recorded twice: (1) Capitol master #22608, recorded in 1959 for AT LARGE, and later included on THE FOLK ERA. Also: Section Two (#9); Seven (#8). (2) ONCE UPON A TIME. Also: Section Two (#23); Three (#11, 12).

Glorious Kingdom by Shane-Reynolds-Stewart. Capitol master #36369, recorded in 1961 for CLOSE-UP. Also: Section Seven (#27); Fifteen (#20).

Goin' Away For To Leave You by John Phillips. Capitol master #36920, done live in 1961 for COLLEGE CONCERT (1962).

Golden Spike by J. Pike. Capitol master #35218, from the GOIN' PLACES sessions of 1961. Released on REDISCOVER (1985).

Gonna Go Down The River by Buddy Mize & Dallas Frazier. Decca master #13,673, from STAY AWHILE (1965).

Goober Peas by Dave Guard. Capitol master #31748, recorded and released in 1959 on HERE WE GO AGAIN. Also: Section Two (#15); Seven (#9).

Good News by Louis Gottlieb. Capitol master #22598, recorded for AT LARGE in 1959. Also: Section Two (#9); Seven (#8).

Goodnight Irene by Huddie Ledbetter & John Lomax. Recorded live in 1966 for ONCE UPON A TIME (1969). Also: Section Two (#23); Three (#11, 12).

Goodnight My Baby by Nick Reynolds. Capitol master #33986, recorded for THE LAST MONTH OF THE YEAR in 1960, and also released as the B side of single 4475. Also: Section Seven (#21).

Goo Ga Gee by Mike Settle. Capitol master #39963, recorded and released in 1963 on SUNNY SIDE.

Go Tell Roger by John Stewart. Decca master #13,865, recorded in 1965 for SOMETHIN' ELSE.

Gotta Travel On by Paul Clayton. Decca master #13,542, recorded and released in 1964 on NICK-BOB-JOHN. Also: Section Three (#8).

Go Where I Send Thee by Guard-Reynolds-Shane. Capitol master #34007, from THE LAST MONTH OF THE YEAR (1960). Also: Section Two

(#13); Seven (#21); Ten (#7).

Grandma's Feather Bed by Jim Connor. THE WORLD NEEDS A MELODY (1973).

Greenback Dollar by Hoyt Axton & Ken Ramsey. Recorded five times: (1) Capitol master #38414, recorded and released in 1962 on NEW FRONTIER. Later collected on THE BEST OF VOL. 2 and THE FOLK ERA. Also: Section Two (#12, 16, 22, 24, 25, 26); Three (#3, 4, 5, 7, 9); Five (#10); Nine (#4, 5, 6); Eleven (#3); Twelve (#2); Fourteen (#3, 10); Fifteen (#14). The original single (4898) is the identical version with the word "damn" covered by a guitar chord, and this censored take also appeared on the *mono* version of CHARTBUSTERS VOL. 2. Frank Hamilton's instrumental cover of the song appeared on SING A SONG. (2) ONCE UPON A TIME. Also: Section Two (#23); Three (#12). (3) Recorded for K-Tel in 1978, and released in Italy on the LEGENDS OF ROCK collection. (4) ASPEN GOLD (1979). Also: Section Two (#18). (5) Recorded in 1981 for the 1982 release of 25 YEARS NON-STOP.

Green Grasses by John Stewart. Recorded twice: (1) Capitol master #32416, recorded as the B side of *Coo Coo-U* in 1959 and later released in Europe on A TRIBUTE TO. A possible contender for inclusion on THE "B" SIDES. (2) Capitol master #38412, assigned to the vaults during the 1962 sessions that produced NEW FRONTIER. Actually John's 1961 Trio "audition" tape, it was finally released in 1985 on REDISCOVER.

Guardo El Lobo by Erich Schwandt. Capitol master #35205, recorded for GOIN' PLACES in 1961. Also: Section Two (#15, 20).

Gue, Gue by Guard-Reynolds-Shane. Recorded twice: (1) Unreleased Capitol mono master #19850, recorded at the 1958 session that produced *Ruby Red*. (2) Capitol master #30201 (also mono), recorded live in 1958 for the 1959 album FROM THE "HUNGRY i", and later issued in Duophonic as part of ENCORES. Also: Section Two (#17). Note: the acappella intro from the studio version was edited into the live track that appeared on the LP.

The Gypsy Rover (see *The Whistling Gypsy*).

Hangman by Nick Reynolds & Adam Yagodka. Capitol master #34634, recorded in 1960 for the 1961 release of MAKE WAY, and later included on THE FOLK ERA and BEST OF VOL. 3. Also: Section Seven (#24).

Hanna Lee by Richard Mills & Stan Jones. Decca master #13,674, recorded in 1965 for STAY AWHILE. Also: Section Three (#8).

Hard, Ain't It Hard by Woody Guthrie. Recorded three times: (1) Capitol mono master #18387, the Kingston Trio's first Capitol track, recorded in 1958 for THE KINGSTON TRIO. Later released in Duophonic on ENCORES. Also: Section Two (#7, 8, 22, 24, 26). (2) ONCE UPON A TIME. Also: Section Two (#23); Three (#11, 12). (3) ASPEN GOLD (1979). Also: Section Two (#18).

Hard Travelin' by Woody Guthrie. Recorded three times: (1) Capitol master #34608, recorded at the 1960 sessions for MAKE WAY (1961). Also: Section Two (#15); Three (#2, 6); Seven (#24). (2) ONCE UPON A TIME. Also: Section Two (#19, 23). (3) 25 YEARS NON-STOP.

Haul Away by Dave Guard. Capitol master #31749, recorded and released in 1959 on HERE WE GO AGAIN. Also: Section Five (#2); Seven (#10).

Hawaiian Nights by Harold Payne. LOOKING FOR THE SUNSHINE.

Hit And Run by John Stewart. Decca master #L14024, recorded in 1966 for CHILDREN OF THE MORNING, and also released as the B side of single 32010.

Hobo's Lullaby by Goebel Reeves. Capitol master #50908, recorded in 1963 for TIME TO THINK. Also: Section Nine (#9).

Home From The Hill by Bronislau Kaper & Mack David. Capitol master #23002, recorded at the 1960 sessions that produced SOLD OUT. Released as the B side of single 4338. Watch for its first LP appearances on THE "B" SIDES (1986).

Honey, Are You Mad At Your Man by Shane-Reynolds-Stewart. Capitol master #38407, recorded in 1962 for NEW FRONTIER. Also: Section Ten (#12); Twelve (#2); Fifteen (#15).

Hope You Understand by John Stewart. Decca master #13,543, recorded and released in 1964 on single 31702 and the album NICK-BOB-JOHN.

The Hunter by Guard-Shane-Reynolds. Recorded twice: (1) Unreleased Capitol master #32394, recorded in 1959 at the *Coo Coo-U* sessions. (2) Capitol master #32417, recorded at the same sessions but later released on SOLD OUT (1960). Also: Section Seven (#13); Eight (#2).

I Bawled by Bob Shane. Capitol master #22595, recorded and released in 1959 on AT LARGE. Also: Section Two (#9); Seven (#8).

If I Had A Ship by Mason Williams. Decca master #13,678, recorded in 1965 for STAY AWHILE. Also: Section Three (#8).

If You Don't Look Around by John Stewart. Capitol master #50931, recorded in 1963 for TIME TO THINK, and also released as the B side of single 5166. Later included in Europe on A TRIBUTE TO. Also: Section Eight (#5).

If You See Me Go by Mike Stewart. Decca master #13,677, recorded in 1965 for STAY AWHILE.

I Like To Hear The Rain by Alex Harvey. LOOKING FOR THE SUNSHINE.

I'll Find You (writer unknown). Unreleased Capitol master from the 1971 *Windy Wakefield* sessions.

I'm A Rake And Ramblin' Boy, adapted by Brown & Gilbert. LOOKING FOR THE SUNSHINE.

I'm Going Home by Fred Geis. Recorded four times: (1) Decca master #13,549, recorded in 1964

for NICK-BOB-JOHN, and also released on single 31730. Also: Section Nine (#10). (2) ONCE UPON A TIME. Also: Section Two (#19, 23). (3) THE NEW KINGSTON TRIO (1970). (4) Recorded in 1979 for ASPEN GOLD, under the title *California.* Also: Section Two (#18).

I'm Going Up Cripple Creek by Jim Connor. Recorded and released in Japan in 1970 on THE NEW KINGSTON TRIO, an album for which no master #s are known.

In Tall Buildings by John Hartford. THE WORLD NEEDS A MELODY (1973).

Interchangeable Love by Mason Williams. Decca master #13,863, recorded in 1965 for SOMETHIN' ELSE.

Isle In The Water by Rod McKuen. Capitol master #51756, recorded live in 1964 for BACK IN TOWN. Also: Section Two (#14).

It Was A Very Good Year by Ervin Drake. Capitol master #35220, recorded in 1961 for GOIN' PLACES, and the last track recorded by the group with Dave Guard. Later included on BEST OF VOL. 3. Also: Section Two (#15, 20, 25); Three (#7); Nine (#8).

Jackson by Billy Edd Wheeler & Gabby Rodgers. Capitol master #39933, recorded in 1963 for SUNNY SIDE. Also: Section Three (#10).

Jane, Jane, Jane by Stan Wilson. Capitol master #37367, recorded early in 1962 for single 4740. Also: Section Nine (#2). A possible candidate for a spot on THE "B" SIDES album in 1986. Later in 1962, background orchestration was added to the

track for SOMETHING SPECIAL, and this version also appeared on BEST OF VOL. 3. Also: Section Fifteen (#12).

Jesse James by Shane-Reynolds-Stewart. Capitol master #36368, John Stewart's first recording with the Kingston Trio. From 1961's CLOSE-UP. Also: Section Three (#2, 6); Seven (#27); Nine (#5).

Johnson Party of 4 by Harold Payne. B side of the 1977 Mountain Creek 45.

Jug Of Punch by Francis McPeake & Ewan MacColl. Capitol master #34640, recorded in 1960 and released in 1961 on MAKE WAY. Also: Section Seven (#23).

Jug Town by Billy Edd Wheeler. From 1973's THE WORLD NEEDS A MELODY.

Just Once Around The Clock (writer unknown). Unreleased Capitol master #22995, recorded at the SOLD OUT sessions in 1960.

Karu by Shane-Reynolds-Stewart. Capitol master #36373, recorded and released in 1961 on CLOSE-UP. Also: Section Seven (#26).

La Bamba by Reynolds-Shane-Stewart. Capitol master #39092, recorded for #16 (1963). Also: Section Two (#13, 15); Nine (#6).

Laredo? by Reynolds-Shane-Stewart. Capitol master #36913, recorded live in 1961 and released in 1962 on COLLEGE CONCERT.

The Last Month Of The Year by Vera Hall, Ruby Pickens Tartt & Alan Lomax. Capitol master #34006, recorded in 1960 for the album of the same name. Also: Section Seven (#19); Ten (#6).

Last Night I Had The Strangest Dream by Ed McCurdy. Capitol master #50909, recorded in 1963 for TIME TO THINK, and also issued on single 5132 and European single 4F 193. Later included on THE FOLK ERA. Also: Section Two (#15, 16); Three (#3, 4, 5, 9); Eight (#5); Eleven (#2).

Last Thing On My Mind by Tom Paxton. Recorded twice: (1) Decca master #13,864, recorded in 1965 for SOMETHIN' ELSE. Also: Section Three (#8). (2) Unreleased Xeres master from the LOOKING FOR THE SUNSHINE sessions.

Leave My Woman Alone by Ray Charles. Capitol master #33626, recorded and released in 1960 on STRING ALONG, and later included on THE FOLK ERA. Also: Section Seven (#17); Ten (#1).

Lei Pakalana by Samuel F. Omar. Decca master #L14026, recorded and released in 1966 on CHILDREN OF THE MORNING.

Lemon Tree by Will Holt. Capitol master #35207, recorded in 1961 for GOIN' PLACES, and later included on THE FOLK ERA and BEST OF VOL. 3. Also: Section Two (#15, 16, 20, 21); Three (#3, 6, 9);

Nine (#7, 8); Eleven (#2); Fourteen (#7).

Less Of Me by Glen Campbell. Decca master #L14032, recorded in 1966 for CHILDREN OF THE MORNING.

Let's Get Together by Chet Powers. Capitol master #51753, recorded live in 1964 for BACK IN TOWN. Also: Section Two (#15, 16); Three (#9); Fifteen (#26, 27).

The Lion Sleeps Tonight (see *Wimoweh*).

Little Boy by Mike Settle. Capitol master #37563, recorded in 1962 for SOMETHING SPECIAL. Also: Section Two (#15); Nine (#4).

Little Light by Reynolds-Shane-Stewart. Capitol master #36909, recorded live in 1961 for COLLEGE CONCERT (1962).

Little Maggie, adapted by Dave Guard. Capitol mono master #18402, recorded in 1958 for THE KINGSTON TRIO. Later re-issued in Duophonic on ENCORES and THE FOLK ERA. Also: Section Two (#7, 8, 15); Three (#2).

Little Play Soldiers by M. Cooper. Decca master #13,557, recorded in 1964 for NICK-BOB-JOHN, and also released on single 31730. Also: Section Nine (#10).

A Little Soul Is Born by John Stewart. Decca master #L14029, recorded in 1966 for CHILDREN OF THE MORNING, and also issued on single 31961.

Lock All The Windows by John Stewart. Decca master #L14031, recorded in 1966 for CHILDREN OF THE MORNING, and also released on single 32010.

Lonesome Traveler (see *Shady Grove/Lonesome Traveler*).

The Long Black Rifle by Lawrence Coleman & Norman Gimbel. Capitol master #22602, recorded in 1959 for AT LARGE. Also: Section Two (#14); Seven (#7); Eight (#1).

Long Black Veil by Marijohn Wilkin & Danny Dill. Recorded twice: (1) Capitol master #38413, recorded and released in 1962 on NEW FRONTIER. Also: Section Ten (#14). (2) LOOKING FOR THE SUNSHINE.

Longest Beer Of The Night by Carson Parks. Recorded and released in 1979 on ASPEN GOLD. Also: Section Two (#18); Five (#12).

Long Time Blues by Mason Williams. Recorded twice: (1) Unreleased Decca master #13,546, recorded at the NICK-BOB-JOHN sessions in 1964. (2) Decca master #13,869, recorded and released in 1965 on SOMETHIN' ELSE.

Looking For The Sunshine by Mickey Newbury. Recorded in 1982 for Xeres single SCH 1-10004, and re-mixed in 1983 for the album of the same name.

Love Comes A Trickling Down by Jonathan Harris. Decca master #13,545, recorded and released in 1964 on NICK-BOB-JOHN.

Love Has Gone by A. Clancy. Capitol master #39059, from the sessions that produced #16 (1963). Released in 1985 on REDISCOVER.

Love's Been Good To Me by Rod McKuen. Decca master #13,539, recorded and released in 1964 on NICK-BOB-JOHN.

Lovin' You Again (writer unknown). THE WORLD NEEDS A MELODY.

Low Bridge by Reynolds-Shane-Stewart. Capitol master #39090, recorded and released on #16 in 1963. Also: Section Fifteen (#17).

Mama, You've Been On My Mind (see *Babe, You've Been On My Mind*).

Mangwani Mpulele by Theodore Bikel. Capitol master #23002, recorded and released in 1960 on SOLD OUT. Also: Section Seven (#14).

Marcelle Vahine by Augie Goupil. Capitol master #39971, recorded and released in 1963 on SUNNY SIDE and as the B side of single 5078. Also: Section Fifteen (#19).

Mark Twain by Geller & Seligson. Capitol master #39058, recorded for 1963's #16. Also: Section Two (#15); Fifteen (#17).

Mary Mild by Bob Shane, Tom Drake & Miriam Stafford. Capitol master #33987, recorded in 1960 for THE LAST MONTH OF THE YEAR. Also: Section Seven (#20); Ten (#10).

Mary Was Pretty (writer unknown). Unreleased Capitol master #35206 from the 1961 GOIN' PLACES sessions.

The Merry Minuet by Sheldon Harnick. Recorded three times: (1) Capitol mono master #30208, recorded live in 1958 and released in 1959 on FROM THE "HUNGRY i". Later re-issued in Duophonic on THE BEST OF and THE FOLK ERA. Also: Section Two (#11, 15, 16, 17); Three (#9); Five (#1). (2) STEREO CONCERT. (3) 25 YEARS NON-STOP.

Midnight Special, adapted by Reynolds-Shane-Stewart. Decca master #13,538, recorded and released in 1964 on NICK-BOB-JOHN. Also: Section Three (#8). The first Decca recording for the Kingston Trio.

Molly Dee by John Stewart. Capitol master #31771, recorded in 1959 for HERE WE GO AGAIN. Also: Section Two (#15); Five (#2); Seven (#9, 12); Twelve (#1).

More Poems by Mason Williams. Decca master #13,547, recorded in 1964 for NICK-BOB-JOHN.

The Mountains O'Mourne by Percy French &

Houston Collisson. Capitol master #23000, recorded and released in 1960 on SOLD OUT. Also: Section Seven (#13).

M.T.A. by Jacqueline Steiner & Bess Hawes. Recorded five times: (1) Capitol master #22563, recorded in 1959 for AT LARGE and single F4221. Later included on THE BEST OF and THE FOLK ERA. Also: Section Two (#9, 10, 11, 13, 15, 16, 22, 24, 25, 26); Three (#9); Five (#7, 8); Seven (#2, 6); Eight (#1); Fifteen (#1, 2). Also released on 78 r.p.m. single F4221 in Canada. (2) Capitol master #36916, recorded live in 1961 for 1962's COLLEGE CONCERT. Also: Section Three (#7). (3) Recorded live in 1966 for ONCE UPON A TIME (1969). Also: Section Two (#19, 23). (4) Recorded as the first half of a medley with *Tom Dooley* for ASPEN GOLD in 1979. Also: Section Two (#18). (5) Recorded in 1981 for the 1982 release of 25 YEARS NON-STOP.

My Lord What A Mornin' by Shane-Reynolds-Stewart. Capitol master #38404, recorded in 1962 for NEW FRONTIER. Also: Section Ten (#13).

My Ramblin' Boy by Tom Paxton. Recorded twice: (1) Decca master #13,544, recorded and released in 1964 on NICK-BOB-JOHN. Also: Section Nine (#10). (2) Decca master #13,550, also recorded at the NICK-BOB-JOHN sessions, but only released on single 31702. Shorter than the LP version.

Nellie by Barry Etris. Recorded twice: (1) THE WORLD NEEDS A MELODY. (2) Unreleased master from the same session (1973).

The New Frontier by John Stewart. Capitol master #38405, recorded in 1962 for NEW FRON-

TIER and single 4898. Also: Section Eight (#4); Nine (#5); Twelve (#2); Fifteen (#15, 26).

New York Girls by Burl Ives. Recorded twice: (1) Unreleased Capitol mono master #19851, from the *Ruby Red* session of 1958. (2) Capitol mono master #30206, recorded live in 1958 for the 1959 release of FROM THE "HUNGRY i", later re-issued in Duophonic on ENCORES. Also: Section Two (#17).

No One To Talk My Troubles To by Dick Weissman. Capitol master #50927, recorded and released in 1963 on TIME TO THINK.

Norwegian Wood by John Lennon & Paul McCartney. Decca master #117,024, recorded in 1966 for single 31922 and CHILDREN OF THE MORNING.

Nothing More To Look Forward To by Richard Adler. Capitol master #36387, recorded at the 1961 CLOSE-UP sessions, and released as the B side of single 4642. A likely title to be found on the 1986 proposed album from Folk Era, THE "B" SIDES.

Oh, Cindy by Guard-Reynolds-Shane-Werber. Capitol master #22604, recorded at the AT LARGE sessions in 1959, and released as the B side of single F4167. It appeared in stereo on the *Tijuana Jail* EP. Later collected in Europe on A TRIBUTE TO. Its first American LP appearance will no doubt be on THE "B" SIDES.

Oh Joe Hannah by John Stewart. Capitol master #39032, recorded and released in 1963 on #16. Also: Section Two (#15); Fifteen (#17).

Oh Mary by J. Pike. Recorded twice: (1) Capitol master #34621 from the 1960 MAKE WAY sessions, released in 1985 on REDISCOVER. (2) see *Don't You Weep Mary*.

Oh, Miss Mary by John Stewart & John Phillips. Capitol master #36912, recorded live in 1961 for the 1962 album COLLEGE CONCERT.

Oh, Sail Away by John Phillips & Richard Weissman. Capitol master #36375, recorded in 1961 for CLOSE-UP, and also released in Europe as the B side of single CL15275. Also: Section Seven (#25).

Oh, Yes, Oh by Dave Guard & Gretchen Guard. Capitol master #34642, recorded in 1960 for the 1961 album MAKE WAY. Also: Section Seven (#23).

O Ken Karanga by Massie Patterson & Lionel Belasco, transcription by Maurice Baron. Recorded twice: (1) Capitol master #36372, recorded and released in 1961 on CLOSE-UP and as the B side of single 4671. Also: Section Two (#14); Seven (#27); Nine (#1, 2). (2) Capitol master #36914, recorded live in 1961 for the 1962 release of COLLEGE CONCERT. Also: Section Three (#7).

Old Joe Clark, adapted by Reynolds-Shane-Stewart. Capitol master #37366, recorded at the

1962 session that produced *Jane, Jane, Jane,* and released that year on SOMETHING SPECIAL and as the B side of single 4808. Later collected on THE FOLK ERA. Also: Section Two (#15); Three (#5); Nine (#3); Fifteen (#9).

Old Kentucky Land by K. Ogermann and J. Nicolas. Capitol master #36859, recorded after the CLOSE-UP sessions in 1961. Sung in German and released in Germany as the B side of single K 22442 in 1961. First released in America on REDISCOVER (1985).

Oleanna by Harvey Geller & Martin Seligson. Capitol master #31768, recorded in 1959 for HERE WE GO AGAIN. Also: Section Seven (#11, 12).

One More Round by Reynolds-Shane-Stewart. Capitol master #39031, released in 1963 on #16 and as the B side of single 4951. Later collected in Europe on A TRIBUTE TO. Also: Section Twelve (#3).

One More Town by John Stewart. Capitol master #37368, recorded at the 1962 *Jane, Jane, Jane* session, and later released on SOMETHING SPECIAL and single 4842. Also: Section Nine (#3, 4, 7); Fifteen (#9, 15). Also recorded instrumentally for SING A SONG by Frank Hamilton.

One Too Many Mornings by Bob Dylan. Tetragrammaton master #7775-BW, recorded live in 1966 and released in 1969 on ONCE UPON A TIME and single T-1526. Also: Section Two (#23); Three (#11, 12).

O Willow Waly by Georges Auric & Paul Dehn. Capitol master #37567, recorded and released in 1962 on SOMETHING SPECIAL.

Parchment Farm Blues, adapted by Jack Splittard & Randy Cierley. Decca master #13,860, recorded and released in 1965 on SOMETHIN' ELSE and single 31860. Also: Section Nine (#11).

Pastures Of Plenty by Woody Guthrie. Capitol master #35204, recorded and released in 1961 on GOIN' PLACES. Also: Section Two (#15, 20); Three (#2, 5).

The Patriot Game by Billy Behen. Capitol master #50932, recorded and released in 1963 on TIME TO THINK. Also: Section Two (#13). A differently edited version was released as the B side of single 5132.

Peace-Loving Gentleman (writer unknown). Unreleased Capitol master by the New Kingston Trio, recorded in 1971 at the *Windy Wakefield* sessions.

Poor Ellen Smith by Shane-Reynolds-Stewart. Capitol master #38406, recorded in 1962 for NEW FRONTIER. Also: Section Two (#15); Ten (#13); Fifteen (#15).

Portland Town by John Stewart. Capitol master

#37564, recorded and released in 1962 on SOMETHING SPECIAL and in Japan as the B side of single CR-1602. Also: Section Three (#5); Fifteen (#12, 13).

Poverty Hill by Fred Hellerman & Fran Minkoff. Decca master #13,540, recorded in 1964 and released that year on NICK-BOB-JOHN.

Pullin' Away by Reynolds-Shane-Stewart. Capitol master #37553, recorded and released in 1962 on SOMETHING SPECIAL. Also recorded instrumentally by Frank Hamilton for SING A SONG.

Put Your Money Away by John Stewart. Decca master #117,025, recorded in 1966 at the *Norwegian Wood* session, and released as the B side of single 31922, as well as on CHILDREN OF THE MORNING.

Raspberries, Strawberries by Will Holt. Recorded three times: (1) Capitol mono master #30583, recorded late in 1958 for single F4114. Also released on the EP of the same name. A possible candidate for THE "B" SIDES. (2) Recorded live in late 1958 for what became STEREO CONCERT (1959). Also: Section Two (#15). (3) Capitol master #22997, recorded and released in 1960 on SOLD OUT. Later included on THE BEST OF and THE FOLK ERA. Also: Section Two (#11, 16, 24, 25, 26); Three (#6, 7, 9); Seven (#15); Eleven (#1); Fifteen (#8).

Razors In The Air by Erich Schwandt. Capitol master #35219, recorded in 1961 for GOIN' PLACES. Also: Section Two (#20); Nine (#1).

Red River Shore, adapted by Jack Splittard & Randy Cierley. Decca master #13,866, recorded in

1965 for SOMETHIN' ELSE. Issued in Japan as the B side of Decca single DS-422.

Remember The Alamo by Jane Bowers. Capitol master #22609, recorded and released in 1959 on AT LARGE. Also: Section Two (#9); Seven (#6).

Reuben James by Woody Guthrie & The Almanac Singers. Recorded twice: (1) Capitol master #36371, released in 1961 on CLOSE-UP. Later included on THE FOLK ERA and THE BEST OF VOL. 2. Also: Section Two (#12, 16, 25); Three (#2, 5, 9); Seven (#25); Fifteen (#14). An instrumental version by Frank Hamilton appeared on SING A SONG. Also: Section Two (#15). (2) ASPEN GOLD (1979). Also: Section Two (#18).

Reverend Mr. Black by Billy Edd Wheeler & Jed Peters. Recorded twice: (1) Capitol master #39044, released in 1963 on #16 and single 4951. Later included on THE FOLK ERA and THE BEST OF VOL. 2. Also: Section Two (#12, 15, 16); Three (#3, 7, 9, 10); Five (#10); Twelve (#3); Fourteen (#3); Fifteen (#18, 22, 28). (2) Recorded in 1981 for 25 YEARS NON-STOP (1982), and also released as the B side of Xeres single SCH 1-10004.

Rider by Bob Shane, Nick Reynolds & Judy Henske. Capitol master #39961, recorded in 1963 for SUNNY SIDE. Also: Section Two (#15).

Riley's Medicine Show (writer unknown). Recorded twice: (1) In 1973 for THE WORLD NEEDS A MELODY. (2) Unreleased alternate version from the same session.

The River Is Wide by Nick Reynolds. Capitol master #34606, recorded in 1960 and released in 1961 on MAKE WAY. Also: Section Two (#15); Seven (#23).

River Run Down by Don MacArthur & John Stewart. Capitol master #39060, released in 1963 on #16.

Road To Freedom by John Stewart. Capitol master #38996, released in 1963 on #16. Also: Section Two (#15); Twelve (#3); Fifteen (#17).

Rocky by K. Ogermann and K. Feltz. Capitol master #36858, recorded in 1961 after the CLOSE-UP sessions. Sung in German and released in Germany as single K 22442 in 1961. First released in America on REDISCOVER (1985).

Roddy McCorley, adapted by Pat Clancy. Capitol master #36915, recorded live in 1961 for COLLEGE CONCERT (1962), and also released in Europe on single CL15367.

Rollin' Stone by Stan Wilson. Recorded twice: (1) Capitol master #31767, recorded in 1959 for HERE WE GO AGAIN, and also released in Japan on single 7P-183. Also: Section Seven (#10). (2) LOOKING FOR THE SUNSHINE (1983).

Roll Your Own, Cowboys (writer unknown). THE

WORLD NEEDS A MELODY (1973).

A Round About Christmas by Nick Reynolds. Capitol master #33989, recorded in 1960 for THE LAST MONTH OF THE YEAR. Also: Section Seven (#20).

'Round About The Mountain by Lou Gottlieb. Capitol master #31755, recorded in 1959 for HERE WE GO AGAIN. Also: Section Seven (#11).

Rovin' Gambler/This Train, adapted by Samuel F. Omar. ONCE UPON A TIME, recorded live in 1966 and released in 1969. Also: Section Two (#19, 23).

Ruby Red by Vance & Pokriss. Capitol mono master #19853, recorded and released in 1958 as the B side of single F4049. Also issued on the *Raspberries, Strawberries* EP. A likely choice for 1986's THE "B" SIDES.

Runaway Song by John Stewart. Decca master #13,871, recorded in 1965 for SOMETHIN' ELSE. Also released as the B side of single 31860, and in Japan on Decca single DS-422.

Run Molly, Run by Bob Shane, Tom Drake & Miriam Stafford. Capitol master #35211, recorded and released in 1961 on GOIN' PLACES. Also: Section Two (#20); Three (#2).

Run The Ridges by John Stewart. Recorded twice: (1) Capitol master #39013, released in 1963 on #16. Also: Section Two (#15); Twelve (#3); Fifteen (#18). (2) Unreleased Nautilus master from the 1979 ASPEN GOLD sessions.

Rusting In The Rain by Rod McKuen. Decca master #13,680, recorded and released in 1965 on STAY AWHILE.

Sail Away (see *Oh, Sail Away*).

Sail Away Ladies by Guard-Shane-Reynolds. Capitol master #31747, recorded in 1959 at the same sessions that produced HERE WE GO AGAIN, and released on the *M.T.A.* EP. A definite contender for inclusion on THE "B" SIDES.

Sally by Dave Guard. Capitol mono master #30582, recorded in late 1959 at the *Raspberries, Strawberries* session, and released as the B side of single F4114. Also issued on the *Raspberries, Strawberries* EP. A likely choice for a spot on 1986's THE "B" SIDES.

Salty Dog by Reynolds-Shane-Stewart. Capitol master #51750, recorded live in 1964 for BACK IN TOWN. Also: Section Two (#15); Three (#4, 7); Fifteen (#26).

San Miguel by Jane Bowers. Capitol master #31766, recorded in 1959 for HERE WE GO AGAIN, and also released as the B side of single 4271. Later included on BEST OF VOL. 3 and A TRIBUTE TO. Also: Section Seven (#11, 12).

Santy Anno, adapted by Dave Guard. Capitol mono master #18396, recorded in 1958 for THE KINGSTON TRIO, and later re-issued in Duophonic on ENCORES. Also: Section Two (#7); Seven (#4).

Saro Jane, adapted by Louis Gottlieb. Capitol mono master #18400, recorded in 1958 for THE KINGSTON TRIO. Later re-issued in Duophonic on ENCORES and THE FOLK ERA. Also: Section Two (#7, 8, 22); Seven (#1).

Scarlet Ribbons by Evelyn Danzig & Jack O. Segal. Recorded twice: (1) Capitol mono master #18752, recorded after the sessions that produced THE KINGSTON TRIO in 1958, and released that year on single F3970, the group's first 45. Also issued on the *Raspberries, Strawberries* EP. A possible candidate for the LP, THE "B" SIDES. (2) Capitol master #22599, recorded in 1959 for AT LARGE, and later included on THE FOLK ERA and THE BEST OF VOL. 2. Also: Section Two (#9, 10, 15, 16, 21); Three (#3, 6, 9); Seven (#6); Eleven (#3).

Scotch And Soda by Dave Guard. Recorded five times: (1) Capitol mono master #18389, recorded in 1958 for THE KINGSTON TRIO. Also released in 1962 as single 4740, and re-issued in Duophonic on THE BEST OF. Also: Section Two (#7, 8, 11, 15, 16, 22, 25): Three (#6, 9); Five (#9); Nine (#2, 8); Eleven (#4). (2) Tetragammaton master #7774-BW, recorded live in 1966 and released in 1969 on ONCE UPON A TIME and single T-1526. Also: Section Two (#19, 23). (3) THE NEW KINGSTON TRIO (1970). (4) ASPEN GOLD (1979). Also: Section Two (#18). (5) 25 YEARS NON-STOP (1982).

Sea Fever by Jane Bowers. Capitol master #34633, recorded in 1960 at the MAKE WAY sessions, and finally released in 1985 on REDISCOVER.

Seasons In The Sun by Rod McKuen & Jacques Brel. Capitol master #50943, recorded and released in 1963 on TIME TO THINK. Also released on single 5166, and later collected on THE BEST OF VOL. 2. Also: Section Two (#10, 12, 16); Three (#7, 9); Eight (#5).

The Seine by Irving Burgess. Capitol master #22603, recorded in 1959 for AT LARGE. Also; Section Two (#10); Seven (#8).

Senora by Jane Bowers and Dave Guard. Capitol master #35213, recorded in 1961 for GOIN' PLACES. Also: Section Two (#15, 20).

Shady Grove/Lonesome Traveler, adapted by Jean Ritchie/Lee Hays. Capitol mono master #30209, recorded live in 1958 for the 1959 release of FROM THE "HUNGRY i", and later re-issued in Duophonic on ENCORES. Also: Section Two (#17).

The Shape Of Things (see *Ballad Of The Shape Of Things*).

She Was Too Good To Me by Richard Rodgers & Lorenz Hart. Capitol master #37578, recorded in 1962 for SOMETHING SPECIAL, and also released as the B side of single 4842. Also: Section Two (#15); Nine (#3).

Sing Out by Mike Stewart. Capitol master #39970, recorded and released in 1963 on SUNNY SIDE.

Sing We Noel by Dave Guard. Capitol master #34043, recorded and released in 1960 on THE LAST MONTH OF THE YEAR. Also: Section Seven (#19); Ten (#7).

Sloop John B by Lee Hays & Carl Sandburg. Recorded three times: (1) Capitol mono master #18391, recorded and released in 1958 on THE KINGSTON TRIO. Re-issued in Duophonic on ENCORES. Also: Section Two (#7, 8, 15, 16, 22); Three (#3, 6, 7, 9); Seven (#1). (2) THE NEW KINGSTON TRIO (1970). (3) 25 YEARS NON-STOP.

Softly As I Leave You by H. Shaper & A. DeVita. Unreleased Capitol master #39091, recorded at the #16 sessions in 1963.

So Hi by Reynolds-Shane-Stewart. Capitol master #51759, recorded live in 1964 for BACK IN TOWN.

Sold American (writer unknown). Unreleased New Kingston Trio master from the 1973 sessions for THE WORLD NEEDS A MELODY.

Some Day Soon by Ian Tyson. Decca master #13,541, recorded in 1964 for NICK-BOB-JOHN.

Some Fool Made A Soldier Of Me by Jerry Fuller. Capitol master #38402, recorded in 1962 for NEW FRONTIER, and later re-issued on THE FOLK ERA. Also; Section Three (#10); Eight (#4); Ten (#11).

Somerset Gloucestershire Wassail by Dave Guard & Eric Schwandt. Capitol master #33993, recorded and released in 1960 on THE LAST MONTH OF THE YEAR and single 4475. Also: Section Seven (#21); Ten (#9).

Sometimes Love Is Better When It's Gone by Mike Settle. Recorded in 1982 and released in 1983 on LOOKING FOR THE SUNSHINE.

Song For A Friend by John Stewart. Capitol master #50950, recorded and released in 1963 on TIME TO THINK, and later collected on THE FOLK ERA. Also: Section Three (#10). It was the Trio's last studio track for Capitol Records.

South Coast by Lillian Bos Ross, Sam Eskin & Rich Dehr. Recorded twice: (1) Capitol mono master #30203, recorded live in 1958 for FROM THE "HUNGRY i" (1959). Also: Section Two (#17, 22). (2) Recorded live in 1958 for STEREO CONCERT (1959).

South Wind by Travis Edmonson. Capitol master #33668, recorded in 1960 for STRING ALONG. Also: Section Seven (#18); Ten (#3).

Speckled Roan by Jane Bowers. Capitol master #34607, recorded in 1960 for the 1961 release of MAKE WAY. Also: Section Seven (#24).

The Spinnin' Of The World by John Stewart. Decca master #L14034, recorded and released in 1966 on CHILDREN OF THE MORNING and single 31961.

Stay Awhile by Reynolds-Shane-Stewart. Decca master #13,681, recorded in 1965 for the album of the same name, and also released as the B side of single 31790.

Stories Of Old by John Stewart. Decca master #13,671, recorded in 1965 for STAY AWHILE. Also: Section Three (#8).

Strange Day by John Stewart & George Yanok. Capitol master #37568, recorded and released in 1962 on SOMETHING SPECIAL.

Take Her Out Of Pity by Shane-Reynolds-Stewart. Capitol master #36382, recorded and released in 1961 on CLOSE-UP. Later included on THE BEST OF. Also: Section Two (#11); Three (#10); Seven (#26); Nine (#8); Ten (#16); Fifteen (#21).

Tanga Tika/Toerau by Eddie Lund/George Archer Ceran. Recorded twice: (1) Unreleased Capitol mono master #18404, recorded at the 1958 sessions that produces THE KINGSTON TRIO. (2) Capitol master #22998, recorded and released in 1960 on SOLD OUT. Also: Section Seven (#14).

A Taste Of Honey by Robert William Scott & Rick Marlow. Decca master #L14028, recorded and released in 1966 on CHILDREN OF THE MORNING.

The Tattooed Lady by Reynolds-Guard-Shane. Capitol master #23002, recorded and released in 1960 on STRING ALONG. Also: Section Two (#15); Seven (#16); Ten (#5). (Note: the master # Capitol has on file for this track is probably incorrect, as it is also assigned to *Home From The Hill*. The general sequence of numbers for the STRING ALONG sessions would indicate that the first three digits for *The Tattooed Lady* would be "336", but what the final two digits might be is anyone's guess.)

Tell It On The Mountain by Stewart-Shane-Reynolds. Capitol master #37566, recorded and released in 1962 on SOMETHING SPECIAL. Also: Section Two (#13); Three (#4, 5); Fifteen (#12).

Tell The Riverboat Captain by Bob Morrison. Capitol master #76966, recorded and released in 1971 by the New Kingston Trio on single 3149. A possible choice for THE "B" SIDES album.

Texas Across The River by Sammy Cahn & James Van Heusen. Decca master #14,210, recorded and released in 1966 on single 32040.

Them Poems by Mason Williams. Capitol master #51761, recorded live in 1964 for BACK IN TOWN. The Trio's last recording for Capitol.

These Seven Men by Mike Stewart. Capitol master #50929, recorded and released in 1963 on TIME TO THINK. Also: Section Three (#10).

They Are Gone by Mason Williams. Decca master #13,868, recorded and released in 1965 on SOMETHIN' ELSE.

They Call The Wind Maria by Frederick Loewe & Alan Jay Lerner. Recorded three times: (1) Capitol mono master #30207, recorded live in 1958 for the 1959 album FROM THE "HUNGRY i", and later re-issued in Duophonic on THE FOLK ERA. Also: Section Two (#17, 22). (2) Recorded live in 1958 for 1959's STEREO CONCERT album, and later included on BEST OF VOL. 3. Also: Section Two (#15, 16); Three (#9). (3) Recorded in 1981 for 25 YEARS NON-STOP (1982).

This Land Is Your Land by Woody Guthrie. Recorded twice: (1) Capitol master #33636, recorded at the STRING ALONG sessions in 1960, and released in 1961 on GOIN' PLACES. Later collected on BEST OF VOL. 3 and A TRIBUTE TO. Also: Section Two (#15, 16, 20, 21); Three (#2, 3, 4, 6, 7, 9); Eleven (#3). (2) THE NEW KINGSTON TRIO (1970).

This Mornin', This Evenin', So Soon by Carl Sandburg. Capitol master #33667, recorded and released in 1960 on STRING ALONG, and collected in Europe on A TRIBUTE TO. Also: Section Seven (#18); Ten (#2). A shortened version was released as the B side of single 4441.

This Train (see *Rovin' Gambler/This Train*).

Those Brown Eyes by Woody Guthrie, Alan Arkin, Bob Carey & Erik Darling. Capitol master #39995, recorded and released in 1963 on SUNNY SIDE.

Those Who Are Wise by John Stewart. Capitol master #39962, recorded and released in 1963 on SUNNY SIDE. Also: Section Three (#10).

Three Jolly Coachmen, adapted by Dave Guard. Recorded twice: (1) Capitol mono master #18388, recorded and released in 1958 on THE KINGSTON TRIO and the B side of single F3970. Later re-issued in Duophonic on THE FOLK ERA and BEST OF VOL. 3. Also: Section Two (#7, 8, 15); Seven (#1). (2) STEREO CONCERT (1959).

Three Song by Mason Williams. Decca master #13,682, recorded and released in 1965 on STAY AWHILE.

Tic, Tic, Tic by Rafael De Leon. Capitol mono master #30200, recorded live in 1958 for 1959's FROM THE "HUNGRY i". Later re-issued in Duophonic on ENCORES. Also: Section Two (#15, 17); Five (#1); Eight (#1).

The Tijuana Jail by Denny Thompson. Recorded three times: (1) Capitol master #22597, recorded in 1959 at the AT LARGE sessions and released that same year on single F4167, as well as the stereo EP *Tijuana Jail*. Later included on THE BEST OF and THE FOLK ERA. Also: Section Two (#11, 15, 16, 22, 24, 25, 26); Three (#3, 6, 9); Eleven (#1). (2) Recorded live in 1966 for the 1969 release of ONCE UPON A TIME. Also: Section Two (#19, 23). (3)

Recorded in 1981 and released in 1982 on 25 YEARS NON-STOP.

Toerau (see *Tanga Tike/Toerau*).

To Be Redeemed by Jane Bowers. Capitol master #38400, recorded and released in 1962 on NEW FRONTIER. Also: Section Two (#15); Ten (#11).

Tom Dooley, adapted by Frank Warner, John A. Lomax & Alan Lomax. Recorded eight times: (1) Capitol mono master #18390, recorded and released in 1958 on THE KINGSTON TRIO and single F4049. Later re-issued in Duophonic on THE BEST OF and THE FOLK ERA. Also: Section Two (#7, 8, 11, 16, 21, 22); Three (#2, 3, 6, 7, 9); Five (#7, 8); Seven (#4); Eight (#2); Nine (#6); Fourteen (#1, 9, 10, 14); Fifteen (#14, 21). Also released on 78 r.p.m. single F4049 in Canada. An instrumental version was recorded by Frank Hamilton for SING A SONG. (2) Recorded live in 1958 for STEREO CONCERT (1959). Also: Section Two (#15); Seven (#3). (3) Capitol master #51760, done live in 1964 for BACK IN TOWN. Also: Section Two (#10). (4) ONCE UPON A TIME (1969). Also: Section Two (#23); Three (#12). (5) THE NEW KINGSTON TRIO (1970). (6) Recorded in 1978 for K-Tel, and released in Italy on the LEGENDS OF ROCK collection. Also: Section Six (#12); Fourteen (#11). (7) Recorded in 1979 for ASPEN GOLD as the second part of a medley with *M.T.A.* Also: Section Two (#18). (8) Recorded in 1981 for the 1982 release of 25 YEARS NON-STOP.

To Morrow by Bob Gibson. Capitol master #33671, recorded and released in 1960 on STRING ALONG. Also: Section Seven (#17); Ten (#4).

Tomorrow Is A Long Time by Bob Dylan. Recorded live in 1966 for the 1969 release of ONCE UPON A TIME. Also: Section Two (#19, 23).

To My Guitar (writer unknown). Unreleased Capitol New Kingston Trio master from the 1971 *Windy Wakefield* sessions.

Try To Remember by Schmidt & Jones. Recorded twice. (1) Capitol master #39014, recorded and released in 1963 on #16. Also: Section Two (#14, 15); Three (#3, 5); Nine (#7); Eleven (#4). (2) THE NEW KINGSTON TRIO (1970).

Turkey In The Straw, adapted by Shane-Connor-Horine. Recorded and released in Japan in 1970 on THE NEW KINGSTON TRIO.

Turn Around by Malvina Reynolds, Allen Greene & Harry Belafonte. Capitol master #50913, recorded and released in 1963 on TIME TO THINK, and later included on THE FOLK ERA. Also: Section Two (#14, 25); Three (#4, 5); Nine (#9); Eleven (#4).

Two-Ten, Six-Eighteen by Rod McKuen. Capitol master #39935, recorded and released in 1963 on SUNNY SIDE, and later in Europe as the B side of single 4F 193. Later included on THE FOLK ERA.

Also: Section Three (#3, 4, 5).

Utawena by Nick Reynolds & Adam Yagodka. Capitol master #34605, recorded in 1960 for the 1961 release of MAKE WAY. Also: Section Seven (#24).

The Unfortunate Miss Bailey by Joe Gottlieb. Capitol master #31763, recorded and released in 1959 on HERE WE GO AGAIN, and later included on THE FOLK ERA. Also: Section Seven (#11).

Verandah Of Millium August by John Stewart & Randy Cierley. Decca master #13,867, recorded and released in 1965 on SOMETHIN' ELSE.

Walkin' This Road To My Town by Al Shackman. Capitol master #51752, recorded live in 1964 for BACK IN TOWN. Also: Section Fifteen (#25, 26).

The Wanderer by Irving Burgess. Capitol master #31765, recorded and released in 1959 on HERE WE GO AGAIN. Also: Section Seven (#10).

Water Boy (writer unknown). Unreleased Capitol master #36388, recorded in 1961 at the CLOSE-UP sessions.

Way Back Home by Jim Connor. Recorded and released in Japan in 1970 on THE NEW KINGSTON TRIO.

Weeping Willow by Shane-Reynolds-Stewart. Capitol master #36384, recorded and released in 1961 on CLOSE-UP. Also: Section Three (#10); Seven (#25).

We Wish You A Merry Christmas by Paul Campbell & Joel Newman. Capitol master #33991, recorded and released in 1960 on THE LAST MONTH OF THE YEAR. Also: Section Seven (#20); Ten (#6).

When I Was Young by Jane Bowers & Dave Guard. Capitol master #33629, recorded and released in 1960 on STRING ALONG. Also: Section Seven (#17); Ten (#1).

When My Love Was Here by John Stewart. Capitol master #36381, recorded and released in 1961 on CLOSE-UP. Also: Section Seven (#26).

When The Saints Go Marching In, adapted by Paul Campbell. Recorded four times: (1) Unreleased Capitol mono master #18753, recorded at the *Scarlet Ribbons* session in 1958. (2) Capitol mono master #30210, recorded live in 1958 for the 1959 release of FROM THE "HUNGRY i", and later reissued in Duophonic on THE FOLK ERA. Also: Section Two (#17); Three (#2, 6). (3) Recorded live in 1958 for STEREO CONCERT (1959). Also: Section Two (#15). Frank Hamilton did an instrumental version of the song for SING A SONG. (4) Recorded live in 1966 for ONCE UPON A TIME (1969). Also: Section Two (#19, 23).

When You've Been Away For A Long Time by John Stewart. Decca master #L14025, recorded and released in 1966 on CHILDREN OF THE MORNING.

Where 'Are You Going Little Boy by John Stewart. Decca master #13,862, recorded and released in 1965 on SOMETHIN' ELSE.

Where Have All The Flowers Gone by Pete Seeger. Recorded six times: (1) Capitol master #23938, recorded and released in 1961 on single 4671 and in Japan on single 7P-259. Later included on THE BEST OF and THE FOLK ERA. Also: Section Two (#11, 16, 22); Three (#2, 3, 5, 7, 9); Nine (#1, 2, 4, 6); Fourteen (#2, 6, 8, 10, 18); Fifteen (#7, 14). (2) Capitol master #36918, recorded live in 1961 and released in 1962 on COLLEGE CONCERT. Also: Section Two (#14, 15, 21). The instrumental version of the song by Frank Hamilton appeared on SING A SONG. (3) Recorded live in 1966 for the 1969 release of ONCE UPON A TIME. Also: Section Two (#19, 23). (4) THE NEW KINGSTON TRIO (1970). (5) Recorded for K-Tel in 1978, and later released in Italy on the LEGENDS OF ROCK collection. Also: Section Six (#12); Fourteen (#12, 13, 17). (6) Recorded in 1981 for the 1982 release of 25 YEARS NONSTOP.

Where I'm Bound by Tom Paxton. Decca master #13,676, recorded and released in 1965 on STAY AWHILE. Also: Section Three (#8).

Wherever We May Go (see *Coming From The Mountains*).

The Whistling Gypsy by Leo Maguire. Capitol master #36370, recorded and released in 1961 on CLOSE-UP. Also: Section Two (#13); Seven (#27).

The White Snows Of Winter by Bob Shane & Tom Drake. Capitol master #34042, recorded and released in 1960 on THE LAST MONTH OF THE YEAR and in Europe on single CL15228. Also: Section Seven (#19); Ten (#8).

Who's Gonna Hold Her Hand by Bob Shane & Tom Drake. Capitol master #33631, recorded and released in 1960 on STRING ALONG. Also: Section Seven (#17); Ten (#4).

Will You Love Me If I Don't Do Coke by Harold Payne. Recorded twice: (1) Unreleased Xeres master from the 1982 LOOKING FOR THE SUNSHINE sessions. (2) Recorded and released in 1983 on LOOKING FOR THE SUNSHINE, with minor lyric changes from the first version.

Wimoweh, adapted by Paul Campbell & Roy Ilene. Recorded three times: (1) Capitol mono master #30205, recorded live in 1958 for the 1959 release of FROM THE "HUNGRY i", and later reissued in Duophonic on ENCORES. Also: Section Two (#15, 17). (2) ONCE UPON A TIME (1969). Also: Section Two (#23); Three (#11, 12). (3) THE NEW KINGSTON TRIO (1970).

Windy Wakefield by Dick Addrisi & Don Addrisi. Capitol master #76974, recorded and released in 1971 by the New Kingston Trio on single 3149. A possible choice for THE "B" SIDES album.

Wines Of Madeira by J. Christie. Capitol master #35208, recorded in 1961 at the GOIN' PLACES sessions. Released in 1985 on REDISCOVER.

With Her Head Tucked Underneath Her Arm by Weston-Lee-Weston. Capitol master #22992, recorded and released in 1960 on SOLD OUT. Also: Section Two (#15); Seven (#15).

With You, My Johnny by Guard-Reynolds-Shane. Capitol master #22991, recorded and released in 1960 on SOLD OUT. Also: Section Seven (#14); Eight (#2).

Woody's Song (see *Folksinger's Song*).

World I Used To Know by Rod McKuen. Capitol master #51757, recorded live in 1964 for BACK IN TOWN. Also: Section Two (#13); Three (#7); Fifteen (#26).

The World Needs A Melody by J. Slate, L. Hinley & H. Delaughter. Recorded twice: (1) By the New Kingston Trio in 1973 for THE WORLD NEEDS A MELODY. (2) Recorded in 1982 for the 1983 release of LOOKING FOR THE SUNSHINE.

A Worried Man by Dave Guard & Tom Glazer. Recorded three times: (1) Capitol master #31764, recorded and released in 1959 on single 4271 and the album HERE WE GO AGAIN. Later collected on THE BEST OF and THE FOLK ERA. Also: Section Two (#11, 15, 16, 21, 22); Three (#9); Five (#3, 9); Seven (#9, 12); Eight (#2); Eleven (#1). Also released on 78 r.p.m. single 4271 in Canada. Also recorded instrumentally for SING A SONG by Frank Hamilton. (2) ASPEN GOLD (1979). Also: Section Two (#18). (3) 25 YEARS NON-STOP (1982).

Wreck Of The John B (see *Sloop John B*).

Yes I Can Feel It by Mason Williams. Recorded twice: (1) Decca master #13,672, recorded and released in 1965 on STAY AWHILE. (2) Decca master #13,704, recorded and released in 1965 on single 31790. The single version features a female back up singer.

You Don't Knock, adapted by Dave Guard. Capitol master #35212, recorded and released in 1961 on GOIN' PLACES, and later included on A TRIBUTE TO. Also: Section Two (#15, 20, 21); Nine (#1); Fifteen (#6).

You're Gonna Miss Me, adapted by Mike Seeger, Tom Paley, John Cohen & Dave Guard. Capitol master #35210, recorded and released in 1961 on single 4536 and the album GOIN' PLACES. Later included on A TRIBUTE TO. Also: Section Two (#20).

You're The One (writer unknown). Unreleased New Kingston Trio master from THE WORLD NEEDS A MELODY sessions in 1973.

Zombie Jamboree by Conrad Eugene Mauge, Jr. Recorded three times: (1) Capitol mono master #30204, recorded live in 1958 for the 1959 album FROM THE "HUNGRY i". Also: Section Two (#17). (2) Recorded live in 1958 for 1959's STEREO CONCERT. Also: Section Two (#15). (3) Recorded in 1981 for the 1982 release of 25 YEARS NON-STOP.

* * * * * * * * *

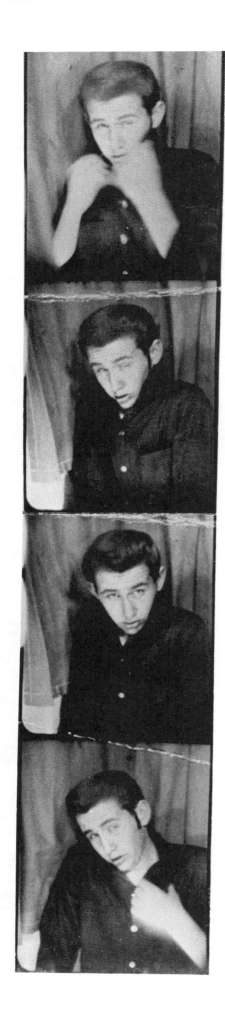

Rare photos of a very young John Stewart, including one taken during a performance by "Johnny Stewart & The Furies", circa 1957. From the personal collection of John Stewart.

John Stewart:
The Making Of A
Modern Day Woody Guthrie
by
Floyd Garrett

Fantasy prelude in three parts:

Part One:

David Baxter walked into a small record store in Boffton, Ohio, in the middle of the last summer of the 1960s. Wingwhammer Records had the reputation of having the rare, the unusual, the fine album; a record collector's record store. And so it was that David went searching for an elusive copy of a bootleg album by Crosby, Stills & Nash called WOODEN NICKEL.

A huge black man behind the counter asked if David required help, and David proceeded to request the illegal album. The black man went into the back room and came back with an album in a plain white jacket, cracked the seal and showed David a label that said simply, "CSN WOODEN NICKEL". David smiled and said, "I'll take it." The black man brought the album up head high and brought it crashing down over his knee, sending WOODEN NICKEL into so much spare change. He walked over to the other side of the store and picked out an album with a bluish cover and an out-of-focus picture of a man and woman in a field of wheat titled SIGNALS THROUGH THE GLASS, by John Stewart and Buffy Ford.

"Now this," said the black man, flashing a huge white smile, "is the real thing."

Part Two:

Four years later, David Baxter missed his bachelor's party the night before his wedding. John Stewart was on the "Midnight Special".

Part Three:

David Baxter, six years later, is divorced from his wife. Reason given by wife: "He spent more time with his damn John Stewart albums than he did with me."

* * * * * * * * *

As I write this there is a fellow by the name of Prince who sits atop the charts, homebased in the heartland of Minnesota. He sings of sex, losing one's virginity, and other such sweaty topics; and is very good at what he does. I'm not quite sure whether he will be listened to in twenty years or even ten years. Top-of-the-chart life is a little like baseball — you're only as good as your last at bat.

What I *am* sure about is that when David Baxter is 64 he will still be listening to his John Stewart albums.

There are no lukewarm John Stewart fans. No one has just one John Stewart album. They have the entire collection or are looking through used record stores for the ones they only have on a tape a friend has dutifully made for them. It is a love affair that has gone on for a lot of years and shows not a bit of wear and tear. So go now. Put on SIGNALS THROUGH THE GLASS, and let's talk John Stewart.

* * * * * * * * *

The Sound and the Furies

Blame it on Elvis if you like. Your John Stewart addiction, that is. John had his own addiction growing up, listening to the Tupelo, Mississippi Flash, Elvis Presley. John recalls the magic moment:

"I saw Elvis Presley at the Pan Pacific Auditorium in L.A. when *Hound Dog* was out. He still had the stand-up bass and The Jordanaires, and it was unbelievable. I was shaken by the concert. I had never seen anything like it in my life. I mean, all that energy coming off the stage, and his voice was so strong, and he was having so much fun doing it . . . and I thought, 'Wow! Rock and Roll!'"

He picked up a guitar, found three chords, started writing songs, and it was all over. Musical history of another kind was being born.

A native of California, John grew up around horses, his father being a horse trainer. This influence, along with an interest in American history (especially the Civil War) found its way into much of John's later music. Between the ages of seven and twelve he penned such lost classics as *Will There Be, L.A. Smog Song* and *Shrunken Head Boogie.* In high school, he and pal George Yanok formed an award-winning comedy act called the "Handkerchief Brothers" (a track from SOMETHING SPECIAL, *Strange Day,* resulted from this collaboration). But it was Elvis who made John pick up the guitar and form his first real group, Johnny Stewart and The Furies. John was the lead vocalist and was joined on guitar by Gil Moreno and Jack Ward. The drums were handled by Bob Zievers, while Ruben Sanchez and Bill Cahill provided back-up vocals. They would cut only one single, *Rockin' Anna/Lorraine* (assisted by Studio Keyboard player Ernie Freeman), on Vita records. Don't rush to the stores to find it. But there was something else blowing in the wind: folk music.

Tom Dooley was on the charts when The Kingston Trio came to do a show at the Pomona County Fairgrounds, and they had an effect on John that was similar to that of Mr. Presley. He unplugged his guitar, took up the 5-string banjo and started writing his own folk songs. His community music credentials allowed him backstage whenever the Trio came to town, and they eventually recorded some of his songs. The first royalty check for *Molly Dee* convinced John to drop out of college and become a professional entertainer.

With the success of The Kingston Trio, as is usually the case in the record industry, it was clone time. Roulette Records needed *their* three-man group, and the answer was The Cumberland Three. Hastily thrown together on a wing-and-a-prayer tip from Frank Werber, the Trio's manager, John gathered together playing companion John Montgomery, with whom he had been performing as "John and Monty," and his former high school choir teacher Gil Robbins. They rehearsed on the plane going to New York, auditioned, got the job, and John started a career that has spanned twenty-six years. The Cumberland Three would put out three albums for Roulette: FOLK SCENE U.S.A., and two Civil War albums, both titled CIVIL WAR ALMANAC (VOL. I being devoted to YANKEES and then equal time to REBELS on VOL. II), all produced by Pete Kameron. Shortly after the final LPs were recorded, John Montgomery left the group (he later joined an obscure act called Saturday's Children). He was ably replaced by Mike Settle, who appeared on the Three's final record, *Old Dog Blue/You Can Tell The World.* On June 13, 1961, The Cumberland Three disbanded. Gil Robbins joined The Highwaymen, Mike Settle joined or formed many groups (including The First Edition), and John Stewart tried-out for a popular folk group (sorry, no hints!)

It is recounted elsewhere in this volume how history stepped in to issue John a new set of cards with The Kingston Trio, but Mr. Stewart accomplished a few other things while he was a member of the KT that deserve at least passing mention. He wrote a song for The Limeliters called *Headin' For The Hills,* and co-wrote (with John Phillips) *Don't Turn Around* for The Journeymen. He very nearly became a *member* of The Journeymen at one point, but reconsidered and remained in the Trio. It was around this time (1963-64) that John wrote the soundtrack for a twenty-two minute film promoting the U.S. Space Program, "With Their Eyes On The Stars," incorporating standard folk songs with his own *Those Who are Wise, Road To Freedom,* and *The New Frontier.* Joining him in the performance were Journeymen Scott MacKenzie and John Phillips, as well as brother Michael Stewart's high school group, The Ridge Runners (named after John's *Run The Ridges*), who later became the successful We Five. (We Five later recorded John's *Love Me Not Tomorrow* and *I Can Never Go Home Again,* plus *If I Were Alone* and *Poet,* co-written with Michael Stewart. Michael later formed another group called "West" that recorded John's *Looking Back Johanna*).

John also was featured on the clandestine "superstar" recording session produced by Nik Venet for Capitol, apparently in 1963. John and such luminaries as Johnny Cash, Kris Kristoffer-

The Cumberland Three
FOLK SCENE, U.S.A.
Roulette R/SR 25121, 1960

Darlin' Corey
Come Along Julie *
The Risin' Canal
Molly Dee *
Brave Bobbie Campbell *
Johnny Reb *

Bull Run *
Along The Colorado Trail
New Land *
Nine Hundred Miles
Save Another Bum
So Long

(* denotes a John Stewart composition)

The Cumberland Three
CIVIL WAR ALMANAC - VOL. 1
Roulette R/SR 25132, 1960

Battle Hymn Of The Republic
Down To Washington
Marching Home
Story Of The Lamb
Tobacco Box
Gonna Get You

Bring The Good Old Bugle
Minnie Balls
Song Of The Hungry
Shipmates Come Gather
The Boys Are Home
Back To Home

The Cumberland Three
CIVIL WAR ALMANAC - VOL. 2
Roulette R/SR 25133, 1960

Hallowed Ground
I Don't Want No Pardon
Lay Ten Dollars Down
Number 292
Aura Lee
The Yellow Rose Of Texas

Goober Peas
Picket's Lament
Hold Our Glasses Steady
Bessie *
The Coward
We'll All Take A Ride

(* denotes a John Stewart composition)

son and Fred Neil billed themselves as *The Nashville Street Singers* for the single release of *The Long Black Veil/Bottom Of The Glass. Will The Circle Be Unbroken* was also recorded at that session.

After the Trio moved to Decca, John produced and wrote *Three Week Hero* for friend Henry Diltz of The Modern Folk Quartet. Recording under the name Pomona Joe Pennyworth, Henry and John were joined on the session by Glen Campbell, Hal Blaine and Joe Osborn. A cover version of the song P.J. Proby was released in England.

* * * * * * * * *

Now let's move forward to 1967. The public decided folk music was dead and turned its back on John and the Trio, so the KT folded, and John turned his full attention to songwriting. Among the vast number of songs he turned out were three that he called his "Suburbia Trilogy": *Daydream Believer, Do You Have A Place I Can Hide* and *Charlie Fletcher.* John Denver, fresh from the demise of what had once been The Mitchell Trio, joined Mr. Stewart for a short-lived duo. They did a demo tape of *Daydream Believer, Do You Have A Place I Can Hide* and Denver's *Leaving On A Jet Plane,* and the tape produced yawns all around. End of duo.

Undaunted, Stewart utilized the access he still had to the Trio's recording studio and produced what has become known (and bootlegged) as the "Columbus Tower Demos". The tape contained some newly recorded versions (or perhaps outtakes) of a few tracks from CHILDREN OF THE MORNING, plus *Come Gather The Time,* a song by the Trio that had not been used on the album. *Way Out There, Any Other Day, Good Time Girls, Only Passing By, Long Life, As The Wheel Starts To Turn, Poor Albert Is Gone, The Dogs Are Waiting In The Park,* and *Come Some Other Morning* were the other titles that apparently never found a home, but The Monkees picked *Daydream Believer* from the pile and took it to the top of the charts for a gold record.

More confident as a songwriter but still insecure about going it alone as a solo performer, John Stewart recruited old friend Henry Diltz and began looking for a third member:

> "I loved the female quality that The Weavers and Peter, Paul & Mary had. I'd been part of three men singing together for seven years, and I was real tired of that sound. I wanted the upper color that you get with a female, and I looked all over — girls from Canada and New York — but couldn't find anyone. Then I finally found Buffy eight miles away from where I lived."

Buffy Ford added the missing element for the new group, but Henry soon found his "other career" as a photographer was demanding a majority of the time, and the trio became a duo. "John Stewart & Buffy Ford" were soon signed to a Capitol recording contract.

* * * * * * * * *

The Capitol Years

We have come to depend on a John Stewart "fix" every year now since 1968. There have been a few gaps in which times we unabashed fans find ourselves sweating and calling a friend with a similar addiction and simply admitting that we are not doing too well. The answer is usually that John will have a new album out soon. And so it has gone year after year. Starting in 1968 with the release of the album SIGNALS THROUGH THE GLASS, we have carried on a love affair that has been the voice of our conscience and our soul.

We were given, in 1968, a pretty heavy load to swallow. Bobby Kennedy gave us a hope that was met with a slug of lead. Vietnam gave us the absolute willies. All John Stewart could do was sit back and deliver *Mucky Truckee River, July, You're A Woman,* and *Draft Age.*

I mean who in the world had the audacity — in the era of Monkees, Beatles, and Jefferson Airplane — to open an album with a solitary mournful 12-string guitar? One has to suspect that producer Voyle Gilmore had a lot of fun with SIGNAL's opening track, *Lincoln's Train.* It is a veritiable feast of overdubbing; voices popping up at you all over the place, as we were taken back to rural America. To 1865. But it wasn't Lincoln; it was Bobby Kennedy that settled into our minds. Assassinations have no concern for time. John and Buffy were in the midst of recording SIGNALS when Senator Kennedy requested their presence as campaign aides. They put the album on hold and went whistle-stopping across the country with RFK. The LP was finished after his death.

This was a political album in a political time. More than that it was a simple yearning for an America that we wanted so desperately in all our full-blown cynicism to believe in.

As James Wyeth alludes to on the back of the album jacket, SIGNALS is a painting for our times. It is hard to imagine the album stripped bare without the haunting string arrangements that never suffocate. The only arrangement that seems remotely out of place is *July, You're A Woman.* This is a song that is an absolute stunner in concert with just John and his guitar. On SIGNALS,

SIGNALS THROUGH THE GLASS
Capitol T/ST 2975, September 1968

Lincoln's Train
Holly On My Mind
Mucky Truckee River
Nebraska Widow
July, You're A Woman

Dark Prairie
Santa Barbara
Cody
Signals To Ludi
Draft Age

(re-issued as Capitol SM 2975, September 1975; Capitol SN-11988, September 1979)

CALIFORNIA BLOODLINES
Capitol T/ST-203, May 1969

California Bloodlines
Razorback Woman
She Believes In Me
Omaha Rainbow
The Pirates Of Stone County Road
Shackles And Chains

Mother Country
Lonesome Picker
You Can't Look Back
Missouri Bird
July, You're A Woman
Never Going Back

(re-issued as Capitol SM 203, March 1975; Capitol SN-11987, September 1979; now listed as Capitol SN-16150)

WILLARD
Capitol ST-540, July 1970

Big Joe
Julie, Judy, Angel Rain
Belly Full of Tennessee
Friend Of Jesus
Clack Clack
Hero From The War
Back In Pomona

Willard
Golden Rollin' Belly
All American Girl
Oldest Living Son
Earth Rider
Great White Cathedrals
Marshall Wind

(re-issued as Capitol SN-11989, September 1979)

however, we are treated to "the attack of the horrible horns." We're talkin' Herb Alpert with his worst hangover, only a dozen of him. Worse yet, on the Capitol re-issue (1975) we are given a different mix with some studio musician who proceeds to throw on a jazzy lead guitar track. Heart be still.

One of the real treats of the album is that it is the biggest body of work we have to date of Buffy Ford. Possessed of one of the most hauntingly beautiful voices, she is the perfect compliment to John. We don't really get to enjoy her again for another three years on a different label. She especially shines on *Dark Prairie* and *Mucky Truckee River*.

So we were given a treat of a duo that never surfaced again, in name at least. SIGNALS THROUGH THE GLASS proved without a doubt that The Kingston Trio had to be left behind and new frontiers explored by John. This was not Kingston material and was just the beginning. It was the prelude to an American classic.

John closed out the Sixties with the release of his first solo album, CALIFORNIA BLOODLINES, an album even the likes of *Rolling Stone* magazine has called a classic and a "must have." A 1978 poll of international music critics (published as a book titled "Rock Critics' Choice: The Top 200 Albums") listed it at #36 of the all-time best LPs. Appropriately, Capitol records, to their credit, saw fit to keep the album in print for over fifteen years. Not a bad track record, considering the axe falls quickly these days to the benefit of the cut-out bins.

This album, which introduces us to Nik Venet as John's new producer, is strictly bare bones Nashville session work and is a real contrast to the string laden SIGNALS; basic guitars, drums, pedal steel and dobro, it is a John Stewart sound that we have not experienced yet.

BLOODLINES has obviously held up with John, as well. Several of the songs still show up in concert from time to time. This album is chock full of classics. The title cut is one of John's simplest and most lovely tunes. *Omaha Rainbow* — another song that grew out of the RFK campaign — gave its name to the outstanding English music magazine that Peter O'Brien has faithfully put out for over ten years. John is featured in each issue. (Most of the quotes in this chapter are from *OR*.). The absolute show stopper of side one, though, is *The Pirates Of Stone County Road*. Simple acoustic guitars throughout, and a mournful John. John has since re-recorded this song a couple of times. It is probably his ultimate slice of Americana.

> ". . . The song is really more a part of an America that is no more — and probably never was. The Nebraska, Kansas part of America with its quiet afternoons and two-story houses, the porches with the swing, the old swimming hole and all of that. That is so indicative of America that is a part of a heritage that we all hold on to."

Side two opens with what seems to be a personal favorite of just about everybody, *Mother*

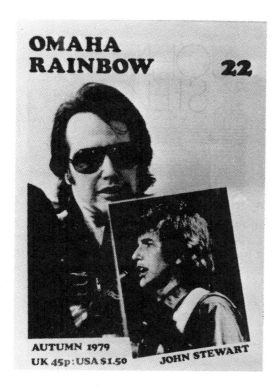

Country, which was also released as a single. In Arizona and California, where it got played on the radio, the record was a big hit. This is another song that John still does in concert, and it will bring a shiver up your spine the first time or the hundreth. As with many of John's compositions, the story *Mother Country* tells is a true one. Mr. Bowie really perished in the Johnstown Flood, and E.A. Stuart really drove that horse "one more time".

We are also treated to *Lonesome Picker,* which was later covered by Glenn Yarbrough, and *Missouri Birds,* later done by Harry Belafonte. Both are memorable songs. The first re-recording of an earlier song also shows up on the second side, as we get an entirely different version of *July, You're A Woman,* later recorded by everyone from Ed Bruce to Robert Goulet. And, of course, the best thing about this one is that somebody obviously told John about the awful horns, and he didn't invite them to this session. Thank you, John.

The last track on the album is *Never Goin' Back,* which had been a minor charter in 1968 by a Sebastianless Lovin' Spoonful, and it even ended up on one of their Greatest Hits LPs. John playfully shouts out the musician credits at the end of this cut.

But classic album status does not translate into mega-sales, and critical acclaim did little to generate consumer interest.

John's next Capitol release was a single, *Armstrong/Anna On A Memory,* two of the best songs he has ever done. The awe-inspiring account of Neil Armstrong's Lunar stroll (his famous "one

giant leap for Mankind" transmission concludes the record) was not only timely, but often misinterpreted.

"I wrote it as it was happening. We went into the studio in two days, and the record was out four days later. It's an example of when a big record company wants to do it, they can really do it; they can crank it out . . . The message of the song was that even though there are ghettoes in Chicago, and people are starving in India and we've completely ravaged the planet, we could for one moment sit there and watch one of our kind walk on the Moon. Where we have really failed, we have also succeeded greatly, but everyone took it as a putdown on the Moonshot. It was banned on radio stations, and they were breaking the record on the air. It got on charts, like at #80 . . . It was on its way, and then it disappeared . . . I think I should have made the song more clear."

It would be John's last charted 45 for ten years in the U.S.A., but in 1972 it suddenly re-emerged in Australia as a big hit.

Chip Douglas, who had produced *Daydream Believer* for The Monkees (and was also another member of The Modern Folk Quartet), was also the producer for the ARMSTRONG album session, but the songs on the single were all that ever were released, as Capitol rejected the finished LP. The rumor still persists that a cassette version (Capitol 4XT-382) leaked out briefly in 1969. Most of the ARMSTRONG tracks were later re-recorded, with the exceptions of *Ain't Enough Water, Looking For The Way* and *Rivers of Light.*

John got permission to return to Nashville and produce his own LP with the band from BLOODLINES. The album had a working title of EARTH RIDER, and John was pleased with the results, but Capitol once more rejected his work. (A single, *The Lady And The Outlaw/Earth Rider*, did manage to get itself released in late 1969, however.) But Capitol still remembered the glowing review that BLOODLINES received, and they decided to spend the bucks on an "outside" producer for one more John Stewart album, and it was an album that had to make you shake your head. If the man couldn't generate sales with *these* session people there was truly no justice in the world. And so we received what would be the last Capitol album, WILLARD. (John did manage to salvage two tracks from his Nashville session to use on WILLARD: *Belly Full Of Tennessee* and *Earth Rider*.)

Produced by heavyweight Peter Asher, who had his hand in some of the best-produced albums of the Seventies, WILLARD included in its supporting cast James Taylor on guitar and vocal, and Carole King on piano. These two were climbing to the top of the heap in 1970 when WILLARD was released, and even this all-star trio could not translate into sales. But WILLARD is still a favorite of many people, and with abundant reason.

There is variety galore on this album. Plenty of country left in the form of the afore-mentioned *Bel-ly Full Of Tennessee* which featured Cajum madman Doug Kershaw on fiddle and an absolutely wailing background vocal; acoustic beauty in *Hero From The War* with John doubling on 12-string and autoharp, and a reprise of the same set-up in *Great White Cathedrals;* and the return of some string arrangements by John Tartaglia, who was also credited with the orchestration on SIGNALS THROUGH THE GLASS.

You couldn't go out and buy an album that painted a picture of earthy Americana better than this. From the front cover drawing by James Wyeth, to the farmboys of the back cover, to the dirt in the grooves, this album told of the America of *Willard, Big Joe,* and *All American Girl.* This was a simple statement about an America that was getting lost in the throes of Vietnam and a loss of innocence that would never be recovered.

So, all-star cast not withstanding, and chock full of more John Stewart classics, it was time to go label shopping; a frustrating occurence that was to be repeated time and again in the years to come.

* * * * * * * * *

The Lonesome Picker, circa 1972. From the collection of Maureen Wilson.

The Warner Brothers Years

Now we come to what must be the two hardest-to-find American released albums in the entire John Stewart collection, THE LONESOME PICKER RIDES AGAIN and SUNSTORM. All the Capitol and RCA albums either stayed in print quite awhile or were reissued in various forms over the years, and the RSO albums were unfortunately mainstays of the cut-out bins for years, but the two Warner albums we only got one shot at, and they disappeared fairly quickly.

Not skipping a year, THE LONESOME PICKER RIDES AGAIN was released in 1971 to the delight of John's growing cult following and to the collective yawns of the majority of the record buying public, who were entering what has to be termed the "dull decade" in terms of musical creativity. John brought in his fourth new producer, this time settling on brother Michael, who gives us a balance somewhere between the beauty of SIGNALS (with nice touches of orchestration by SOMETHING SPECIAL KT stringman Jimmie Haskell) and the stark acousticness of WILLARD's finest moments. We also get two live cuts for the first time and, as usual, the host of solid session people we had come to expect on a John Stewart production.

Just An Old Love Song starts the set off with a lonesome harmonica played soulfully by the unsinkable Henry Diltz. We are also introduced to "The Dump Trucks", John's backup singers for the session that included Diltz, Michael Stewart, Buffy Ford, Jennifer Warnes, Peter Asher, and sister Kate Taylor. They continue to add nice touches throughout the album.

Also on side one we get the return pleasure of a duet with Buffy, on *Bolinas,* that absolutely dwarfs any of the work she did on SIGNALS. A very simple guitar, bass, vocal arrangement makes this cut one of the standout tracks on the album.

The following piece, *Freeway Pleasure,* is probably the album's finest moment, as we are given just John and his guitar in one of his most personal statements about life on the road and the yearning to be "home" all at the same time.

But no discussion of this album would be complete without once again mentioning *Daydream Believer.* A monster hit by precious little Davy Jones and those hairy Monkees in 1967 (it would be revived blandly by Anne Murray in 1980), the royalties from this song bought the bologna and peanut butter sandwiches for many years. John gives it his own treatment, and it was obviously a fun cut for him with his cut-up fade out at the end. That song led the way into *Crazy,* which is another of the album's beauty cuts in its simplicity of ar-

rangement, and it lets John shine sans Dump Trucks or Buffy.

The final songs on the album, *Wild Horse Road* and *All The Brave Horses,* give us a beautiful two-cut concept on John's continuing love affair with horses that started with *Mother Country* on CALIFORNIA BLOODLINES. Taken on another level, they are odes to the heroic leaders of our times, who always seem to be cut down in their prime. The first cut, *Wild Horse Road,* is again a simple production, and it peacefully leads into the big production finale of *All The Brave Horses,* which brings back Buffy and all the Dump Trucks and a full blown string arrangement. Fair warning: a poor pressing of this cut will send you to hide in the closet, because the production on this cut was really "up front", but it closed out such a nice concept that you could hardly argue about that minor point. This album vaulted itself into favorite status among many Stewart collectors for years to come.

Talk about continuity, we finally have a repeat in the production department as Michael Stewart is once again assigned the knob duties, and the session people remain pretty much the same for SUNSTORM, John's second and final album for Warners. But this album was also a study in contrasts. It offers us an absolutely outstanding side one and a side two that is almost forgetable, if one can call anything by John forgettable.

There are at least three "firsts" on this album that should be noted. SUNSTORM gives us the first duo writer's credit with *An Account Of Haley's Comet* assisted by John's father, John S. Stewart. We also have ROCK (read: rock and roll) with *Bring It On Home,* where for the first time the bass line and electric guitars of ace session men Larry Carlton and Presley mainstay James Burton scorch throughout. Our third first is the inclusion of the song *Sunstorm,* taken from the would-be motion picture "Harkin", the rejected script for which must be tucked away rotting in some movie mogul's vault.

Anyway, as stated, the first side of SUNSTORM is a winning mixture of John Stewart material, but it is totally different from all the preceding stuff in that there is a rock edge to the aforementioned *Bring It On Home,* as well as *Arkansas Breakout,* the closing cut on the side.

But the side opens simply enough with *Kansas Rain,* with another dose of yearning for a vanishing America, and just the right touch of brokenhearted cynicism for the home country we want so much to love.

Cheyenne, the second cut on the side, has become a favorite of many Stewart fans, and it is easily SUNSTORM's showcase tune.

THE LONESOME PICKER RIDES AGAIN
Warner Bros. WS 1948, November 1971

Just An Old Love Song
The Road Shines Bright
Touch Of The Sun
Bolinas
Freeway Pleasure
Swift Lizard

Wolves In The Kitchen
Little Road And A Stone To Roll
Daydream Believer
Crazy
Wild Horse Road
All The Brave Horses

SUNSTORM
Warner Bros. BS 2611, April 1972

Kansas Rain
Cheyenne
Bring It On Home
Sunstorm
Arkansas Breakout

An Account Of Haley's Comet
Joe
Light Come Shine
Lonesome John
Drive Again

CANNONS IN THE RAIN
RCA Victor LSP-4827, March 1973

Durango
Chilly Winds
Easy Money
Anna On A Memory
All Time Woman
Road Away

Armstrong
Spirit
Wind Dies Down
Cannons In The Rain
Lady And The Outlaw

(re-issued as RCA Victor AYLi-3731, February 1981)

Side two is a different story. Sometimes a side takes a while to grow on you, and there have been times of patient waiting when all of a sudden something clicks, and you can't get said side off your turntable, and the landlord is banging at your door to play something else. Please! Well, I'm still waiting. One can understand the inclusion of *An Account Of Haley's Comet* as a tribute to John's father, but all the songs on this side just seem to lack that certain something out of a whole that says "John Stewart Classic." There *are* nice touches here and there: *Joe* starts out as a nice little number until we are dumped on by overly-produced Dump Trucks near the end; *Light Come Shine* is another neat statement on religious hypocrisy, until we are again Dump Trucked on; and *Lonesome John* at least gives us a reason to play this side of the album. *Drive Again* would fit more neatly on side one, as it is decidedly rock and gives us some good drumming and percussion, and the return of a few horns to the production (although this time tastefully in the background). The fact that the album contains only ten songs just adds to the negatives.

John Stewart hated (and still hates) SUNSTORM and the Warner Bros. years in general. When he departed the label, both albums were immediately deleted from the catalog. This is as good a place as any to mention that *Omaha Rainbow's* Peter O'Brien has recently re-issued SUNSTORM in Great Britain on his fledgling Sunstorm Records (catchy name!), and it is reported that THE LONESOME PICKER RIDES AGAIN will be accorded a similar honor in 1986. (Both albums feature new covers, as the original photos were lost by Warners.)

I owe it to you ultra-serious Stewart collectors to note that a promotional record was released to radio DJs in 1971, titled "The John Stewart Mouthful" (PRO 504). Side one was a live club monolog called *The Bad Old Days,* in which John humorously recalled his sexually-unfulfilled school days, and side two was a cut from LONESOME PICKER, *Little Road And A Stone To Roll.* It was also during the Warner years that he made a rare guest appearance on an album by Chris Darrow, who was a member of John's band at the time. The song (on which John played guitar) was *Alligator Man,* and the album was titled ARTIST PROOF (Fantasy 9403).

Since I seem to be in a time warp right now (we were about to enter the year 1973, remember?), this might be a good time to mention the *other* John Stewart. I don't know who he was or what became of him, but he formed a duo with Scott Walker (of Walker Brothers fame) in the late Sixties, thereby getting his name into the *Schwann Catalog* and confusing a lot of people. Even Glenn A. Baker confused the two Stewarts in his otherwise excellent liner notes for the Australian collection THE BEST OF JOHN STEWART WITH THE KINGSTON TRIO.

All that having now been covered, we leave Warner Bros., label shopping again, after an uneven statement from John Stewart — SUNSTORM (it's no wonder they didn't know where to put his music in record stores) — and wondering "what's next." None of us were prepared for the birth of a classic: CANNONS IN THE RAIN.

* * * * * * * * *

The RCA Years

In a sense, we turn back. With CANNONS IN THE RAIN, we return to Nashville for the recording sessions as opposed to sunny California. And for the first time we have a new version of a Kingston Trio song (from the COLLEGE CONCERT album) written by John and Papa John Phillips, *Chilly Winds.* This has to be a favorite of just about everybody, because not only does John still include it in his shows, but the current Kingston Trio also showcases this song in its act.

But first it was rumor time. John was going to be in a movie "Pat Garrett And Billy The Kid", directed by the original inventor of slo-mo violence, Sam Peckinpah, who was fast becoming a major Hollywood legend and bad boy. This mouth-watering news was finally squelched when Kris Kristofferson took the role (even a supporting role evaded our hero when Bob Dylan was cast), and we were left with *Durango,* the lead-off cut on CANNONS. The opening banjo lick left no mistake as to the direction this album was going. This was probably John's most "country" album with Fred Carter, Jr., veteran of several former sessions, spinning the production dials and all sorts of "name" country session people manning the instruments. Hargus "Pig" Robbins took over on keyboards, "Goodtime" Charly McCoy on harp, and Pete Drake on the pedal steel. The Dump Trucks are gone and in their place we get the veteran Nashville Edition, plus the ever present Buffy. Bergen White takes over the orchestration chores with some fairly mainstream arrangements that don't hinder or particularly add to the overall effect, either. John really enjoyed making this album and lists it as one of his personal favorites.

So we lead off with the tasty banjo-led *Durango,* which recounts for us the tale of the film role that wasn't to be for John. Then we get our taste of the first Kingston Trio re-issue with *Chilly Winds,* which John dedicates to Nick and Bob. After trying to live down a past that included a then-thought "monkey on the back" stint with the Trio, John pays tribute to a legacy that he is now very proud of. (The single version released has some additional pedal steel).

CANNONS also includes *Anna On A Memory* (side one) and *Armstrong* (side two), both re-recordings of the 1969 Capitol single. Both songs, in this incarnation, are just beautifully folky and are a real contrast to the earlier Chip Douglas productions. Which versions are your favorites probably depends on which ones you heard first.

Leading off side two, the new *Armstrong* provides a beautiful lead-in for one of the album's showcase pieces, *Spirit.* The song is yet another lyric masterpiece of longing for an America that in 1973 was just about torn apart with the dual tensions of Vietnam and Watergate. The other masterpiece on the side comes in the form of the title cut, *Cannons In The Rain.* Dedicated to John's Mom and Dad, it is easily the most beautiful mixture of acoustic guitar, piano, and strings on the album. But it is John's clear vocal that really shines on this cut and makes it the album's winner. This is one John Stewart album that is extremely hard to pick apart, because although it contains the usual standout tunes mentioned, it is very much an album that must be taken as a whole to really be appreciated. Although not a concept album per se, each cut seems to have its place and seems to blend quite nicely into the next. Says Mr. Stewart of CANNONS:

> "...It was one of the first albums that I really had a hand in producing. Fred and I produced it. I've always believed that an

album should have a mood and a texture to it, and this was the first album I had done that I thought had a mood from beginning to end. We made it in the great RCA Victor studios down in Nashville, great warm chambers, and we really thought the album out, and we really worked on it and tried to lean it up and bring some color to it. I think we succeeded. It's a good album."

But, once again, as we were now used to, beauty did not translate into sales, so we could only shake our heads in wonder when the next set showed up in 1974, THE PHOENIX CONCERTS, a live album; and not only a live album, but a *double* live album.

This time we are delivered a double dose of Dynaflex, the potato chip-thin equivalent of what RCA calls vinyl, and the stack mentality that gives us side four on the back of side one. We also get a dazed and crazed looking John in some type of uniform on the cover, which might have made a bad cover for The Cumberland Three. Overdose of Vitamin E, indeed. But so much for the minor quibbling.

The inside is what counts, right? And what we get is new and vintage John Stewart and a return of Nik Venet to the producer's control board. (It was Venet's idea to do the album in Arizona, where John was a *star*.) All the previous albums are represented in one form or another, and there are a couple of new additions. Plus we get an idea of what it was like to see (or at least hear) John on tour. Not bad for the price of a couple of pesos.

Starting off the set is a new song, *Wheatfield Lady.* This song was also released as a single but as a studio version that was much clearer and crisper, as well as being a great stereo mix. But for now on the album this live version is not bad for openers. Of the next three old songs that are dusted off for new treatment, the clear standout is an eerie version of *The Pirates Of Stone County Road.* With John's new spoken intro and Buffy's voice interweaving here and there, it was the definitive version for more than a decade. Side one closes out with John's rousing send-up of *Runaway Fool Of Love,* a song he wrote for his idol, Elvis Presley, at the request of RCA. Sadly, Elvis never recorded it, but John liked the song so much that he did a studio version that was released as a single at that same time.

Roll Away The Stone opens up side two with another plea to the country: just what are we doing to our land? It features some dandy and subtle pedal steel work by Dan Dugmore, and good work by the chorus, this time pared down to just Buffy, old buddy Mike Settle, and Denny Brooks. Next we

THE PHOENIX CONCERTS
RCA Victor CLP2-0265, June 1974

Wheatfield Lady
Kansas Rain
You Can't Look Back
The Pirates Of Stone County Road
The Runaway Fool Of Love

Roll Away The Stone
July, You're A Woman
The Last Campaign Trilogy

Oldest Living Son
Little Road And A Stone To Roll
Kansas
Cody
California Bloodlines

Mother Country
Cops
Never Goin' Back

WINGLESS ANGELS
RCA Victor APL1-0816, April 1975

Hung On The Heart
Rose Water
Wingless Angels/Survivors II
Some Kind Of Love
Survivors

Summer Child
Josie
Ride Stone Blind
Mazatlan/Adelita
Let The Big Horse Run

(re-issued as Pickwick/Camden ACL 7080, May 1980)

FIRE IN THE WIND
RSO RS-1-3027, October 1977

Fire In The Wind
Rock It In My Own Sweet Time
On You Like The Wind
The Runner
Morning Thunder

Promise The Wind
Boston Lady
18 Wheels
The Last Hurrah
The Wild Side Of You

get a dose of that John Stewart humor like we got on ONCE UPON A TIME (the last Trio live album) in the intro to *July, You're A Woman.* This is the third time around for this one, and is a nice lead into the *Last Campaign Trilogy,* a moving tribute to Robert Kennedy. A new song, *The Last Campaign,* leads into two done earlier on the LONESOME PICKER album, *Wild Horse Road* and *All The Brave Horses.* The overall effect of the eight-minute *Trilogy* is quite stunning.

Several things are worth mentioning about side three. We get another song that has stuck in John's sets until this day. *Kansas* is almost a forgettable song, but just try to get rid of it. Once you're turned on to it, you're done for. (The lyrics have gone through some revisions over the years, and the song is now a bit more optimistic than the original that we have here on PHOENIX.) We also get another verse for *California Bloodlines* in the deal, and how bad can that be? The other cuts on the side are re-readings, including an exceptional version of *Cody,* featuring a fine assist from a shining Buffy.

If there is a disappointment to this album, it has to be side four, which contains what must be considered a rather safe walk-through of *Mother Country,* and then another new song, *Cops,* which hasn't been heard from since. But then we have the saving grace of a rousing, show-stopping version of *Never Goin' Back* for the final number that lets the members of the band stretch out a bit and makes us wish that next Saturday night we could go down to the local concert hall and see John, Buffy and the whole gang do the same show again

just for us. So despite John's oft-expressed objections about the drummer not being right and the organ not being plugged in (picky, picky), the album comes off as a fan's delight. It also produced another first for stalwart devotees of Stewart, *The Phoenix Concerts Songbook.*

Before we go label shopping again, and I mean desperately this time, we get one more album from RCA, WINGLESS ANGELS. Now, I have to admit straight-up that it took me five years to like this album, but now the needle finds it on a regular basis. Maybe it was the front and back cover with the flyer get-up. I just threw my hands into the air and said, "Now what, John?" So it sat on my shelf and then became an instant classic.

Really, there are all sorts of reasons to like this album at first glance. Crack session men are once again on hand to help out: Pete Abbot, engineer for the early Trio recordings, plys his trade here; Nik Venet is back for a recordbreaking third crack at production central; a vocal assist is provided by old friend John Denver (a year earlier, John and Buffy had added back-up vocal to *Sweet Surrender* on Denver's BACK HOME AGAIN album); and there is the resurfacing of an old name, Dave Guard, who helped arrange a cut. Notable in her absence (John refers to her as "the missing part") is Buffy, a no-show for the first time in seven years. Strings once again come to the forefront on side one in the capable hands of Perry Botkin, Jr.

Why I didn't catch the beauty of side one from the start is a total mystery, because there is not a throw-away cut in the lot. The favorite cut of many fans seems to be *Some Kind Of Love,* with the lead piano of Tom Keene as the dominant intrument instead of the guitar. Lyrically, this is John at his best. Closing out the side we turn from love to politics with *Survivors,* the song that the Peoples Bicentennial Committee wanted to make the new National Anthem. With the first few lines of the

John Stewart. From the personal collection of Maureen Wilson.

song we have the voice and conscience of America at work. If Woody Guthrie had seen these times and lived to write the songs of this era, he would have written this song. John Denver adds high tenor, and it is a nice contrast. Stewart's performance of the song on "The Smothers Brothers Show" (April 28, 1975) helped launch it as a single that should have been a hit. A special shorter version was released to DJs, in hopes of creating more air play.

Side two is a biting contrast to side one, which as a whole is very quiet and laid back; the last three songs on side two, on the other hand, finish with a knockout punch. *Ride Stone Blind,* the Dave Guard assisted number, makes you wonder what a whole album of this stuff would have sounded like. Following that we have a coupling of *Mazatlan* with the public domain *Adelita* (as in *Farewell Adelita,* ala KT), which leads into a new horse song, *Let The Big Horse Run,* which brings to a rousing finish the RCA era. Before finishing the books on this album let us note that for the first time we have a co-author (excluding John's Father). Michael Cannon helps out on two cuts, *Wingless Angels* and *Summer Child.* (Cannon also co-wrote *Rodeo Mary,* which did not appear on WINGLESS ANGELS but later showed up on the excellent British collection of John's RCA years, FORGOTTEN SONGS OF SOME OLD YESTERDAY,

which also contained the studio version of *Wheatfield Lady* and a previously unheard live version of *Let The Big Horse Run.* Another Stewart composition from the RCA period, *Bertha,* remains unreleased.)

But now we're talking the end of the line. Right? Three major labels; three strikes and you're out. We've been to Capitol: the logical start ("We got a lot of miles out of the Trio and we will out of John Stewart"); three albums. Then two shots on the label that gave us Looney Tunes and a carrot-munching rabbit. And finally three shots with a label who wanted to retire on the profits of John Denver. Now where do we go? To the fans.

* * * * * * * * *

The RSO Years

If you're John Stewart you have to shake your head. You've now been in the music business for almost two decades. You've been at the top of the heap with the Trio, and because of that you've been accused of not "paying your dues." You've been pink slipped by three labels. You're playing bars for rent money. You look around at guys like Harry Chapin and Gordon Lightfoot who are doing music somewhat like your own, but who have their occasional hits, and you shake your head. You look at the lesser talent, a Jim Croce maybe, and you maybe say, "what do I gotta do? *Die* first?" But there's *the music.* There's always the music . . .

So you go to the fans. The rabid fans. The fanatics. The core. The cult. And you say: there's this label, RSO; there's this guy Al Coury; how 'bout dropping him a line? And the cult, the core, the fanatics played post office with Al Coury, RSO head honcho, and we were about to get our John Stewart fix.

There's two things you have to notice about FIRE IN THE WIND, John's first of three RSO albums. Number one is that Buffy's back, and with a smiling John Stewart on the back cover. Up to now we had no idea John could smile, except for a half-hearted try on WINGLESS ANGELS. And secondly, John once again poses as poster child for the American Cancer Society, sucking all that fire into his lungs. All right. I know. Picky, picky, picky. This has nothing to do with the inside stuff.

And we're talking a nifty package here folks; once again unlike anything John had put out before. From the opening scorch guitar of *Fire In The Wind,* John's journey into eroticism, to the starkly autobiographical 12-stringish *The Last Hurrah,* this was a varied album, cut by cut, with only two songs that could be called filler (*On You Like The Wind* and *Wild Side Of You*).

It wasn't until I saw John open his "Gold" tour show with *Fire In The Wind* that I came to appreciate this powerful song. Completely different from anything John had done, it was a superb opener.

Rock It In My Own Sweet Time changed course immediately back to folk. Along with *Boston Lady* and *The Last Hurrah* on side two, acoustic fans would know John had not abandoned his roots entirely.

Rounding out side one is *The Runner,* another fine acoustic piece with the fine harmonica of Mickey Raphael thrown in, and *Morning Thunder,* yet another in a long line of John Stewart "horse" songs.

Side two opens up politically with *Promise The Wind,* John's mid-term report card to Jimmy Carter and the good ol' boys with their sunny southern smiles. So if Jimmy was "sellin' us the Lord", where the heck is John's song about what Ronnie's sellin' us in the Eighties?

Boston Lady is next; a nice acoustic guitar number with all sorts of fine images in it. This leads into a rousing *18 Wheels,* which would have made a great country single but was never released in such form. The heads at RSO should have known that *any* song that mentions Merle Haggard in it is a sure fire hit — for *anybody,* for crying out loud.

John, for the first time is *credited* with a hand in the production chores. Along with singer-songwriter Mentor Williams, John helped produce three songs and took over the control board completely on *Morning Thunder, Boston Lady* and *The Last Hurrah.* One can almost visualize John walking into the studio alone at three o'clock in the morning and sitting down and doing *The Last Hurrah.* Other firsts to note is that we now have the wonderful Chris Whalen manning the bass and somebody named Buffy Ford *Stewart* on background vocals (and the knot is tied). John actually produced a Buffy solo track during the FIRE IN THE WIND sessions. That unreleased song was *Louisianne,* a composition of John's that he never recorded himself.

John Stewart didn't hear any hits on the album and wanted *The Last Hurrah* to be the last track on side two — a closing cut to his recording career, but Al Coury wouldn't hear of it. Stewart would get one final shot with RSO, whether he liked it or not.

And the songs began to come out of John's cerebrum at an amazing rate (they still do!): *Susan On The Silver Screen, Virginia, Sky Blue Eight, Easy Fever, Zapata* (later recorded by The White Mountain Singers), *The Old Gunfighter, Keeping That In Mind, The Duchess, Hardtime Town, Rock In My Road, If I Never Go East Of Denver Again, You Can't Let The Little Things Get You Down, Snakes Of Nuevo Laredo, Tracks In The Grass, Cooler Water Higher Ground, If I Knew What Love Is, Come And See Me When You're Older, Those Oldies But Goodies.* Some of these songs surfaced on bootleg tapes, but most of them simply never got beyond the demo stage, as RSO did not hear the makings of that elusive hit record anywhere in the pile.

Down but not out, John paid the rent by doing songs for TV movies like "Go West Young Girl" and original radio commercials for Levi's jeans ("San Francisco, 1950: most men diggin' gold, 'cept a man named Levi Strauss, so the story's told . . .").

But FIRE IN THE WIND wasn't to be the picture drawn in *The Last Hurrah.* You see there was this guy named Lindsey Buckingham, who as a youngster was much like some of us: zonked out on Kingston Trio albums. He took that penchant for folk music and learned how to play guitar off of John's Trio contributions, and he turned it into the Fleetwood Mac "Big Mac Attack". And a mutual musical love affair was about to be born.

Nick Reynolds and John Stewart could not get Fleetwood Mac's album, RUMOURS, off of the turntable. Lindsey Buckingham was hammering his guitar like a banjo, and they looked at each other and said "what is going on here?" And so it was that John took up the electric guitar, which he hadn't had much success with, and learned *his* licks from Lindsey. This mutual admiration wasn't kept in the closet for long, and John knew that Lindsey just had to produce his next album. And that album was to be *it* for RSO if no hit was produced. John remembers:

> "Lindsey's influence on my life was very much the same as what Elvis had done and what the Trio had done: he'd flipped a switch in my head that made the world look entirely different to me."

They finally met through mutual acquaintance Walter Egan, and Lindsey agreed to produce John's album. With that news RSO gave John the key to the studio, but Mr. Buckingham's other duties kept him away from the sessions for days at a time, and John began to realize that *he* would have to be the producer, with as much input from Lindsey as he could get.

> "Linsdey cranked the volume up real loud as he said, 'You've got to get inside the mix, John' . . . and 'I'm turning the knob until it sounds right.' You know, a very Zen answer . . . so I lost my fear of

the board and started cranking EQ like crazy, figuring out what to do. He said, 'You've got to do it like the old Trio records, like *Seasons In The Sun* and *Honey, Are You Mad At Your Man'*, and I was trying to think, 'What does he mean?' Then one day . . . an actual light went off in my head and I went, 'Right. It's got to be hypnotic, it's got to be repetitious, and it's got to be simple.' So I scrapped three of the tracks, went back in and learned how to do it. I never told RSO until it was out that I'd really produced it. They thought it was Lindsey playing the guitar on there and it was me . . . When it was out I told Al and he said, 'Well, it's really good, John.' . . . I was having more fun than I'd ever had in the studio.''

It is with a mixture of tears and apprehension that you greet the news that someone you've followed for years has "made it." You have the satisfaction, to be sure, of saying to those friends that shook their heads at you collectively for so long, "See, I told you so!" But also it means that someone is not "yours" anymore. He now belongs to the general public. In John's case it was to be a brief romance.

I've got to say right off the bat that BOMBS AWAY DREAM BABIES is probably the least satisfying album of any of John's solo efforts. There *were* golden moments, to be sure. What BOMBS AWAY did do is let us tell our friends, "Hey, wait a minute! If you think *this* is good wait till you hear this other stuff!" There is something about this album, though, that bothers me, and I'll be damned if I can put my finger on it. So it is with some degree of irony that I point out "BADB" contains John's greatest moment in the sun, *Gold*.

You couldn't believe it when you first heard it played on the radio. John Stewart was being played on the radio! There was no where you could go in the summer of '79 without hearing the record. What was going on here? First of all, there is no way you can say anything bad about *Gold*. It is a remarkable piece of pop music. I suppose the question that begs to be asked is would it have been the hit it was if only Mary Torrey held background vocal court? As it is, we will never know. It is one of those unanswerables. So we get torrid backing vocals from Mary Torrey *and* blond star Stevie Nicks. Whether you like the woman or not, Ms. Nicks added a "presence" to a fine John Stewart song. And it was a *hit,* as in #5 on the national charts. Stevie also added her vocals to the second single from the album, *Midnight Wind,* which reached the Top Forty despite some unnecessary pruning of length by RSO.

Well, that's what you have to talk about first, obviously. We have a John Stewart album with an honest-to-goodness pair of hits to help push the album (and John along with it) into the Top Forty pop establishment. Now let's get picky.

This album has Lindsey Buckingham written all over it. I am a huge fan of Lindsey Buckingham's, so I was delighted to see my two heroes together, playing and producing pop music. And not unlike

close encounters of the fourth kind in the back of your Dad's Chevy, there is a lot of hit and miss here. Those of us who have come to love Lindsey's and John's albums know we can always expect the unexpected, but there are also a few givens: up-front crisp guitars, torrid drumming and throwing away the metronome.

Lindsey is credited as being "producer-at-large", John is given the producer's credit, and this album is well produced, to be sure, but it also ends up being a very uneven album. And there comes the part you can't put your finger on. Although there are only two songs on this album I genuinely don't like (*Over The Hill* and *Comin' Out Of Nowhere*), things just do not add up to make this a really great album.

Besides *Gold* and *Midnight Wind,* side one also provides us with the third single from the album, *Lost Her In The Sun.* Why this song was picked as the third single instead of the far more commercial *Heart Of The Dream* (which grew out of an earlier song titled *The Sun Tries Shining*) is another one of those baffling questions, but it did get considerable airplay on FM stations and provided John with his third Top Forty hit. (Sheet music was published for all three songs, and a songbook for the album soon followed.) Then we get a new cutting of *Runaway Fool Of Love* with the ever distinctive Lindsey helping out on vocals and electric guitar.

I wanted so much to like side two's opening cut, *Over The Hill.* Besides featuring Lindsey on the

background vocals it also had Mary Kay Place, who not only was the late, great Loretta Haggers of "Mary Hartman, Mary Hartman" fame, but also the owner of two fine solo albums for Columbia records. Sadly, her talent here is all but wasted. This was just not a shining moment for the album and not a good way to start off a side.

In contrast, we get the album's premiere shining moment on the next cut, with a crisp, clear rendition by John and Lindsey of the old CHILDREN OF THE MORNING cut, *The Spinnin' Of The World.* This is the acoustic masterpiece of the album with John throwing in a dulcimer guitar for good measure. But it is the interplay of John and Lindsey on harmony vocals that is the centerpiece here. Anyone seeing the KT Reunion show on PBS, which featured a live version of this song, knows exactly what I mean. This cut alone was worth the price of the album.

You also want to like *Comin' Out Of Nowhere.* Any song that features the rising from the grave of Dave Guard (who also is credited with creating the album's title) on backing vocals, *and* a cameo appearance by daughter Catherine Guard — and *still* doesn't work — is a crime. But, bingo! This song leaves me nowhere, indeed. But as uneven and unsatisfying as this album was, its success bought John Stewart the right (and the obligation) to create a sequel, which would be his third and last RSO album.

But before we tackle that one, let's talk about what happened because of *Gold. Cash Box* named John runner-up to Michael Jackson as "Comeback

BOMBS AWAY DREAM BABIES
RSO RS-1-3051, May 1979

Gold
Lost Her In The Sun
Runaway Fool Of Love
Somewhere Down The Line
Midnight Wind

Over The Hill
The Spinnin' Of The World
Comin' Out Of Nowhere
Heart Of The Dream
Hand Your Heart To The Wind

JOHN STEWART IN CONCERT
RCA Victor AFL1-3513, February 1980
(re-mixed re-issue of eight tracks from THE
    PHOENIX CONCERTS, plus two (*) previously
    unreleased live tracks)

Wheatfield Lady
Kansas Rain
You Can't Look Back
Kansas
California Bloodlines

Mother Country
Oldest Living Son
July, You're A Woman
Freeway Pleasure *
Let The Big Horse Run *

FORGOTTEN SONGS OF SOME OLD YESTERDAY
RCA PL 43155, March 1980 (Great Britain)

Wheatfield Lady *
You Can't Look Back
July, You're A Woman
Let The Big Horse Run *
Cody
California Bloodlines
Mother Country

All Time Woman
Anna On A Memory
Armstrong
Cannons In The Rain
Hung On The Heart
Road Away
Rodeo Mary *

(* denotes previously unreleased track)

Artist of the Year." He was featured in *People* and in just about every major and minor music magazine in America. Mayor Sam Yorty presented him with the "Key To The City" of Los Angeles. John began showing up on TV again, including a gawdawful appearance on "Solid Gold" that somebody should have been shot for, and he even spent a whole day (October 3, 1979) in one of the "Hollywood Squares."

All of this was not lost on John's former labels. Nik Venet was producing a play-on-record for Capitol called THE CHICAGO CONSPIRACY TRIAL (Capitol SABB 12020), and he tapped John to do the narration. In addition, Capitol put out *new* re-issues of John's three LPs. Warner Bros. in Great Britain re-issued his *Daydream Believer* on 45, and as mentioned earlier RCA in London compiled the FORGOTTEN SONGS album, all this in spite of the fact that *Gold* wasn't even a hit in England! RCA stateside called John and Nik back to the mixing board to prune the double PHOENIX album down to a single LP called JOHN STEWART IN CON-CERT. John has referred to the new mix as "dog doo", and with some justification, but at least it gives us an additional previously unreleased live track, *Freeway Pleasure.* The industry was geared-up and waiting for John Stewart to repeat the success of BOMBS AWAY DREAM BABIES, but it was not to be.

The infinitely more satisfying and far less popular DREAM BABIES GO HOLLYWOOD was the follow-up to BOMBS AWAY. This album was a fine mixture of rock & roll and folk; possibly the finest blend of the two genres we will ever receive from anybody.

From top to bottom this is a first-rate effort with John producing a top notch cast of performers,

leading them through his own brand of studio magic. The mix here is a little muddier than BOMBS AWAY and a little heavy on the supporting vocals, but these ten tracks were to be the greatest state-of-the-art production ever waxed by John. Apparently comfortable with the electric guitar now, John takes on the whole chore of "guitar player." Chris Whalen again handles the bass, and the background vocals are handled by a bevy of veterans, including old friend Henry Diltz, Phil Everly, Nicolette Larson, Linda Ronstadt, and with all the vocals arranged by Wendy Waldman.

RSO released a special one-sided LP to radio stations called the DREAM BABIES GO HOLLYWOOD RADIO INTERVIEW DJ ALBUM (RSO 8046), and it featured John "answering" questions listed on the back of the jacket that could be dubbed-in by any DJ.

Side one of the *real* album starts out with a hard driving *Hollywood Dreams,* a song whose original title was *New Orleans* until John figured out that nobody dreams about becoming a star in New Orleans. This slides into the quiet *Wind On The River* (with the harmonies of Phil Everly) and slides just as easily back to pounding rock with *Wheels Of Thunder.* This featured some absolutely riveting drumming and guitar work and left little doubt with anyone that the Kansas prairies had been left in the dust of your first car and that hot date on a Saturday night. Side one is rounded off with a two-parter, *Monterey* and *(Odin) Spirit Of The Water,* two tales of the sea that are the album's high water mark. *Odin,* however, sank as the album's only American single. Like *Midnight Wind* before it, the 45 version was unjustifiably edited before release.

Side two works just as well with the classic cut

DREAM BABIES GO HOLLYWOOD
RSO RS-1-3074, March 1980

Hollywood Dreams
Wind On The River
Wheels Of Thunder
Monterey
(Odin) Spirit Of The Water

Lady Of Fame
The Raven
Love Has Tied My Wings
Nightman
Moonlight Rider

BLONDES
Allegiance AV431, December 1982

Tall Blondes
The Queen Of Hollywood High
Girl Down The River
The Eyes Of Sweet Virginia
Judy In G Major

You Won't Be Going Home
Jenny Was A Dream Girl
Blonde Star
Golden Gate
Angeles

BLONDES
Polydor 2480 701, February 1983 (Sweden)
(earlier mix of the domestic release)

All The Desperate Men *
Tall Blondes
The Queen Of Hollywood High
Girl Down The River
The Eyes Of Sweet Virginia
Judy In G Major

You Won't Be Going Home
Jenny Was A Dream Girl
Same Old Heart *
When The Night Was Ours *
Golden Gate
Blonde Star

(* denotes tracks not released in USA)

of *Love Has Tied My Wings,* a magical moment of studio overdubbing and fun, with just sizzling acoustic guitar licks and stomping. Somehow, in my mind at least, this is the closing chapter to the story begun by *Freeway Pleasure* on the LONESOME PICKER album.

Next came the song John wrote for Linda Ronstadt, *Nightman.* This would have undoubtedly made a great single by anybody, but it was only released in such form by John — and in England — where it died of neglect. Closing out the album is the very Lindsey Buckinghamish *Moonlight Rider,* a mixture of splendid counter-point guitars and drumming that sent everybody packing. And just·as that song ends so abruptly, so did the RSO chapter on John Stewart. Probably one of the greatest questions of all is how in the world can a label produce megahits like SATURDAY NIGHT FEVER and GREASE and still lose their collective shirts? John, unfortunately, was caught in the bath of RSO's red ink, and that was that. Chapter closed. Ended. But hey, there's always other labels. Right?

* * * * * * * * *

The Blonde And The Budgie

This time we had to sweat things out quite a bit. It would be two years before there was another John Stewart album. As usual, the wait was well rewarded and filled with a few diversions.

A good review for DREAM BABIES GO HOLLYWOOD got John on the cover of *BAM Magazine;* RCA re-issued WINGLESS ANGELS and CANNONS IN THE RAIN on budget labels; a fine retrospective of John's career was presented on radio stations far and wide in December of 1980 on the "Robert W. Morgan Special Of The Week"; and RSO put the lock on things with a back-to-back hits 45 re-issue of *Gold/Midnight Wind.* Lindsey Buckingham in 1981 released his first solo album, LAW AND ORDER (Asylum 5E 561), which contained a flattering (if somewhat unintelligible) track called *Johnny Stew.*

1982 found Mr. Stewart working occasionally with former Boston sensation Chuck McDermott, who a bit earlier had moved to California and started "The Chuck McDermott Band." The two hit it off and sounded good together, and John began using Chuck and members of the band on his demos. (At one point, John seriously considered making a trio with Chuck and Buffy, "Darwin's Army," described as "a cross between the Kingston Trio and the Band.") DREAMS ON A SHINGLE was the working title of a bare bones acoustical album

John and Chuck McDermott. Photo by Judy Jones.

Chuck and John in concert. Photo by Judy Jones.

that John tried unsuccessfully to peddle to a few labels that year. Such songs as *Wings Of St. Michael* (later done by The White Mountain Singers), *Tears Of The Sun, Hot On The Trail, Under Heavy Fire* and an intended return tip-of-the-hat to Lindsey titled *Tear Down The Sky (Liddy Buck)* were among the songs that were left behind when SHINGLE evolved into a "concept" album about the mythical California Girl. It was at this point that John was signed by Allegiance Records.

Allegiance specializes in signing established artists with a cult following. Besides John they also revived Donovan from whatever limbo he had been in. They also specialize in no advances and no promotion. It's been said that they've taken the art of not selling albums (and still staying in business) and turned it into their own unique style. So we get BLONDES. This is one album you can be sure will *not* turn up in the cut-out bins, mainly because it barely made it into the stores in the first place. We get a smiling John with an even toothier Chuck McDermott on the back cover, and three lovely ladies on the front. We also get a splendid production on the shoestring budget, two out-and-out classics, and a host of other good songs.

Produced by John with an assist from Chuck, it is doggone nice to hear harmony again. Anybody who saw John in the past few years with Chuck by his side knows what a great addition Mr. McDermott has been. Chuck's own talent is enormous. Unfortunately, in 1985 Chuck moved back to the New England area, and John (although he inherited most of Chuck's band!) became a solo act once again. But we get a couple of albums here with the able hand and voice of Chuck in the mix, and he is a pleasant addition to the "John Stewart Sound." (Chuck's album, THE TURNING OF THE WHEEL, was released in England by Sunstorm Records in 1986.)

Supporting cast members again include Chris Whalen on bass, Lindsey on backing vocals for one cut, and ditto Linda Ronstadt. But John and Chuck are the stars here.

And once again you have to shake your head right off the bat. One of the puzzling questions throughout John's career has been the selection of singles. This time *The Queen Of Hollywood High* (which evolved from an earlier demo called *Field Where The Angels Dance*) was chosen over the much more commercial *Tall Blondes.* I can only call this the "Stevie Nicks Syndrome." *Queen* had Linda R. (a "star") on backing vocals, while *Tall Blondes* was just John and Chuck. Unfortunately, *Tall Blondes* is by far the superior song. Besides being the lead cut, it just about jumps out of your speakers. It would have been a sure fire hit if released at the beginning of the summer, since it had "summertime single" written all over it. Release *Tall Blondes,* promote the album by spreading the BLONDES poster (featuring one of the girls from the cover) far and wide, and the story might have changed from here on out.

Settled in-between two pieces of filler is the first John Stewart classic to come down the pike in a long time, *The Eyes Of Sweet Virginia.* Another in a long line of "Virginia" songs, it is an acoustically outstanding piece of work, and John and Chuck have fun with the harmony. Certainly this is one of the album's highpoints.

Jenny Was A Dream Girl on side two features the helping hand of Lindsey Buckingham and was reportedly going to be the second single but never saw the light of day. It's positioned perfectly next to *Blonde Star,* a searing song about a Welch witch of some repute.

But now it's classic time again. You go into your room about midnight, turn all the lights off, and you put on *Golden Gate,* shut the door and shake your head. Again. How could anybody write a song so beautiful and yet have it fall on deaf ears? Showcasing just John and his guitar, *Golden Gate* is possibly his finest studio moment. Ever.

We need to ask a lot of questions about a lot of John's albums, but possibly BLONDES makes that need a bit more obvious, as we have a Swedish counterpart to this album that is radically different. Released on Polydor, the whole package is first class. The front cover gives a nod to Chuck, and the back is much easier to read. But it's the guts of the album that are really different.

Side one leads off with *All The Desperate Men.* This was released as the European single, and it seems hard to imagine it not being a hit here in this country, yet it was left off the American album entirely. The reason given is that the American BLONDES was a concept album, and *All The Desperate Men* didn't fit the concept. But hey, we're talking *survival* here folks, and *Desperate Men* (like *Tall Blondes*) had hit single written all over it. The rest of side one remains essentially the same.

"What do you mean, you don't know the words? You wrote the song!!" Photo by Judy Jones.

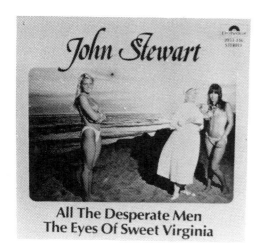

All The Desperate Men
The Eyes Of Sweet Virginia

The face lift comes on side two. Here we get two more additions and a deletion. We pick up *Same Old Heart* and *When The Night Was Ours* and lose *Angeles.* Also, *Golden Gate* and *Blonde Star* are flip-flopped in a move that made absolutely no sense.

What also is different are the mixes. The Swedish album is the more intimate and simpler affair, and I suppose it's really a matter of taste. The Swedish production tends to be a little flatter than its American counterpart, probably because the master was made from an earlier, less refined mix. You pick.

No matter what form you're discussing, you have to call this album (or albums) a bit uneven and unsatisfying. BLONDES was a radical departure from the RSO years and signaled either a return to simpler days or less money to play with in the studio. Take your pick again.

The next time we hear from John is July of 1983, as he sings *Ticket For The Wind* over the closing credits of the incredibly awful movie, "Smokey & The Bandit Part 3." The song (which isn't half bad) is given the dubious honor of being the lead-off track on the mini-LP soundtrack (MCA-36006).

As REVENGE OF THE BUDGIE (November 1983) is given lengthy treatment elsewhere, let me make just a few passing comments on it. Anytime we can get Nick Reynolds into a recording studio it's bound to be a treat. And of course there is Lindsey again and Gary "Buddy" Busey thrown in on vocal in the bargain. So let's just ask the obvious question: If Allegiance can't afford to promote the albums they've got already, what are they doing buying up a label like Takoma, which BUDGIE was released on? Okay, enough. It is a John Stewart product, and who cares what label it's on, right? Suffice it to say that side one is worth the ticket price, and let it go at that. And good luck finding this album, too. (John's best new song on BUDGIE, *Dreamers On The Rise,* was featured that year in an awful movie called "Hot Dog," but it was sung by none other than Chuck McDermott!)

Possibly the Allegiance experience more than anything else convinced John that — label politics be damned — something drastic needed to be done. Well, John, why not start your own label?

* * * * * * * * *

It's Not The End, It's The Beginning
(here's to Errol Flynning)

Launched in 1984, Homecoming Records is off to a slow but promising start. Anybody who knows quality music has got to be impressed by what John is trying to create with his new label. Given half a chance, Homecoming will become the Windham Hill (the first class jazz label) of folk music. But the label has to start small, and the first package we get is a sampler called THE GATHERING (HC-00100). In it we are given the hope of not one but four upcoming releases, of which to date we've only received two. But there is such promise in all the material gathered here that we won't quibble about timetables. THE GATHERING stands up by itself as one of the finest albums issued anywhere in 1984.

Selections from John's own CENTENNIAL lead off both sides of the album. CENTENNIAL is an all instrumental album, and the first thing you're tempted to say is "What? An instrumental John Stewart album?" But the stuff is so darn beautiful, you wonder why the guy didn't do it earlier. The

cuts from CENTENNIAL previewed on THE GATHERING are portions of *Behind The Wheel, The Plains* and *The Wilderness*.

Also by John on the album is a new version of *The Pirates Of Stone County Road,* originally off the CALIFORNIA BLOODLINES album some fifteen years earlier. This is now the definitive version with its smokey 12-string intro. *Pirates* is a preview cut from the album THE LAST CAMPAIGN. Both THE LAST CAMPAIGN and CENTENNIAL are part of a series called the "American Journey."

Rounding out THE GATHERING are two offerings from Heriza and Ford and three short offerings from Bruce Abrams. Heriza and Ford give us two stunningly beautiful cuts from their album HEARTS TOGETHER, due to be released in 1986. Both *East Of Eden* and *Call It A Day* are written by Katherine Heriza and Buffy Ford Stewart and feature absolutely perfect harmony. Any fan of Buffy's has to be pleased, and HEARTS TOGETHER will reportedly feature two new John Stewart compositions. Bruce Abrams cuts are from the to-be-released EP called DELANCEY STREET and are more top-notch instrumental guitar work (featuring some lovely Irish ballads).

Even though this album is only a sampler, it is so satisfying that it leaves you crying for more. And how can you ask for anything more from a sampler? With the thought of four new records from the stables of John Stewart productions, and a sneak preview of each, which do you put out first? Well, the answer was *none* of them. Because of the nature of Homecoming Records (it being basically acoustic and soothing to the tired turntable), there was the need for another outlet for "normal" John Stewart projects. With the appropriately titled Affordable Dreams label invented, John released an LP called TRANCAS, an album that was originally intended to be his second Allegiance outing.

There are a lot of things about TRANCAS that cry bare bones production, but for a first offering on a new label it's not bad. It starts off with what was a throwaway bit in the movie "Smokey & The Bandit Part 3" (yes, you actually had to sit through this piece of muck to catch it, because it wasn't released on the soundtrack) called *It Ain't The Gold.* This would have made a sure fire hit during the Olympics if it had been released as a 45. *Reasons To Rise* shows us that John still reads the newspapers. The song is about the gentleman who has devoted his life to giving us the answer to Mount Rushmore: a mountain-size tribute to Crazy Horse. Possibly the nicest cut on the side is *Chasing Down The Rain.* Very simply produced with quiet acoustic guitars and a soft synthesizer, it is John in his best form.

Side two opens with perhaps the best tune on the album, *Bringing Down The Moon.* Nice acoustic guitars and lovely harmonies added-on by mainstay Chuck McDermott make this one of those instant John Stewart classics. The other highlight of side two is the song *The American Way.* Again, just John's voice with the quiet acoustic guitars and a touch of soft synthesizer.

TRANCAS finds John producing again and playing all instruments this time except for an awfully annoying (at times) set of electronic drums. Let's hope the drums are a passing fancy. I know Lindsey uses them, John, but at times they are just plain obnoxious. The only help John seems to get here on TRANCAS is on the vocals, with Buffy, Chuck, Nick Reynolds and Teresa Tate joining in. All-in-all, the album has a sort of pleasant "pop" feel to it. Not exactly commercial, and far from ever being dull, John has once again for the most part come up with something completely different and beyond common record store classification.

1984 continued to be a banner year for Stewart fans, as John released CENTENNIAL hot on the heels of TRANCAS. The what and why of the album was best described by John in the pages of the *Homecoming Celebrator:*

> "I've always been a fan of Aaron Copland and Virgil Thompson. I've had an album of American music in the back of my head for as long as I can remember. I incorporated some old folk melodies, but it's pretty much new American themes.
>
> It's a lot different doing an album without vocals. Instrumentals let your imagination run wild. They give you the landscape and you supply the characters. Lyrics give you a lot of information and they do create pictures, but instrumentals let you create your own pictures.
>
> I wanted an album that would make

TRANCAS
Affordable Dreams AD-01, June 1984

It Ain't The Gold
Reasons To Rise
Pilots In Blue
Chasing Down The Rain
'Till The Lights Come Home

Bringing Down The Moon
All The Lights
Rocky Top
The American Way
The Chosen

CENTENNIAL
(from the "American Journey" series)
Homecoming HC-00200, June 1984

The Plains:
    Distant Wagons
    Wichita Cross Winds
    Betsy From Pike
    Indian Springs
The Wilderness:
    Grand Canyon Summer
    The Hooliann
    Montana Crossing
    After The Rain
    The Launch Of Apollo 11

Behind The Wheel
The Gold Rush

THE LAST CAMPAIGN
(from the "American Journey" series)
Homecoming HC-00300, January 1985

Clack Clack/Oldest Living Son
Kansas
The Pirates Of Stone County Road
Dreamers On The Rise

Cody
Spirit/Survivors
Hearts And Dreams On The Line
Crying In The Storm
Last Campaign Reprise (Clack Clack)

you feel . . . physically, more relaxed. Music is the medicine of the future."

Impeccably produced by John (who played all the instruments, as well), CENTENNIAL would be the crowning achievement in any other artist's career, but for Mr. Stewart it is just a resting place. This album needn't take a backseat to any instrumental album released that year. Critics may talk about guitarist Michael Hedges or harpist Andreas Vollenweider producing *the* instrumental albums of the year, but they've obviously not heard CENTENNIAL. This album sets the standard for all future releases on Homecoming Records.

But the next one to be served-up on the vinlyl platter is a hard one for any artist — including John Stewart — to better. I've painted you some thumbnail sketches of most of the man's work, but now you'll have to excuse me if I get a bit windy about THE LAST CAMPAIGN.

Part of the way we pass on the heritage of our country to our children is through music. From the fife and drum of the Revolutionary War, the Civil War laments of the blue and gray, and the trail songs of the west, music has always been part of the fabric of our lives; "in our very souls," John Stewart would say.

It is hard to write about any John Stewart album without a whiff of history and a sense of rite of passage, and THE LAST CAMPAIGN is steeped in both. We've lived with a lot of these songs for some seventeen years, as long as we've lived with the memory of the death of Robert Kennedy. For many of us that death was an ending to a chapter in this country's history. So why, at this late date, is THE LAST CAMPAIGN such a politically timely album? Optimism. If ever we needed an album that shows us where we came from and rekindles some fine old dreams for our future, it is now. Perhaps coincidentally, President Reagan recently quoted from the Book of Stewart while presenting the Medal of Freedom to the late Senator's family in a ceremony at the White House.

What we get from Homecoming in 1985 is a brilliant tribute to both Robert Kennedy's spirit, and a John Stewart feast of re-recorded favorites with two new songs, as well. More than just something to tide us over till his next album, THE LAST CAMPAIGN is both haunting and downright mesmerizing. Besides getting new, crisp, expertly engineered recordings of some classics, we get to see how John has matured as a guitarist (as if we needed convincing after the brilliant CENTENNIAL) and as an arranger.

Side one offers us five previously recorded selections: the coupling of *Clack Clack/Oldest Living Son* off the WILLARD album; a studio version of *Kansas,* available only live before CAMPAIGN,

retitled *You Can't Go Back To Kansas;* an absolutely haunting version of *The Pirates Of Stone County Road* (previously sampled on THE GATHERING); and favorite BUDGIE cut, *Dreamers On The Rise.*

All the cuts take advantage of modern recording techniques that enhance their previous conformations, especially evident on *Kansas,* since the live recording was so technically mediocre. Chuck McDermott adds vocals to *Kansas* and *Dreamers On The Rise.* Even though Chuck has moved to the East Coast, let's hope that John continues to go to him like a bullpen ace for vocal assistance.

Side two holds the two "new" entries to the recording library, the brilliant *Hearts And Dreams On The Line* and the energetic *Crying In The Storm.*

Side two also gives us the only dud; the only song not transformed anew into a gem — the coupling of *Spirit/Survivors.* They both fit into the theme of the album, so it's not that. I think the problem is that *Spirit,* in its original version on CANNONS IN THE RAIN, is perfect; so why re-do perfection? But all we're really quibbling about here is John hitting a single instead of the usual homerun. Some people are never satisfied.

As usual, no mention of a John Stewart album is complete without an observation about the always able backing support of Buffy Ford Stewart. Her stunning vocal contributions to John's albums continue, highlighted on CAMPAIGN by *Cody.* The lady can do no wrong.

Whether it is because the majority of this material is familiar, or because it just stands by itself as an excellent album, I found this the most satisfying record of John's in years. It didn't have the "manufactured" feel — of portions of TRANCAS. Somehow John makes us feel, once again, "the dust . . . in our eyes and in our clothes . . .", yet points his finger out there, to the future, as Robert Kennedy did, daring us to put our hearts and our dreams on the line.

TRANCAS, CENTENNIAL and THE LAST CAMPAIGN. After so many long dry spells we get three John Stewart albums within seven months. Pinch me, I must be dreaming!

1985 also saw Homecoming release an album by The Modern Folk Quartet (MOONLIGHT SERENADE) and sign such artists as Margo Jones and Larry Cansler. Larry and John have an interesting cassette for joggers in the works called THE RUNNER, VOLUME ONE, the executive producer of which is a gentleman named Terry Ransom. Terry's other big project at present is a fabulous songbook/scrapbook to be titled "The John Stewart Anthography." Yum!

Homecoming began 1986 with the limited release

of a John Stewart cassette called SECRET TAPES '86, a sort of "legalized bootleg" to raise funds for other projects. Among the tantalizing titles on the tape are: *Home From The Stars, Spirit In The Light, Seven Times The Wind, The Price Of The Fire, Illegals, The City, Jenny At The Wheel, Prison Without Walls, Going Home, The River* (yet another instant classic), *China Sky, Unchained Beast, Hearts Of The Highland, Summer Sun's Cold, The Children* and *Justiceville,* John's rallying cry for help for the homeless. All this plus a live medley of *California Bloodlines/Chilly Winds/Cheyenne* makes for quite a package!

A couple of titles we've heard mentioned (*Always Young* and *Hunger In Your Heart*) aren't here, but perhaps they're being saved for Homecoming's proposed live double album of JOHN STEWART'S GREATEST HITS. This will hopefully be recorded later in the year and will consist of half new material and half "old favorites" from a poll conducted in the *Homecoming Celebrator.* I can hardly wait!

If you're at all like me then once or twice in your life you've wanted to thank John personally for all the pleasure his music has given you. On at least two occasions, such thanks have been set to music and recorded. A British group called Kid Gloves did it with a song titled *Let Him Sing His Song (John Stewart's Song)* in 1972, and American Jeff

McDonald released his own *Thank You, Lonesome Picker* in 1985. This kind of reverence for someone still alive is rare, indeed. But so is John Stewart.

* * * * * * * * *

So folks, we've followed that Lonesome Picker through stints with a couple of Trios and a solo career spanning, all-in-all, some quarter of a century. We've done our best to supply you with the titles of every Stewart composition we've ever heard of, and there probably aren't more than another five hundred or so that we've missed. Not too prolific, is he?

John Stewart has left us — even if he quits tomorrow — with a body of music that can stand up with the very best, as well as a lot of head shaking and unanswered questions. We must ask ourselves why this individual — who has given his life to American music and ranks with Woody Guthrie, Pete Seeger and a small handful of other artists as one of the last truly "American" songwriters — has been relegated to cult status.

Well, we can ask all we want, and shake our heads all we want, and just where will that get us? As for me, it's midnight, it's raining, and I think I'll just put *Golden Gate* on the turntable and leave some things unanswered. I think that's what David Baxter would do if he were here.

* * * * * * * * *

John Stewart Non-Kingston Trio Singles:

Johnny Stewart:

Rockin' Anna/Lorraine, Vita 45-V-169, 1957

The Cumberland Three:

Come Along, Julie/Johnny Reb, Roulette R-4247, 1960
So Long/Hallowed Ground, Roulette R-4287, 1960
Old Dog Blue/You Can Tell The World, Roulette R-4357, 1961

The Nashville Street Singers:

The Long Black Veil/Bottom Of The Glass, Capitol 5017, August 1963

John Stewart:

Mother Country/Shackles And Chains, Capitol 2469, April 1969
July, You're A Woman/She Believes In Me, Capitol 2538, June 1969
Armstrong/Anna On A Memory, Capitol 2605, August 1969
The Lady And The Outlaw/Earth Rider, Capitol 2711, December 1969
Marshall Wind/Clack, Clack, Capitol 2842, September 1970
Daydream Believer/Swift Lizard, Warner Bros. 7525, September 1971
Light Come Shine/Little Road And A Stone To Roll, Warner Bros. 7552, March 1972
Arkansas Breakout/An Account Of Haley's Comet, Warner Bros. 7592, May 1972
Chilly Winds/Durango, RCA Victor 74-0970, April 1973
Wheatfield Lady/Anna On A Memory, RCA Victor APBO-0109, May 1974
The Runaway Fool Of Love/July, You're A Woman, RCA Victor PB-10003, July 1974

Survivors/Josie, RCA Victor PB-10227, May 1975
Promise The Wind/Morning Thunder, RSO RS 894, January 1978
Fire In The Wind/Promise The Wind, RSO 007 (2090 286), 1978 (England)
On You Like The Wind/Morning Thunder, RSO 2090 274, 1978 (England)
Gold/Comin' Out Of Nowhere, RSO RS 931, May 1979
Midnight Wind/Somewhere Down The Line, RSO RS 1000, August 1979
Lost Her In The Sun/Heart Of The Dream, RSO RS 1016, November 1979
Daydream Believer/Just An Old Love Song, Warner Bros. K 17583, March 1980 (England)
(Odin) Spirit Of The Water/Love Has Tied My Wings, RSO RS 1031, April 1980
Nightman/Love Has Tied My Wings, RSO 61, 1980 (England)
Gold/Midnight Wind, RSO RS 8021, February 1981 (re-issues)
The Queen Of Hollywood High/Judy In G Major, Allegiance 3900, January 1983
All The Desperate Men/The Eyes Of Sweet Virginia, Polydor 2053 316, March 1983 (Sweden)

"Just wait till '88!" Concept and photo by Joe O. Ray.

Revenge Of The Budgie

by
Allan Shaw

As previously mentioned, on November 7, 1981, The Kingston Trio (Bob Shane, Roger Gambill and George Grove) got together with former members Dave Guard, Nick Reynolds and John Stewart, and special guests Mary Travers, Lindsey Buckingham and Tom Smothers for a show that was billed as "The Kingston Trio and Friends: Reunion". The show was taped for later broadcasting on Public Television and was apparently one of that network's more successful fund raising specials in 1982.

The March 12, 1982 issue of *The Wall Street Journal* carried an article by Roy Harris, Jr., of *The Journal's* Los Angeles bureau entitled "The Kingston Trio's Weird Reunion". The gist of Mr. Harris' article was that the camaraderie of the Trio's early days 25 years previously was clearly lacking and, in many respects, the Reunion show was a strained rehash of the frictions that caused Dave Guard to leave the group in 1961. Among other things he said, "For one thing the three men don't seem to like each other much anymore, and despite the program have little apparent desire to sing together again." He concluded the article by saying, "In other words, enjoy the Reunion. It may be another 20 years for the next one."

Although Mr. Harris made some valid observations, by failing to even mention John Stewart and his role in the "second Kingston Trio", he seriously misled those of his readers who were not avid Kingston Trio fans, befuddled those who were, and arrived at a conclusion that, at least in part, was

John Stewart, Lindsey Buckingham, and Nick Reynolds strike a pose at the photo session for the REVENGE OF THE BUDGIE cover. Photo by Henry Diltz.

proven wrong only two years later.

Briefly, for the uninitiated (if there really are any), the Kingston Trio was formed in 1957 by Dave Guard, Nick Reynolds and Bob Shane and achieved almost instantaneous success. Following disagreements as to musical direction, Dave Guard left the group in 1961 to be replaced by John Stewart. This configuration (to use Bob Shane's descriptive word) of the Kingston Trio sang together until 1967 at which time the three members went their separate ways.

Although some fans dispute the legitimacy of the present configuration of the Kingston Trio, which contains only Bob Shane of the original three members, there is almost universal agreement that the "original" Trio continued until the 1967 breakup. Sure, there are and probably always will be those who argue over whether they preferred the "Guard Trio" or the "Stewart Trio", but almost no one denies that both configurations rightly bore the name.

Yet Mr. Harris appears to have missed this. Although he appears to have been at the reunion show, he must have left early and not seen, while the "Guard Trio" was performing, an enthusiastic John Stewart standing in the wings yelling "Give us more, Dave." He apparently didn't feel the enthusiasm on the stage or in the audience when the "Stewart Trio" performed, nor does he appear to have heard Mr. Stewart say, "It's a real trip to sing with you guys again." He also could not have heard John say, at the conclusion of the song *Reuben James,* "I can't believe it, I blew the banjo solo," followed by Nick Reynolds' immediate retort, "Perfect, you always did!" And certainly, had he seen the Trio members hugging each other following the finale, he wouldn't have said, "Notice, however, that there's no embracing among the old buddies, and that they don't joke among themselves — ". Nick Reynolds himself summed it up beautifully when he said, "Sure we were all a bit nervous at first, after all those years. But once we got into that first song, it really came alive again. All the barriers were down for a few minutes."

So where does this lead? To another Reunion? Well, no, but *yes,* sort of. It depends on one's definition of a reunion, and if two of the original four getting together in the studio and recording an album counts as a reunion, then we have one. And thereby hangs the tale of REVENGE OF THE BUDGIE, a tale as unusual as that of the *first* reunion.

In Jack Rubeck's April 1980 interview with Nick Reynolds in *Goldmine,* Nick said, regarding a reunion album: "Well . . . there's always a possibility. Maybe when we're sixty years old we'll do

something like that. — I don't know. I'm just really skeptical about the whole thing, because it requires a lot of money to do it, and it takes time away from my family. — I just can't run off and leave for six weeks without moving everybody down to Los Angeles or wherever the recording studios are. I guess I don't want to."

And so it stood until after the November 1981 show. Nick stayed on his ranch and tended it, while John continued to perform and record his solo albums. But that show, with the excitement and enthusiasm of the audience and John's expressed joy at singing with Nick and Bob again lit the spark. Nick had been away from home for only 10 days for the reunion show, but began to think that maybe it would be fun to sing with the Trio and record again after all.

He wasn't anxious though, and John wasn't pushing. Although they were together on several occasions and talked of another Trio reunion or of Nick doing some vocals on one of John's future albums, it didn't get much further than that. Each of them had other things on his mind. Dave Guard suggested that he, Nick and John record an album, but after much initial enthusiasm, Dave left the West Coast to pursue other horizons.

It was then that Steve Fiott entered the picture. Steve, a folk singer himself as founder and member of The White Mountain Singers, and a close personal friend of both John and Nick, heard of their conversations, picked up the ball and began to push. Although Steve says that he "didn't have to push too hard", Nick Reynolds is emphatic in saying, "Without Steve's encouragement it wouldn't have happened."

Regardless, it was what they needed. Although both Nick and John favored the idea, neither was quite ready to put it together. Nick didn't have the time nor inclination to learn and record the ten to twelve songs normally on an album, and a trip to the studios in Los Angeles for only one or two songs just wasn't worth it. So Steve suggested four songs, enough for an EP, and yet little enough to not keep Nick away from his ranch and family for more than a few days. An EP also offered the advantage of costing less than a complete album, an attractive proposition when no one had the slightest idea of the chances for commercial and financial success of the record. Steve got to work on the logistics of producing the record, and further solidified his role as the catalyst that brought everything together.

And so it was arranged. In a series of phone conversations John and Nick began to discuss which songs they would like to record for the EP. Both agreed that they would like to include songs composed by John, so John sent Nick tapes of

Nick Reynolds, Steve Fiott, John Stewart at the REVENGE OF THE BUDGIE recording session. Photo by Henry Diltz.

several of his songs, including *Dreamers On The Rise* and *Cheyenne.* Although all the songs John sent had been written some time earlier, only *Cheyenne* had previously appeared on one of John's domestically released albums (SUNSTORM, 1972). They also considered other songs, including several that they had sung together while with the Kingston Trio, and discussed doing an Hawaiian song as well.

Despite all their conversations, they initially agreed upon only *Dreamers On The Rise* as being one of the four songs to definitely be included on the record. Nick said about that song, "When I first heard *Dreamers On The Rise* it just killed me. It was done so perfectly. I didn't know how we could do it any better, but I wanted to do it."

So Nick took all the songs John sent, put them together on one tape so he could listen to them together and compare them, and began working out harmonies as he had done so often with The Kingston Trio. Before long he was ready to go,

although, as he later reported, "I made a point of taking that tape with us in the car, and all the way down I kept working on harmonies and arrangements. I took the whole family with me, and when we got down there we rented a house just a few doors down from John."

In the meantime John had been talking with Lindsey Buckingham, a close friend and old Trio fan who had appeared on a couple of John's albums and at the 1981 Reunion show. When John mentioned to Lindsey that Nick was coming down to Los Angeles to record an EP with him, Lindsey was intrigued, offered his services in any way and asked to attend the recording session. He also reminded John of a tune he had written as an instrumental and played for John and Nick at the Kingston Trio Reunion show. John remembered that both he and Nick liked the tune, so suggested that he put words to it, and that he and Nick record it as well. Lindsey quickly accepted that offer, as well as one that he participate in recording

Lindsey Buckingham makes some musical suggestions to Nick Reynolds at the BUDGIE SESSION. Photo by Henry Diltz.

the album. So by the time Nick arrived in Los Angeles with his family, there was yet another song to be recorded for possible inclusion on the EP. And although it hadn't been definitely decided to include that song, Nick later acknowledged that having Lindsey interested in the record and being a part of it was one of the factors that helped him decide to go ahead with it.

Following Nick's arrival, several informal pre-studio rehearsals were held at John's house. During the course of these, and as singers are wont to do, John and Nick sang a number of songs that came to mind, including several that had been sung by the Kingston Trio. Although they initially weren't consciously looking for songs to include on the EP, but were generally just having a good time together and singing familiar songs from days gone by. As they continued to sing they came to realize that they needed an old Trio song to really make the record click.

Among the old Trio songs they sang as a warm up song was *Buddy Better Get On Down The Line,* which had been sung and recorded by The Kingston Trio on the STRING ALONG album. John's son Mikael had caught them doing the song on tape, and as he played it back it caught

Nick's attention. "We need something like that" he said. "Let's do that or something like that." John started to play it on the guitar, and they quickly warmed up to it. After they finished a couple of run throughs of it, Nick said, "Hey, that's great! Let's see if we can't put some new words to it and make a new arrangement and include it." Before long it was done, and *Buddy Won't You Roll Down The Line* was ready to be recorded for the EP. The only other Trio song considered for the EP was *Pullin' Away,* but that never got past the warm-up stage.

Lindsey Buckingham was at John's house for many of these informal sessions and as he contributed his input to the songs and to the record in general, his role quickly expanded from its original one of providing instrumental accompaniment on three of the songs to also providing ALL the guitar parts on *Hiding In The Shadows* and additional vocals on *Buddy Won't You Roll Down The Line.*

Another interesting sidelight of the story is that on this song (*Buddy Won't You Roll On Down The Line*) Nick and John (and Lindsey) were also joined in their vocals by actor Gary Busey, who had previously proved his musical abilities as the star of the movie "The Buddy Holly Story." During one of the recording sessions Gary walked in and was introduced to the others by John, who then said, "It would be great to have Gary sing on *Buddy* with us." And so it happened. Nick Reynolds is particularly effusive in his praise of Gary and his participation in and contribution to the song, and says, "His appearance, and whatever he brought, was a key element in the song. Gary was a big part of *Buddy* and brought a lot of magic to it."

Although *Buddy,* perhaps the most exciting song on the album, has an interesting story behind it, the other songs also have their own stories. Nick Reynolds describes *Living On Easy* as a "nice little naughty song" that he suggested and to which he and John wrote new arrangements from the original Hawaiian public domain version. Trio fans will recognize strong similarities to *Lei Pakalana,* a track on CHILDREN OF THE MORNING. *Same Old Heart,* although one of John Stewart's compositions, was included despite his initial reluctance regarding it. As Nick tells it, he liked the song and wanted to include it, but John was against it. Nick persisted, however, and was supported by Lindsey Buckingham. Finally they prevailed upon John to include it during the recording sessions and ultimately on the album. The BUDGIE version is more up-tempo and cheerful than the one that appeared on the Swedish release of John's BLONDES album.

The last song, *Angel On The Road Shoulder,* although under consideration from the early stages was not included until nearly the last minute and, as a matter of fact, was not even

Takoma TAK-7106, released November, 1983

side one:

1 *Buddy Won't You Roll Down The Line*
2 *Dreamers On The Rise*
3 *Cheyenne*

side two:

1 *Living On Easy*
2 *Hiding In The Shadows*
3 *Angel On The Road Shoulder*
4 *Same Old Heart*

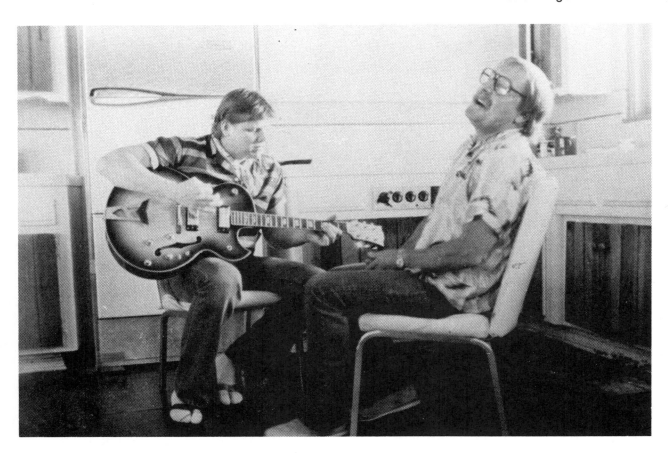

Gary Busey impresses Nick Reynolds with some impromptu jamming during a recording break. Photo by Henry Diltz.

recorded until September, whereas all the other songs were recorded in June. Basically what happened was that the four songs originally intended for the EP had become six songs, and that created its own problem of what to do. Only four songs would fit easily on an EP, and even if they could have squeezed a fifth or even a sixth song on, Nick and John couldn't agree on dropping even one song, let alone two. Again, Steve Fiott, who was executive producer of the album, suggested a solution: go to a ten inch or twelve inch record that would include seven songs, and market it as a "mini LP." A few phone calls and some fast talking later, and it was decided upon. But at that point they were out of studio time and didn't have a seventh song. However, everyone realized that Nick would have to return to Los Angeles at a later date to do some re-mixing, so it was agreed that a seventh song would be recorded then. *Angel On The Road Shoulder* was decided upon; Nick worked out his part over the summer, and when he returned in September it took only a few minutes for John and Nick to go over it together and record it.

Then came the nitty-gritty of putting it all together. Carla Frederick (who had recorded the album) handled the mixing, assisted by John and Nick, and by Lindsey Buckingham on *Hiding In*

The Shadows. Lindsey also took on the chore of writing the liner notes and, after considerable discussion the cover art was decided upon, as was the title of the album. As a further link to the past, although it was not intended to be that, the photography was done by Henry Diltz, a commercial photographer and member of The Modern Folk Quartet, who had done many of John's LP cover photos.

The album's cover pictures and title have a story behind them too. Although none of the participants will repeat the joke, they all allude to it being a joke about a "budgie" that produced the series of photos gracing the cover and showing John laughing heartily over something. Although John was initially reluctant, he did agree to using the series of photos on the cover.

Despite the reluctance to telling the story behind the cover photos, John and Nick do tell the story behind the title. It seems that "Budgie" was a nickname for Nick during the Kingston Trio days, although he hadn't been addressed by that appelation in years. However, the name was revived to be used as a name for the entity of Nick, John and Steve Fiott that produced the album. Subsequently, in discussing a name for the album, and referring to his long absence from the recording scene, Nick said, "How about RETURN OF THE

Nick, John, Gary Busey and Lindsey Buckingham between takes at the Shangri-La Recording Studio. Photo by Henry Diltz.

BUDGIE?'' Immediately upon his saying this, Nick reports, John turned to him and, "with a gleam in his eye said, 'How about *REVENGE* OF THE BUDGIE?'" And so it came to be. As an afterthought, the little character with the four-string guitar (the "budgie") was added to throw additional humor into the picture.

If one word were to be used to try and describe the feeling one gets in listening to the album, that one word would be "exciting." One word scarcely does the job though, as it was best and briefly described by Barry Alfonso in his review in *BAM Magazine,* a review that Nick Reynolds describes as the "Best review I've gotten in my life!" Mr. Alfonso said,

"The title to this mini-LP is the tip off — what's contained here is played for fun. This reunion between two former Kingston Trio stalwarts could've easily been a ponderous exercise in nostalgia. Rather than serving up the same old folky fare of the Trio, however, BUDGIE is an intriguing blend of traditional American music and newfangled technopop arrangements.

"The lead tracks on each side are the best examples of this experiment. Both tunes — *Buddy Won't You Roll Down The Line* and *Living On Easy* — are hoary folk standards, but dressed up in drum machines and oscillating synthesizers, they sound almost as contemporary as A Flock Of Seagulls (and a whole lot more tuneful). On top of the computer-based instrumentation, Reynolds and Stewart layer shimmering acoustic and electric guitars, creating a mini wall of sound. If this description sounds familiar, take a listen to Lindsey Buckingham's recent work and hear similar "folk moderne" dabblings. Buckingham was a party to BUDGIE, singing and/or playing on several tracks and co-writing one tune, *Hiding In The Shadows,* with Stewart.

"Before you conclude that this is some Buckingham project with surrogate singers, it should be said that Reynolds and Stewart's personalities are not lost in the instrumental work. A warmth and easy-going friendliness comes through in their close vocal harmonies — you can hear the years of music-making they've put in together. Stewart's songwriting contributions to BUDGIE are not unlike his past work: a bit overly sentimental at times, but still charming in their simplicity and sincerity.''

John Stewart was reluctant to be quite as effusive as Nick in his opinion of the review, but it was obvious that he was quite pleased with it. Describing the album as ''hi-tech folk'', he agreed with Nick and said that the *''BAM* review is a great review!''

The *BAM* review and other feedback on the album was most gratifying to Nick. Although he was quite excited about the album from the moment the first tracks were cut in the recording studio, he was initially also somewhat apprehensive about the reception it would receive among old Trio fans. Except for his appearance on the Reunion television show, on which he sang and played songs that had been big hits for The Kingston Trio in the past, this was his first venture onto the entertainment scene for 16 years, and the first time ever that he had done anything other than with The Kingston Trio or in a Kingston Trio style. Within days after the album was released he was curiously asking for the reaction of the ''old Trio fans''. Having always been proud of his work

Nick and Lindsey listen to a playback. Photo by Henry Diltz.

and highly sensitive to its acceptance by the public, he was fascinated to learn that old Trio fans were enjoying listening to it as much as he and John had enjoyed making it. Less than three months after the album was first released he wrote, ''Everyone who has heard the BUDGIE has honestly loved either all or part of it a lot, old Trio fans to young kids who don't know a thing about me or the Trio. There are certain songs that cover the different spectrums. John and I subconsciously made the song choices and arrangements and it turned out to be sort of a 'sampler' of what we do, and it really is.''

As Barry Alfonso so perceptively observed in his review of the album, no small part of the good feeling on the album and the good feeling one gets in listening to the album comes from the years that Nick and John spent singing together and the close personal relationship that developed during that time. Lindsey Buckingham expressed this beautifully in the album's liner notes when he said, ''I was also intrigued because although John and Nick's blend has remained, their musical collaboration has been dormant for 16 years. Yet once the sessions had begun, any initial fears gave way to confidence and a sense of catharsis for all. Every day I was reminded of the importance that personal chemistry plays in the making of good music, and when we were done, I came away feeling privileged to be involved, happy to have been able to give back a small part of that which Nick and John had given me before.''

John Stewart put it even more eloquently by saying, ''To both Lindsey Buckingham and myself, who have been working in the record industry and recording studios for years and years, working with Nick again was a classic example of the fact that chemistry and attitude cannot be aided by electronics. The human aspect of record making cannot be replaced by technology where, in the last analysis, it is still people communicating with people.''

With all those good words and euphoria, one would tend to think that all was well. Unfortunately it wasn't. John and Nick would have liked BUDGIE to have been but the first of many recordings together, but recognized that the commercial success of BUDGIE was an essential prerequisite to that happening. However, lack of promotion, air play and adequate distribution thwarted the album's potential for success.

Although almost all ''hard core'' Trio fans were able to obtain the record, it wasn't always easy. And, although there is a fairly large contingent of those ''hard core'' Trio fans, there are a lot more old Trio fans who would likely have bought the record if they had been aware of it and could easily have found it. But that wasn't the case. Also, of course, and of even greater consequence, is that there is a large group of record buyers that are a generation or two younger than Nick Reynolds and John Stewart and who, although they might recognize the Kingston Trio name, aren't going to recognize the individual names nor associate them with the sounds to be found on BUDGIE. Without adequate air play, promotion, distribution and sales, BUDGIE has so far ended up being an only child.

Although Takoma Records executives criticized the original publication of an early version of this chapter (in *GOLDMINE,* June 22, 1984) as being unfair and inaccurate in its description of their efforts (or lack thereof), and complained that it didn't accurately tell "our side of the story," our requests of them for specifics have gone unanswered. Citing the old adage of actions speaking louder than words, we have excised some of our remarks and leave it to our readers to judge, from their knowledge of and ability to find the album (other than from Kingston Korner), whether or not the promotion and distribution of the album was what it should have been.

Nick Reynolds expressed both his frustration with the situation and his confidence in the album when he wrote, several months after the album's release, "The air play has been fairly good for an album with no promotional material to get it on the air. No material has been given out by Takoma as to who, why, or what the album is about. Most young DJs and record store owners don't even

know who 'Nick Reynolds' is or was. Really, I'm not being egotistical, but the fact remains that if Takoma could get it together enough to have the 'old Trio record buyers' aware of the BUDGIE existence, we could probably sell thousands of records. 'They' (that age group) have almost no choice of what to buy, and they're just waiting for some old friends to drop by with something new. — It's such a thrill to sing and record with John, I hate to have it end with lack of enthusiasm from the record company."

And so it stands, at least for now. Is Nick right in his heartfelt belief that there is still a substantial market for the type of music, or at least its evolutionary successor, that rocketed The Kingston Trio to the height of the pop charts 25 years ago? Or, are Nick and John, and hence by implication The Kingston Trio, simply "yesterday's act" that no longer has a substantial following from the past and has little appeal to the record buyers of today? There are those of us with thinning and/or graying (or both) hair who fervently believe Nick is right, not only because we like the record ourselves, but also because our children (who are the real record buyers of today) are equally enthusiastic about it. But whether we are right or wrong, we would like to be proved such by the album having the promotion and air play it deserves so that the entire listening and record buying public has the opportunity to hear and buy it.

* * * * * * * * *

Nick reviewing some film in his theatre, "The Star."

Linda and Nick Reynolds at home with their children, Jennifer, John and Annie. Photo by "The World", Coos Bay, Oregon.

John Stewart. November 7, 1981. Photo by Jack Rubeck.

EPILOGUE

I had the advantage of being both a fan and a member of The Kingston Trio.

I was under the spell of the songs and the way they were sung long before I became a member of the band. The Trio's songs had adventure, romance, humor, melody, and they were easy to sing and play. What more could you ask?

I found that after I joined the group I was part of finding the songs and putting them together. I also found that I could no longer look forward to the next Kingston Trio album, as I was now *making* the next Kingston Trio album.

The albums that Dave, Nick and Bob made inspired a generation of fans and performers, including me. The albums that impressed me the most were THE KINGSTON TRIO, FROM THE "HUNGRY i", AT LARGE, HERE WE GO AGAIN and SOLD OUT. These records set the standard of excellence that everyone who followed tried to attain.

Of the albums Nick, Bob and I made, COLLEGE CONCERT seems to have held up well over the years. It captured the energy and fun that we had on stage. As far as the studio recordings go, NEW FRONTIER was our best effort. We worked hard on that record, and I think it shows.

I'll never forget the first song I sang on stage with Nick and Bob. It was *Darlin' Corey,* and the sound of the band singing full-out on stage almost knocked me over. I had been in other folk groups. Good folk groups they were, too, but *this* group was special. It had a magic that even the entrance of a new voice couldn't diminish.

It was the most fun I ever had.

The Kingston Trio was the best example of a fact that has proven itself true over the years: "In pop music, attitude is everything."

John Stewart
Malibu, California
February, 1986

About the Contributors

ELIZABETH ANNE WILSON was born in Ames, Iowa on October 21, 1954. Before moving to her current place of residence in San Diego, California (where she has become an aspiring novelist), she lived for many years in Bountiful, Utah, and graduated magna cum laude from the University of Utah, where she majored in English.

Elizabeth contributed "The Dave Guard Interview" to this book, and she singles out Dave for special thanks. She lists STRING ALONG, THE LAST MONTH OF THE YEAR, STAY AWHILE and COLLEGE CONCERT as her favorite Kingston Trio albums, and adds: "I was four when *Tom Dooley* became a hit, and my parents were fans from the beginning, so I've been listening to the KT ever since I can remember. They have a way of making the listener feel as though he or she is a part of the act. The KT have never had to rely on gimmicks or a deafening decibel level; their talent, dedication and good humor were all they ever needed."

* * * * * * * *

PAUL LEWIS SURRATT, JR. was born in Greenville, South Carolina on December 27, 1947, and he has also lived in New York and California, with time-out for a four-year cruise off the coast of Vietnam as a member of the U.S. Navy. He is currently a video researcher living in Studio City, California and is the President and Founder of the Archives of Music Preservation, an organization devoted to collecting rare video tapes of recording artists. His name appears in the credits of many awards shows and music specials, including "The Kingston Trio & Friends: Reunion." Paul got his show biz start with The Shilohs, the folk group that spawned the legendary Gram Parsons. He later was a member of the Rockville Junction, and for the past ten years has been half of a folk duo known as LeCorn & Surratt.

Paul contributed "The Frank Werber Interview" and many of the rare photos that appear in this book, and he was also the source for the quotes from engineer Pete Abbot. In addition, he drew upon his vast knowledge of the Trio to provide a considerable amount of background information for Ben, Jack and Allan to work with. He would like to express his thanks to Ron and Bob Furmanek, John Phillips, and Frank Werber, as well as to John, Bob, Nick, Dave, George and Roger. His favorite KT albums: "All of Them!" When asked to sum up the Trio's influence on his life, Paul stated: "They were my inspiration for the Archives, for being with Gram, everything. They opened my eyes to the music business. Let me put it another way — I still own a Martin guitar and a Vega banjo."

* * * * * * * * *

FLOYD ROBERT GARRETT was born in Los Angeles, California on January 20, 1951, and spent four years at Indiana University of Pennsylvania (with a History major and an English minor) before settling in as a writer in a suburb of Cleveland, Ohio, for many years. He currently resides in Colorado Springs, Colorado, where he is an Executive Recruiter.

Besides creating the John Stewart chapter, Floyd has also produced a flock of short stories, a play (*Dreamers On The Rise,* with music by J. Stewart) and a novel (*Bringing Down The Moon*). He offers his thanks to his parents, John Stewart, Whammer and Jill. He lists AT LARGE, STRING ALONG and TIME TO THINK as his favorite Trio LPs, and adds that "*Scotch And Soda* will live forever." Says Floyd about the Trio's influence: "I was eight when the Trio were number one on the charts. I would like to think that each generation has a special group that they will always feel tender about. The Beatles were too big. But once upon a time, before lite beer, before angel dust, before Richard Nixon, MTV, and footnotes in music like Boy George, there lived *in our hearts* a group called The Kingston Trio. And they were not just 'fashion' but musicians and personalities that forever altered our lives. I can no longer try to explain what the music of John Stewart (the 'soul of America') means to me. So raise another glass to Trios old and new; Oh, Mother Country, I do love you."

* * * * * * * * *

WILLIAM J. BUSH was born in West Palm Beach, Florida on August 25, 1946, and he has lived in Boston, Massachusetts and Portland, Maine. He earned his B.S. and M.S. at the University of Illinois and currently resides in Seminole, Florida, where he is a partner in a nearby Tampa advertising agency.

Besides contributing the chapter on Trio instruments, Bill has also appeared in the pages of *Guitar Player* and *Frets* and is a contributor to *The Guitar Player Book.* He has two solo books in the works, the working titles of which are *Folk Revival* and *History Of 50s Rock & Roll.* He wishes to thank Nick, John, Bob and Dave, and lists his favorite KT albums as TIME TO THINK, #16 and NEW FRONTIER. Says Bill: "The Kingston Trio opened my ears to a whole new world of music beyond rock and roll. They showed us taste, style, humor; a 'class' act that set the standard."

* * * * * * * * *

MICHAEL ALLAN SHAW was born in Evanston, Illinois on July 14, 1940. He earned his B.A. at Colorado State University, his J.D. at the University of Denver College of Law, and his M.B.A. at Chicago's DePaul University. (It should be noted that while attending Colorado State University, Allan was a very active officer of that institution's Ballad & Folk Song Club; formed a group called the Highlanders, which achieved some degree of local notoriety; and upon at least one or two occasions sang around an intra-school campfire with a University of Colorado student named Judy Collins. He later sat in on the 1964 recording sessions for the album THE SLIGHTLY IRREVERENT MITCHELL TRIO.) Allan has lived in Tokyo, Japan; Calgary, Alberta; and Vancouver, British Columbia. He now resides in Naperville, Illinois, where (after eighteen years of corporate law with major retailing concerns) he has opened a private law practice. He is the former Folk Music Editor of *Goldmine,* a volunteer worker for *Come For To Sing,* a member of the Fox Valley Folklore Society, a member of the advisory board of the World Folk Music Association, President and co-owner of Folk Era Productions, and the President of Kingston Korner, Inc., as well as the current editor of the *Kingston Korner Newsletter.*

Allan contributed all or part of several chapters in this book, and his writings on folk era artists appeared frequently in his *Goldmine* column, "The Folk Scene". He would like to thank Ben, Jack,

George, Bob, Roger, John, Nick and Dave, and lists as his favorite KT albums THE KINGSTON TRIO, THE LAST MONTH OF THE YEAR and TIME TO THINK. Says Allan about the Trio's profound influence on his life: "I just can't put it into words."

* * * * * * * * *

JACK A. RUBECK was born in Portland, Oregon on April 2, 1944, and he still resides there. He has two years of college under his belt and works in the Revenue Protection division of the U.S. Postal Service. He is also the Vice President — Western of Kingston Korner, Inc.

Besides "The Nick Reynolds Interview" and parts of several other chapters in this book, Jack's writing credits include four years as a folk columnist for *Goldmine.* He singles out Jack Howard, Brian Bukantis and Ben Blake for special thanks, and lists AT LARGE as his favorite Trio LP and *When My Love Was Here* as favorite song. Says Jack: "AT LARGE was the first record I ever heard on a hi-fidelity system, and it introduced me to the multiple pleasures of true-to-life sound, unique singing styles, and imagination-provoking songs."

* * * * * * * * *

BENJAMIN SCOTT BLAKE was born in Bangor, Maine on April 12, 1949, and he has lived in Tucson, Arizona; West Palm Beach, Florida; Willimantic, Connecticut; as well as Houlton, Springfield and Presque Isle, Maine. He has a B.A. in English from Eastern Connecticut State University, and his former occupations include a 1969 stint as a disc jockey (rumor has it he was fired for refusing to remove ONCE UPON A TIME and *Armstrong* from the turntables). He currently resides in Norwich, Connecticut, and drives a milk and ice cream vending route to support his writing habit. He was also the original editor of the *Kingston Korner Newsletter* and is the Vice President — Eastern of Kingston Korner, Inc.

Besides all or part of several chapters in this book (and his role as coordinating editor of the project), Ben's writing credits include four years as a folk columnist for *Goldmine,* a published account of the KT Reunion in *Omaha Rainbow,* and poetry that has appeared in *Rolling Stone* and various literary magazines. He would like to thank Tom McCabe, Paul Just, Jack, Allan, Wings, Lorie, and the long-time readers and supporters of Kingston Korner. He lists TIME TO THINK, STRING ALONG and THE LAST MONTH OF THE YEAR as his favorite KT albums. Says Ben of the Trio's influence: "Thanks, guys."

About Kingston Korner

The year was 1977, and Los Angeles record dealer John F. Howard did not realize that he was about to create a monster. For some time he had been selling used Kingston Trio albums by mail to customers in Oregon (Jack Rubeck) and Connecticut (Ben Blake), and it was in Howard's nature to accompany his shipments with witty retorts about his customers' questionable tastes in music. Rubeck and Blake (to Howard's chagrin) replied in kind, extolling the virtues of their favorite group. After a few exchanges of this nature, Howard decided he'd had enough and sent the pair of KT fans each other's names and addresses. "You two deserve each other!" Howard admonished.

After only a few letters, Rubeck suggested to Blake that they might co-write a column about the Trio for a record collectors' magazine he had discovered called *Goldmine.* "Sure," Blake replied. "We'll call it 'Kingston Korner'!" And so it was that "KK" began, premiering in the pages of *Goldmine* in the September, 1978 issue. Letters immediately began pouring in to the fledgling folksters, each proclaiming something to this effect: "I thought I was the only one left alive who still liked these guys!" One of the first to utter these immortal words was an Illinois KT fan named Allan Shaw, who subsequently became one of KK's biggest supporters, contributing many "Folk Profiles" and album reviews to the column.

A solid network of Trio fanatics kept the column alive and kicking for thirty-one installments, plus an April, 1979 cover story on John Stewart. But all good things run their course, and KK took its final bow in the December, 1981 issue. Allan Shaw soon took up the slack with a column called "The Folk Scene," the initial appearance of which — subtitled "Kingston Korner Revisited" — ably covered the excitement of the November 7, 1981 Trio Reunion (at which Shaw, Rubeck and Blake were awestruck invited guests at both the concert and "wrap party", even getting to say a few words before the national cameras of *Entertainment Tonight*).

"Kingston Korner" was over, but the mail kept pouring in from all over the globe. Writer's cramp — plus a sense of duty to long-time readers — brought about the creation of the *Kingston Korner Newsletter,* the first ten issues of which were crude photocopies that fans could obtain for the price of a postage stamp.

And so it might have remained but for the intervention of the hand of fate, in the form of a suggestion from Bob Shane to Allan Shaw. Bob knew Allan was one of the Trio's biggest fans and collectors, so he asked him to consider having some business cards printed up for the Trio to give to record-seeking fans at their many concerts. A few phone calls later, and Shaw, Rubeck and Blake had formed "Kingston Korner, Inc.". Our boys had suddenly entered the record business! Color catalogs were printed, mailing lists and magazine advertising were purchased, and beginning with issue #11, the *Newsletter* became a multi-paged, professionally printed publication. Headquartered in Allan's basement, Kingston Korner, Inc. soon became a second full-time job for him, in addition to which he soon found himself dabbling in the world of concert promotion. (Allan's first outing was a date for the Trio; they arrived on time, but their instruments did not! His second concert was with John Stewart and Chuck McDermott; their instruments arrived as scheduled, but John and Chuck missed the flight!)

Kingston Korner today is a growing, fan-oriented business concern that daily ships records and tapes worldwide to admirers of the Trio and John Stewart, and they have recently added the work of Glenn Yarbrough, The Limeliters, The White Mountain Singers, Peter, Paul & Mary, The Brothers Four, Schooner Fare, and the entire roster of artists (including The Modern Folk Quartet) of John Stewart's new label, Homecoming Records. In addition, KK, Inc. now distributes the new Folk Era label. The publication of THE KINGSTON TRIO ON RECORD is yet another milestone on what will hopefully be a long road of service to fans of fine music everywhere.

* * * * * * * * *

To be included on Kingston Korner's mailing list and receive a complimentary copy of the latest issue of *Kingston Korner Newsletter,* please send your name and address to:

Kingston Korner, Inc.
6 South 230 Cohasset Road
Naperville, IL 60540 USA

Thank You

The authors of this book would like to thank as many people as we possibly can remember who helped provide facts, photos and inspiration. (Personal thank-yous have been extended in the "About the Contributors" section.) Some of the names should be bigger than others, but what the heck. As the Trio has been known to say, "Close enough for folk music."

We are indebted to **Frank H. Gildner, Jr.,** the editor and publisher of *The Evansville Review,* Evansville, Wisconsin. He not only printed "The Kingston Trio On Record", but was responsible for its layout and overall appearance. Without his experience and judgment, we would have been lost.

Also our gratitude is extended to **Alice "Susie" Hoffman** whose extraordinary efforts in overseeing the typesetting for THE KINGSTON TRIO ON RECORD resulted in a seemingly impossible task being completed in an amazingly short time.

Special thanks are extended to **Frank Shelley** for the thankless task of printing and sizing the seemingly endless photos of the records that fill this little volume.

Maureen Wilson and **Maia Rehlin** provided the lion's share of the non-U.S.A. information to be found in the book. In addition, Maureen donated her extensive KT and John Stewart scrapbooks to the cause.

Adair Stevens must be given due credit for uncovering that vast source of information that is the "Guard Collection" at the Meir Library, University of Wisconsin-Milwaukee. **Richard Johnston,** whose extensive notes were housed therein, must be thanked for his permission to draw upon said notes, as well as for his encouragement regarding our project.

We are forever in debt to **JoAnn Young,** intrepid producer of "The Kingston Trio & Friends: Reunion", who made us feel more important than we really were. November 7, 1981 will always be a great source of inspiration and fond memories for all of us, and we will remember JoAnn as the person who "pulled off the impossible".

Finally, we would like to thank **Nick Reynolds** and **John Stewart** for taking time out of their busy schedules to write a few words for us. They have added an air of credibility to this book (and certainly added to its sales!) that might otherwise have appeared to be lacking.

And to all of those people and organizations listed below, for a thousand things, large and small, we thank you.

Pete Abbot
Robert Adams
Bob Allen
William Allen
Arnie Amber
Lou Antonicello
Archives of Music Preservation
Kristin Baggelaar
Michael Bailey
Robert Balboni
John Barbour
Bob Barker
Dave Batti
Ed Becker
Herm Becker
Terry Behling
Totte Bergstrom
Tom Berilla
Billboard
Lloyd Binosheattle
Joe Biscontini
Richard Blaisdell
Elizabeth Blake
Lorelei Blake

Peter Bollen
Allan Bone
Ken Branen
Lindsey Buckingham
Bruce Buckley
Ron Busch
William Bush
Mike Callahan
Camera 3 Productions
Canadian River Music
Canadisc
Candlelite Music:
    David Lipman
Capitol Records:
    Bobby Colomby
    John Groomer
    Jack Reynolds
    Pete Welding
Robin Carter
Cash Box
Dorathea Center-Harlowe
Dick Cerri
Chnito Productions:
    Ross Meurer
    Tomm Rivers

Jim Connor
Larry Crawford
James Cyphers
Don D. Davis
Don D. Davis
Doug Delio
Henry Diltz
Jeff Fessenden
Jurgen Feub
Dan Field
Louis Field
Jim Fiorilli
Steve Fiott
Frets
Fuji Productions:
    Russ & Nikki Gary
Paul Gajdos
Daniel Galender
Catherine Gambill
Roger Gambill
Richard Gardner
Floyd Garrett
Rod Geddes
Vivian Gildner
Voyle Gilmore

Bill Goetz
Goldmine:
    Brian Bukantis
    Trey Foerster
    Jeff Tamarkin
    Rick Whitesell
Jean Goodman
Lou Gottlieb
Tom Green
George Grove
Dave Guard
Ed Gunny
Rod Harrington
Bob Haworth
Heritage Music Review:
    Doug Bright
John Hilvert
Richard Hogan
Homecoming Records
Pat Horine
John F. Howard
DeWayne Johnston
Judith Jones
Phil Jones
Stan Kaess

Bernard Kamaroff
Casey Kasem
Harold Kazakoff
Bruce Kirkman
Michael Kotzen
J.E. Kowalczyk
Steve Kruckemeyer
Charlie Kucharski
Thomas Lamb
Dave Larson
Jeff Larson
Tom Larson
Spencer Leigh
Kevin Lewis
Lonesome Picker Records
Dennis Loren
Brownie Macintosh
Phil Marchesseault
Tim Marmack
Barry Martin
Paul Martin
MCA Records:
    Kenn Scott
Chuck McDermott
Jeff McDonald
Bruce McFarland
Kurt Meier
Mark James Meli
Bob Meyers
Donald Milton

Toru Mitsui
Mobile Fidelity Sound Lab:
    Michael Grantham
Bill Montella, Jr.
Bill Morehead
Robert W. Morgan
Orrie Morrison
D.L. Mortensen
Jim & Charlene Murphy
National Academy of
    Recording Arts & Sciences
Nautilus Recordings:
    Baxter Boyington
Tanya C. Newbury-Smith
Bernard Nicksich
Sharon Ober
Peter O'Brien
Omaha Rainbow
Open System Project
William Padden
John Parisi
Dow Patterson
Tom Payne
Frank Pesice
Tom Pickles
Terry Pliner
Theodore Presser Company:
    Henson Markham
Terry Ransom
Joe O.Ray

RCA Victor Records:
    Lorene Lortie
    Marguerite Renz
Record Industry Association
    of America
William Regets
Lennart Rehlin
Dean Reilly
Jane K. Reynolds
Linda Reynolds
Phil Reynolds
Steve Rosenberg
RSO Records:
    Al Coury
    Ronnie Lippin
Tom Rush
Joe Sachs
Cliff Schroeder
Ben Schubert
Hansi Schwarz
Jack Scott
Bob Senior
Bob Shane
Genevieve Shaw
Ian Shaw
Trevor Shaw
Wes Smith
Paul Sobotor
Jack Splittard
Buffy Ford Stewart

Sunstorm Records
Paul Surratt
Molly Swan
Gary Tennant
Mary Travers
University of Wisconsin-
    Milwaukee, Meir Library,
    Special Collections:
    Allen Kovan
    Stanley Mallach
Richard Vining
Larry Waggoner
Jean Ward
Robert Ware
Bill Warren
Ronald Weinger
Frank Werber
Bob Westfall
David Wheat
Elizabeth Wilson
Marci Wilson
Rod Wilson
World Folk Music Association
Frank Wright
Xeres Records:
    Nick & Jane Heyl
Annie Yarbrough
Bill Zorn
Eric Zorn

In addition, Frank Shelley would like to thank the following people for their assistance:
    Kathy Vanaria, Full Frame Productions, Boston
    Diane Letourneau, Alan Ross, Master Color Service, Boston

* * * * * * * * *

The Kingston Trio in concert, April 1, 1986, Crown Uptown Theatre, Wichita, Kansas. Left to Right: Carey Blade (bass), George Grove, Bob Shane, Bob Haworth, Ben Schubert (tenor guitar). Hidden behind Bob Shane is Tom Green (drums). Photo by Dave Larson.

INDEX

The Kingston Trio, Bob Shane, Nick Reynolds and John Stewart in an unusual and seldom seen publicity photo. Photo courtesy of the Archives of Music Preservation.

In January, 1961, Capitol Records produced a 4-page flyer promoting the release of MAKE WAY. Since it is such a unique and interesting piece of Kingston Trio record memorabilia, it is here reproduced in its entirety. From the collection of Allan Shaw.

The Kingston Trio

MAKE WAY! THE KINGSTON TRIO

NEW ALBUM SURE TO HIT GOLD ALBUM PAYDIRT !!

"MAKE WAY! THE KINGSTON TRIO," a brand-new album by the best-selling group in the business today, is a cinch to hit gold album paydirt.

So far, four Trio albums have struck it gold-album rich. They are: THE KINGSTON TRIO, which contains a noteworthy nugget named "Tom Dooley"; FROM THE HUNGRY i; THE KINGSTON TRIO AT LARGE; and HERE WE GO AGAIN.

Two later releases, SOLD OUT and STRING ALONG, will move momentarily into that golden million-seller circle.

All, of course—plus the Trio's end-of-the-year package, THE LAST MONTH OF THE YEAR — have been Billboard chart champions.

The new album, MAKE WAY! THE KINGSTON TRIO, looks to pan out likewise. It's in the same folk-flavored vein as its powerpacked predecessors.

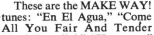

GOLD ALBUM NO. 1

These are the MAKE WAY! tunes: "En El Agua," "Come All You Fair And Tender Ladies," "Jug Of Punch," "Bonny Hielan Laddie," "Utawena," "Hard Travelin'," "Hangman," "Speckled Roan," "The River Is Wide," "Oh, Yes, Oh!," "Blow The Candle Out" and "Blue Eyed Gal."

The tunes for this new album, and all the tunes for all the Trio albums, are selected only after the group has screened hundreds of songs from almost as many sources.

"We are not students of folk music," says Dave Guard, the 6-foot-3-inch former Stanford University graduate student. "The basic thing for us is honest and worthwhile songs, songs that people can pick up and become involved in. Like ancient poetry, songs like that are successful because the audience participates in what the artist is doing."

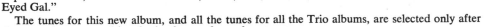

GOLD ALBUM NO. 2

"We don't collect old songs in the sense that the academic cats do," affirms the wiry Nick Reynolds. "We get new tunes to look over every day. Each one of us has his ears open constantly to new material or old stuff that's good."

"Good songs," adds Bob Shane, "are songs that can be made to live during the performance."

And that's exactly what each song sung by the Trio does— it lives. Millions of fans all over the world, from Tallahassee to Timbuctu, attest to the fact.

How has this fabulous success — these astounding record sales and sold-out personal appearances — effected the group?

Bob Thomas, of the Associated Press, answered the question when he wrote: "No act in show business today is hotter than The Kingston Trio, three young men who refuse to act like show people. Mind you, they're not square. They're as hep as any collegiates, which they were just a few years ago. But they refuse to be swept away by their whirlwind success."

A success, to be sure, that already has become a legend.

GOLD ALBUM NO. 3

GOLD ALBUM NO. 4

THE TRIO: FROM CAMPUS TO HUNGRY i TO CAPITOL TO "TOM DOOLEY" TO NUMBER 1 IN THE NATION

In 1957, the three clean-cut young men—Dave Guard, Bob Shane and Nick Reynolds—who are The Kingston Trio were pounding the textbooks in colleges near San Francisco. Dave, the acknowledged leader of the group, was an honor student at Stanford University. Nick and Bob were a few miles away at Menlo College.

A common interest in the native rhythms of all the countries of the world led to the formation of the Trio. But little did they dream that their backroom harmonizing in student hangouts around Stanford would lead to the success they enjoy today.

One evening in the Spring of 1957, the boys were concertizing in a colorful spot hard by the Stanford campus, The Cracked Pot. In the audience was San Francisco publicist Frank Werber, who numbered among

Frank Werber, the Trio's manager

his accounts, the esoteric nightspot, the Hungry i, Werber recognized the group's tremendous audience-pleasing talent, signed them to a personal management contract and began grooming the Trio for a professional debut.

After weeks of intensive rehearsal. The Kingston Trio was booked for brief appearances at the Hungry i, Facks II and other San Francisco bistros. They then were signed for one week by San Francisco's famed new-talent showcase, The Purple Onion. They were extended another week, then another, finally ended up spending seven months.

Word of the sensational new trio leaked across the country and they packed up their guitars, banjos and bongos and headed East. First stop was Chicago and Mr. Kelley's where, every night, cash customers formed a serpentine outside, clamoring to see the hottest property in show business. In New York City, at the Blue Angel and the Village Vanguard, the story was the same.

For their first national TV appearance, the Kingstons ran off with one of the top plums of all, Playhouse 90. On May 1, 1958, they appeared in "Rumors of Evening," playing airline pilots as well as displaying their considerable musical talents. Following this, the boys returned to San Francisco and a summer-long stint at the Hungry i.

CAPITOL CONTRACT

In January of that year, the Kingston Trio had been signed to a long-term exclusive recording contract by Capitol artist and repertoire producer Voyle Gilmore, a native

The beaming Kingston Trio received its first gold record for "Tom Dooley" from Max Callison, Regional Manager, Capitol Records Distributing Corp. The occasion was a cocktail party hosting the Trio in New York City in January, 1959.

San Franciscan. Their first long-playing album, "The Kingston Trio," was released the following June. It sold well, but was by no measure a "smash hit"—at first!

Contained in the album, though, was a haunting, century-old folk song, "Tom Dooley." Disk jockeys in scattered spots around the country, principally Salt Lake City, played the song constantly. At the request of several C R D C sales branches, a single record of "Tom Dooley" was released in the Fall of 1958. The Tom Dooley saga is pretty much legend by now.

The recording gained momentum from the day of its release, shot to the top of the national best-seller lists and remained on the charts for months afterward. Their album also took a firm grip on the top rungs of the charts. That "Tom Dooley" created a national furor is an understatement. So great was the interest in "Tom Dooley" and The Kingston Trio that Life and Newsweek, among other national magazines, devoted pages to chronicling the colorful events.

The Kingstons maintain a torrid schedule of personal appearances. In a recent period of less than two weeks played engagements

**The Trio, on one of its many
sold-out personal appearances.**

in New York City; Billings, Montana; Seattle; Vancouver; Portland; Los Angeles; San Diego, Rexburg, Idaho; Salt Lake City; Tucson and Washington, D.C. Barely breathing hard, the boys sandwich in newspaper interviews, visit disk jockeys, autograph records in stores and, in short, do just about anything to help promote their appearance wherever they are playing.

Music has always been an accepted part of the lives of Dave Guard, Nick Reynolds and Bob Shane. Dave and Bob were born and brought up in Hawaii where they strummed ukuleles and sang native songs only shortly after they learned how to walk. Throughout their teens, Bob and Dave sang and played on the beach at Waikiki, taking time out to attend Punahou School, skin dive and ride surfboards whenever they could. In addition to the songs of Hawaii, they learned the music of the South Pacific and the Orient from visiting yachtsmen and travelers.

Nick was born "stateside" in Coronado, Calif., just outside San Diego. The son of a career Naval officer, Nick was a seasoned world traveler before he entered high school. Each time the family moved, Nick (who notes that "Dad plays a swingin' guitar") added a new set of songs to his repertoire.

WHAT'S IN A NAME?

How did the boys come to call themselves The Kingston Trio? They and their manager picked the name because they felt it suggested Calypso music, so popular when they were starting out.

Garbed in natty, striped "ivy-league" shirts open at the collar, charcoal gray slacks, white socks and gleaming shoes, The Kingston Trio presents a striking appearance on stage. They are festooned with guitars or banjos and their bongos and conga drums are within reach. They have no formal written arrangements of the songs they sing, but each is letter perfect.

Dave is married to the former Gretchen Ballard, of Pasadena, Calif., whom he met at Stanford. They have a daughter, Catherine Kent Guard, born June 1, 1958. Despite the rugged schedule he and the other boys have set for themselves, Dave manages to read a book a day. He worked his way through Stanford (B.A., Economics, 1956), still got a B average. His mother and father, a civil engineer, still reside in Honolulu.

Nick was married in September 1958 to Joan Harris whom he met when the Trio was at the Hungry i and she was a comedienne at a club up the street. She later worked as assistant to the Trio's manager, Frank Werber. Between trips, Joan and Nick live an idyllic life on a houseboat, anchored on San Francisco Bay. Nick used to be an avid sports-car racer but gave it up in 1955 after a close friend was killed. He presently owns a Fiat-Nardi-Vignale sport coupe, reportedly the only one in the United States.

Bob is married to Louise Brandon, daughter of a prominent Atlanta, Ga. corporation lawyer. Bob is a bull fight afficionado and mariachi fan. Like Nick, he also is a waterskier. When Bob and Dave lived in Hawaii, they had a comedy diving act which was in great demand.

NATION'S TOP ARTISTS

And that about sums up The Kingston Trio. Except to mention their *four* gold album awards (it'll soon be five) and the fact that they're the hottest selling group in the nation.

THE TRIO IN ACTION—A SHOELESS SESSION, A TV BIT, A POOLSIDE REHEARSAL, A SAN FRANCISCO STROLL

FRONT VIEW!

VOYLE GILMORE, (left), who has produced all the Trio's albums, chats with the shoeless Trio between "takes".

BACK VIEW!

STILL SHOELESS (as always when recording) the boys are shown with their manager, Frank Werber.

TV TIME!

SINGIN' AND STRUMMIN' on a recent TV appearance. The Trio is much in TV demand, too, and has appeared on many top shows.

REHEARSAL!

REHEARSAL AT POOLSIDE. The boys are perfectionists and rehearsal is followed by more rehearsal until each song is letter-perfect.

ON TOP OF THE WORLD!

THAT'S SAN FRANCISCO in the background, the city that brought the group its first success and started The Kingston Trio on its record-breaking trip to the top of the musical world.

9 BEST-SELLING ALBUMS BY THE KINGSTON TRIO 9

THE KINGSTON TRIO — T-996

Three Jolly Coachmen • Wreck Of The "John B" • Bay Of Mexico • Sara Jane • Banua • Tom Dooley • Fast Freight • Hard, Ain't It Hard • Santy Anno • Scotch And Soda • Coplas • Little Maggie

FROM THE HUNGRY I — T-1107

Tic, Tic, Tic • Gue, Gue • Dorie • South Coast • Zombie Jamboree • Wimoweh • New York Girls • They Call The Wind Maria • The Merry Minuet • Medley: Shady Groove; Lonesome Traveler • When The Saints Come Marching In

STEREO CONCERT — ST-1183

Banua • Three Jolly Coachmen • South Coast • Coplas • They Call The Wind Maria • Zombie Jamboree • Tom Dooley • The Merry Minuet • Raspberries, Strawberries • When The Saints Come Marching In (Stereo Only)

THE KINGSTON TRIO AT LARGE — (S)T-1199

M.T.A. • All My Sorrows • Scarlet Ribbons • Remember The Alamo • Blow Ye Winds • Corey, Corey • The Long Black Rifle • Early Mornin' • The Seine • I Bawled • Good News • Getaway John

HERE WE GO AGAIN — (S)T-1258

Molly Dee • Across The Wide Missouri • Haul Away • The Wanderer • 'Round About The Mountain • Oleanna • The Unfortunate Miss Bailey • San Miguel • E Inu Tatou E • A Rollin' Stone • Goober Peas • A Worried Man

SOLD OUT — (S)T-1352

El Matador • The Mountains O'Mourne • Don't Cry Katie • Medley: Tanga Tika; Toerau • With Her Head Tucked Underneath Her Arm • Carrier Pigeon • Bimini • Raspberries, Strawberries • Mangwani Mpulele • With You My Johnny • The Hunter • Farewell Adelita

STRING ALONG — (S)T-1407

Bad Man's Blunder • The Escape Of Old John Webb • When I Was Young • Leave My Woman Alone • This Mornin', This Evenin', So Soon • Everglades • Buddy Better Get On Down The Line • South Wind • Who's Gonna Hold Her Hand • To Morrow • Colorado Trail • The Tattooed Lady

THE LAST MONTH OF THE YEAR — (S)T-1446

Bye, Bye, Thou Little Tiny Child • The White Snows Of Winter • We Wish You A Merry Christmas • All Through The Night • Goodnight My Baby • Go Where I Send Thee • Follow Now, Oh Shepherds • Somerset Gloucestershire Wassail • Mary Mild • A Round About Christmas • Sing We Noel • The Last Month Of The Year

MAKE WAY! THE KINGSTON TRIO — (S)T-1474

En El Agua • Come All You Fair And Tender Ladies • Jug Of Punch • Bonny Hielan Laddie • Utawena • Hard Travelin' • Hangman • Speckled Roan • The River Is Wide • Oh, Yes, Oh • Blow The Candle Out • Blue Eyed Gal